OVERCOMING Adversity

BASEBALL'S TONY CONIGLIARO AWARD

EDITED BY BILL NOWLIN AND CLAYTON TRUTOR

ASSOCIATE EDITORS: GREG ERION AND LEN LEVIN

Society for American Baseball Research, Inc.
Phoenix, AZ

OVERCOMING ADVERSITY: BASEBALL'S TONY CONIGLIARO AWARD

Edited by Bill Nowlin and Clayton Trutor
Associate editors: Greg Erion and Len Levin

ISBN 978-1-943816-43-9
ebook ISBN 978-1-943816-42-2

Cover and book design: Gilly Rosenthol

Photography credits:

National Baseball Hall of Fame—all cover photos.
The B&W photos on the cover are L to R: Jim Eisenreich, Jim Abbott, and Jim Mecir.
The Hall of Fame also provided the photographs on pages 16, 23, 30, 36, 48, 64, 81, 88, 99, 112, 158, 201, and 203.

The following photographs were all provided courtesy of the various teams and enterprises:
Angels Baseball - pages 43, 78.
Baltimore Orioles - pages 58, 94.
Boston Red Sox - pages 9, 71, 138, 163, 170, 174, 179, 190.
Matt Dirksen/Colorado Rockies - page 126.
Detroit Tigers - page 53.
Pittsburgh Pirates - page 131.
San Diego Padres - pages 194, 195.
Skip Mihos/Tampa Bay Rays - pages 117, 147.
The Topps Company, Inc. - pages 199, 200.
Washington Nationals Baseball Club - page 185.

Society for American Baseball Research
Cronkite School at ASU
555 N. Central Ave. #416
Phoenix, AZ 85004
Phone: (602) 496-1460
Web: www.sabr.org
Facebook: Society for American Baseball Research
Twitter: @SABR

CONTENTS

INTRODUCTORY ESSAY

By Clayton Trutor

ON AUGUST 5, 1990, THE Boston Red Sox organization announced the establishment of the Tony Conigliaro Award. The annual prize would honor the memory of its namesake, a local hero turned Red Sox legend who died that February. The Tony Conigliaro Award would be presented each January by the Boston chapter of the Baseball Writers Association of America to a major-leaguer who had overcome adversity "through the attributes of spirit, determination, and courage," just as "Tony C" had during his short and tragic, yet remarkable and inspiring life and career.[1] This biographical collection honors Conigliaro and the 29 remarkable men who have won the award that bears his name, every one of whom has persevered through physical or personal hardship as they pursued a major-league baseball career.

I first heard the name "Tony Conigliaro" about two months before he passed away. My mother bought me a VHS tape for Christmas entitled *Yaz: From Fenway to Fame*. The 45-minute, WSBK-produced documentary paid tribute to Carl Yastrzemski's career at the time of his 1989 induction into Cooperstown. This baseball-obsessed 8-year-old watched the Sean McDonough-narrated video dozens of times between Christmas morning and the end of winter break. All January I subjected my lunch tablemates to recitations on the 1967 Impossible Dream season. Being Vermonters, many of them were also Red Sox fans. None of them yet shared my nostalgia for a time more than 10 years before any of us were born. Figuring prominently in my orations was a player I referred to as "the local kid," mimicking the way Dick Williams spoke of Tony Conigliaro in the video's file footage.

Yaz: From Fenway to Fame featured a montage of home runs by Yaz and Tony C from the spring and summer of 1967 that clearly had a major impact on me. I told everyone who would listen that Tony Conigliaro was my favorite baseball player. I told them about the Boston-area teenager who was signed by his hometown team, got called up to the big leagues while still in his teens, emerged immediately as one of the American League's most feared sluggers, became the youngest player in history to win the home-run crown, led the '67 Red Sox toward their first pennant in a generation, suffered career-threatening facial injuries when he was hit by a pitch in the midst of the pennant race, and came back 20 months later to become once again one of the league's top sluggers. Many of the adults I told this said that he was their favorite player, too.

Tony C was one of theirs, both regionally and generationally. Long before talk of "Red Sox Nation," fans across New England took great pride in a fellow New Englander starring for the *Olde Towne Team*. New England's long winters and short springs stack the deck against even the best members of the region's ballplaying fraternity. Merely making a major-league roster would have ensured his status as a local hero. Conigliaro's emergence as a bona-fide big-league star inspired a unique sense of awe in fans from Presque Isle to Pittsfield. Moreover, Conigliaro was arguably the first member of my parents' generation, the Baby Boomers, to become a major-league baseball star. At age 20, he led the American League in home runs with 32 in 1965. More than just their contemporary, Conigliaro shared in his generation's passions, most notably through his love for rock 'n' roll music. Conigliaro, whose voice bore a strong similarity to Gary Lewis's, recorded a series of singles for RCA in the mid-1960s and became a popular nightclub singer in the Boston area, performing renditions of his own tunes as well as top-40 hits of the day.[2]

The reverence with which my elders spoke of Conigliaro only grew in the weeks after his death on February 24, 1990, eight years after he suffered a debilitating heart attack that required his family to provide him with convalescent care for the rest of his life. My prompting was not the only reason that the adults around me commenced with an outpouring of love for Tony C. His death moved baseball fans everywhere, many of whom caught but a glimpse of his tragically abbreviated career and the emotional and financial struggles his family faced in the last years of his life. For New Englanders of a certain age, though, the loss of Conigliaro was the loss of an icon whose triumphs and tragedies helped to define their youth. By establishing an award in his honor, the Boston Red Sox organization demonstrated its attentiveness to the meaning that millions of their fans attached to the life and career of Anthony Richard Conigliaro.

The annual presentation of the Tony Conigliaro Award to a current major leaguer who has overcome personal adversity serves a number of purposes. It runs counter to contemporary cynicism about the motivations of professional ballplayers by honoring a player whose character merits the kind of attention that other athletes receive for their shortcomings. The award reminds Conigliaro's contemporaries of his legacy as a professional baseball player and as a man of courage and determination. Most importantly, the award introduces him to baseball fans too young to remember his career through the prism of a contemporary player. Specifically, the Tony Conigliaro Award serves to immortalize its namesake by honoring a player who embodies the same personal qualities.

The authors of this modest volume hope to contribute to the award's legacy by recounting the lives and professional careers of Conigliaro and the men who have been honored in his name. As you will learn, the players profiled in this book surmounted a wide range of physical and personal hardships. Some of the recipients recovered from serious injuries, including 1993 awardee Bo Jackson, who returned to the major leagues after reconstructive hip surgery. Several of the recipients are cancer survivors, including Jon Lester (2007), who recovered from non-Hodgkin's lymphoma and pitched the Boston Red Sox to victory in the deciding game of the 2007 World Series. Some recipients overcame personal tragedy, including Mark Leiter (1994), who persevered after the death of his 9-month-old son to earn a spot in the California Angels starting rotation. Some of the recipients overcame disabilities, such as Curtis Pride (1996), who was born deaf. Some of the recipients overcame life-threatening circumstances, such as Wilson Ramos (2014), who was kidnapped at gunpoint in his native Venezuela in 2011. The 2015 recipient of the Tony Conigliaro Award, St. Louis Cardinals pitcher Mitch Harris, missed five years of professional baseball to serve his country in the US Navy after his graduation in 2008 from the Naval Academy.

The Tony Conigliaro Award is unique among honors in professional sports. Its closest cousin among honors presented by Major League Baseball, the Comeback Player of the Year Award, was established in 2005 to honor players whose on-the-field performance returned to form after a decline in a previous season or seasons. The Pro Football Writers Association of America and the Associated Press present National Football League Comeback Player of the Year Awards that bear a closer relation to the Tony Conigliaro Award. Both awards honor athletes who have re-emerged as productive players after a decline in performance, serious injury, or personal hardship. From 1980 through 1985, the National Basketball Association had a Comeback Player of the Year Award, but replaced it in 1986 with a Most Improved Player Award. The National Hockey League offers no such award.

In June 2015 I got the idea for doing a book focused on the winners of the Tony Conigliaro Award while corresponding with two of the leading lights of the SABR Biography Project, Mark Armour and Bill Nowlin (my co-editor and the man who has shepherded this project into being). I have been contributing to the SABR Biography Project for the past three years. From the time I finished my first biography, I had been hoping to play a significant role in bringing a biography book project into being. Serendipitously, I had just finished David Cataneo's outstanding biography, *Tony C: The Triumph and Tragedy of Tony Conigliaro* (Rutledge Hill Press, 1998). Cataneo's beautifully written and detailed account of Conigliaro's life rekindled my boyhood interest in the Red Sox slugger. Putting together a book that profiled the recipients of the Tony Conigliaro Award seemed like a great way to channel my renewed enthusiasm for one of the most remarkable men in baseball history.

NOTES

1   Nick Cafardo, "Red Sox Notebook," *Boston Globe*, August 6, 1990: 41.

2   Jason Ankeny, "Tony Conigliaro," AllMusic.com. Accessed online on March 13, 2016: allmusic.com/artist/tony-conigliaro-mn0002034222/biography.

THE RED SOX AND THE TONY CONIGLIARO AWARD

THE **T**ONY **C**ONIGLIARO **A**WARD was the brainchild of Boston Red Sox Vice President of Public Relations Dick Bresciani. The first award was presented in 1990, in honor of Red Sox outfielder Tony Conigliaro, who had died in February 1990 at the age of 45. "Bresh," as he was widely known, died of complications from leukemia in November 2014.

Red Sox Senior Director of Public Affairs Pam Kenn talked about the process in an interview on November 18, 2015, not long before Mitch Harris was selected as the 2015 recipient.

"Bresh started it. Bresh came up with the idea," said Kenn. He knew Tony and kept it going through 2013. Pam Kenn picked up the ball. "I'd been involved in the administration of the process in the past—mostly, getting the guys to come to the dinner. Shortly before he died, he actually pointed me to the files, with the previous letters and all that he'd done before. It's mostly correspondence, tallies from voting, things like that.

"It's been the same process every year. At the end of the season you have a good sense of your team and how the year went and who was good and all that. We reach out to each PR director, or PR staff, and ask for a nomination from their team. We attach a brief paragraph about Tony C and how he had overcome adversity—spirit, courage, and determination are the three things that we look for—and then each team submits nominations to us."

There haven't been as many teams nominating as in earlier years, perhaps because they don't know if one of their players would be able to attend the dinner and receive the award. As the organizing force behind the award, the Red Sox leave it up to each team to decide who they might wish to nominate.

"We tell them who had won before, but we don't tell them what each person has overcome. We provide that information, and we let them decide. A lot of times they'll come back and ask, 'Is this someone who would fit?' Most of the time we just say, 'Yes, nominate whoever.'

"The Padres last year nominated Dave Roberts. Normally, it's a player but this was the case of a coach. We're open to things like that. We really are open. It's not just physical adversity. There are Tommy John guys. There are people like Dewon Brazelton who overcame … even Wilson Ramos last year, he overcame a very tough upbringing, and a kidnapping.

"I think Dave tugs at our heartstrings. Tony C was a player. It's really up for interpretation. These were Bresh's parameters, which I would respect and want to hold to, but I think there's some flexibility."

The Red Sox ask for nominations by a certain date, typically right at the beginning of November. At the time of the interview, the Red Sox had narrowed the list down to five candidates to present to the committee.

Who's on the committee? In 2015, it consisted of three people from Major League Baseball—Pat Courtney, Phyllis Merhige, and Katy Feeney. Both Richie and Billy Conigliaro were on the committee. There was also a fan, Brenda Cook, for the past few years. "I think we may have gotten her through the BoSox Club." The committee changes every once in a while. Bill Ballou, former president of the Boston chapter of the Baseball Writers Association of America, said the committee included the president and most recent past president of the BBWAA. "There are some sports editors as well." Broadcaster Joe Castiglione was on the committee in 2015.

"There are basic parameters but I do think it has changed in the past, of who actually votes. Scott Lauber voted on behalf of the *Herald* last year. Mike Lynch. Howard Ulman. Brenda Cook. Joe Sullivan. Joe Castig. Phyllis, Pat, and Katy."

After Gordon Edes was named Red Sox Historian in 2015, he joined Pam in overseeing the award. "We revamped the committee selecting the award," he said, "giving it a more national composition, because it is an award for which any major leaguer is eligible. We had committee members from *USAToday*, Yahoo!, ESPN, Fox, and MLB.com, as well as a more varied group of local participants. Billy and Richie Conigliaro each had votes. We also revamped the selection process, no longer just relying on clubs to nominate candidates. Committee members are also urged to do so; for example, it was my idea last year to nominate 2015 winner Mitch Harris, one of four players I personally nominated last year, and we had numerous nominations from our committee this year.

"Once we gathered nominations, I sent out bios of the candidates, we had a conference call to discuss the candidates, and the vote took place a week later. It is my goal to have a revolving number of committee members in the future."

The Red Sox are involved in organizing the list but a glance at the list of honorees over the years shows that Red Sox players are not overly represented. There have been three Tampa Bay Rays, three Red Sox, and three Angels over time. To some extent, the final selection represents which ballclubs have been more diligent in the nomination process. "The Angels nominated somebody this year. The Rays are usually pretty on top of it. They did tell us they don't have a nomination this year."

There were a couple of years there were ties, simply because that's how the vote came out. The process is open for review, and any such review may result in future change. For now, it seems to work well.

It is considered a major-league award, given by the ballclub. The Red Sox pay for the recipient's airfare, hotel, and other expenses.

—Bill Nowlin

HOW THE AWARD IS SELECTED — THE 2016 TONY CONIGLIARO AWARD

A look into how 2016 honoree Yangervis Solarte was selected is reflected in the following press release from the Red Sox on December 25, 2016. The text that follows is the press release in full:

San Diego Padres infielder Yangervis Solarte has been selected the winner of the 2016 Tony Conigliaro Award in voting conducted by a 20-person committee of media members, Major League Baseball executives, Red Sox officials, and members of the Conigliaro family.

Solarte received 11 first-place votes and a total of 62 points, based on a 5-3-1 points system for first-, second- and third-place votes. Phillies catcher Tommy Joseph, who had three first-place votes, and Royals catcher Salvador Perez tied for second with 23 points apiece. Marlins pitcher Jose Fernandez (4), Pirates pitcher Ryan Vogelsong (1) and Indians pitcher Perci Garner (1) received the other first-place votes.

The Conigliaro Award has been given every year since 1990 in memory of the former Red Sox outfielder, whose career was tragically shortened by a beanball in 1967 and whose life ended in 1990 at the age of 45. It is awarded to a "Major Leaguer who has overcome adversity through the attributes of spirit, determination and courage that were trademarks of Tony C."

The award is scheduled to be presented at the Boston Baseball Writers Dinner on Thursday, Jan. 19, 2017 at the Marriott Copley Place. To purchase tickets, please contact Ashley Walenta at awalenta@sportsmuseum.org or call (617) 624-1231. More information on the dinner can be found here. http://www.sportsmuseum.org/events/boston-baseball-writers-annual-dinner.aspx

Solarte was nominated for the award by his team, the San Diego Padres. In September, Solarte's 31-year-old wife and mother of their three children, Yuliette Pimentel Solarte, succumbed to cancer. Solarte left the club in July to spend four days at his wife's side; a week after her death, he returned to the club, their three daughters and his mother accompanying him to San Diego.

"It feels a little different, and she's gone now, but at the end of the day those things are out of our control,'" Yangervis said upon his return. "Those things are up to God and that was his decision. We fought. We were hoping that she'd be around for a little bit longer, but here we are."

Megan Otto, the Padres' manager of player and family relations, nominated Solarte.

"For Yangervis, 2016 has been one of the most personally challenging years that he will have in his lifetime," she wrote. "Dealing with personal loss and missing time to due to injury, and yet he still managed to produce the best year of his career."

Solarte earlier in the season also missed six weeks due to a hamstring injury. In 109 games, he batted .286 with a career-high 15 home runs and career-best 71 RBIs.

"He's had a heck of a year," Padres manager Andy Green said. "With what he's been through at home, his ability to still perform on a baseball field has honestly been astounding to me."

Conigliaro, a native of Swampscott, Mass., at 19 hit a home run in his first at-bat at Fenway Park in 1964. A year later, 1965, he became the youngest player to lead his league in home runs when he hit 32 in 1965, his second full season in the big leagues. He also became the youngest American League player to reach 100 home runs when he hit No. 100 at 22 years and 197 days, just 65 days older than the major league record holder, Mel Ott (22 years, 132 days).

Conigliaro's early promise of greatness went unfulfilled after he was struck in the face by a pitch from Jack Hamilton of the Angels on Aug. 18, 1967, fracturing his left cheekbone, dislocating his jaw, and severely damaging the retina in his left eye. It was the only hit batsman of the season for Hamilton, and just one of 13 in the span of an eight-year career.

Conigliaro missed all of the 1968 season, but returned to play two more years in Boston, hitting a career-high 36 home runs for the Sox in 1970, when he also drove in 116 runs. He was traded after the season to the California Angels, but declining vision led him to announce his retirement in 1971. He attempted another comeback for the Red Sox in 1975, but ended his career after batting just .123 in 69 plate appearances.

Congliaro suffered a massive heart attack in 1982, and died eight years later at the age of 45.

These people comprised the committee that conducted the voting:

- Pat Courtney, chief communications officer, Major League Baseball
- Phyllis Merhige, senior vice president, club relations, MLB
- Katy Feeney, senior vice president, scheduling and club relations, MLB
- Pam Kenn, Boston Red Sox VP, community, alumni and player relations
- Gordon Edes, Red Sox historian
- Billy Conigliaro, brother, Tony Conigliaro
- Richie Conigliaro, brother, Tony Conigliaro
- Tim Brown, Yahoo! Sports
- Steve Buckley, *Boston Herald*
- Uri Berenguer, play-by-play Red Sox Spanish-language broadcast team
- Joe Castiglione, WEEI radio play-by-play broadcaster
- Doug Glanville, ESPN
- Steve Hollingsworth, 2015-16 president, BoSox Club
- Jon Paul Morosi, MLB.com and MLB Network
- Bill Nowlin, author and baseball historian
- Dave O'Brien, NESN Red Sox play-by-play broadcaster
- Jorge Ortiz, *USA Today*
- Nilson Pepen, host and producer, Conversando de Deportes
- Grace Pontius, Class of 2018, Mount Mansfield (Vt.) Union High School
- Jayson Stark, ESPN.com

THE BASEBALL WRITERS ASSOCIATION OF AMERICA AND THE TONY CONIGLIARO AWARD

BILL BALLOU OF THE *Worcester Telegram* is a longtime BBWAA member and, as chairman for several years, was involved in the decisions as to which players would be recipient of the Tony Conigliaro Award.

Bill was interviewed interviewed by Bill Nowlin on July 8, 2015 about the process.

"My first year as chairman was 2006, but I've been involved with the dinner since 1988. The first one was Jim Eisenreich in 1990. He was very gracious. I remember Dickie Thon, the next one, getting here very early and spending three hours talking with people in the headquarters lounge at the Sheraton. A very pleasant guy. Curtis Pride—there have been a lot of very gracious winners. And some of them did not have real significant major-league careers. You look at the list. It's been very eclectic, all the way from Jim Eisenreich to Curtis Pride to Tony Saunders. He's not a household name, by any means. Dewon Brazleton was one of the nicest guys that we've had there. Baldelli, much more prominent guy, and then Tony Campana—few people would have known about Campana except for this.

"There have been a lot of really interesting ones. Mike Lowell came to the dinner before he was a member of the Red Sox. He was with the Marlins then. It's interesting how many of them later wound up playing for the Red Sox. Lowell. Curtis Pride. Mercker. Freddy Sanchez. Baldelli.

"I remember sitting next to Joaquin Benoit at the 2011 dinner—he won in 2010—and talking with him at length about lots of different topics—about what it was like to play in Tampa Bay, why Joe Maddon was such a good manager, the things that he did. It's always of interest to talk with these guys because of their perspectives—different perspectives often than we get in Boston."

The original inspiration was Red Sox executive Dick Bresciani. "For years, he was the main liaison between the Red Sox and us. His particular history with the Red Sox as an employee goes back to the early 1970s, and as a fan back even before that. He had a very good idea how important Tony Conigliaro was at the time he was here. Most fans now know Conigliaro as a sort of historical figure whereas Bresciani knew him as a real player, a real person, and realized what an impact he had on Boston baseball in the Sixties and early Seventies.

"We're always looking for ways to honor new people. One of the things about the dinner—this has always been a Red Sox award. We've always had the current and the past chairman vote on the media side. That's one of our duties."

As Pam Kenn notes, the number of teams nominating has seemed to decline in recent years. Perhaps this book will help prompt more nominations. "Every team is invited to nominate somebody, but there's not as many nominees as there were. There was a time we might have eight or ten, and now it's down. I'm not sure why that is. It might be that the kind of career-shattering injury that used to happen isn't commonplace any more. Guys like Lowell and Lester were both cancer survivors; there are always going to be those off-the-field issues as well.

"I remember the discussion with John Lackey. I remember when we talked about Lackey at our BBWAA meeting, it was not just that he came back from Tommy John but that his comeback was so dramatically good. The nature of how good it was is probably what swayed everybody. You could probably have 30 Tommy John surgery comebacks every year but I think the nature of his comeback and how it all played out in the end was probably what swayed him.

"We don't control the nominees. If your team doesn't want to nominate anybody, you don't. We may have only had four or five three people to vote on that year, and he may have been the best candidate of all of those.

"I think the interest around baseball has tailed off. Maybe it needs to be promoted more in some fashion. No one broadcasts it. They broadcast it one year, but it's just people handing out awards and giving speeches. It's not great television. It's not that exciting. News people can do little clips on it, but it's not exciting.

"The interest at the Red Sox is still high, but we've been pretty good about awarding it to non-Red Sox players. As you would expect, if your team takes the time to nominate you for this award, they generally are very good about getting the players to come to the dinner to accept the award. We've had a lot of really good guests that way. The Red Sox take care of the travel and all. Airfare and hotel. We've had a real good cross-section of guys from out of town coming in.

"The Red Sox want to do this. We [BBWAA] are happy to serve as a forum for presenting the award, and having it as part of our dinner, but we don't do any of the research on it, we don't do any of the contacting of teams on it....

"Pam has been very conscientious about this. When she was the P.R. director, she was always very conscientious in terms of getting guys in and she always worked very hard at it."

In April 2016, Bill added a thought:

"The most recent Conigliaro Award winner, Mitch Harris for the 2015 season, was an unconventional choice who turned out to be one of the most popular picks. Harris had no injury. He was honored for making it to the majors after fulfilling his military service commitment following his graduation from the Naval Academy.

"Fans at the 2016 dinner were very vocal in their admiration of what Harris had overcome to make the big leagues. The choice further broadened the base of where we can look to find good Conigliaro candidates."

TONY CONIGLIARO

BY BILL NOWLIN

NO MATTER HOW YOU MEASURE it, Tony Conigliaro's career got off to a terrific start, but tragedy repeatedly intervened and the great promise of his early years remained unfulfilled. A local boy made good, Tony was born and raised in the Boston area, signed with the hometown team, and made his major-league debut in 1964 soon after he turned 19 years old. In his very first at-bat at Fenway Park, Tony turned on the very first pitch he saw and pounded it out of the park for a home run. By hitting 24 home runs in his rookie season, he set a record for the most home runs ever hit by a teenager. When he led the league in homers with 32 the following year, he became the youngest player ever to take the home run crown. When he hit home run number 100, during the first game of a doubleheader on July 23, 1967, he was only 22—the youngest AL player to reach the 100-homer plateau. He hit number 101 in the day's second game.

As if that wasn't enough, Tony Conigliaro was a bona-fide celebrity and singer with a couple of regional hit records to his credit.

Tony C was born on January 7, 1945, in Revere, Massachusetts, a few miles north of Boston, and grew up both there and in East Boston, where he first played Little League ball at age 9. Tony and his younger brother Billy (b. 1947) were obsessed with baseball, playing it at every possible opportunity, usually with the support and guidance of their uncle Vinnie Martelli. "He used to pitch batting practice to me for hours, till my hands bled," wrote Conigliaro in his autobiography *Seeing It Through*.[1] In his very first at-bat for the Orient Heights Little League team, Tony hit a home run over the center-field fence. He credited coach Ben Campbell for giving him tremendous encouragement in youth baseball.

Tony confessed that at a very early age, "I discovered how much I hated to lose."[2] His teams didn't lose that often. By the time he was 13 and in Pony League, they

were traveling out of state in tournament play. Tony went to high school at St. Mary's in Lynn, where his father, Sal, was working at Triangle Tool and Dye. Sal and Tony's mother, Teresa, were very supportive of his athletic endeavors and were a fixture at Tony's various ballgames.

As both a shortstop and pitcher, Tony had already come to the attention of scouts like Lennie Merullo and Milt Bolling and by the time he graduated claimed to have had as many as 14 scouts tracking him. In his final couple of years, he recalled batting over .600 and having won 16 games on the mound, and remembered his team winning the Catholic Conference Championship. He played American Legion ball in the summers, with the same .600 batting average. The Red Sox asked Tony to come to a 1962 workout at Fenway Park, where both he and Tony Horton showed their stuff. When the Legion season ended and Tony's father

courted bids, Boston's Milt Bolling and Red Sox farm director Neil Mahoney made the best bid at $20,000 and Tony signed with the Red Sox.[3] He was sent to Bradenton for the Florida Instructional League.

It was Conigliaro's first time far from home, and he didn't stand out that well at winter ball. In the spring of 1963, he was invited to the Red Sox minor-league camp at Ocala. He did well there, and was assigned to Wellsville in the New York-Penn League. Before he reported, he went home to see his girlfriend, got in a fight with a local boy, and broke his thumb. He wasn't able to report to Wellsville until the end of May. That was the end of Conigliaro's pitching career, but the scouts were looking at his hitting more than his pitching anyway. Tony did well at Wellsville, batting .363, hitting 24 homers, and winning the league's Rookie of the Year and MVP awards. He played that autumn at instructional league in Sarasota and was added to the Red Sox' 40-man roster. The next spring, 1964, the Sox brought him to their big-league spring training headquarters in Scottsdale, Arizona.

Boston's manager was Johnny Pesky who, as it happened, lived on the same street in Swampscott to which the Conigliaro family had recently moved: Parsons Street. Pesky saw the fire in Tony Conigliaro and played him that spring; Tony hit a monster home run off Cleveland's Gary Bell on March 22, the first day his parents came to visit him in Scottsdale. Ted Williams admired Conigliaro's style and told him, whatever he did, "Don't change that solid stance of yours, no matter what you're told." Ted told reporters, though, "He's just a kid; he's two years away."[4]

Johnny Pesky saw otherwise. Tony C was 19 and only in his second year in Organized Baseball, but he made the big-league club as the center fielder for the Red Sox. Pesky was taking a chance on a relatively untested player, but the 1964 Sox, frankly, didn't have a great deal of talent.

Conigliaro's first major-league game was in Yankee Stadium on April 16. In his first major-league at-bat, against Whitey Ford, he stepped into the box with men on first and second, and grounded into a double play. His third time up, he singled and finished the day 1-for-5. The next day, April 17, was the home opener at Fenway Park. Tony was batting seventh in the order, facing Joe Horlen of the White Sox. He swung at Horlen's first pitch and hit it over the Green Monster in left field, and even over the net that hung above the Wall. Tony Conigliaro, wearing number 25, took his first home-run trot. Tony told writers afterward that he always swung at the first good pitch he saw. "I don't like to give the pitcher any kind of edge," he said.[5]

In that same spirit, Conigliaro crowded the plate. And pitchers, quite naturally, tried to back him off the plate. He was often hit by pitches, and suffered his first injury on May 24 when Kansas City's Moe Drabowsky hit him in the left wrist, causing a hairline fracture. Fortunately, Tony missed only four games.

Back in the lineup, back pounding out homers, Tony hit number 20 in the first game of a July 26 doubleheader against Cleveland. In the second game, he got hit for the fifth time in the season, by Pedro Ramos. It broke his arm. This time he missed a month, out until September 4. Conigliaro finished the season with 24 homers and a .290 average.

In 1965, under manager Billy Herman, Tony played in 138 games and hit 32 more homers, enough to lead the league, though his average dipped to .269. During the June free-agent draft, there was more good news for the Conigliaro family: The Red Sox used their first pick to select Tony's younger brother, Billy. Tony was struck yet again by another ball on July 28, when a Wes Stock pitch broke his left wrist. It was the third broken bone Tony had suffered in just over 14 months. He simply refused to back off the plate. Orioles executive Frank Lane intimated that Red Sox pitchers could defend Tony a bit better by retaliating.

Suffering no serious injuries in 1966, Tony got in a very full season, seeing action in 150 games. He banged out 28 homers and drove in 93 runs, leading the league in sacrifice flies with seven. His average was .265 and the Boston writers voted him Red Sox MVP. The Red Sox as a team, though, played poorly in these years. In 1966 they were spared the ignominy of last place only because the Yankees played even worse. Boston ended the year in ninth place, 26 games out of first, and the Yankees ended in tenth, 26½ games behind the Orioles. In his first three years in the majors, the highest that one of Tony's teams finished was eighth place in 1964.

Tony C's brilliant play shone all the more because of the colorless team around him. The local boy made good was a teenage heartthrob and the 6-foot-3 handsome star attracted a lot of attention from local girls, and girls on the road. Assigning older players as roommates to provide a stabilizing presence didn't do the trick. Dick Williams wrote in his autobiography, "I never saw him. Not late at night, not first thing in the morning, never. I was providing veteran influence to a suitcase."[6] In the early part of 1965, Tony Conigliaro the pop star released his first recording. He recorded a couple of singles and might have developed a career in this area, but kept his focus on baseball.

Billy Conigliaro joined his brother as the two traveled together to spring training in 1967. Tony was hit by a fastball in early workouts and he hurt his back as well. Billy was sent out for more seasoning; he first made the big-league club in 1969. Tony got off to a slow start, batting well enough but without much power. He didn't hit his third home run until June 11. And he still crowded the plate. Johnny Pesky told author David Cataneo, "He was fearless of the ball. He would just move his head, like Williams did. A ball up and in, Tony would just move his head. He thought the ball would never hit him."[7]

The Red Sox surprised everyone with their play in 1967. Conigliaro contributed as well. One game that stood out was an extra-inning affair at Fenway on June 15. Boston was hosting the White Sox and the game was scoreless for ten full innings. Chicago took a 1-0 lead in the top of the 11th, but Joe Foy singled and then Conigliaro hit a two-run homer off John Buzhardt for a walkoff win. The win moved the Red Sox up by percentage points to put them in a tie for third place, just four games out of first, and the next day's *Boston Globe* referred to the "Impossible Dream" season the Red Sox team was having for itself.

It was on July 23 that Tony hit the 100th and 101st home runs of his major-league career. The Red Sox were just a half-game out of first place. It was a tight race, with Boston hanging just out of first, but never quite making it on top. As late as August 14, the Red Sox were in fifth place—but only three games out.

On the 17th, Tony's partner in the music business, Ed Penney, was visiting his sons at the Ted Williams Baseball Camp in Lakeville, Massachusetts. Ted warned Penney, "Tell Tony that he's crowding the plate. Tell him to back off." He said, "It's getting too serious now with the Red Sox." Penney remembered, "I told him I would. I'd see him the next night. When we were walking across the field to get the kids, and Ted was going up to the stands to make some kind of talk, he turned around and yelled over to me and said, 'Don't forget what I told you to tell Tony. Back off, because they'll be throwing at him.'"[8] Penney did tell him, before the game the very next night. Tony was in a slump at the time, and told his brother Billy he couldn't back off the plate or pitchers wouldn't take him seriously. If anything, he was going to dig in a little closer.

The Red Sox were facing the California Angels the next day—August 18—and Jack Hamilton's fourth-inning fastball came in and struck Tony in the face, just missing his temple but hitting him in the left eye and cheekbone. Tony later wrote that he jerked his head back "so hard that my helmet flipped off just before impact."[9] He never lost consciousness, but as he lay on the ground, David Cataneo wrote, Tony prayed, "God, please, please don't let me die right here in the dirt at home plate at Fenway Park."[10] Tony was fortunate to escape with his life, but his season—and quite possibly his career—was over. Conigliaro had been very badly injured.

The 1967 Red Sox made it to Game Seven of the World Series before the bubble burst. It had nonetheless been a tremendous year for the team, and reignited the passion for the Sox in the city of Boston. Since 1967, tickets for Fenway Park have been hard to come by. Tony, however, felt he'd let the team down. He was down on himself and downplayed his contribution in the drive to the pennant. His teammates were the first to reassure him that they never would have reached the postseason had it not been for his contributions early on. There is little doubt, though, that Conigliaro was missed in the World Series itself. George Scott was unambiguous in his assessment: "I've said it a million times, if Tony had been in the lineup, we would have won. He was one of those guys. Reggie Jackson was a big-game player. Tony was that kind of player."[11]

There was concern Conigliaro might lose the sight in his left eye. He tried to come back in spring training, but there was just no way. His vision was inadequate, and his doctor told him, "I don't want to be cruel, and there's no way of telling you this in a nice way, but it's not safe for you to play ball anymore."[12] Tony C wouldn't quit, though, and against all odds, his vision slowly began to improve. By late May, he was told he could begin to work out again. Tony also learned new ways to see the ball. When he looked straight on at the pitcher, he couldn't see the ball, but he learned to use his peripheral vision to pick up the ball and was able to see well enough by looking a couple of inches to the left. Tony wanted badly to get back into baseball. He spent a good amount of time in the late summer of 1968 trying to learn to become a pitcher, and started several games in the Winter Instructional League for the Sarasota Red Sox beginning on November 4, but he rolled up a record of 0-3, giving up 15 runs in one game, and developed a sore arm as well. He played in the outfield on the days he wasn't pitching and he began to connect for a few solid hits. He gave up the idea of pitching, emboldened to try to come back as a hitter in spring training 1969.

Not only did Tony make the team in 1969, but he broke back in with a bang, hitting a two-run homer in the top of the tenth during Opening Day in Baltimore, on April 8. The O's re-tied the game, but Tony led off in the 12th and worked a walk, eventually coming home to score on Dalton Jones's sacrifice fly to right. Tony delivered the game-winning hit in the fourth inning of the home opener at Fenway Park on April 14, though admittedly it wasn't much of a hit. He came up with the bases loaded and wanted to break the game open. Instead, he sent a slow dribbler toward Brooks Robinson at third, and beat it out as Ray Culp scored from third. Tony C was back. It was never easy, and the various books on his struggle document how hard he had to work at what once seemed so effortless, but Tony played in 141 games, hit 20 home runs, and drove

in 82 runs. Tony won the Comeback Player of the Year Award. There wasn't any question who would win it.

The 1970 season was Tony's best at the plate, with 36 homers and 116 RBIs. He also scored a career-high 89 runs. Brother Billy had made the Red Sox, too, in 1969, getting himself 80 at-bats and acquitting himself well. Billy became a regular in 1970, appearing in 114 games and batting .271. Add his 18 homers to Tony's 36, and the resulting total of 54 set a record for the most home runs by two brothers on the same major-league club. On July 4 and September 19, they each homered in the same game.

In October the Red Sox traded Tony. Stats aside, they knew that Conigliaro was playing on guts and native talent, but may have sensed that his vision was still questionable. His trade value was as high as it likely ever would be. Not even waiting for Baltimore and Cincinnati to finish the World Series, they packaged Conigliaro with Ray Jarvis and Jerry Moses and swapped him to the California Angels for Ken Tatum, Jarvis Tatum, and Doug Griffin. Even years later, Red Sox executives neither explained nor took credit (or responsibility) for the trade. The news stunned the baseball world—and Red Sox fans in particular. As author Herb Crehan wrote in *Red Sox Heroes of Yesteryear*, referring to Boston's then-mayor, "it was as if Mayor Menino were to trade the USS Constitution to Baltimore for the USS Constellation."[13] Ken Tatum may have been the key to the trade; the Sox were after a strong reliever and he'd done very well for California.

Tony was crushed, and as Crehan noted, he "never adjusted to life as a California Angel." David Cataneo wrote, "Tony C and Southern California just didn't happen."[14] Conigliaro batted just .222 in 1971, with only four homers and 15 RBIs just before the All-Star break. His headaches had returned. He wasn't feeling well. Cataneo mentioned a string of ailments, from a bad leg to a pinched nerve. Tony even put himself in traction for an hour before every game. Some of the Angels lost patience with him and began to mock him. Finally, fed up, he packed his bags and left the team after the July 9 game, announcing his retirement. He also told reporters that he simply couldn't see well enough, but took the Red Sox off the hook for having dealt tarnished goods. "My eyesight never came back to normal. ... I pick up the spin on the ball late, by looking away to the side. I don't know how I do it. I kept it away from the Red Sox. ... I had a lot of headaches because of the strain to see. ... My search for that damn baseball."[15]

When he heard the news that Tony had left the Angels, Billy Conigliaro exploded in the Red Sox clubhouse, telling reporters that the reason for the trade to California in the first place had been Carl Yastrzemski, that Yaz had all the influence on the ballclub. "Tony was traded because of one guy—over there," he charged, indicating Yastrzemski. Yaz "got rid of Pesky, Ken Harrelson, and Tony. I know I'm next. Yaz and Reggie [Smith] are being babied, and the club better do something about it."[16]

Billy was part of a major ten-player trade with Milwaukee, but the trade was not made until October. Billy never rejoined the Red Sox. Tony did, but it took a while.

An eye exam Tony underwent after returning to Boston showed that the blind spot in his vision had grown considerably; his vision was deteriorating once more. Tony hadn't given up yet and in October 1973 talked about wanting to mount another comeback with the Angels in 1974. It appears that the Angels wanted him to play for their Salt Lake City affiliate, to see how he worked out, but Tony was past wanting to play for a minor-league team and so stayed retired. Late in 1974, he wrote to the Red Sox asking for another shot at a comeback and GM Dick O'Connell said he could come to spring training, but not at financial cost to the Red Sox. If he was willing to pay his own way, he was welcome to give it a try. The Angels graciously granted Tony his outright release in November 1974. The Red Sox offered him a contract with the Pawtucket Red Sox, which he signed on March 5, 1975.

Tony took up the challenge, and he had an exceptional spring. On April 4 he got word that he had made the big-league team. Opening Day 1975 was four days later, at Fenway Park on April 8, and Tony was the designated hitter, batting cleanup. With two outs and Yaz on first, Tony singled and Yaz took third. The crowd gave Tony C a three-minute standing ovation. Perhaps Milwaukee pitcher Jim Slaton and his batterymate, Darrell Porter, were caught a little off-guard; the Red Sox scored a run when Tony and Yaz pulled off a double steal.

Tony's first home run came three days later, off Mike Cuellar in Baltimore. With a first-inning single the following day, he drove in another run, but his .200 average after the April 12 game was the highest he posted for the rest of the season. He appeared only in 21 games, for 57 at-bats, and was batting just .123 after the game on June 12. He was hampered by a couple of injuries; it just wasn't working out. The Red Sox needed to make room on the 25-man roster for newly acquired infielder Denny Doyle and they asked Tony to go to Pawtucket. After thinking it over for a week, he agreed to and reported, traveling with the PawSox, but getting only sporadic playing time. Manager Joe Morgan said, "He had lost those real good reflexes," and teammate Buddy Hunter told David Cataneo, "Any guy who threw real hard, he had trouble with." Hunter added, "He was dropping easy fly balls in the outfield."[17] In August Tony Conigliaro finally called it a day, and retired once again, this time for good. "My body is falling apart," he explained.[18]

Before too long, Tony found work as a broadcaster, first in Providence and then in the San Francisco area. He lost a nice gig in the Bay Area in early 1980, but filled in with other stations. In a life full of setbacks, even the health-food store Tony owned in California was lost to mudslides in December 1981.

In early 1982, though, Tony learned that Ken Harrelson was leaving his job as color commentator with Channel 38 in Boston, the Red Sox station. Now there was a job with appeal! He interviewed for the position on the day he turned 37, January 7, 1982. The audition went very well, and he was told he'd got the job. Tony had a couple of other stops to make, and then planned to return to the Bay Area to pack up his gear for the move back to Boston.

On January 9, 1982, Billy Conigliaro was driving Tony to Logan Airport when Tony suffered a heart attack in the car. Though rushed to the hospital, Tony suffered irreversible brain damage and was hospitalized for two months before being discharged into the care of Billy and the Conigliaro family. He lived another eight years before succumbing at age 45 on February 24, 1990.

SOURCES

Cataneo, David, *Tony C.* (Nashville, Tennessee: Rutledge Hill Press, 1997).

Conigliaro, Tony, with Jack Zanger, *Seeing It Through* (New York: Macmillan, 1970).

Crehan, Herb, *Red Sox Heroes of Yesteryear* (Cambridge, Massachusetts: Rounder Books, 2005).

Williams, Dick, with Bill Plaschke, *No More Mr. Nice Guy* (San Diego: Harcourt Brace Jovanovich, 1990).

Thanks to Wayne McElreavy for considerable assistance with this profile.

NOTES

1 Tony Conigliaro, with Jack Zanger, *Seeing It Through* (New York: Macmillan, 1970), 130.

2 *Seeing It Through*, 133.

3 *Seeing It Through*, 145, 146. Some contemporary press reports put the figure at $25,000.

4 *Seeing It Through*, 167.

5 *Seeing It Through*, 178.

6 Dick Williams, with Bill Plaschke, *No More Mr. Nice Guy* (San Diego: Harcourt Brace Jovanovich, 1990), 73.

7 David Cataneo, *Tony C.* (Nashville, Tennessee: Rutledge Hill Press, 1997), 65.

8 Interview with Ed Penney on August 15, 2006.

9 *Seeing It Through*, 10.

10 Cataneo, 108.

11 *Seeing It Through*, 124.

12 *Seeing It Through*, 82.

13 Herb Crehan, *Red Sox Heroes of Yesteryear* (Cambridge, Massachusetts: Rounder Books, 2005), 179.

14 Cataneo, 195.

15 Cataneo, 202, 203.

16 Cataneo, 203. For more on Billy Conigliaro's feelings on the subject, see his biography for SABR's BioProject.

17 Both the Morgan and Hunter statements are in Cataneo, 223.

18 Associated Press wire story, August 23, 1975.

JIM EISENREICH

By Scot Johnson

ST. CLOUD, MINNESOTA, NATIVE Jim Eisenreich retired from baseball in 1998, capping a career that spanned 15 major-league seasons and included two World Series appearances. Still, with all of his success, Eisenreich's baseball career may be most remembered for how it was almost ended before it ever really started.

Eisenreich was born on April 18, 1959, in St. Cloud, the middle of five children of Cliff and Ann Eisenreich. He was introduced to baseball almost immediately and began to play when he was 7 at Southside Park in St. Cloud. Right around that time, young Jim began to display some strange, unexplainable symptoms. His face would tic and jerk, or he would clear his throat uncontrollably. His peers made fun of young Jim, and teachers assumed that was just trying to draw attention to himself, that he could stop the behavior any time he wished.

As strange as Jim's behavior was, he was also well known at an early age for his baseball skills. Though teased often, Jim was usually the first chosen when teams were decided for pick-up baseball games. All the Eisenreich children were involved in youth sports in St. Cloud, and both of their parents attended most of the family sporting events. Eisenreich referred to his family later as a "strict Catholic" family but very close. His father, Cliff, taught school at the local reformatory. His mother, Ann, was a homemaker.

Eisenreich continued to stand out as a ballplayer at St. Cloud Tech High School and later followed his father's footsteps to St. Cloud State University. St. Cloud State head baseball coach Jim Stanek remembered recruiting Eisenreich: "He was 5-foot-9 and 140 pounds, not very big but he could hit the ball."[1]

Eisenreich matured quickly and was a starter for the varsity team by his sophomore season. He was the team's leading hitter and earned all-conference honors. In his junior year in 1980, Eisenreich continued to impress. Despite his .385 batting average and second consecutive all-conference season, he wasn't even considered the top prospect at his school. The scouts were watching infielder Bob Hegman, who was getting a look from several major-league teams. Eisenreich's head coach at the time, Denny Lorsung, wrote to the Minnesota Twins to thank them for some tickets and suggested that they take a look at Eisenreich.

Whether or not Lorsung's letter made a difference, Jim Eisenreich was drafted by the Minnesota Twins in the 16th round of the 1980 amateur draft and signed with the team shortly after. It wasn't too long before Eisenreich was opening some eyes in the Twins' organization. Just weeks after he signed, he hit his first professional home run, a grand slam for the Elizabethton Twins that came just weeks after he signed. Though his team only managed to finish fourth, Eisenreich was named Co-Player of the Year in the Appalachian League. At the end of the 1980 season, Eisenreich played five games with Class-A Wisconsin Rapids of the Midwest League.

He returned to Wisconsin Rapids for the 1981 season and improved on his 1980 success, batting .311 with 23 home runs and 99 runs batted in (RBIs) for a fourth-place team. His performance, combined with an organizational youth movement, earned him a non-roster invitation to spring training with the Twins before the 1982 season. Eisenreich eventually made the major-league team as the starting center fielder and was one of 10 players with less than a year of major league experience to make the Twins' Opening Day roster that year. Among the other young players on that team were Kent Hrbek, Gary Gaetti, and Ron Washington.

Eisenreich's speedy promotion through the minor leagues seemed to be paying off for the Twins early in the 1982 season. Through April 25, Eisenreich was batting .324 with a couple of home runs. It was about that time that his childhood problems resurfaced. At first, Eisenreich and the baseball media dismissed it as

a simple case of rookie nerves. On April 30, Eisenreich began a string of five consecutive games in which he pulled himself out of the lineup early due to "twitches and facial grimaces."[2]

"I just get nervous," Eisenreich said to Patrick Reusse in a May 1982 issue of *The Sporting News*. "When I think about it and try to correct it, I make it worse. The more I do it, the madder I get at myself. When I forget about it and have fun, I am okay."[3]

Eisenreich continued to have success at the plate during this time, but the final straw came at Fenway Park on May 4. Prior to the game, a Boston newspaper ran a story on Eisenreich's condition, which was still being treated as a simple case of nerves. Even Eisenreich's teammates found the initial symptoms somewhat comical at the time, so it was probably not surprising that the Red Sox fans began to taunt Eisenreich early in the game. Fans in the bleachers chanted insults at Eisenreich, and the symptoms progressively became worse. By the third inning, Eisenreich was still shaking violently and began to have trouble breathing, a result of hyperventilation, causing him to remove himself from the game.

Twins manager Billy Gardner tried to write Eisenreich's name into the lineup during the ensuing series in Milwaukee, but Eisenreich was unable to play in any of the games. On one occasion, Eisenreich ran from the outfield, into the dugout, tearing his clothes off while saying that he couldn't breathe. He was taken to the emergency room that night, where teammate Mickey Hatcher looked on as doctors tried unsuccessfully to calm Eisenreich down using tranquilizers. Eisenreich was placed on the disabled list shortly after and was admitted to St. Mary's Hospital in Minneapolis on May 9.

After an unsuccessful attempt to return in late May, Eisenreich and the Twins pulled the plug on the 1982 season in early June. Eisenreich sought multiple medical opinions on his condition, which only added to his frustration. "I don't know what's wrong with me. No one else does. If I go to four doctors, I get four different opinions."[4] The initial diagnosis was agoraphobia, and Eisenreich was put on medication to help reduce hyperventilation. He also tried self-hypnosis and different kinds of medication to control seizures. There was talk in the Twins' organization that Eisenreich might have been well enough to return in September, but the medication he was on made him unable to perform at the level to which he had become accustomed.

The spring of 1983 brought with it new hope for Eisenreich and the Twins. Jim reported to camp believing that his problems might be behind him. A .400 batting average in spring training seemed to confirm that. As the Twins broke camp, all reports were that Eisenreich was set to start in center field and lead off in the batting order.

But after the second game of the 1983 season, seemingly out of nowhere, Eisenreich told Billy Gardner and Twins vice president Howard Fox that he wanted to retire, saying that baseball was not "worth it" anymore and that he was no longer enjoying the game. With that, Eisenreich headed home for St. Cloud. The Twins convinced him to go on the disabled list rather than retire, hoping that Eisenreich might return. His mind was made up, however, and despite several overtures by the Twins, Eisenreich remained in St. Cloud for the rest of the 1983 season, where he passed the summer by playing softball four nights a week.

The same pattern repeated in the spring of 1984, when Eisenreich attempted another comeback. He managed to appear in 12 games for the Twins before he once again announced his retirement. As they did the year before, the Twins organization tried to convince Eisenreich to give it another try. The Twins were always high on his talent. In the spring of 1984, Calvin Griffith said of Eisenreich, "a natural ballplayer like this might only come once in a lifetime."[5] Manager Billy Gardner, around the same time, suggested that Eisenreich's presence in center field "added 10 additional victories."[6]

The relationship between the Twins and Eisenreich finally came to an end on June 4, 1984, when Jim refused a minor-league rehabilitation assignment. The Twins negotiated to pay Eisenreich for the rest of the season if he requested retirement, which he did. The parting seemed mostly amicable, with only a hint of frustration coming from Calvin Griffith, who seemed upset that Eisenreich had not tried new medication. The Twins brought up a young Kirby Puckett from the minors to replace Eisenreich in center field.

Eisenreich spent the next three years in St. Cloud working as a part-time painter, working in an archery shop, and playing semipro baseball with the St. Cloud Saints, where he remained retired from the majors until October of 1986. Eisenreich's former teammate at St. Cloud State, Bob Hegman, had become the Kansas City Royals' administrative assistant for scouting and player development. Through his correspondence with some of the other coaches in the semipro league, Hegman found that Eisenreich was excelling on the field and stood out among the other players like a "man playing on a girls' softball team."[7] Hegman recommended Eisenreich to Royals general manager John Schuerholz, and ultimately Eisenreich was invited to Royals' camp as a non-roster player for the spring of 1987, his rights purchased from the Twins for the waiver price of $1.

At the time the Royals signed Eisenreich, Dick Howser was Kansas City's manager. Howser resigned in February of 1987, however, and the Royals hired Billy Gardner to be their new manager. (Howser was attempting to comeback as manager after resigning the previous season because of a brain tumor; however, he was too sick to manage and died in June of 1987). Gardner had been the manager with the Twins during Eisenreich's stint with Minnesota. Gardner remembered the frustration of Eisenreich's first attempt to play major-league baseball, but he wanted to keep an open mind and was openly rooting for Eisenreich to succeed with the Royals.

Within the media coverage of Eisenreich's return, the first mention was made of Tourette syndrome. Jim told reporters that he believed Tourette syndrome was what had been causing the problem, not agoraphobia, as had been originally diagnosed and widely publicized. There was some skepticism from the media, and Eisenreich's original doctor stood by his first diagnosis. Still, to Eisenreich, the new understanding of his affliction gave him the confidence to try major-league baseball again.

Tourette syndrome is described by the Tourette Syndrome Association (TSA) as a neurological disorder that becomes evident in early childhood or adolescence before the age of 18 years. Tourette syndrome is defined by multiple motor and vocal tics lasting for more than one year. The first symptoms usually are involuntary movements (tics) of the face, arms, limbs or trunk. These tics are frequent, repetitive, and rapid. The most common first symptom is a facial tic (eye blink, nose twitch, grimace) and is replaced or added to by other tics of the neck, trunk, and limbs.

These involuntary (outside the patient's control) tics may also be complicated, involving the entire body, such as kicking and stamping. Many persons report what are described as premonitory urges—the urge to perform a motor activity. Other symptoms such as touching, repetitive thoughts and movements, and compulsions can occur.

There are also verbal tics. These include grunting, throat clearing, shouting, and barking. Occasionally, the verbal tics may also be expressed as the involuntary use of obscene words or socially inappropriate words and phrases and gestures. Despite widespread publicity, such behavior is uncommon with tic disorders.

Most people with Tourette syndrome and other tic disorders lead productive lives. There are no barriers to achievement in their personal and professional lives. Persons with Tourette syndrome can be found in all professions. A goal of the Tourette Syndrome Association is to educate both patients and the public of the many facets of tic disorders. Increased public understanding and tolerance of Tourette syndrome symptoms are of paramount importance to people with Tourette syndrome. Medication and counseling can help patients and their families cope with the illness.[8]

Eisenreich just wanted a chance, and the Kansas City Royals were ready to offer that to him. He started the 1987 season with Memphis in the Southern League. In 70 games with Memphis, Eisenreich batted .382 with 11 home runs and a league-leading 10 triples. Those numbers quickly led to a spot on the major league roster, and Eisenreich made his return to the big leagues on June 22, 1987, in a game at Oakland.

The Royals team that Eisenreich joined was in the heat of a race for the American League West lead with the Twins. Eisenreich's first major-league hit since 1984 came in a game against the Twins, and he was a major contributor in a series that saw Kansas City win three out of four from Minnesota in late June and early July. On July 1, it was Eisenreich's run-scoring double in the bottom of the ninth inning that defeated his former team. The next day, Eisenreich had a home run and four RBIs in the Royals' 10-3 victory in the series finale

Eisenreich didn't get caught up in his success in 1987. He told *The Sporting News*, "I know people are making a big thing about this, but I don't consider this a comeback, not yet . . . if I can play the whole season and be successful, then I'll know I'm back."[9] Eisenreich did finish the season, and, though his team did not win the division, he stuck it out and returned to the Royals the following season.

The 1988 season was a tough one for Eisenreich on the field. In the middle of the summer he experienced Class AAA for the first time in his career when he was sent down to Omaha. Eisenreich finished the season hitting just .218 with Kansas City

Both Eisenreich and the Royals got off to a great start in 1989. During the team's 17-9 start, Eisenreich batted .333 with 10 RBIs. Thanks to the hot stretch early on, Eisenreich played his first full season as a major-league regular. The season was such a success that Eisenreich beat out Bo Jackson to earn the Royals' Player of the Year award, as voted by the Kansas City media in the winter of 1989.

Eisenreich stayed with the Royals and remained an everyday player until Hal McRae became manager at the end of 1991. McRae used Eisenreich as a fourth outfielder out of spring training in 1992 despite the fact that Eisenreich had had an excellent spring. After the Royals got off to a 2-16 start, McRae made some changes that included using Eisenreich more, though he still was primarily a platoon player for the rest of the 1992 season.

That offseason brought changes for Eisenreich, who tested the free-agent market and ultimately signed with the Philadelphia Phillies in January 1993. For Eisenreich, the move meant that he would play in the National League, where he would spend the balance of his career. The Phillies brought him in as part of an aggressive offseason in which they acquired veterans Milt Thompson and Pete Incaviglia in addition to Eisenreich.

Though he was originally signed by the Phillies to be the fourth outfielder, Eisenreich quickly became the platoon partner of Wes Chamberlain in right field. The 1993 season may have been the best of Eisenreich's career to that point. Not only did he have great individual success, his team went to the World Series. Eisenreich's three-run home run in Game Two of the Series was a key factor in one of Philadelphia's two victories over the Toronto Blue Jays.

The Phillies lost the 1993 World Series in heartbreaking fashion, but Eisenreich's contributions earned him a contract extension with the Phillies. He continued to put up good numbers even though he was kind of the odd man out in the Philadelphia outfield for most of his time there. During the 1996 season, it was reported that the Phillies were shopping Eisenreich aggressively, despite the fact that he was having one of his best seasons at the plate. In December of 1996, at the age of 37, Eisenreich signed as a free agent with the Florida Marlins.

Once again Eisenreich came to a team that was making noise in the offseason. The Marlins, a franchise in only its fifth year, added veterans Bobby Bonilla and Moises Alou in addition to Eisenreich, who served primarily as a back-up left fielder. Once again team success followed, and the Marlins won the National League Wild Card in 1997 and advanced to the World Series, where Eisenreich once again was a contributor, this time in a seven-game World Series victory for his club. Eisenreich hit his second World Series home run in Game Three and was on second base when Edgar Renteria hit the series-winning single in the bottom of the 11th inning of Game Seven. "It was the greatest moment of my career," he told Bradford Doolittle. "We'd just won the World Series. I kind of pinch myself and kick myself, it's just amazing. It actually happened. Right after that, if you remember those old boom boxes, where you'd slowly turn them up to max, that's how the stadium was. And it stayed there for like an hour. That was unbelievable, the best time I ever had." [10]

In May of 1998, Eisenreich was traded to the Los Angeles Dodgers in a blockbuster deal that, among other things, briefly moved Mike Piazza to Florida. Eisenreich finished his major-league career in Los Angeles and retired after the 1998 season.

Throughout his later years in baseball, Eisenreich became an inspiration for others dealing with Tourette syndrome. He would regularly receive calls from people asking him how he overcame Tourette to have success in the major leagues. In 1996, Eisenreich and his wife, Leann, founded the Jim Eisenreich Foundation for Children with Tourette syndrome. Eisenreich now lives in Kansas City with his wife and four kids. He continues to travel the country, telling his story to children and families in order to get the message out about Tourette syndrome, often doing so at major-league baseball stadiums, where the foundation hosts presentations and outings for Tourette-affected families. The foundation also provides resource guides for teachers, principals, counselors, and school support staff on Tourette syndrome and gives an annual Children's Most Valuable Player Award to major-league players and alumni who have made a significant positive impact on the lives of children. Past winners have included Sean Casey, Kirby Puckett, Barry Larkin, and Arizona Diamondbacks general manager Joe Garagiola Jr.

Note: an earlier version of this biography appeared in the book *Minnesotans in Baseball*, edited by Stew Thornley (Nodin, 2009).

SOURCES

In addition to the sources cited in the Notes, the author also consulted:

Reusse, Patrick. "Eisenreich Says He Won't Be Back," *The Sporting News*, April 18, 1983.

Elliott, Tom. "One Last Chance," *St. Cloud Times*, February 26, 1987.

Elliott, Tom, "The Story of a Comeback," *St. Cloud Daily Times*, July 2, 1987.

Covitz, Randy. "Eisenreich Is Doing It Every Day," *The Sporting News*, September 11, 1989.

Preiss, Rick. "Cliff Eisenreich Devoted Life to Family, Teaching," *St. Cloud Times*, April 27, 1990.

Abicht, Anne. "MVP: Jim Eisenreich's Dream is Reality," *SCSU Outlook*, Summer 1990, 106.

Urdahl, Dean. *Touching Bases with our Memories: The Players Who Made the Minnesota Twins 1961-2001* (St. Cloud, Minnesota: North Star Press, 2001).

Young, Joseph. "Phillie Spirit Invades Holy Spirit as Students Cheer Famous Alumnus," *St. Cloud Visitor*, October 21, 1993.

Jim Eisenreich Foundation: http://tourettes.org.

Tourette Syndrome Association: http://www.tsa-usa.org.

NOTES

1   Dave Anderson, "Eisenreich Move No Shock to Ex-coach," *St. Cloud Times*, March 7, 1983.

2   Patrick Reusse, "Twins Rookie Battles a Nervous Disorder," *The Sporting News*, May 17, 1982: 32.

3   Ibid.

4   Patrick Reusse, "Eisenreich Hopes to Shake Affliction," *The Sporting News*, March 14, 1983: 30.

5   Patrick Reusse, "Eisenreich Again Says He is Retiring," *The Sporting News*, June 18, 1984: 12.

6   Patrick Reusse, "Eisenreich Giving It One More Try," *The Sporting News*, March 12, 1984: 48.

7   Michael Martinez, "Eisenreich Says He's Set To Try Again," *New York Times*, December 15, 1986.

8   For a summary of Eisenreich's background, diagnosis, and treatment that enabled him to return to baseball, see Jeff Shera, "When Anxiety Comes to Bat," *New York Times*, March 8, 1987.

9   Bob Nightengale, "Eisenreich: Illness or Anxiety," *The Sporting News*, March 23, 1987.

10   Bradford Doolittle, "Jim Eisenreich: No Place To Hide," *Baseball Prospectus*, July 5, 2012.

DICKIE THON

BY BOB LEMOINE

"I'm lucky to be alive. I'm happy to be alive. I'm doing everything I can to play again. It would be a plus. But there are more important things."
Dickie Thon, 1985[1]

SOME BASEBALL CAREERS ARE remembered for a single moment. It could be a hit to win the World Series, a strikeout to break a record, a diving catch, or a costly error. Dickie Thon's career is remembered for one moment … a pitch that got away. At a time when he was quickly becoming one of the rising shortstops in the National League, Thon's career and life changed forever when a pitch hit him in the left eye, leaving him with permanent partial blindness. Because of that one pitch, we will never know how great a player Dickie Thon could have been, but because of that one pitch, we know how great a man is Dickie Thon, who through faith and perseverance overcame a debilitating injury and persevered through a 15-year major-league career.

Richard William Thon was born on June 20, 1958, in South Bend, Indiana, to Frederick "Freddie" Thon Jr. and Evangeline Thon. Freddie played baseball at Notre Dame, but arm problems curtailed his career. He was in South Bend completing his undergraduate degree in business when Dickie was born. The family moved back to Puerto Rico, and Thon grew up in the Rio Piedras section of San Juan, where his great-grandfather had settled after migrating from Germany.[2] Thon's grandfather, Fred Thon Sr., pitched for the San Juan Senadores of the Puerto Rican Winter League and turned down a Brooklyn Dodgers contract since he was making more money as an engineer.[3] "From the time I was little," Dickie said, "I saw how important baseball was to the people of Puerto Rico. My grandfather told me stories about his days with San Juan in the 1940s and early 1950s. He talked about Monte Irvin, Joshua Gibson, and others who

came down here."[4] Thon remembered at the age of 5 meeting Irvin, who was visiting Fred Sr. Irvin, Dickie said, was "nice, polite, and strong." Young Thon also grew up cheering for baseball heroes Orlando Cepeda and Roberto Clemente.[5]

Thon was not the only player in his family to suffer an eye injury; his brother Frankie suffered the same fate on the baseball field. Playing American Legion baseball in San Juan in 1978, Frankie was hit in the face by a catcher's throw, and lost partial vision. Frankie played in the San Francisco Giants minor-league system, but vision problems forced him to retire in 1981.[6]

In his teenage years, Thon played for Bayamón in the Puerto Rico Winter League. He was signed by the California Angels as an amateur free agent in 1975. He spent the 1976 season with Class-A Quad Cities (Davenport, Iowa) of the Midwest League, batting .276 in 69 games at shortstop. Tom Sommers, then the Angels' director of minor-league operations, called Thon "the best natural-looking infielder I've ever seen."[7]

Thon spent 1977 with Class-A Salinas (California) and Triple-A Salt Lake City. Dick Miller of *The Sporting News* wrote, "The best prospect in the [Angels'] farm system is a 19-year-old shortstop named Dickie Thon."[8] Thon spent 1978 and the beginning of 1979 at Salt Lake City. He was called up and made his major-league debut on May 22, 1979, when he replaced Bobby Grich at second base in the eighth inning of a game the Angels were losing to the Milwaukee Brewers. Thon singled in his first at-bat, against Rich Hinton of the Chicago White Sox in the second game of a doubleheader on May 27 at Chicago.

Thon took advantage of his opportunities, going 6-for-16 (.375) through June 17 while filling in for the injured Grich and Bert Campaneris, impressing manager Jim Fregosi. "It looks like he has all the tools to play up here," Fregosi said. Said Thon: "I'm learning all the time from both Jim Fregosi and (coach) Bobby Knoop. They really know this game."[9] On September 6 Thon doubled home Don Baylor in the eighth inning with the go-ahead run in a 10-9 win over Chicago. The win kept the first-place Angels three games ahead of Kansas City, and the team went on to win the American League West. Thon pinch-ran and scored in Game Two of the ALCS against Baltimore in his only appearance in the series, won by Baltimore three games to one. Thon finished with a .339 batting average in 56 at-bats. As a rookie Thon met teammate Rod Carew, whom he would mention as the most influential player in his career.[10]

Thon started at Salt Lake City in 1980 and in 40 games blistered minor-league pitching, batting .394. He was recalled and went 5-for-5 in his first game back, on May 28 against Texas. "I was lucky on a couple of hits but I feel really good at the plate," he said after the game. "I feel comfortable here and I know I can hit big-league pitching."[11] "I was nervous and excited at the same time," he recalled in 2016.[12] Thon was 10-for-14 in his first three home games, batted a torrid .462 in May, and finished the season with a .326 batting average with runners in scoring position. "I'm just trying to fit in," he said. "I'm not that good yet. I have to be patient. I'm real excited about playing here."[13] Thon finished the season batting .255 in 80 games for a dismal 65-95 Angels club. In the winter he returned to Puerto Rico and won a batting title with Bayamón, hitting .329, with a league-best 46 runs and 82 hits in the 60-game schedule.

Thon's chances of starting for the Angels in 1981 were slim, however, with stable veterans Grich, Campanaris, Rick Burleson, and Freddie Patek on the roster. Thon was traded on April 1, 1981, to the Houston Astros for starting pitcher Ken Forsch. "We were looking for an established, experienced pitcher who can throw a good number of innings," Angels executive vice president Buzzie Bavasi said. "While we are terribly sorry to lose Dickie, as far as this club is concerned, the future is now."[14]

In the strike-shortened 1981 season, Thon played a utility-infielder role for Houston, backing up veteran Craig Reynolds. He batted .274 in 95 at-bats, with a .337 on-base percentage. Thon also feasted on home cooking and left-handed pitching, batting .308 at home (compared with .250 away) and .370 against left-handers (compared with .184 against righties). His on-base percentage from August to October was .422 and his batting average was .409, helping the Astros win the National League West for the second half of the season, the unique setup due to the players strike. Thon cooled off in the postseason, batting only .182, and the Astros lost the Division Series to the Dodgers. Thon returned to Puerto Rico in the offseason and batted .333 for Bayamón, winning another batting title.

Thon replaced Reynolds as the starting shortstop in 1982 and asserted himself as one of the top shortstops in the National League, with the glove and the bat. He led the National League in triples (10) and was ninth in stolen bases (37). He was fourth in the league among shortstops in fielding percentage (.975), his range factor per game (putouts and assists divided by games played) was fourth, and a total zone runs average for shortstops (calculating the number of runs above or below average a player is worth to the team) ranked him second behind Ozzie Smith. "I am not really doing anything differently," Thon said. "I'm just getting the chance to play."[15] Thon compiled a 21-game hitting streak from July 24 to August 13, batting .308 over that stretch, and had a four-hit game two days after the streak ended, going 4-for-5 with three doubles against Cincinnati. He hit his first major-league home run in his 567th at-bat, off Bob Walk in Atlanta on June 29. Thon finished the season batting .276 with 3 home runs and 36 RBIs for the 77-85 Astros. His 6.1 WAR (wins above replacement) statistic was sixth in the league for position players.

The 1983 season was Thon's breakout season, and his statistics were among the leaders in the National League in several offensive and defensive categories. His value to the improved 85-77, third-place Astros was immense, and his 7.4 WAR was first in the league among position players. Thon was seventh in at-bats (619), six in plate appearances (686), seventh in hits (177), and fourth in total bases (283). He ranked first in shortstop assists (533), third in putouts (258), and second in double plays turned as a shortstop (114).

His .299 batting average in April was following by three months of .300 or better. Thon had a 12-game hitting streak from May 12-26 and three two-home run games, on June 17, 28, and July 9. His 14th-inning walk-off home run on August 10 beat San Diego. His power was a surprise even to him. "I wasn't thinking home run tonight," he said after the San Diego game. "I just wanted to get on base."[16] Thon made the 1983 All-Star team and stroked a pinch-hit single off Rick Honeycutt. "I saw Willie Mays sitting next to me," Thon remembered from the event. "That was a thrill."[17] His final numbers — .286 batting average, .341 on-base percentage, .457 slugging percentage, 20 home runs, 79 RBIs — were good enough to give him seventh place in the National League MVP voting.

Thon got off to a good start in 1984, batting .375 in the first four games of the season. Then his life changed forever on April 8, in a game at Houston's Astrodome.

Thon used a batting stance that leaned into the plate. New York Mets pitcher Mike Torrez had caught him looking in his first at-bat on a called third strike on the outside part of the plate. In his next at-bat, Thon crept even closer to the plate. Torrez decided to pitch him inside. "After I got him away, I decided to bring it in," Torrez recalled. "He has a tendency to crowd the plate and lunge for balls so I thought I'd jam him. It was a strategy decision, nothing more. But my ball was sailing that day."[18]

Torrez yelled a warning to Thon after releasing the ball, but Thon didn't hear it. Plate umpire Doug Harvey said he saw the ball move about 10 inches, starting waist-high and moving upward until it glanced off Thon's ear flap, then struck him above the left eye.[19] "When I saw where the ball was, it was too late to get out of the way," Thon said.[20] "He ducked," Torrez said, "but he ducked into (the pitch)."[21] Thon said in 2015 that he continued to relive that moment in his dreams: the ball coming right at him, and himself powerless to move.[22]

The Astrodome crowd went eerily silent as team physician William Bryan and manager Bob Lillis bolted to the field. "I heard a bone break," Dr. Bryan said. "I heard the ball hitting the bone, like a dull thud."[23] Thon didn't get up. "I kept thinking, 'I want to

live'" he said. 'I want to see my family again.' I didn't know how bad it was. I was scared. I said, 'Is this really happening?'"[24]

At Methodist Hospital, X-rays revealed a fracture of the orbital rim, the bone above the left eye. "It was an accident, the pitch sailed on me," Torrez said after the game. "I feel awful. He's a good young ballplayer. I just hope to God he's all right. My thoughts will be with him and his family tonight."[25] Torrez called Thon and apologized. "He told me he was real sorry," Thon said. "I believe him. It's one of those things. It's part of the game."[26]

Frankie Thon's wife, Blanca, who was watching the game, became so distraught that she went into labor and gave birth prematurely to Freddie Francis Thon.[27] (Notwithstanding, Freddie represented the fourth generation of Thons in professional baseball, and played for several minor-league teams from 2004 to 2011.)

Thon's 1984 season was over, and his road to recovery was beginning. "I'm not really ever emotional about it and I'm not afraid of getting back in," Thon said later in 1984. "But in the morning, when I wake up, that's when I think about it. I don't blame Mike Torrez. I blame myself. I think, 'Why did I let this happen?' I just stood there."[28]

Three days after he was hit, Thon had surgery on the left orbital bone, but the blurred vision continued. "I hope the Good Lord will help me recover quickly," he said. "It's tough to work hard in spring training to get ready, then have something like this happen. But I'll be back."[29] "I feel for my brother (Frankie)," said Thon. "And I feel him in me. He never had a chance to play in the majors. I have to come back, for me and for him."[30]

An eye examination measured the vision in his left eye as 20/300, and Thon could neither read nor drive. By June 1 his vision had improved to 20/50, but there was still scar tissue behind the retina. He was examined by Stephen J. Ryan, an expert in retina damage at the University of Southern California. "It has to improve on its own," Thon said. "The doctors say I can adjust (to seeing a blurry ball) in time. If it's a matter of work, I'll do it. I'm not down and I'm not giving up."[31] "I have no depth perception," he said. "Glasses won't help right now. ... I've tried batting practice, but the ball is a blur." While dressing and being on the Astros bench during home games kept him in the game and relaxed, "the problem starts when I drive home and I can't always tell how far the traffic light is," he said.[32]

With time off, Thon took business courses at a community college. "I took a course on sports psychology that really helped," he said.[33] He also continued eye exercises that involved following marks on a golf ball and reading numbers on a spinning record.[34] An exam in the fall showed Thon's vision improved to 20/40. "If you take a piece of wax paper and crinkle it up," Dr. Bryan said, "then try to straighten it out, it still has wrinkles. The ophthalmologists tell us that's how the back of Dickie's eyeball looks. It [beaning] affected his visual acuity—his ability to read letters—and his depth perception."[35]

Thon returned to the field in late 1984 in the Arizona Instructional League. He played in five games and had five hits.[36] He played winter ball for the San Juan Metros,[37] hitting a home run in his first game but going 0-for-6 with two errors in his next two games. "I asked to be removed from the lineup," said Thon,[38] who felt he was being used by the team owner as a promotional gimmick.[39]

In spring training 1985, Thon was hopeful. "My timing is bad," he said. "I'm rushing everything. I don't do anything smoothly. Hopefully it's getting better. I'm seeing the ball better and better. Sometimes it's hard to overcome the fear of being hurt. I'm trying to concentrate on seeing the ball and getting out of the way. I know I can do it. It's something I am working on. I have a lot of faith in God. If he wants me to play again, I will."[40]

Thon's career pre-injury was that of a young and promising star. The post-injury Thon was a much different player, one who had to constantly battle physical and mental hardships. "I didn't enjoy the game the same way," he said in 2015. "It was more work for me. Before, it was fun. After that, it was, 'I gotta do this to work for my family, to work for my future.'"[41]

Thon was the Astros' starting shortstop on Opening Day in 1985. A crowd of 42,876 gave him a lengthy standing ovation, and were thrilled to see him single and score the Astros' first run of the season in a 2-1 win over the Dodgers. "This is a big step," he said. "I was anxious about it. The regular season is different from spring training. I wanted a groundball hit at me early to get it out of the way. And the first hit helped."[42] "We were rooting so hard for him that when he came back in the dugout after that first hit, it was as if every player on our team had gotten that hit," manager Bob Lillis said.[43] "He has so much determination that I knew it was just a matter of time until he made it back," said teammate Jose Cruz.[44]

Thon struggled early on, batting .200 in April, striking out 11 times in 40 at-bats, and batting .163 in June, striking out 13 times in 43 at-bats. "They know I'm not going to get worse, but they don't know if I'm going to get better," he said of the 20/40 vision in his left eye. "I've got to be patient with myself."[45] Batting just .207, he went on the disabled list on May 19. He returned to the field in mid-June, but by July 10 was batting .193. Thon batted .299 with five home runs over the remainder of the season, lowering his strikeouts and raising his season batting average to .251.

With a new two-year contract, Thon arrived at spring training in 1986 optimistic. "This year I feel a lot better than I did last year at this time," he said. "I think the best thing I can do is play and get the competition. That's what I need." He reported that his left eye vision was 20/30, "but I'm getting used to it and seeing the ball good. I wasn't confident last year. I had a lot of friends and a lot of players back me up. I have a lot of faith. I'm working hard."[46] Thon slumped at the plate, but played in 106 games, platooning with Craig Reynolds and facing mostly left-handed pitching.

Complaining of blurred vision, Thon, hitting a paltry .205, went on the disabled list on June 5. When he returned on June 23, he batted .280 the rest of the season, and .300 in the September Western Division title run. Thon was on the field as Mike Scott threw a no-hitter against San Francisco, clinching the National League West. "Very good pitching and very steady infield. Good outfield, good bench, and [manager] Hal Lanier did a great job," Thon remembered.[47] Batting eighth, Thon belted a home run off Sid Fernandez of the Mets in Game Four of the NLCS, giving the Astros a 3-1 victory and tying the series at two games apiece. He played in all six games, going 3-for-12 at the plate, as the Astros lost to the Mets.

Thon left spring training without permission on March 14, 1987, complaining of vision problems. He had gone hitless in eight at-bats, striking out twice, and had made three errors. He underwent a 2½-hour eye examination, with results showing no improvement. Thon also requested psychiatric assistance. His agent, Tom Reich, stated, "Dickie is suffering from a lot of stress. Obviously, at this point, Dickie isn't ready to play." Thon had no desire to return. "I don't know when I'll go back to Florida," he said. "They want to make me make a decision right away, but I'm not going to do it."[48] The team fined Thon $1,000 a day for his absence. He returned to Puerto Rico to see a specialist.[49] Thon returned to the team in May, but left again July 3 after batting .212 and complaining of continual eye problems. "I feel sad because I wish I

could have done more for the team," Thon said. "I feel a lot for this team. I feel I'll always be one of them."

Thon was placed on the disqualified list after an unsatisfactory meeting with Astros GM Dick Wagner. "The way [Wagner] has been dealing with my situation, I won't be around here anymore," Thon said. "It's difficult to walk away from a game I'd do anything to play."[50]

Thon's career with the Astros was over, but in 1988 the San Diego Padres were looking for a shortstop to back up Garry Templeton. Thon signed with the Padres as a free agent and played against left-handed pitching, batting .264 in 95 games, but was frustrated with his role. He asked the Padres to trade him. "I had to erase a stigma," Thon said. "I knew by then I could play, but I had to convince others that I could."[51] After the season he was traded to the Philadelphia Phillies. In the winter before the 1989 season, Thon worked in Puerto Rico with Ken Duzich, who was both a hitting instructor and vision specialist. "Dickie was left-eye dominant," Duzich said, "I recommended he open up his head a little bit more so that the right eye had better vision."[52]

Thon no longer crowded the plate but stood away, allowing his right eye to compensate for his left. He also switched from a 34- to a 38-ounce bat.[53] Thon had his best season since 1983, batting .271 in 136 games with 15 home runs, the most among NL shortstops. On September 12 he hit a walk-off home run to beat the Mets 2-1 in a September in which he batted .357. "I think he's back," Phillies manager Nick Leyva said. "And after all the things Dickie has gone through, you have to feel good for him. He's been through a lot of adversity."[54] Thon was just glad for the opportunity to play. "I'm just trying to go out and play as hard as I can every day," he said. "I feel good right now, and I'm getting the chance to play. I think playing so much has made a big difference."[55] He was rewarded with a 1990 contract for $1.1 million in base salary.[56] He continued as the everyday shortstop in 1990, playing in 149 games with a .255 batting average and 8 home runs. On July 13 he hit two home runs at the Astrodome, to the polite applause of the fans, as the Phillies defeated the Astros 4-2. "I feel good about the Houston fans,"

Thon said. "They have always been good to me. I'm glad I did something they liked."[57]

Thon downplayed being labeled "courageous" when he was awarded the 1990 Philadelphia Sports Writers Association's Most Courageous Athlete Award. "My wife is more courageous than me," he said. "She's had three (caesarean sections), and she wants to have another baby. That's being courageous."[58]

Thon had a nearly identical 1991 season for the Phillies, batting .252 with 9 home runs and 44 RBIs. He slumped in July, and heard the boos from Philly fans. "It bothers me a little bit," Thon said. "I know that always comes when you struggle, but I just want people to know that I play hard, and I think I've been doing my job."[59] Thon's time in Philadelphia came to a close when the Phillies did not offer him a contract for 1992.

In December of 1991 Thon was presented the second annual Tony Conigliaro Award. Conigliaro was a Boston Red Sox player who also suffered vision problems after a beaning in 1967. The annual award is presented to the major leaguer who overcomes "an obstacle and adversity through the attributes of spirit, determination and courage."[60] Thon was a well-deserved recipient.

Shortly after receiving the award, Thon returned to Texas when he signed as a free agent with the Rangers. "This is like home, and it's a very good club," Thon said.[61] A team with many offensive weapons was plagued with one of the worst pitching staffs in the league, and the Rangers finished 77-85 in 1992. A bone bruise on his right shoulder forced Thon to miss most of August and September,[62] and he was released after appearing in 95 games, batting .247 with 4 home runs and 37 RBIs. He returned to the Puerto Rican Winter League with major leaguer Juan Gonzalez and led Santurce to defeat San Juan in the finals. The series attracted 90,369 fans to the ballpark for the six games, including a record crowd of 23,701 in Game Six.[63]

Thon signed with the Milwaukee Brewers for 1993.[64] He batted .396 in April, and singled home the winning run against Toronto on June 25, spoiling ex-Brewer Paul Molitor's return to Milwaukee. Thon played in 85 games, batting .269 with one home run. After the season the Brewers declined his $350,000 option, and he signed a minor-league contract with Oakland in February of 1994. But he retired a month later, complaining of not seeing the ball well in the field.[65] "It's a tough break," said A's manager Tony La Russa. "He's always been a guy I'd like to have on my club. It was just the wrong time of his career ... defensively; he didn't really react like I know he could."[66] Thon's 15-year career, which took him from a promising young star to a gritty survivor, was over.

In a 2015 interview with Greg Hanlon of vicesports. com, Thon revealed that the scar tissue behind his retina still had not fully healed, and that his vision and depth perception troubles continued to plague him. Driving and reading were still difficult. Thon played for 10 years while having vision in one eye described as "looking through a sheet of wax paper." No one except his wife, Sol (short for Maria Soledad), knew the extent of his disability. Thon became good at guessing the answers during the eye tests, officially giving him 20/30 vision he likely didn't really have. "I was afraid they wouldn't give me a chance to play," he said.[67]

In 1996 Thon was the Astros' minor-league baserunning and infield instructor. Later he returned to Puerto Rico and continued to be involved with the winter league, working with the Cangrejeros de Santurce club, as well as youth baseball. Thon's family is known for its success in athletics. His wife, Sol, was a volleyball player on the Puerto Rican National Team; daughters Soleil, Vanessa, and Mariana were collegiate volleyball players at Rice, Tulsa, and South Florida; and son Dickie Joe Thon, an infielder, was drafted by the Toronto Blue Jays in the fifth round of the June 2010 amateur draft, and received a $1.5 million signing bonus. As of 2016 he was still playing in the Blue Jays farm system. "He earned more by signing than I did in my best year," his father joked.[68]

In 2011 Thon and Torrez met face-to-face for the first time since the beaning. Torrez again apologized, but Thon repeated what he had said 27 years earlier: It's just part of the game. A devout Catholic, Thon said he looked instead to the blessings of his life instead of the hardships. "I've had a lot of good things happen to me. I try to think about it that way," Thon said.[69]

Asked by the author to describe anything important he would want conveyed in this biography, Thon said: "One thing I've learned is that [you should] always believe in yourself and accomplish everything you want in life, with hard work and determination. Don't listen to negative stuff. Always concentrate on believing that you can accomplish anything if you are willing to work hard."[70]

SOURCES

In addition to the sources cited in the Notes, the author also benefited from the Dickie Thon file at the Baseball Hall of Fame Library, Cooperstown, New York.

NOTES

1   Gordon Edes, "Dickie Thon Is the Latest Big League Player to Attempt a Comeback From a Serious Beaning: GAME'S NIGHTMARE," *Los Angeles Times*, March 18, 1985.

2   Greg Hanlon, "Lost Greatness, Scar Tissue, and Survival: The Life of Baseball's Brief Superstar, Dickie Thon," Vice Sports. Retrieved March 8, 2016, sports.vice.com/en_us/article/lost-greatness-scar-tissue-and-survival-the-life-of-baseballs-brief-superstar-dickie-thon.

3   Mason Kelly, "Thon Family Bound By History," *Bakersfield* (California) *Californian*, July 16, 2006. Retrieved January 30, 2016, bakersfield.com/sports/2006/07/16/thon-family-bound-by-history.html.

4   Thomas E. Van Hyning, *Puerto Rico's Winter League: A History of Major League Baseball's Launching Pad.* (Jefferson, North Carolina: McFarland, 2004), 108.

5   Dickie Thon, mail correspondence with the author, September 2016.

6   Thon correspondence with author.

7   Earl Gustkey, "Angel Officials Keep an Eye on the Minors," *Los Angeles Times*, April 23, 1976: 8.

8   Dick Miller, "Rich Angels Ask: Which Niche for Grich Next Year?" *The Sporting News*, October 22, 1977: 31.

9   Pete Donovan, "Angels…Who are Those Guys?" *Los Angeles Times*, June 23, 1979: D8.

10   Thon correspondence with author.

11   Jim Shulte, "Thompson, Thon Lead Angels' Win Over Texas," *San Bernardino* (California) *County Star*, May 29, 1980: D3.

12   Thon correspondence with author.

13   Dick Miller, "Thon Hits a Ton, and Angels Think of Trade," *The Sporting News*, June 28, 1980: 10.

14   Associated Press, "California, Houston Swap Two Players," *Santa Cruz* (California) *Sentinel*, April 1, 1981: 49.

15   Hal Bodley, "Thon Earns His Stripes at Short for the Astros," *USA Today*, June 29, 1983: 5C.

16   Associated Press, "Thon's 16th Homer Gives Astros the Win," *Baytown* (Texas) *Sun*, August 11, 1983: 2-C.

17   Thon correspondence with author.

18   Craig Wolff, "A Fearless Moment Keeps Its Hold on Dickie Thon," *New York Times*, June 17, 1984. Retrieved January 31, 2016. nytimes.com/1984/06/17/sports/a-fearless-moment-keeps-its-hold-on-dickie-thon.html?pagewanted=all.

19   Ibid.

20   Ray Didinger, "The Future Is a Blur for Dickie Thon," *The Sporting News*, September 24, 1984: 58.

21   Ibid.

22   Hanlon.

23   Ibid.

24   Ibid.

25   Ibid.

26   Associated Press, "Thon Afraid of Not Being Able to Play Again After Being Hit by Pitch to Head," *Big Spring* (Texas) *Herald*, April 11, 1984: 10. Retrieved March 27, 2016, bill37mccurdy.com/2015/06/06/the-night-dickie-thon-went-down/.

27   Wolff, "A Fearless Moment."

28   Ibid.

29   "Thon Has Surgery," Associated Press clipping in Thon's Hall of Fame file marked 4/12/1984.

30   Wolff, "A Fearless Moment."

31   Ibid.

32   Craig Wolff, "Thon Now Looks to 1985," *New York Times*, June 16, 1984.

33   Ron Fimrite, "You Can't Keep a Good Man Down," *Sports Illustrated*, April 16, 1990.

34   Ibid.

35   Edes.

36   Ibid.

37   Associated Press, "Thon to Make Comeback in Winter League," *Albany* (New York) *Times Union*, undated article in Thon's Hall of Fame file.

38   Hal Bodley, "Dickie Thon: Astros Shortstop Battles Blurry Vision, Doubts in Comeback," *USA Today*, January 22, 1985.

39   Edes.

40   Ibid.

41   Hanlon.

42 Neil Hohlfeld, "Thon Makes Opening Night to Remember," *The Sporting News*, April 22, 1985: 24.

43 Ibid.

44 Neil Hohlfeld, "Thon Now Appears Back in Stride," *The Sporting News*, September 9, 1985: 18.

45 Jack Etkin, "Astros' Thon Praying Path to Lineup Clears," *Kansas City Times*, May 2, 1985.

46 Fred McMane, "Thon's Fight Back Nearly Completed," *Tampa Tribune*, March 13, 1986.

47 Thon correspondence with author.

48 "Thon Asks for Help," *Albany Times Union*, March 23, 1987.

49 "Thon Given Ultimatum," *Albany Times Union*, March 18, 1987; "Thon Will be Back," *Albany Times Union*, March 19, 1987.

50 "Thon Doesn't Plan Return to Astros," *New York Post*, July 7, 1987.

51 Fimrite.

52 Van Hyning, 108.

53 Hanlon.

54 Bill Brown, "Thon Has Completed Long Journey," *The Sporting News*, September 25, 1989.

55 Ibid.

56 Unknown clipping in Thon's Hall of Fame file, marked 2/19/90.

57 "Thon's Blasts Light Up Night for Phillies," *New York Daily News*, July 15, 1990.

58 Paul Domowitch, "Thon: My Wife Is More Courageous," *Philadelphia Daily News*, February 13, 1990. Retrieved March 27, 2016, articles.philly.com/1990-02-13/sports/25880359_1_courage-dickie-thon-mike-torrez-fastball.

59 Diane Pucin, "Struggling Thon Not Ready for the Scrap Heap Just Yet," Knight-Ridder News Service story published in the *Albany Times Union*, August 4, 1991.

60 "Tony Conigliaro Award," Baseball Reference Bullpen. Retrieved March 27, 2016, baseball-reference.com/bullpen/Tony_Conigliaro_Award.

61 Randy Galloway, "Thon's Voice Will Be Heard in Clubhouse," *Dallas Morning News*, April 2, 1992.

62 United Press International, "Rangers' Thon on DL," August 7, 1992. Retrieved February 27, 2016, upi.com/Archives/1992/08/07/Rangers-Thon-on-DL/1406713160000/.

63 Van Hyning, 108.

64 Ed Glennon, "Brewers Sign Thon," *Rockford* (Illinois) *Register Star*, March 31, 1993: 5D.

65 "Thon Retires," *Stamford* (Connecticut) *Daily Advocate*, March 3, 1994: C2.

66 "Eyesight Fading, Thon Retires," *Santa Cruz* (California) *Sentinel*, March 3, 1994: B-3.

67 Hanlon.

68 Marc Seide, "Seniors Storied Childhood Paves Way to USF," *The Oracle*, October 26, 2010. Retrieved March 27, 2016, usforacle.com/news/view.php/690131/Seniors-storied-childhood-paves-way-to-U; Bob Elliott, "Thon's Father Knows Best," *Toronto Sun*, August 23, 2010.

69 Hanlon.

70 Thon correspondence with author.

JIM ABBOTT

BY RICK SWAINE

LEFT-HANDED PITCHER JIM Abbott is probably the most celebrated athlete with a major disability of his era. Born with a deformed right arm, Abbott was already a national hero before signing a professional contract with the California Angels in 1988. As a sophomore pitcher for the University of Michigan in 1987 he was named the best amateur athlete and the top amateur baseball player in the nation, and became the first U.S. pitcher to beat the Cuban national team in Cuba in 25 years. As a junior he garnered a gold medal as a member of the 1988 U.S. Olympic baseball team, crowning his amateur career by beating Japan in the final game in Seoul, South Korea. In his first season in professional baseball, he won a spot in the starting rotation of the pennant-contending Angels without an inning of minor-league seasoning and established himself as a topflight major-league pitcher.

Abbott's right arm ends about where his wrist should be. He doesn't have a right hand, just a loose flap of skin at the end of his underdeveloped arm. Otherwise, he was a strapping 6-foot-3 200-pounder in his prime whose physique could have served as a model for the ideal baseball player.

Abbott, who retired in 1999, pitched with a right-hander's fielder's glove perched pocket-down over the end of his stubbed right arm. At the conclusion of his delivery, he would deftly slip his left hand into the glove and be ready to field the ball. After catching the ball, he would cradle the glove against his chest in the crook of his right arm and extract the ball with his left hand, ready to make another throw. Observers invariably marveled at how smoothly and efficiently he could catch and throw the ball with one hand.

Jim Abbott's parents were still teenagers when he was born in Flint, Michigan, on September 19, 1967. Having a child at such as young age was difficult enough, especially a child with a disability, but Mike and Kathy Abbott resolved to make their son's life as normal as possible. Mike Abbott sold cars and worked as a meatpacker and Kathy took courses at home while raising Jim. Eventually both parents finished college and went on to successful careers, Mike in management and Kathy as a teacher and later an attorney. Jim's parents always encouraged him to try things and helped him acquire confidence. "We decided that if Jim wanted to [play sports] then to let him try," said Mike Abbott in a 1998 USA Today interview. "I helped out with some things. But in the end it was all Jim. It had to be."[1]

Jim started showing an interest in sports at an early age. Trying to nudge him toward a sport that didn't depend on the use of his hands, his parents bought him a soccer ball. But, Jim didn't really like soccer. After all, every other kid in the neighborhood was playing baseball so that's what he wanted to do. Ironically, it was Jim's younger brother, Chad, who became a soccer player.

So Jim Abbott began developing the remarkable hand-eye coordination that would allow him to do with one hand what others did with two. He spent hours throwing a rubber ball against a brick wall and catching it on the rebound. His father helped him develop the technique for handling his glove-hand switch which allowed Jim him to throw and catch the ball with the same hand. Over the years he continued this drill, moving closer and closer to the wall and making the glove transition faster and faster.

When Jim began school, he was fitted with a mechanical hand made of fiberglass and metal. But he hated the prosthesis, which he called a "hook," because it frightened some of his classmates and made him self-conscious. Eventually his parents stopped making him wear it.

At the age of 11, Jim joined a Little League team and threw a no-hitter in the first game he pitched. Despite his early success, most people figured the competition would soon pass him by. In fact, at every

step, from Little League on, he kept hearing that his playing days would probably end at that level. But at each new level, Jim proved his doubters wrong. When he entered high school at Flint Central, his new coach doubted Jim would be able to defend his position adequately. But Jim actually fielded well enough to play first base and the outfield when he wasn't pitching.

Even his hitting was exceptional. Jim batted from the left side, wrapping his left hand around the bat and the stub of his right arm. He was able to generate remarkable power, blasting seven homers and batting an excellent .427 as a senior. On the mound that year he won ten games and lost three with an incredibly low 0.76 ERA and averaged more than two strikeouts per inning pitched.

Jim was also the backup quarterback for Flint Central until the end of his senior year when he started the last three games, passing for 600 yards and six touchdowns. In addition, he was the squad's punter, averaging 37.5 yards per kick as a senior. His first national exposure came when his high school football accomplishments were featured on NBC's *The NFL Today* pregame show.

Abbott was drafted by the Toronto Blue Jays out of high school in the 36th and last round of the draft, but turned down their $50,000 bonus offer to attend the nearby University of Michigan. Despite the major league offer and his high school achievements, colleges with top baseball programs didn't heavily recruit him. There were still some reservations about his disability, and Abbott himself admitted to having some initial doubts about his ability to play college baseball. But they were quickly dispelled. As a freshman he was named Most Courageous Athlete for 1986 by the Philadelphia Sportswriters Association after posting a record of six wins against two losses. The season was not without embarrassment, however. After his first college game, the modest young hurler was mortified and suffered an unmerciful razzing from his teammates when the press held the team bus up for an hour to interview him.

Over the next two seasons, Jim continued to develop as a pitcher and began to think seriously about a career in professional baseball. In 1987 he pitched the Wolverines to first place in the Big Ten Eastern Division standings and then to the conference championship and threw a shutout in the NCAA tournament. For the season he won 11 games against three losses. He then earned a spot on the U.S. national amateur baseball team, Team USA, and on the warm-up tour threw his three-hit complete-game victory against the vaunted Cuban team in front of 50,000 spectators. In the Pan American Games, he not only carried the flag for the U.S. delegation, but also won two games without giving up an earned run as Team USA captured a silver medal. For the year, his efforts earned him the Sullivan Award, being chosen over hurdler Greg Foster and basketball star David Robinson as the outstanding amateur athlete in the country. He then beat out future major-league stars Jack McDowell, Robin Ventura, and Ken Griffey Jr. for the coveted Golden Spikes Award, given to the top amateur baseball player.

Abbott had another fine season at Michigan in 1988, becoming the first baseball player to ever be named Big Ten Conference Player of the Year. He then pitched the U.S. Olympic Team to victory over

Japan with a 5-3 complete-game effort, which he still considers his biggest thrill in sports.

After his Olympic triumph, Abbott decided to forgo his last year of college eligibility to enter the professional ranks. He was selected by the California Angels with the eighth pick in the first round of the amateur draft and negotiated a $207,000 bonus. As happened whenever Jim moved up to another level in sports, skeptics came out of the woodwork to question whether a player with one arm could perform at the next level. The familiar old questions about his ability to defend his position resurfaced.

On bunts and slow rollers Abbott often didn't have time to field the ball with his glove and make the transfer. So he usually discarded the glove and fielded bunts barehanded. In high school, an opposing coach once ordered the first eight batters to bunt. After the first one reached base, Jim shut down the bunting game by retiring the next seven in a row. Of course, he had to pass the same test in college and the big leaguers would also give it a try. But once again, Abbott answered with great coordination and quick reflexes.

The 1989 edition of the Angels that Abbott joined as a rookie was a talented team — legitimate pennant contenders. They'd finished fourth to Kansas City in 1988 and featured a solid pitching staff that had been bolstered by the off-season acquisition of veteran ace Bert Blyleven, who already had more than 250 major-league victories under his belt. It didn't seem likely that a raw, 21-year-old rookie could crack the rotation.

Up to that time only 15 players had made their professional debut in the major leagues since the establishment of the amateur draft in 1965. Still fewer enjoyed successful careers while most quickly faded into oblivion. Everyone assumed Abbott would be farmed out to gain needed experience, but he made the team out of spring training and edged into the starting rotation. Injuries to other members of the rotation, as much as his own performance, allowed Abbott to make the opening day roster, but there was still a good deal of second-guessing. Many felt Abbott's retention was more about public relations than fielding the best roster.

It's true Abbott was a media sensation. His first spring appearance was in a "B-game" that had to be moved from a practice field to the main stadium to accommodate the throng of fans and media representatives. At the postgame press conference, Abbott patiently discussed his pitching/fielding motion. "I've been doing this since I was 5 years old. Now it's as natural as tying my shoes," he said to reporters, leaving them to contemplate the complexity of tying one's shoes with one hand.[2]

As with the beginning of every new phase in his career, Abbott's first regular season start was a major event. The media, including four television crews from Japan, converged on Anaheim Stadium in full force for the grand debut. Jim lasted less than five innings and racked up his first major league loss, but left to a standing ovation from the huge crowd. *Baseball America* ranked his debut second only to Jackie Robinson's breaking of the color barrier in terms of historical significance.

After another defeat, Abbott beat the Baltimore Orioles in his third start and settled down to pitch good baseball the rest of the season. He ended the year with 12 wins against the same number of losses. The dozen victories were the most major league wins by a pitcher in his first professional season since long-forgotten Ernie Wingard won 13 in 1924 for the old St. Louis Browns before fading into obscurity.

The Angels finished the 1989 season in third place and Abbott was voted the club's Rookie of the Year. He was also named the Most Inspirational Player by the Anaheim chapter of the Baseball Writers Association of America.

Abbott's deft handling of the constant public pressure may have been his most impressive accomplishment, however. Handsome and articulate, he was interviewed countless times by the major networks and publications. He turned down repeated book offers, and received tons of mail — including a personal telegram from Nolan Ryan before his first start. Hall of Famers Ernie Banks and Bobby Doerr asked for his autograph, and 363-game-winner Warren Spahn called him his hero. Jim studied communications in college and was better prepared than most 21-year-old rookies to handle the crush. His maturity and cooperation with the press and the public won him a legion of loyal supporters and he naturally became an inspirational role model for kids with all kinds of disabilities.

Questions about his ability still remained, however. Abbott had trouble holding runners on base and his fielding was weak. He was the second easiest pitcher in the league to steal against and he had a rather low fielding percentage. By his own admission, he missed many plays that he should have made.

Abbott experienced a disappointing 1990 sophomore season, compiling a 10-14 won-lost record. He got off to a terrible start in 1991, suffering four straight losses to begin the season after an unimpressive spring performance. Calls for his demotion to the minors lit up the phone lines to the sports talk shows, but the club stuck by him and he managed to turn the corner.

In fact, he ended up enjoying a breakthrough campaign. Although the Angels faded after the All-Star Game, Abbott won eleven games after the break to finish 1991 campaign with an 18-11 won-lost mark and a stingy 2.89 earned run average. In the voting for the American League Cy Young Award, the most prestigious pitching honor in the league, he placed third as Roger Clemens of the Red Sox captured the trophy for the third time. Abbott's 1991 record is even more impressive when the lack of run support provided by the Angels hitters is taken into account. According to a concept for rating pitcher performance developed by noted baseball statistician and author Bill James, Abbott led the American League in "tough losses" with eight.

Another highlight of Abbott's excellent 1991 campaign was a 375-foot triple he drove into the gap in a spring training contest against the San Francisco Giants. Since the Angels were in the American League where the designated hitter is used, Abbott didn't get to bat during the regular season. The triple was his first hit in a major-league uniform and the pitcher drove his teammates crazy talking about it.

In December 1991 Jim married Dana Douty, who had grown up in the Anaheim area. What should have been a very satisfying offseason for young Jim Abbott

was marred by antagonistic salary negotiations, but he eventually signed a one-year contract for $1.85 million, which made him the highest-paid fourth-year pitcher in baseball history at that time.

The 1992 season was another memorable one for him, but for all the wrong reasons. The Angels won only 72 games and finished fifth in the seven-team American League Western Division. Despite pitching well all year, Abbott posted a dismal 7-15 won-lost record. But his sparkling 2.77 ERA was a more accurate indicator of the quality of his efforts. Throughout his career Abbott routinely suffered from poor run support, but in 1992 the Angels backed him with the lowest run-support figure in the American League since the adoption of the designated-hitter rule in 1973.

To top it off, in December 1992 Abbott was swapped to the New York Yankees for three minor-league prospects when the Angels couldn't sign him to a long-term agreement. The Yankees, who hadn't participated in a postseason game in more than a decade, were hungry for a pennant going into the 1993 season. They'd signed Wade Boggs and Jimmy Key as free agents and acquired Paul O'Neill and Abbott in trades and looked like a solid contender. Abbott and agent Scott Boras, who'd rejected a four-year, $4 million-per-season offer from the Angels in October, immediately ran into problems negotiating a contract with the Yankees. They ended up in arbitration, where the Yankees' $2.35 million offer beat out Abbott's $3.5 million request. The Yankees' negative arguments confused and upset the young hurler. "Why did they trade for me if that's what they think?" he wondered. It was an early sign that the sensitive pitcher might have a tough time in the Bronx. Nevertheless, Abbott tried to embrace the city and the team. But, his entire term in New York was frustrating and his performance was mediocre.

One of the few bright spots was a September 4, 1993, no-hit victory over the Cleveland Indians in the midst of a tight pennant race. The no-hitter catapulted Abbott back into the national spotlight and once again focused on the unique accomplishments of a baseball player performing, and performing exceptionally well, with one hand.

But a little more than a week after his no-hit gem, Yankees owner George Steinbrenner publicly blasted Abbott for not doing the job, even questioning the pitcher's courage. Steinbrenner's outburst, with his team only a game and a half out of first place, seemed to take the heart out of the club, and they limped home to a second-place finish, seven games behind Toronto. Abbott finished with a record of 11 wins against 14 losses.

Abbott's second season in New York started out as turbulently as the first. Before spring training even started, "The Boss" blamed Abbott's mediocre 1993 performance on his charity work and frequent visits with disabled children. "Jim Abbott's got to give 100 percent of his attention to baseball!" Steinbrenner demanded.[3] Abbott, who'd been selected for the prestigious "Free Spirit Award" for his work with children, was stunned and actually found himself having to defend his charitable efforts. Another confrontation occurred when the Yankees invented a new glove for him with a flap that was supposed to hide his grip on the ball from the opposing first base coach's sight. The theory was that Abbott was tipping his pitches because he wasn't able to pitch out of his glove like other pitchers. Jim warmed up with the new glove before his second start of the season, but couldn't get comfortable with the new device and refused to use it in a game.

The 1994 season ended in mid-August when the players went on strike. Abbott's final tally for the abbreviated season was nine wins and eight losses. On December 23 the Yankees decided not to tender an offer for the 1995 season and he became a free agent. He was expected to sign with the Angels, who'd just named Marcel Lachemann, Jim's favorite pitching coach, as their manager. But the Chicago White Sox came up with a better offer.

Abbott pitched respectably in Chicago, but the Sox traded him to the Angels when they dropped out of the Central Division race early. The Angels, who were in the thick of the Western Division race, welcomed Jim back with open arms. He won five games and lost four for California, but the team came up a game short in its quest for the division title. For both teams combined his won-lost record was 11-8 and he posted a 3.70 earned run average, a substantial improvement over his performance in New York.

Before the 1996 season, Jim signed a new three-year deal with the Angels and reported to spring training set for a big season. But he posted a woeful 2-18 won-lost record, accompanied by a horrendous 7.48 earned run average. Even a midseason trip to Vancouver, the first minor league action of his career, didn't help. His poor performance continued the next spring and the Angels released him, eating the final two years of his $7.8 million contract.

Out of baseball at the age of 29, Jim Abbott went home to spend time with his wife and new baby daughter, and devote more time to his many charitable activities.

After sitting out the entire 1997 season, Abbott attempted a comeback with the White Sox. He worked his way back pitching in the Sox system for Hickory, Winston-Salem, Birmingham, and Calgary before a late-season trial call-up to Chicago. With the White Sox, he won all five of his starts and in the offseason he received the Tony Conigliaro Award, which is presented annually to the player who best overcomes obstacles and continues to thrive through adversity.

The miracle comeback was not to continue, however. The White Sox weren't confident that Abbott's resurgence was for real and didn't re-sign him for the 1999 season. He signed with the Milwaukee Brewers but was released in July with a 2-8 won-lost mark and 6.91 earned run average. He did provide some final heroics, though. Since Milwaukee was in the National League where the designated hitter isn't employed, Abbott got a chance to bat, and on June 15, 1999, he lined out the first base hit by a one-handed batter in the major leagues in more than 50 years since one-armed outfielder Pete Gray played for the St. Louis Browns in 1945.

Immediately after his release by Milwaukee, Jim announced his retirement from baseball. He now has two children and lives in California. He is in demand as a motivational speaker and is still heavily involved in children's charities. He's associated with Amigos de los Ninos, a California organization that aids groups that care for children, has twice been named the March of Dimes Athlete of the Year, and received the Freedom Forum's Free Spirit Award for his charitable work. He's still very involved in disabled children's causes and continues to make appearances for various charitable organizations. In 2004 he was inducted into the Michigan Sports Hall of Fame.

What happened to Jim Abbott's promising career? How could a pitcher who was considered to have the best stuff of any left-hander in the league in 1993 be through six years later at 31 years of age? The most popular explanation is that the opposition was able to read his pitches because he couldn't shield the ball with his glove. Likewise, base runners were able to take advantage because he couldn't conceal his pickoff move to first base. Other experts insisted that he was bunted out of the league.

Abbott, however, refused to blame his disability. He maintained that the problem was that his fastball started to lose velocity fairly early in his career and it was too big an adjustment to go from power to finesse. In his earlier years, his fastball consistently approached 95 mph, but by the end of his career he was topping out around 85 to 90 mph.

For his major-league career, Jim Abbott won 87 games and lost 108 with a 4.25 earned run average. Yet, he had as much of an impact as any player who played the game, giving renewed hope to thousands with disabilities. He once estimated that he had at least one scheduled meeting with a disabled child during every road series of his career.

"My experiences, added up, make me feel like I've had a Hall of Fame career," Abbott said when announcing his retirement from the game.

Note

This article is an adaptation of a profile of Jim Abbott in Rick Swaine, *Beating the Breaks: Major League Ballplayers Who Overcame Disabilities* (Jefferson. North Carolina: McFarland, 2004).

SOURCES

Books

Bernotas, Bob, *Nothing to Prove: the Jim Abbott Story* (New York: Kodansha American, 1995).

Gutman, Bill, *Jim Abbott Star Pitcher* (New York: Grey Castle Press, Inc., 1992).

Online Aids

CBS Sportsline, March 31, 1997, "Veteran Lefthander Jim Abbott Released by Angels." cbs.sportsline.com/mlb, (unknown access date)

Lowe, John, "Abbott retires at 31: 'It's time to admit reality.'" *Detroit Free Press*, July 27, 1999, freep.com/sports/baseball/qaabbott27, (3/22/03)

"Former 'M' star, Abbott, bats in 1st MLB game." *The Michigan Daily Online*, April 9, 1999, pub.umich.edu.daily/1999/apr/04-09-99/sports/sports6, accessed (9/6/02)

Seguine, Jim, "Jim Abbott returns to baseball." *Michigan Today*, Summer 1999, umich.edu/~newsinfo/MT/99/Sum99/mtloj99, (9/6/02)

Rolfe, John, "Jim Dandy," turnerlearning.com/efts/bball/jimdandy.htm, (9/6/2002)

"Jim Abbott: Career Notes," espn.go.com/mlb/profiles/notes/4038.html, (10/2/02)

Speakers Platform: Featuring the Finest Keynote Speakers, speaking.com/speakers/jimabbott.html, (10/3/06)

NOTES

1   Tim Wendel, "Return Engagement: After sitting out a year, Jim Abbott makes an improbable comeback." *USA Today Baseball Weekly*, September 9-15, 1998

2   Rick Swaine, *Beating the Breaks: Major League Ballplayers Who Overcame Disabilities* (Jefferson, North Carolina: McFarland, 2004), 13.

3   Daily News Wire Services, "Boss: Abbott Must Focus On Work," Philly.com, February 26, 1994.

BO JACKSON

By Norm King

THEY WERE UBIQUITOUS. THEY were funny. And for a while during the late 1980s and early 1990s, the Nike commercials that showed Bo Jackson playing everything from baseball to cricket to hockey—wearing the uniform of the storied Montreal Canadiens no less—brought the phrase "Bo Knows" into popular culture.

These commercials played on Jackson's astounding athletic abilities. His abundant speed, power, agility, and quickness allowed him to play in the NFL and baseball's major leagues. Although he wasn't the first athlete to play two sports professionally—Jim Thorpe holds that distinction—he was the first to become an All-Star in the two leagues in which he played and the first to rise to prominence in the media-driven sports world of the late twentieth century.[1]

Bo Jackson was born on November 30, 1962, in Bessemer, Alabama, the eighth of Florence Jackson Bond's 10 children born. A fan of the television show *Ben Casey*, Florence, who worked as a housekeeper, named her son Vincent Edward Jackson, after the show's star, Vince Edwards.[2] Young Vincent could never be confused with the program's caring namesake; he was such a difficult youngster, that his family began referring to him as a boar hog. That eventually was shortened to Bo, and the nickname stuck.

Jackson inherited two traits from his absentee father, A.D. Adams, size and a terrible stutter. The size made him big, tough, and athletic, while the stutter made him a target of ridicule among other children. What he did not get from his father was discipline.

"We never had enough food," Jackson wrote in his autobiography. "But at least I could beat on other kids and steal their lunch money and buy myself something to eat. But I couldn't steal a father. I couldn't steal a father's hug when I needed one. I couldn't steal a father's whipping when I needed one."[3]

While not a very good student at McAdory High School in McCalla, Alabama, he found an outlet for his anger and energy in sports. He won two state high-school decathlon titles, but it was his prowess on the football field and baseball diamond as a senior that attracted the scouts. He averaged 10.9 yards per carry as a running back, and smacked 20 home runs in a 25-game baseball season. The New York Yankees drafted him in the second round of the 1982 draft, but Jackson accepted a football scholarship to Auburn University instead.

Jackson had a legendary football career at Auburn. He rushed for 4,303 yards (still a school record as of 2016) with 43 touchdowns during his four years as a Tiger. His 1,786 rushing yards as a senior won him the Heisman Trophy as college football's most outstanding player in 1985.

Yet, as good as he was at football, his goal was to play professional baseball. "My first love is baseball," he said, "and it has always been a dream of mine to be a major league player."[4]

Baseball scouts thought Jackson could make that dream come true. After watching him play on April 13 and 14, 1985, one scout wrote: "A complete type player with outstanding tools; can simply do it all and didn't even play baseball last year. A gifted athlete; the best pure athlete in America today."[5]

As highly regarded as he was, Jackson's baseball career was almost derailed by an NCAA rules violation, a violation he felt was caused deliberately by the Tampa Bay Buccaneers, who planned to draft him number 1 in the NFL draft. Prior to the draft, they flew Jackson to Tampa in owner Hugh Culverhouse's private jet for a physical examination. Even though Buccaneer officials told Jackson that it was within NCAA rules to accept the flight, it was nonetheless a violation. Jackson was suspended for the second half of his senior baseball season.

"I think it was all a plot now, just to get me ineligible from baseball because they saw the season I was having (after hitting .401 in 1985, Jackson was batting .246, with 7 home runs and 14 RBIs in 21 games in 1986) and they thought they were going to lose me to baseball," he said in an ESPN documentary on his life. "(Like) if we declare him ineligible, then we've got him."[6]

If it was a plot, it failed; the Bucs selected Jackson first overall in the 1986 NFL draft, but he declined their offer of a four-year deal worth between $5 million and $7 million, opting to play baseball instead. The Kansas City Royals chose Jackson in the fourth round of the 1986 major-league draft. (The California Angels had drafted him in 1985, but he didn't sign with them, either.) While his contract with the Royals was not as lucrative as what the Buccaneers offered, Jackson still inked a solid deal, three years for $1 million.

The Royals sent Jackson to the Memphis Chicks, their affiliate in the Double-A Southern League, where he performed poorly at the plate early on—he had a .105 average after 10 games—but Chicks manager Tommy Jones wasn't concerned. "Prior to (Jackson's) first game, I said it would take three weeks for him to get comfortable and to adjust to life in baseball," Jones said. "After three weeks, I felt we could make some evaluations. Until then, I don't think it would be fair."[7]

That approach proved wise, as Jackson improved steadily. After 53 games, his batting average had risen to .277, with 7 homers and 25 RBIs. These numbers prompted the Royals, having an offyear after winning the World Series in 1985 (they finished with a 76-86 record), to call him up on September 1, when major-league teams could expand their rosters. He made his debut on September 2, playing right field against the Chicago White Sox, and getting his first major-league hit off 41-year-old Steve Carlton. His first home run came 12 days later when he hit a solo blast in the fourth inning off Seattle's Mike Moore. Jackson remained with Kansas City for all of September, and hit .207 with two home runs and nine RBIs in 25 games.

Jackson left no doubt about his work ethic by how hard he trained for the 1987 season, his first full year with the Royals. He worked with Hal Baird, his Auburn baseball coach, in January, and even Baird

noticed a difference in Jackson's intensity. "He was far more diligent in his work habits," Baird said. "I saw more dedication, more willingness to work, than I had ever seen before."[8]

That preparation paid early dividends, as Jackson made the team after very nearly starting the season at Triple A. A few days before the season started, general manager John Schuerholz had decided to send Jackson to the minors for more experience, but then changed his mind after doing something he had never done before. "I talked to several of our veterans—George Brett, Hal McRae, Frank White," Schuerholz said. "I had never done that before, but they told me they thought he could help us."[9]

Jackson made Schuerholz look like a pretty smart guy in the season's first few days. He went 4-for-5 with three RBIs in a 13-1 pasting of the Yankees on April 10. He followed that performance up with a game for the ages on April 14 against the Tigers. He went 4-for-4, with two home runs—including a grand slam—and seven RBIs in a 10-1 laugher over the Tigers. Two weeks later, Jackson got some interesting news when the Los Angeles Raiders chose him in the seventh round of the NFL draft.[10] Naturally this sparked great media interest, so Jackson put a sign over his locker that read: Don't be stupid and ask football questions. OK!"

Regardless of the intelligence of the fourth estate, newspapers reported in July that Jackson was going to sign with the Raiders. Jackson responded to the speculation at a news conference when the Royals were in Toronto on July 11. "Any way you look at it, I have to do my job with the Kansas City Royals before I can do anything else," he said. "Whatever comes after baseball season is a hobby for Bo Jackson."[11]

Jackson's teammates were not happy when he announced that he had reached terms with the Raiders on July 14 during the All-Star break. Even before he signed with the Raiders, some players felt he was only with the team because of his drawing power. There was also the sense that the front office treated Jackson differently than the other players. Most major-league contracts at the time included clauses prohibiting players from participating in off-field activities that could jeopardize their baseball careers, yet Jackson was allowed to play a violent contact sport. One anonymous Royal expressed his unhappiness by changing the sign above Jackson's locker to read: "Don't be stupid and ask any baseball questions."

Fans weren't happy, either, in part because the enmity between the Raiders and the hometown Kansas City Chiefs was palpable. When he took the field in the team's first game after the season resumed, fans booed him lustily. Some even threw toy footballs that were printed with the words: "It's a hobby." Of course, fans being fans, they cheered him just as lustily when he made a spectacular tumbling catch in the fifth inning.

Coincidentally or not, Jackson's play suffered in the second half of the season. He was benched for extensive periods because he was striking out at a prodigious rate — 27 strikeouts in 64 at-bats between July 16 and August 7. After hitting .254 with 18 home runs, 45 RBIs, and 115 strikeouts before the All-Star break, Jackson played in only 35 games in the second half, with four home runs, eight RBIs and another 43 strikeouts. He would have struck out 221 times if he had played in all 162 games.

While Jackson's decision to play two sports was controversial, it also had its lighter moments. In a New Year's Day 1987 column of tongue-in-cheek predictions, *Kansas City Times* writer Bill Tammeus wrote that Jackson would sign a contract to play with the National Hockey League's Buffalo Sabres, then join the Ice Capades as a hobby. Jackson did receive — and this is true — an offer to play basketball with the Orange County Crush of the fledgling International Basketball Association, a league whose players could be no taller than 6-feet-4. The offer, which Jackson turned down, was a publicity stunt.[12]

After playing seven games with Los Angeles and scoring four touchdowns (including one on a 91-yard run against Seattle, the longest run from scrimmage in the NFL that season), Jackson returned to the Royals for 1988, but not before working with Auburn coach Baird again in the offseason. Baird was not impressed with what he saw.

"There's a real need for some concentrated instruction," Baird said. "I can't believe he didn't go to [Triple-A] Omaha last year. I think (the Royals) made concessions and misjudged him a little."[13]

The media reported that Jackson faced competition for the left fielder's spot from rookie Gary Thurman. It wasn't really much of a contest, as Jackson batted .298, with 5 home runs and 12 RBIs in Florida, while Thurman hit .185 and struck out 16 times in 65 at-bats.[14] Jackson went north as the Royals' starting left fielder. He got off to a good start, too; after going 3-for-4 with a two-run homer and a stolen base in a 7-6 Royals win over Texas on May 16, teammate George Brett said: "Bo Jackson proves he belongs here. He still has a lot to learn, but he learns every time he goes out there."[15]

By the end of May Jackson was hitting .309, with 9 home runs and 30 RBIs. But then fate chose to intervene on June 1 when he tore a hamstring muscle running out a groundball. He missed 28 games, and his batting average began falling on his return. By season's end it was down to .246. He hit 25 home runs, one behind team leader Danny Tartabull, and had 68 RBIs. His 146 strikeouts — including nine consecutive whiffs between September 16 and September 19 — were the fourth highest in the American League. He led junior-circuit left fielders in assists, with 12.

If Jackson has a favorite Beatles song, it may be "Come Together," because that's what happened for him in 1989. He started off hot again, so hot that by the All-Star break he had 21 home runs, just four shy of his 1988 total. Even his strikeouts created a sensation; he got his teammates' attention when he broke a bat in two over his knee after striking out against the Twins on May 9. "Some jaws dropped and some eyes got real big in the dugout after that one," said Royals coach John Mayberry.[16]

Jackson's own jaw may have dropped when he saw the results of fan balloting for the 1989 American League All-Star team, as he led the American League, with 1,748,696 votes. He took full advantage of his moment in the sun, batting leadoff for the AL squad and going 2-for-4, including a 448-foot home run to center field and a stolen base as the American League defeated the National League 5-3. He garnered All-Star Game MVP honors, and the admiration of NL manager Tommy Lasorda.

"Bo Jackson was exciting, really" Lasorda said. When he hit (his home run), I thought it sounded like he hit a golf ball. He's awesome and exciting."[17]

But injuries disrupted Jackson's season yet again when the regular season resumed. He missed 15 games between July 23 and August 8 with sore thigh muscles, an injury he had prior to the All-Star break. Unlike previous years, however, his numbers didn't fall off a cliff, and he finished with 32 home runs, 105 RBIs (both career highs), 26 stolen bases, and a .256 batting average. He did lead the league in one category, with 172 strikeouts.

After his third season with the Raiders, in which he played in a career-high 11 games—he also had the longest run from scrimmage for the season, a 92-yard scamper against Cincinnati—Jackson started 1990 by fulfilling a promise to his mother. He had vowed to her that he would earn his college degree, and in January of that year he began taking classes at Auburn toward that end. He received a bachelor's degree in family and child development in 1995. Sadly, his mother died in 1992 and never saw him graduate.

"I will be the first in my family to get a degree from a major college," Jackson said. Hopefully, that will influence my younger relatives in the family as far as nieces and nephews to go on to college to try to be something or someone."[18]

Jackson's propensity for striking out went beyond the diamond and into the arbitration hearing room in February. He was seeking $1,900,001, but the arbitrator ruled in the Royals' favor. Still, he earned a $1 million salary for the season, which, of course, followed the usual route of great start followed by serious setback. On July 17 he was on pace to hit .270 for the season with 39 home runs and 117 RBIs (albeit with 206 strikeouts) when he hurt his shoulder diving for a fly ball hit by fellow two-sport athlete Deion Sanders. He missed 38 games, but continued to hit well on his return, finishing with a .272 average, 28 home runs, and 78 RBIs in 111 games.

Jackson should have known from his arbitration experience that Bo didn't know gambling, because in 1990 he bet once too often that the punishment he received playing football would not affect his baseball career. Jackson could have made sports history when he was selected to play in the NFL Pro Bowl after the season, which would have made him the first athlete to play in all-star games in two different sports. That was not to be, however, as he suffered a hip injury in a Raiders 20-10 playoff win over the Cincinnati Bengals on January 13, 1991, when he was tackled after a 34-yard run. He didn't play in the AFC Championship Game against the Buffalo Bills—which was probably just as well because the Raiders lost 51-3. He never played football again.

Jackson and the Royals managed to avoid an arbitration hearing when he signed a one-year, $2.4 million deal with the team for the 1991 season. The contract didn't really matter, because his hip injury wasn't getting any better. He had developed a condition called avascular necrosis, which meant that his hip cartilage and bone were deteriorating. When spring training came around, he was still walking around on crutches and clearly unable to play. The Royals placed him on waivers on March 18.

Jackson wasn't out of work long enough to apply for unemployment benefits. On April 3 he signed a three-year, $8.15 million contract with the Chicago White Sox, although "only" $700,000 was guaranteed. White Sox owner Jerry Reinsdorf likened the signing to buying an insurance policy. "It's like life insurance," he said. "You pay the premium, the premium is gone. But if it turns out you die, your family is very happy you had the insurance. If he comes back, we'll be thrilled."[19]

Jackson carried out his rehabilitation under the supervision of the White Sox medical staff. They gave him permission in mid-June to walk without the crutches he had been using since suffering the injury. A month later he started taking some batting practice and did some soft throwing. His workouts continued through August, then on August 25 he began a six-game minor-league rehabilitation assignment. Finally, on September 2, Jackson played his first game of the season against, ironically, the Royals. He went hitless in three at-bats as the DH, but drove in a run with a sacrifice fly. He played in 23 games, hit three home runs and had 14 RBIs, all at the DH spot.

Jackson was very happy to have returned to the field but the following offseason was full of bad news for him. On October 10 his football career effectively ended when he failed a physical given by the Los Angeles Raiders doctors. He made it official one month later when he announced his retirement from football. He joined the White Sox for spring training, but it was evident early on that he was not ready to play. The bat was there, but he wasn't going to be much good on the basepaths. "I have to say if my running was like my hitting I'd be satisfied," Jackson said. "But I'm not. I'm very down on myself for the way I'm running."[20]

Jackson had his damaged hip replaced with a prosthetic ball and socket in Chicago on April 4, 1992. The prognosis was that he would be able to run after he recovered from the operation, but not at the level of a professional athlete. Jackson didn't listen to the prognosis. "Medical and athletic experts figured Jackson would not be heard from again," wrote Ron

Flatter. "Apparently there were no Bo Jackson experts to be heard."[21]

Jackson let nothing stand in his way from getting back on the ballfield, even his mother's passing on April 27. His rehab was carried out under the watchful eye of White Sox trainer Herm Schneider, and although progress was slow, it was steady. Even with several hours a day of exercise and training, he walked with a limp until July, and didn't begin his running program until January. Amazingly, he was ready to go for spring training, and on March 4 played his first baseball game in more than a year, going 1-for-3 in an 11-10 loss to Pittsburgh. His status with the White Sox wasn't confirmed until the team finally decided to keep Jackson on March 24.

One might wonder why Jackson would put himself through all that work and discomfort—after all, he didn't need the money. The answer lies in a promise he made to his mother. Before she died, she asked if he was attempting a comeback. He said that if he did, his first hit would be for her. On April 9, 1993, he faced a pitcher in a regular-season game as a pinch-hitter in the bottom of the sixth inning. Facing the Yankees' Neal Heaton, he took the first pitch for a strike, then deposited the next pitch over the right-field wall for a home run.

"Lucky for me and unfortunately for the pitcher, I hit a home run," Jackson recalled. "But that hit meant more to me than anything, because I kept my word, my promise, to my mom. I could have retired that night."[22]

Jackson didn't retire that night, but went on to play in 85 games that year, both in the outfield and at DH. He smacked 16 home runs, batted in 45 runs and hit .232. He also made his only career appearance in the postseason, going 0-for-10 with six strikeouts as the White Sox lost the ALCS in six games to the Toronto Blue Jays.

Jackson's offseason was busy. His remarkable comeback from the hip-replacement surgery, and the intense effort he put in to attain that achievement, was honored when he won both the Tony Conigliaro Award and *The Sporting News* American League Comeback Player of the Year Award. (Andres Galarraga won in the National League.) On the playing side, Jackson rejected an offer of salary arbitration by the White Sox, choosing instead to take the free-agent route. He signed with the California Angels, the team that first drafted him in 1985.

Jackson had a good season in a part-time role for California, playing left and right field and at DH. He appeared in 75 games and batted a career-high .279, with 13 home runs and 43 RBIs in 201 at-bats. One of his season highlights was a five-RBI day at Detroit on May 26. But even before his season was cut short by the players' strike, he began to talk about retiring. "When I left college, my lifelong goal was to be retired from professional sports when I was 34 years old (he was 31 at the time)," he said. "Because I don't think I'll start living until after that."[23]

Jackson ended up retiring even sooner than that. The strike delayed the opening of spring training in 1995, and once it resumed, Jackson, who was a free agent, received calls from a few teams, but decided enough was enough. "I got to know my family [during the strike]," he said in explaining why he retired. "That looks better to me than any $10 million contract."[24]

After retiring from sports, Jackson began working in numerous business and charitable activities. As of 2016, he ran a training complex for athletes in Lockport, Illinois. Among his charitable endeavours is the *Bo Bikes 'Bama* campaign. Tornadoes can cause devastating damage in Alabama, so every year he, his celebrity friends, and other participants cycle across his home state to raise money for the construction of community storm shelters.

Jackson and his wife, Linda, as of 2016 lived in Chicago and have two sons Garrett and Nicholas and a daughter Morgan.

SOURCES

In addition to the sources cited in the Notes, the author used the following:

Auburntigers.com.

ESPN.com.

Footballdb.com.

Observer-Reporter (Washington, Pennsylvania).

Pro-football-reference.com.

Sports Illustrated.

Stutteringhelp.org.

Swaine, Rick. *Baseball's Comeback Players: Forty Major Leaguers Who Fell and Rose Again* (Jefferson, North Carolina: McFarland & Company. 2014).

NOTES

1 Thorpe played six seasons in the majors and eight years in the NFL.

2 *Ben Casey* was a medical drama televised on ABC from 1961 to 1966.

3 Ron Flatter, "Bo Knows Stardom and Disappointment," espn.go.com.

4 Ibid.

5 Matt Snyder, "Bo Jackson's 1985 Scouting Report (Hint: He was good at baseball)," cbssports.com, May 7, 2013.

6 Greg Auman, "When Bucs Blew It By Drafting Bo Jackson," *Tampa Bay Times*, April 24, 2015. The incident left Jackson with a bad taste in his mouth, and he warned the Buccaneers that drafting him would be a waste of a pick. The Buccaneers nevertheless chose him number 1 overall in the NFL draft, but he never signed with them.

7 "Bo's Slow Start Doesn't Concern His Manager," *The Tennessean* (Nashville), July 10, 1986: 7-E.

8 "Jackson Leaves Almost All in Awe," *St. Louis Post-Dispatch*, April 19, 1987: 4F.

9 John Sonderegger, "Heirs Apparent: Jackson Gets Into Swing With Royals, Big Leagues," *St. Louis Post-Dispatch*, May 10, 1987: 11F.

10 Jackson was eligible for the 1987 draft because he did not sign with the Buccaneers in 1986.

11 ESPN Sportscenter, July 11, 1987. Jackson was often criticized as being arrogant for referring to himself in the third person. In fact, he was using a speech therapy technique he learned to prevent stuttering.

12 According to the Association for Professional Basketball Research (apbr.org), the International Basketball Association existed from 1988 to 1892 as the World Basketball League.

13 Rick Hummel, "Classy Horton Not Bitter Over Being Traded," *St. Louis Post-Dispatch*, February 14, 1988: 3G.

14 Thurman ended up playing in 424 major-league games over nine seasons.

15 "Jackson Continues Hot Pace," *Constitution-Tribune* (Chillicothe, Missouri), May 17, 1988: 6.

16 Bill Coats, "Eye Openers," *St. Louis Post-Dispatch*, May 13, 1989: 2C.

17 "Royals' Bo Jackson Is MVP in American League Victory," *Macon* (Missouri) *Chronicle Herald*, July 12, 1989: 2.

18   Marsha Sanguinette, "Eye Openers," *St. Louis Post-Dispatch* January 20, 1990: 6C.

19   Murray Chass, "White Sox Decide to Gamble on Bo Jackson," *New York Times*, April 4, 1991. Note that baseball-reference.com lists his 1991 salary at $1,010,000.

20   Bill Madden, "Bo Jackson's Baseball Career Appears Over," *Southern Illinoisan* (Carbondale, Illinois), March 7, 1992: 4B.

21   Ron Flatter, "Bo Knows Stardom and Disappointment," espn.com.

22   Lindsay Berra, "#TBT: Bo Jackson Misses a Full Season, Homers in First At-Bat," mlb.com, April 9, 2015. Jackson later had the ball bronzed and placed it on his mother's grave.

23   Mike Terry, "Bo Knows Life After Baseball," *San Bernardino County* (California) *Sun*, July 10, 1994: C1.

24   "Well What Do You Know?," Bo Retiring from Baseball," *The Tennessean*, April 4, 1995: 6C.

MARK LEITER

BY CLAYTON TRUTOR

MARK LEITER WAS A RIGHT-handed pitcher who appeared in 335 games over 11 major-league seasons between 1990 and 2001 (1990-1999, 2001). He started 149 games and appeared in relief 186 times. Leiter pitched for eight clubs: the New York Yankees (1990), Detroit Tigers (1991-1993), California Angels (1994), San Francisco Giants (1995-1996), Montreal Expos (1996), Philadelphia Phillies (1997-1998), Seattle Mariners (1999), and Milwaukee Brewers (2001). Tall (6-feet-3) and lanky, Leiter was the middle of three baseball-playing brothers. His older brother, Kurt, spent four seasons as a pitcher in the Orioles' minor-league organization (1982-1984, 1986). His younger brother, Al, was a two-time All-Star (1996 and 2000) and pitched for the Yankees, Blue Jays, Marlins, and Mets for 19 seasons (1987-2005). Mark's son, Mark Jr., as of 2015 was in his third year as a starting pitcher in the Philadelphia Phillies' minor-league organization.

Mark Sr. is perhaps best known for the persever-ance he displayed in the face of personal tragedy, which led the Boston Chapter of the Baseball Writers' Association of America to name him the winner in 1994 of the Tony Conigliaro Award, given annually to the major leaguer who "best overcomes an obstacle and adversity through the attributes of spirit, deter-mination, and courage that were the trademarks of Conigliaro."[1]

Mark and Allison Leiter's second son, Ryan Alexander, born in July 1993, was diagnosed with a rare genetic disorder, Werdnig-Hoffman disease, also known as spinal muscular atrophy (SMA), a condition similar to amyotrophic lateral sclerosis (ALS), the disease that killed Lou Gehrig. Ryan Leiter's battle with SMA lasted throughout the winter of 1993-1994. Eventually he lost the use of his limbs and the ability to be fed orally. As Ryan's disease entered its final stages in March 1994, the Tigers released Mark during spring training. On March 21, 1994, the California Angels signed Leiter to a free agent minor-league contract. In the final weeks of spring training, Leiter won a spot not only on the Angels' major-league roster, but in their starting rotation. On April 4, 1994, Opening Day, nine-month-old Ryan Leiter died in his mother's arms, hours after saying goodbye to his father for the last time, who was on a flight to Minnesota with the Angels for their season opening series. Soon after their son's death, the Leiters created the Ryan Leiter Fund, which raises money to aid families who are struggling with SMA. The Boston BBWAA chapter honored Mark Leiter for his personal strength, perseverance, and generosity amid family hardship.[2]

Mark Edward Leiter was born on April 13, 1963, in Joliet, Illinois, to Alexander Leiter, a merchant seaman, and Maria Leiter, a homemaker. One of seven siblings (six brothers and a sister), the Leiters relocated to Ocean County, New Jersey, soon after Mark's birth.[3] Raised on the Jersey Shore, Leiter graduated from Central Regional High School in Bayville, New Jersey, in 1981. He starred on the baseball team along with his brother Al, who was a freshman during Mark's senior year, and classmate Jeff Musselman, who later pitched for the Blue Jays and Mets (1986-1990). Mark played baseball at Connors State Junior College in Warner, Oklahoma, a perennially nationally-ranked junior college team, and in 1983 he played far closer to home at Ramapo College in Mahwah, New Jersey.[4]

The Baltimore Orioles selected Leiter in the fourth round of the January 1983 amateur draft.

He spent the summer of 1983 with the Bluefield Orioles of the Rookie-level Appalachian League and the Hagerstown Suns of the Class-A Carolina League. At Bluefield he had a 2-1 record in six starts with a 2.70 ERA, but he struggled to a 1-5 record with a 7.25 ERA in eight starts in Hagerstown.

Leiter returned to Hagerstown in 1984. As a starter he posted an 8-13 record with a 5.62 ERA in 27

in the season to be promoted to Triple-A Columbus in May. His 9-6 record against International League competition earned him a long look at the pitching-strapped Yankees' spring training in 1990 before he was returned to Columbus. After posting a 9-4 record in 30 appearances, 14 of which were starts, the 27-year-old Leiter was promoted to the Yankees in late July.

Leiter made his major-league debut on July 24, 1990, against the Texas Rangers. Pitching in relief, he surrendered a single and a walk but no runs in 1⅓ innings, finishing the game in a 4-1 defeat. Leiter struggled in his next three appearances, and in early August the Yankees sent him back to Columbus. Called up again after the International League season, Leiter pitched in four more games for the Yankees, finishing his rookie season with a 1-1 record and a 6.84 ERA. His final appearance of the season, which also proved to be his final appearance in a Yankees uniform, was a high note: a seven-inning no-decision start against the Detroit Tigers in which he surrendered only one run.

In March 1991 the Yankees traded Leiter to the Tigers for infielder Torey Lovullo. Leiter started the season with the Triple-A Toledo Mudhens but joined the Tigers in late April. Before the All-Star break he worked primarily as a long reliever. After the break, he made 15 starts, posting a 9-7 record for the season for the second-place Tigers.

Leiter's 1992 season bore a striking resemblance to 1991, as he alternated between long relief and the rotation, a consistent presence on Detroit's staff. He started in 14 of his 35 appearances, with eight wins and five losses. Leiter spent much of the 1993 season in the same mode, alternating between long relief and a back-end starter. His old shoulder trouble returned, forcing him to the disabled list for much of the season's second half and contributing to the club's decision to release him the following spring, but not before Leiter underwent his fourth arthroscopic shoulder surgery.[6]

Leiter signed with the California Angels shortly after the Tigers let him go, and earned a spot in the Angels rotation. After victories in his first two decisions that year, Leiter's ERA ballooned to more than 5.00 in subsequent starts, and in mid-May he was

appearances. Leiter worked nearly twice as many innings (139⅓) in 1984 as he had in his first season (72⅔), demonstrating an ability to eat up innings even if he struggled on the mound. He spent most of the 1985 season in Hagerstown, working primarily as a reliever and gaining eight saves in 34 games. Leiter received a late-season promotion to Double-A Charlotte, where he was 1-0 in five relief appearances.

Leiter's baseball career took a dramatic turn during spring training in 1986. He injured his right shoulder badly enough to require season-ending surgery. One missed season turned into three as his shoulder didn't take to surgical repairs. Three shoulder surgeries over a three-year period kept Leiter out of baseball in 1986, 1987, and 1988. While he rehabilitated his shoulder, he worked as a corrections officer at the Ocean County Jail.[5]

The Orioles released Leiter in June 1988. In September the Yankees signed him to a minor-league contract. Leiter started the 1989 season with Class-A Fort Lauderdale, where he pitched well enough early

sent to the bullpen. Leiter spent the remainder of the season as a middle and long reliever, working his ERA down to 4.72 in 40 appearances.

Released after the season, Leiter signed with the San Francisco Giants in April 1995. The pitching-deprived Giants added him to their rotation, and he went 10-12 in 29 starts with a 3.82 ERA. Leiter returned to San Francisco in 1996, signing a one-year deal worth $1.5 million, more than twice what he made the previous season. Manager Dusty Baker had enough confidence in Leiter to make him the Opening Day starter (a road loss to the defending world champion Atlanta Braves.)[7] The rocky start to the season presaged a difficult year for Leiter. Through July he was 4-10 with a 5.19 ERA. On July 30, the day before the trade deadline, the Giants traded Leiter to the Montreal Expos for two pitchers, left-handed starter Kirk Rueter and right-handed reliever Tim Scott. The trade proved far more beneficial to the Giants. Leiter pitched well for the Expos, posting a 4-2 record and a 4.39 ERA for the contending Expos, who fell two games short of the wild card. (Rueter spent more than a decade with the Giants, becoming the franchise's winningest left-handed pitcher since they moved to the Bay Area five decades earlier.)

After the season, Leiter built on his late-season momentum and signed a two-year, $3.9 million deal with the Philadelphia Phillies, the team he grew up rooting for on the Jersey Shore. In 1997 Leiter struggled to a 10-17 record in 31 starts for the Phillies, with an ERA of 5.67 against early "steroids-era" National League hitting. The Philadelphia press came down hard on Leiter, a high-profile free-agent who wasn't panning out on a last-place Phillies team. The coverage spurred Leiter to speak out against the "mean" and "negative" ways in which the Philadelphia media portrayed him.[8] In 1998 the Phillies moved Leiter to the bullpen, where he split his time between long relief and closing duties. Leiter, now 35, excelled in the bullpen, appearing in 69 games and posting a 7-5 record with a 3.55 ERA and 23 saves.

After the 1998 season, the Phillies exercised a one-year, $1.3 million option on Leiter but traded him to the Seattle Mariners for left-handed pitcher Paul Spoljaric. Despite his struggles with the Phillies, Leiter looked back fondly on his time with the team. "I only played here two years in my career. And it was the biggest thrill, he said in 2013. "I don't think there was a guy who loved playing for the Phillies more than I did. I know there are guys who played here for so many years and were so great. But to grow up as a kid coming here and dreaming about being on the field at the Vet someday and then getting to do it? That was amazing."[9]

Leiter pitched in only two games for Seattle, going on the shelf in early May with recurring shoulder problems. He missed the rest of the 1999 season and was released after the season. He also sat out the 2000 season. Meanwhile the injured Leiter bounced from the Mariners to the Pirates to the Rockies to the Mets to the Brewers in a series of trades and free-agent signings between 1999 and 2001, never once seeing major-league action in the 23 months between May 1, 1999, and April 5, 2001.

Leiter spent the 2001 season, which proved to be his last, as a reliever and spot starter for the Milwaukee Brewers, appearing in 20 games scattered across another injury-riddled season. After the season the Brewers declined an option on Leiter's contract and, at 38, he retired. Leiter retired with a career record of 65-73 and an ERA of 4.57. He pitched in 335 games in 11 seasons, 149 of which were starts.

As of 2015 Mark and Allison Leiter resided in Lacey Township, New Jersey. After retiring, Mark established The Leiter Advantage, to offer pitching lessons to players.[10] The Leiters' son Mark Jr. was a standout pitcher at Toms River North (New Jersey) High School and at the New Jersey Institute of Technology, where he earned first-team All-Great West Conference honors during his senior year and set a school record during his senior year with 103 strikeouts, including a school-record 20 in a May 2013 game against Chicago State. The Philadelphia Phillies selected the junior Leiter in the 22nd round of the June 2013 amateur draft. He finished the 2015 season with the Double-A Reading Fighting Phils.[11]

SOURCES

In addition to the sources cited in the Notes, the author also consulted Baseball-Reference.com and Baseball-Almanac.com.

NOTES

1   Christopher Smith, "St. Louis Cardinals' Mitch Harris, a Navy Lieutenant, Wins Tony Conigliaro Award Given by Boston Red Sox," *Masslive.com*, December 15, 2015. Accessed on March 1, 2016: masslive.com/redsox/index.ssf/2015/12/st_louis_cardinals_mitch_harri.html.

2   Peter Schmuck, "Leiter Raises Awareness, Money After Losing Infant Son to Disease," *Baltimore Sun*, June 13, 1994: C1; Claire Smith, "Baseball: A Son's Fight Against Death Inspires a Father," *New York Times*, April 24, 1994. Accessed on March 1, 2016: nytimes.com/1994/4/24/sports/baseball-a-son-s-fight-against-death-inspires-a-father.html; "Mark Leiter Back to Work," *New York Times*, April 10, 1994. Accessed on March 1, 2016: nytimes.com/1994/04/10/sports/baseball-mark-leiter-back-to-work.html; Nick Cafardo, "Baseball Writers' Dinner Notebook," *Boston Globe*, January 20, 1995: 44. For more information on aiding families dealing with SMA, see curesma.org.

3   "Obituary: Karl Alexander Leiter," Legacy.com, January 10, 2013. Accessed on March 1, 2016: legacy.com/obituaries/app/obituary.aspx?pid=162251944

4   "Gary Vaught," *University of Indianapolis Athletics*. Accessed on March 1, 2016: athletics.uindy.edu/mobile/staff.aspx?staff=6.

5   Tim Kurkjian, "The Comeback Kids," *Sports Illustrated*, September 23, 1991. Accessed on March 1, 2016: si.com/vault/1991/09/23/106783131/baseball; Peter Schmuck.

6   "It's Business: Tigers Waive Leiter, Bolton," *Owosso Argus-Press*, March 16, 1994: 9.

7   Paul Hagen, "Giants' Baker Saw Potential in Leiter," *Philadelphia Inquirer*, April 8, 1997. Accessed on March 1, 2016: articles.philly.com/1997-04-08/sports/25528949_1_phillies-fairy-tale-mark-leiter.

8   Alex Beam, "For Every Lash, There's a Backlash," *Boston Globe*, December 10, 1997: C1.

9   Paul Hagen, "Leiters Relish Connection with Phillies," MLB.com, November 1, 2013. Accessed on March 1, 2016: mlb.com/news/article/63606778/.

10   Claire Smith; for Mark Leiter's pitching school, see leiteradvantage.net.

11   Doug Hall, "Mark Leiter Jr.: Continuing the Leiter Legacy," *27 Outs Baseball*, June 2013. Accessed on March 1, 2016: 27outsbaseball.com/philadelphia-phillies/leiter-jr-legacy-baseball; "Mark Leiter Jr. Strikes Out 20," ESPN.com, May 3, 2013. Accessed on March 1, 2016: http://espn.go.com/college-sports/story/_/id/9240724/mark-leiter-jr-fans-20-college-game.

SCOTT RADINSKY

By Gregory H. Wolf

"**I**F YOU DO STINK IT UP TODAY, YOU get to come out the next day and get another shot," said Scott Radinsky. "That's why I love being a reliever."[1] A hard-throwing left-hander, Radinsky was never afraid of failure, or a challenge. He made a big jump from Single A to the majors, debuting with the Chicago White Sox in 1990. After leading the staff in appearances for three straight seasons (1991-1993), he was diagnosed with Hodgkin's disease, underwent chemotherapy and radiation treatment, and missed the entire 1994 season. Still weak when he returned to the South Siders a year later, he moved on to the Los Angeles Dodgers in 1996 and had three productive seasons. After Radinsky overcame cancer, two elbow operations, including Tommy John surgery, ended his career.

Radinsky was more than just a dependable middle reliever and occasional closer who appeared in 557 big-league games in parts of 11 seasons. Described by Jeff Torborg, his first big-league skipper, as "a young, aggressive athlete," and a "raw, strong, hard-throwing kid—a free spirit," Radinsky was a brutally honest realist whose greatest passion might have been music, and he served as a frontman in several critically acclaimed Los Angeles-based bands, including Pulley, which was still performing as of 2016.[2] "I'm a punk rocker," he told Franz Lidz of *Sports Illustrated* in 1997.[3] "I'm crazy about playing ball, but it's just a sideline."

Nobody ever confused Radinsky with a quiet, deferential company man. Throughout his playing career and as he transitioned into a respected minor- and major-league coach, Radinsky refused to conform to the expectations of the big money, corporate world of baseball, and proudly displayed his punk-rock ethos of anti-establishment, individuality, and anti-authoritarianism. Contrary to expectations, that attitude made Radinsky a well-liked player and trusted mentor to prospects. "I'm not a fan of the act you have to put on to be a big leaguer," he continued in *Sports Illustrated* with refreshing detachment. "You play for some guy in a skybox. You're like a puppet. You've got to do everything textbook, or you lose your job. You want to warm up, but the umpire stops you because he's waiting for a TV commercial to end. What I like about punk is that it's anticommercial. It's pure."[4]

Scott David Radinsky was born on March 3, 1968, in Glendale, California, about eight miles north of Los Angeles. His parents were Marshall L. Radinsky, a native of West Virginia, and Boston-born Barbara (Kornetsky) Radinsky. Scott had played some Little League ball, and was coached by his father, who worked for JME Signage, but he was more interested in skateboarding and the burgeoning Southern California punk-rock scene than in organized sports. "I was an angry, rebellious kid," admitted Radinsky.[5] By the age of 15 he co-founded the band Scared Straight, which released its first record in 1984.

Radinsky grew up a Dodgers fan, but didn't follow major-league baseball too closely. As a member of the Simi Valley High School baseball team, Radinsky played the way he sang—full throttle with little discipline. He evolved from a disinterested first baseman as a sophomore on the junior-varsity squad to closer as a junior, and then as a senior burst on the scene with the force of a speeding, 90-second Minor Threat song as one of the region's best starting pitchers. "Scott had absolutely no mechanics," said his coach, Mike Scyphers. "He just got the ball and threw it."[6] At 6-feet 3 and weighing about 170 pounds (he'd add another 20 pounds in the course of his career), Radinsky (14-1, 0.72 ERA with 180 strikeouts in 100⅓ innings) attracted big-league scouts as Simi Valley was ranked the number-one high-school team in the country in 1986.[7] On June 2 the White Sox selected the 18-year-old graduating senior in the third round with the 75th overall pick in the amateur draft. "Once I found out [professional baseball] was a reality," Radinsky revealed about discovering that he was drafted, "I think the option of school was out the door. To get that opportunity was awesome. I wasn't really familiar with the White Sox, but you learn pretty quick."[8]

The teenage Radinsky commenced his professional baseball career in the Rookie-level Gulf Coast League in 1986. After two undistinguished campaigns as primarily a starter, he was converted into a full-time reliever, but missed most of the 1988 season with an assortment of injuries. With just 127⅓ innings under his belt, Radinsky put it all together in 1989 with South Bend in the Class-A Midwest League, earning All-Star honors with a circuit-best 31 saves and sparkling 1.75 ERA in 61⅓ innings while fanning more than four batters for every walk he issued (83 to 19) for the league champions.

Coming off a last-place finish in the AL West in 1989, the White Sox were in desperate need of left-handed relief and looked to Radinsky, as a nonroster player in spring training, for help in 1990. "[He's] maybe the strangest kid in camp," suggested sportswriter Alan Solomon in the *Chicago Tribune*.[9] With Bobby Thigpen firmly established as the closer, Radinsky unexpectedly made the squad, joining holdover Ken Patterson as the relief corps' sole southpaws. "Rad," as his teammates began calling him, was unintimidated by his surroundings, and quickly became a fan favorite. He cranked up his punk-rock music in the clubhouse and possessed an unflappable and unconventional demeanor not normally associated with baseball players, like riding his bike from his apartment in downtown Chicago to and from Comiskey Park. After retiring the only batter he faced in his debut in the season opener against the Milwaukee Brewers on April 9, Radinsky got off to what Bill Jauss of the *Tribune* called a "sensational" start, yielding just one earned run and seven hits in his first 17 appearances, covering 14⅓ innings.[10] "'Rad' has an outstanding arm," gushed manager Torborg. "And he's got poise. He has that attitude: 'I don't care who's up. I'll get him out.'"[11] Radinsky boasted a stellar 1.87 ERA as late as July 4, but suddenly hit a brick wall, as if his internal amp had been quickly unplugged. Thereafter he posted a demotion-inspiring 10.13 ERA as he struggled with his control and showed the effects of overwork. While the White Sox had a 25-game turnaround to win 94 contests and finish in second place, Radinsky demonstrated the kind of self-awareness and introspection that came to characterize his approach to pitching. "When I came out of high school," said Radinsky, "I thought I knew everything about pitching. Well, I'm learning. … I've learned you can't throw without a thinking plan, without pitching sequence."[12]

Radinsky was a willing and enthusiastic student. In his rookie campaign, he proved his mettle as a workhorse (62 appearances), but needed to avoid the big inning (4.82 ERA in 52⅓ innings) to ensure his future in the big leagues. In 1991 Rad emerged as one of the best set-up men in the AL and one of the most coveted relievers in majors. While Thigpen failed to reproduce his otherworldly numbers from the previous season (a major-league record 57 saves and 1.83 ERA), Radinsky proved to be the staff's most consistent reliever, pacing the club with a 2.02 ERA, and tying Thigpen with a team-high 67 appearances for the second-place White Sox. Occasionally thrust into the role of closer, Radinsky saved eight games, but also blew seven chances.

"Radinsky is a barbed original, a punk-loving, jock-loathing lefty," opined sportswriter Franz Lidz.[13] Like the adrenaline rush he got by listening to a two-minute, guitar-infused song by Black Flag, Radinsky seemed ideally suited to the high-pressure, intense lifestyle of a reliever, where everything is calm until that sudden burst of energy on the mound. "I love the five minutes I'm actually in the game," he told Lidz. "Those five minutes are why I come to the ballpark and put up with the writers, the dress code, the team meetings, the authority of the dugout, the major corporation that is baseball."[14]

No dilettante, Radinsky recognized that being a relief pitcher was more than facing two or three batters in a game 70 times a season or accumulating stats readily digested in the newspapers. It required physical and mental dedication with as much action and even more preparation behind the scenes to which the average fan was impervious. "A lot of people don't realize if you see 60 or 70 games you have to look at the person who threw in those games," Radinsky said. "Out of the 70 games I did get in, there were probably 30 other games I was one pitch away from getting in that I didn't get in and I was just as hot and ready to go."[15]

"Rad has already gotten that mental state," said Thigpen in spring training in 1992 about Radinsky's potential as a closer. "Rad wants to do it. He's confident he can."[16] Back in the role as set-up man, Radinsky got off to another scorching start, with a 1.64 ERA over his first 25 starts. When Thigpen struggled and was booed mercilessly by the Comiskey Stadium crowd, Radinsky finally had a chance to test his nerves as a closer. "I said in spring training that there's a lot of clubs that don't have one closer, and we're sitting with two of them," said pitching coach Jackie Brown.[17] From July 22 to August 22, Radinsky picked up a save in 10 of 12 chances and posted a 1.32 ERA in 14 appearances. Despite Radinsky's success, manager Gene Lamont used a closer by committee over the last five weeks with the emergence of another hard-throwing right-hander, future All-Star Roberto Hernandez. The 24-year-old Radinsky appeared in a team-high 68 games (tied for seventh most in the AL) with an impressive 2.73 ERA and 15 saves (eight blown chances) for the third-place Pale Hose.

Led by a pair of 25-year-old sluggers, MVP Frank Thomas and Robin Ventura, and arguably the best quartet of young starting hurlers in the league (Cy Young Award winner Jack McDowell, Alex Fernandez, Wilson Alvarez, and Jason Bere), the 1993 White Sox cruised to their first AL West crown in 10 seasons. Radinsky appeared in 73 games (second most in the league) while Hernandez served as primary closer (38 saves). Radinsky was also transforming into a LOOGY (left-handed one-out only guy). He averaged only about two outs per appearance, logging 54⅔ innings (4.28 ERA) while hampered by a severely strained groin in June. In the White Sox loss to the Toronto Blue Jays in the ALCS, he appeared in four of the six games, yielding four runs (two earned) while registering just five outs.

Health-conscious, Radinsky maintained an active offseason workout regimen of mountain biking and hiking in Southern California. He also toured with

his band. "I guarantee you," said the pitcher-singer, "there is no aerobic workout that a major league baseball player does that's better than playing live for 45 minutes."[18]

Radinsky faced his biggest challenge in February 1994 when he was diagnosed with Hodgkin's disease, a type of lymphoma. "When I got the news it totally sucked," said Radinsky of learning that he had cancer. "That's the worst news you can get."[19] He underwent surgery at Sarasota Memorial Hospital and returned to his home in Simi Valley to recuperate. "It was tough to deal with," he said about the months of radiation and aggressive chemotherapy. "But it was no problem. I had a schedule to do and did it."[20]

His White Sox teammates were understandably floored by the news. "It hasn't sunk in yet," said pitcher Jack McDowell. "It's not something you can prepare for."[21] During spring training White Sox players wore a patch of Radinsky's number 31 on their jersey.

Far from wallowing in self-pity and facing the prospects that his professional baseball career might be over, Radinsky perceived his ordeal as just another bump on the road and as a chance to spend time with his wife, Darlenys (the sister-in-law of White Sox player Ozzie Guillen), and catch up with friends in LA. "I'm about in the same shape I'd be, having to go to spring training," said Radinsky in early May. "Other than not being able to pitch competitively to real hitters, really good hitters, I'm staying in shape. I'm riding my bike, throwing every day, pitching in a league on Sundays."[22] He also volunteered as a coach at his former high school. Radinsky surprised his teammates and coaches with his health and appearance during the White Sox' three-game series against the California Angels in mid-May. After throwing on the side for Lamont, Radinsky harbored hopes that he might return to the team in September, just weeks after his chemotherapy was scheduled to finish. That plan was derailed by the baseball strike, which interrupted the season on August 12 and lasted 232 days.

The White Sox showed their loyalty to Radinsky by signing him to a one-year contract for the 1995 season, thus giving him a shot to stage a feel-good comeback. With his characteristic nonchalance, Radinsky relished the moment, but maintained his unique brand of humor. "Comeback?" he responded when queried about his return to the club, "What did I miss?"[23] After an 18-month absence from major-league baseball, Radinsky took the mound for the first time in an exhibition game on April 14 (the season had been delayed the end of the strike on April 2), yielding a run and three hits in an inning. "I just wanted to get through an inning, and have some fun," said Rad.[24] After easing along during spring training, Radinksy yielded a leadoff single to Greg Vaughn in the ninth, then retired the next three batters in the season opener on April 26 against the Brewers. "Feels good to finally have a little adrenaline flowing through my body again," said the tightly-wound southpaw.[25] The effects of Radinsky's lengthy layoff were noticeable. He was easily fatigued, struggled with his control, and landed on the DL in mid-July with a serious groin pull. With a 7.03 ERA, Radinsky was sent to Class-A South Bend for a rehab stint, but return to the club was far from certain. But after tossing 9⅔ scoreless innings for South Bend,

Radinsky was back with the White Sox in mid-August. He regained his mid-90s heater and yielded just three earned runs in his final 17 appearances (11⅔ innings), suggesting his career was far from over.

In December 1995 Radinsky was honored with the sixth annual Tony Conigliaro Award for his inspirational return to baseball. He received the award the following January, at the annual dinner hosted by the Boston chapter of the Baseball Writers' Association of America.

Notwithstanding Radinsky's success at the end of 1995, the White Sox did not re-sign him when he was granted free agency in December 1995. "I was crushed when they let me go," Radinsky said in *Sports Illustrated*. "I would have accepted any contract, even a minor-league contract."[26] Few teams expressed interest in a 27-year-old middle reliever who had posted a dismal 5.45 ERA in his return after missing a season due to Hodgkin's disease. The Los Angeles Dodgers took a chance on the hometown product, and signed Radinsky to a minor-league contract in January 1996. "I'm getting the same movement [I used to]," said Radinsky excitedly about his pitches during spring training. "And I know because of the reaction of the hitters."[27] Radinsky surprised everyone with a sturdy spring and was tapped by skipper Tommy Lasorda, in his last of 22 seasons at the helm of the only organization he ever knew, to open the season with the Dodgers.

Radinsky enjoyed the best stretch of baseball in his big-league career in his three years with the Dodgers (1996-1998), posting a stellar 2.65 ERA in 195 appearances. In his first 24 appearances with the club, he yielded only one earned run (in 21⅔ innings) and punched out 19. "You can't help but love him," praised Lasorda. He's a super guy to have on the team."[28] In the Dodgers' three-game sweep at the hands of Atlanta Braves in the NLDS, Radinsky pitched twice, recording four outs and issuing a walk.

After a staff-leading 75 appearances in 1997, Radinsky was named the Dodgers' closer in 1998 with the offseason departure of former All-Star Todd Worrell. Described by LA sportswriter Jason Reid as having "nasty stuff," Radinsky was successful in his first 10 of 12 save opportunities and posted a stellar 1.35 ERA through May 27.[29] Thereafter he hit a rough patch, blowing five saves in six chances and losing the closer's role. On June 4 the Dodgers acquired Cincinnati's red-hot closer, Jeff Shaw (1.81 ERA), who eventually led the NL in saves with 42. Radinsky once again paced the staff in appearances (62) and posted a sub-3.00 ERA for the third consecutive season.

Granted free agency after the 1998 season, Radinsky signed a lucrative two-year deal with the St. Louis Cardinals worth a reported $5 million. Rad seemed perfectly suited for Redbirds skipper Tony LaRussa who pioneered the use of the LOOGY in the late '90s and early 2000s. However, the 31-year-old hurler never found his rhythm, struggled with his control, and his ERA skyrocketed to 6.62 on June 11 after his second consecutive meltdown. Bothered by elbow tenderness the entire season, Radinsky landed on the DL after an appearance on July 26. According to Mike Eisenbath of the *St. Louis Post-Dispatch*, team physicians diagnosed "sizable chips" in Radinsky's left elbow, which were surgically removed in August, ending the reliever's season.[30] "I don't know what normally comes out of arms," Radinsky told Cardinals beat writer Rick Hummel, "but I was pretty much blown away by it."[31]

Despite expectations to the contrary, Radinsky began the 2000 season on the DL. According to the *St. Louis Post-Dispatch*, he suffered from a "strained left forearm."[32] I'm frustrated," said the reliever bluntly. "It's almost embarrassing."[33] He made his season debut on June 1, and lasted less than one batter. After throwing just three pitches, he was removed because of elbow pain, and was placed in the DL again.[34] LaRussa was roundly criticized by the local media for failing to send Radinsky on a minor-league rehab assignment. The *Post-Dispatch* reported that doctors subsequently determined that Radinsky required season-ending and potentially career-threatening Tommy John surgery and performed the operation on June 9.[35]

Radinsky wasn't ready to retire, even after two elbow operations and Hodgkin's disease. He signed a minor-league deal with the Cleveland Indians, spent most of the 2001 seasons in Double A and Triple A, and made his final two big-league appearances, with

the Tribe, when the rosters expanded in September. Released by the Indians in March 2002, Radinsky appeared in 18 games for the Calgary Cannons, the Florida Marlins' Triple-A affiliate in the PCL, in his final attempt to return to the majors.

At the age of 34, Radinksy retired in 2002. In parts of 11 seasons in the majors, he appeared in 557 games, carved out a 3.44 ERA in 481⅔ innings, and posted a 42-25 record with 52 saves.

Radinsky returned to Los Angeles and his wife, Darlenys, with whom he had three children, daughters Shylene and Rachael, and son Scott. His hiatus from baseball did not last long. After helping the Cleveland Indians in the Arizona Instructional League in 2004, Radinsky was hired by Cleveland in 2005 as a pitching coach for their affiliate in the Class-A South Atlantic League. He moved through the farm system over the next five seasons, then served as Cleveland's bullpen coach (2010-11) and pitching coach (2012). "I enjoy player development," said Radinsky. "I enjoy watching guys get from A-to-B-to-C-to-D, and maybe have the opportunity to get to the big leagues."[36] He related well to his players, who were fully aware of the challenges he had overcome in his playing career. Radinksy had the reputation as a "trust your stuff" coach, who was as much as psychologist as he was mentor.[37] After three seasons as pitching coach in the Dodgers organization, Radinsky was named the bullpen coach for the Los Angeles Angels in 2016.

As of 2016, Radinsky resided in Los Angeles. A man of varied interests, he continued to tour with his punk band, Pulley, and devote time to Skatelab, a skateboard park he co-founded in the 1990s.

SOURCES

In addition to the sources noted in this biography, the author also accessed the *Encyclopedia of Minor League Baseball*, Retrosheet. org, Baseball-Reference.com, the SABR Minor Leagues Database, accessed online at Baseball-Reference.com, and *The Sporting News* archive via Paper of Record. Special thanks to Bill Mortell for his assistance with genealogical research.

NOTES

1   Alan Solomon, "Radinsky Waits for Closing Time," *Chicago Tribune*, April 21, 1992: C3.

2   Hillel Kuttler, "Out of a Job, but Not Missing a Beat," *New York Times*, August 25, 2012.

3   Franz Lidz, "Punk With a Nasty Delivery. Dodgers Reliever Scott Radinsky Throws Smoke and Sings Music That Burns," *Sports Illustrated*, July 28, 1997.

4   Ibid.

5   Ibid.

6   Ibid.

7   Vince Kowalik, "Only 1 Stop Remains for Simi Valley Southern Section Baseball," *Los Angeles Times*, June 2, 1993: 8; Vince Kowalik, "Scyphers Addresses One Final Objective," *Los Angeles Times*, June 5, 1993: 10.

8   Devon Teeple, "Interview with Scott Radinsky: MLB Player/Coach, Punk Rock Frontman, Entrepreneur, *AXA Entertainment*, December 12, 2012. examiner.com/article/interview-with-scott-radinsky-mlb-player-coach-punk-rock-frontman-entrepreneu.

9   Alan Solomon, "Sox Pitching Blurred," *Chicago Tribune*, March 28, 1990: A6.

10 Bill Jauss, "Bullpen Rose. Ideal Set-up for This Pair," *Chicago Tribune*, June 30, 1990: 8.

11 Ibid.

12 Ibid.

13 Lidz.

14 Ibid.

15 Teeple.

16 *The Sporting News*, July 6, 1992: 12.

17 Solomon, "Radinsky Waits for Closing Time."

18 *The Sporting News*, February 22, 1999: 59.

19 Teeple.

20 Paul Sullivan, "Still Laid Back. Radinsky Back. Sox Pitcher Puts Disease Behind Him," *Chicago Tribune*, April 9, 1995: 9

21 "White Sox Reliever Radinsky Is Examined for Growth on Neck," *Los Angeles Times*, February 22, 1994: 5.

22 Jeff Fletcher and Mack Reed, "Simi Coach Is Removed Amid Inquiry," *Los Angeles Times*, May 4, 1994: 1.

23 Sullivan, "Still Laid Back. Radinsky Back. Sox Pitcher Puts Disease Behind Him."

24 Ibid.

25 Paul Sullivan, "Word War. Sore Spot for Selig, Fehr," *Chicago Tribune*, April 27, 1995: 10.

26 Lidz.

27 Jerome Holtzman, "Scott (Players Love Him, Man) Radinsky Popping His Old Heater," *Chicago Tribune*, June 18, 1996: 3.

28 Ibid.

29 *The Sporting News*, February 16, 1998: 23.

30 Mike Eisenbath, "Cardinals Notebook," *St. Louis Post-Dispatch*, August 14, 1999: 4OT

31 Rick Hummel, "Obstacles Don't Intimidate Radinsky," *St. Louis Post-Dispatch*, February 19, 2000: 3OT.

32 Rick Hummel, "Rick Ankiel Is Sharp in Pitching for Scoreless Inning," *St. Louis Post-Dispatch*, March 30-2000: C2.

33 Ibid.

34 Rick Hummel, "Radinsky Returns to DL After 3-Pitch Comeback," *St. Louis Post-Dispatch*, June 4, 2000: D10.

35 Rick Hummel, " 'Tommy John' Surgery Ends Radinsky's Year; McGwire, Vina, Howard Are Back in Outfield," *St. Louis Post-Dispatch*, June 10, 2000: 4OT.

36 Teeple.

37 Kuttler.

CURTIS PRIDE

By David Laurila

URTIS PRIDE'S FIRST BIG-league hit came on September 17, 1993, when he was a member of the Montreal Expos. It was a pinch-hit, two-run double in the seventh inning of a win over the Philadelphia Phillies, whom the Expos were battling for first place in the National League East. As he stood on second base, he could feel the 45,757 strong at Stade Olympique roaring their approval.

"The crowd was on their feet giving me a standing ovation that lasted for about five minutes," remembered Pride. "I felt the cheer. It was so loud, as if the crowd was trying to get me to hear their applause. It was very emotional."[1]

Pride was born deaf. He would go on play professionally for 23 years, including parts of 11 seasons at the major-league level. A left-handed-hitting outfielder who stood 6 feet tall and weighed a little over 200 pounds, he primarily served in a reserve role. Of his 199 big-league base hits, 50 came off the bench, including 29 as a pinch-hitter.

Curtis John Pride was born on December 17, 1968, in Washington, DC. His father, John, worked for the US Department of Health and Human Services for 38 years before retiring. His mother, Sallie, was a nurse before becoming a stay-at-home parent once Curtis was found to be deaf.

When Pride was 2 years old, his family moved to Silver Spring, Maryland, where he was enrolled in the Montgomery County Public School System's Auditory Service infant program. He was then "mainstreamed" into the local school system from seventh grade until his graduation from John F. Kennedy High School in 1986. He was the only hearing-impaired student at the school.

There was no history of deafness in Pride's family. (Audiologists found him to be 95 percent deaf in both ears as a result of his mother having rubella — German measles — while she was pregnant.) His parents decided to raise him using an oral approach "because of its advantages in the hearing world." He became a proficient lip-reader and, according to a former teammate, had enough speech that he could be reasonably well understood. It wasn't until later in life that he learned American Sign Language (ASL).

Language limitations didn't prevent Pride from becoming an accomplished student and an elite athlete. Aided by good genes — his father played basketball and track in college — Curtis excelled in multiple sports. In 1985 he was named one of the top 15 youth soccer players in the world for his performance in the FIFA U-16 World Championship, in Beijing, China. He would later tell the *Guardian* that soccer was his best sport, but baseball was his favorite sport to play.

In 1986 Pride received a full basketball scholarship to the College of William and Mary, where he was a starting point guard. Academically, he graduated from high school with a 3.6 GPA before going on to earn a degree in finance, in 1990. Had his dreams of becoming a professional athlete not panned out, Pride was planning to become a financial adviser.

The New York Mets selected Pride in the 10th round of the 1986 draft. That meant decision time. It is rare that a young athlete attends college and plays professional baseball at the same time, but heeding the advice of his father, that's exactly the road he chose. For the next five years, Pride's offseasons were spent in the classroom, while his summers were spent honing his skills in the minor leagues.

Pride was just 17 years old when he debuted with the Kingsport Mets of the rookie-level Appalachian League. He appeared in 27 games, logging five hits, one of them a home run, in 46 at-bats. His inexperience showed, as he went down on strikes 24 times.

Pride returned to Kingsport for his age-18 and -19 seasons, putting up better numbers as he matured. Even so, there were developmental obstacles. For one, his academic schedule demanded that he finish his

spring semester before resuming baseball activities. That meant no spring training and a late start to the season. Needing to be back at school by the beginning of September, he couldn't attend the fall instructional league.

From Kingsport, Pride continued his slow climb up the minor-league ladder, spending a year each in Pittsfield, Columbia, St. Lucie, and Birmingham. In 1993, at age 24, he finally broke through. He did so with the Expos, with whom he had signed as a sixth-year minor-league free agent.

Pride began his eighth professional season with Double-A Harrisburg, but he wasn't there for long. A .356 batting average and 15 home runs in 50 games earned him a promotion to Triple A. Once in Ottawa, Pride hit .302 in 301 plate appearances. His athleticism on display, he swiped 50 bases between the two stops. The Expos called him up in September.

Pride's pinch-hit double in the extra-inning win over the Phillies was the beginning of something unique. His second big-league hit was a pinch-hit triple. His third was a pinch-hit home run. His fourth was a pinch-hit single. At season's end, Pride was 4-for-9 and had hit for the cycle. Every one of his at-bats had come as a pinch-hitter.

The 1994 season was disappointing for both player and team. The Expos had the best record in baseball when the players strike ended any hopes of bringing a championship to Montreal. Meanwhile, Pride spent the entire campaign in Ottawa, hitting a lackluster .257 with 9 home runs.

The 1995 season marked a return to the big leagues, as well as continued reserve-role usage. Pride's first two hits were of the pinch-hit variety, and the next four came in games he'd entered as a defensive replacement. It wasn't until his 37th big-league game that he recorded a hit as a member of a starting lineup. He had just 11 hits all year, in 63 at-bats. Half of his season was spent in Ottawa, where his slash line was .279/.339/.448. Come October, he was a free agent for the second time.

Pride, then 26 years old, signed with the Detroit Tigers in March. He went on to have his best season. In 95 games he hit .300/.372/.513, with 10 home runs in 301 plate appearances. He looked ready to establish himself as an everyday player, but it wasn't to be.

"I was finally given a chance to play on a regular basis, and was able to produce the way I was capable," explained Pride. "The next year they gave my starting position to a rookie. I let that affect my mental attitude and performance."

During the offseason, Pride was presented the Tony Conigliaro Award to honor a player who has overcome "an obstacle and adversity through the attributes of spirit, determination, and courage that were trademarks of Conigliaro."

Thrust back into a supporting role in 1997, Pride hit a lackluster .210 in 79 games, nearly half of which came off the bench. In August the Tigers released him. The Red Sox picked him up, but gave him only two at-bats. The first resulted in a pinch-hit home run, at Fenway Park. The second was a pinch-hit strikeout. At the end of the season, he was cut loose once again.

The roller coaster continued in 1998. Signed by the Atlanta Braves, Pride went on see action in 70 games, but he started just 19 times. He hit a creditable .252/.325/.411, but that wasn't enough for him keep his job. He was released in December.

Pride reached a crossroads in 1999. The Kansas City Royals inked him to a contract in late February, but released him less than two weeks later. A wrist injury that required surgery was a primary reason, but other factors were at play as well. The journeyman outfielder was now 30 years old, and his track record was admittedly spotty. His allure to big-league organizations was growing dimmer.

Undaunted, he soldiered on. Once his wrist was healed—and with his options limited—he signed with the Nashua Pride of the independent Atlantic League. Rusty from being on the shelf most of the summer, he recorded just a pair of hits in 32 at-bats.

Pride battled his way back to the top, but the roller coaster never stopped. From 2000 to 2008 he played for nine organizations—seven in affiliated ball, and two more in indie ball—and over that time he was either traded or released on 10 separate occasions. Amid the turmoil, there were moments in the sun.

After getting a second cup of coffee in Boston, in 2000—this time nine games—Pride returned to Montreal the following year for his second go-round with the Expos. He hit a respectable .250 in 76 at-bats. From there it was on to the Pirates' organization, where he hit .296/.362/.436 for Triple-A Nashville.

Continuing an all-too-familiar trend, he was set free at the end of the 2002 season.

With no better offers forthcoming, the resilient 34-year-old returned to Nashua to begin the 2003 season. Sixteen games in, with a .344 batting average on his stat sheet, he was signed by the New York Yankees. Most of his time was spent in Triple A, but he did get into four games with the big-league club. His lone hit, which came in his third at-bat in a Yankees uniform, was a home run.

The following three years were at the same time atypical and emblematic of his career. Pride was in the Anaheim Angels organization from 2004 to 2007, breaking a string of nine consecutive seasons in which he switched allegiances at least once. Signed to a one-year contract each time, he continued to hit well in the minors, but receive a paucity of time in the major leagues. He came to the plate just 86 times in an Angels uniform.

Pride's last hurrah in professional baseball came close to home. In 2008, at the age of 39, he hooked on with the Atlantic League's Southern Maryland Blue Crabs. When that 89-game stint came to an end, he'd concluded a 23-year career that saw him play in 421 big-league games, 1,296 minor-league games, and 136 independent-league games.

Pride's major-league numbers are modest. In 989 plate appearances, he logged 199 base hits and batted .250/.327/.405. His minor-league numbers are far superior, particularly in Triple A. One rung below the majors, he batted .291/.384/.468 over 2,914 plate appearances.

Why Pride didn't get more opportunities at the highest level—and why he jumped from organization to organization—is somewhat of a mystery. Asked if his deafness played a role, Pride wouldn't speculate as to whether he was discriminated against. All he'd say was, "Teams appreciated my ability on the field, and more importantly, I was a very good team player." A former teammate concurred, adding that effort was never a problem—he took pride in every aspect of the game, from hitting to fielding to base-running.

During his career, Pride played for some of the top managers in the majors. Among them were Felipe

Alou (Montreal Expos), Bobby Cox (Atlanta Braves), Mike Scioscia (Los Angeles Angels), and Joe Torre (New York Yankees).

Pride didn't stay away from the sport for long. Shortly after retiring, he accepted the head coaching position at Gallaudet University, the country's only liberal-arts college for the deaf. In 2014 he led the team to a school record 27 wins. Since taking over the position in 2009, Pride has become fluent in ASL.

Pride resides in Wellington, Florida, with his wife, Lisa (who is hearing), and their two children, both of whom have hearing loss. Noelle, who was 12 years old in November 2016, has bilateral cochlear implants. Colten, 9 years old at the same point 2016, is deaf in his left ear.

Along with his wife, Pride runs the Together with Pride Foundation, whose mission is to "support and create programs for deaf and hard of hearing children that focus on the importance of education and the learning of life skills along with promoting a positive self esteem."[2]

In 2010 President Barack Obama announced the appointment of Pride to the President's Council on Fitness, Sports and Nutrition. The council is a committee of volunteer citizens who advise the president through the secretary of health and human services about opportunities to develop accessible, affordable, and sustainable physical activity, fitness, sports and nutrition programs for all Americans.

In January 2016, Baseball Commissioner Rob Manfred announced that Major League Baseball had appointed Pride as an "Ambassador for Inclusion." In his role, he "provides guidance, assistance and training related to MLB's efforts to ensure an inclusive environment." That includes "serv(ing) as a resource for individuals in the baseball family regarding issues related to disabilities."[3]

Pride's story is perhaps best encapsulated in a quote he gave to the *New York Times* in 1993:

"It's my life. I was going to do whatever I wanted."[4]

SOURCES

In addition to the sources cited in the Notes, the author consulted Baseball-Reference.com and the following sources:

gallaudetathletics.com/sports/bsb/coaches/pride_curtis?view=bio.

signingsavvy.com/blog/174/Living+Loud%3A+Curtis+Pride+Major+League+Baseball+Player.

theguardian.com/football/blog/2015/may/06/curtis-pride-the-deaf-usa-soccer-prodigy-who-turned-to-pro-baseball.

NOTES

1   All quotations from Curtis Pride come from an email interview with the author in November 2016.

2   togetherwithpride.org.

3   m.mlb.com/news/article/161261386/curtis-pride-is-mlbs-ambassador-for-inclusion/.

4   Joe Sexton, "Expos' Pride Can Feel the Cheers," *New York Times*, September 25, 1993. nytimes.com/1993/09/25/sports/baseball-expos-pride-can-feel-the-cheers.html.

ERIC DAVIS

BY NORM KING

IN A 1987 *SPORTS ILLUSTRATED* article on teammate Eric Davis, Cincinnati Reds outfielder Dave Parker said, "Eric is blessed with world-class speed, great leaping ability, the body to play until he was 42, tremendous bat speed and power, and a throwing arm you wouldn't believe."[1]

Parker was right on all counts but one; Davis suffered far too many injuries and endured too much serious illness to allow him to play into his fifth decade. But he had all the tools, and when his body was right, he was one heck of a ballplayer. He had enough power and speed to earn membership in the 30-30 club—very nearly becoming the first 40-40 hitter—and was a good enough center fielder to earn three Gold Gloves during his career. He won a World Series with Cincinnati in 1990, but later in his career defeated a far more ruthless and dangerous opponent, colon cancer.

Eric Keith Davis was born on May 29, 1962, in Los Angeles, one of three children born to Jimmy and Shirley Davis; his siblings include an older brother, Jim Jr., and a sister, Sharletha. Eric's father worked for Boys Market, a grocery-store chain. The family lived in very tough South Central Los Angeles, and Jimmy would go to the playground with his sons not only to shoot hoops, but to protect them from the dangers that lurked in the neighborhood. On one occasion, someone at the playground was shooting a gun wildly.

"Here I was, there to protect Eric, but the shooting was so close, I panicked," said Jimmy." All I could say was just, 'Eric, hit the dirt.' We all ran behind the school. That's the kind of area it is. It's a blessing he got out without getting hurt."[2]

It wasn't unusual for kids in that area to be enticed into the drug culture. Davis was often offered narcotics as a youngster, but avoided the trap of addiction by playing sports. He played baseball and basketball at Fremont High School and often went up against childhood friend, rival, and future major leaguer Darryl Strawberry, who played at Crenshaw High School. Davis's favorite sport was basketball, and he never took baseball seriously until his senior year in high school, when he hit .531 with 50 stolen bases. Numbers like those tend to draw scouts' attention; it was at that point that baseball superseded basketball as a career path.

"I guess the first time I took baseball seriously was when the scouts started paying attention to me," said Davis, who played shortstop in high school. "Darryl (at Crenshaw) always had more scouts watching him. There weren't too many scouts who would come down to Fremont looking for talent."[3]

A few teams did scout Davis, including the Dodgers and Brewers, but it was the Reds who signed him after selecting him in the eighth round of the June 1980 draft. His first stop was up the coast with the Eugene Emeralds of the short-season Northwest League. He didn't set the world on fire immediately, hitting only .219 in 33 games as an 18-year-old. He hit only one home run, but he made it count—it was a two-run walk-off blast in the bottom of the ninth against the Central Oregon Phillies on August 18.

Davis worked his way up through the minors showing an impressive combination of speed and power; the power was especially surprising because although he was 6-feet-2, he played at only 165 pounds. He hit 48 home runs and stole 141 bases between 1981 and 1983, earning him a place on the Reds' 40-man roster prior to the 1984 season. The Reds also decided to take advantage of Davis's speed for defensive purposes by switching him from shortstop to the outfield, beginning in 1981 at Eugene.

Being on the 40-man roster doesn't guarantee a trip up north with the big club, and such was the case with Davis, who began the 1984 campaign with the Wichita Aeros, Cincinnati's affiliate in the Triple-A American Association. But sometimes you have to get a break to succeed; in Davis's case, a hamstring injury to Duane

Walker on May 17 earned Davis his first call-up to the majors. That Davis was hitting .311 with 10 home runs and 35 RBIs on the farm didn't hurt.

Even as a rookie, Davis showed that he could both do magical things on a ballfield and lose playing time due to injury. The injury occurred when he hurt his knee sliding in a July 19 game against the Mets. He was benched for a while in the hopes that the injury would improve but the team finally put him on the disabled list on August 14. He returned on September 1 and celebrated by hitting five home runs in four games.

As impressed as he was by Davis's power outburst, Reds manager Pete Rose was more concerned that he make contact rather than just aim for the long ball. "I told him to just be quick with the bat and the homers will come," Rose said. "I told him, too, that I'd be watching him like a hawk. The kid understands. He has a chance to be the best player on this club."[4]

Maybe the kid didn't understand as much as Rose thought. He went north with the team after spring training in 1985 and turned some heads on Opening Day when he stole second and third on successive pitches during the Reds' 4-1 win over Montreal. From that point on, about the only thing Davis turned was Rose's stomach, for by June 4 he was hitting only .189, with 31 strikeouts in 90 at-bats. That's when Rose sent Davis down to the Triple-A Denver Zephyrs, where he hit .277 in 64 games with 15 home runs, 38 RBIs, and 35 steals. The Reds recalled him in September, and Davis remained with the parent club the rest of the year. He admitted that returning to the minors was good for him. "The only thing good about going back was that it helped me mentally," he said. "It was a test of my character, especially when I failed after all the media hype last spring."[5]

Davis made the parent club again in 1986, when the Reds left spring training with seven outfielders. Rookies Paul O'Neill and Kal Daniels won jobs in Florida to join holdovers Davis, Parker, Eddie Milner, Nick Esasky, and Max Venable. As he did the previous season, he impressed on Opening Day, belting a three-run homer to lead Cincinnati to a 7-4 win over the Phillies. Unlike 1985, however, he stuck around

awhile and began exhibiting some of the power and speed that had Reds executives salivating.

Davis really began to prove himself when Esasky went on the disabled list on June 14 with sore thigh muscles. After starting 12 games in April, he had been benched in early May when he was hitting .214 with 4 home runs, 12 RBIs, and 17 stolen bases in 98 at-bats. He started sizzling as soon as he resumed a regular role, hitting .371 in his first 25 games after Esasky's injury, with 8 home runs, 19 RBIs, and 23 stolen bases. The Reds lost anyway, 8-4.

Davis joined some select company on August 25, 1986, when he hit his 20th homer of the year, off the Pirates' Rick Rhoden. The blast qualified him for entry into the exclusive 20-60 club (20 home runs and 60 stolen bases), joining future Hall of Famers Joe Morgan and Rickey Henderson. He eventually reached the 20-80 echelon, with 27 homers and 80 steals to go with a .277 batting average, 71 RBIs, and a .901 OPS.[6]

Davis credited batting coach Billy DeMars with his improvement as a hitter, because DeMars changed his approach at the plate, getting him to tighten up his swing and go with the pitch instead of trying to pull everything. This meant that instead of trying to hit an outside pitch to left (Davis was a right-handed hitter), he could hit it to right, and with authority.

The lessons Davis applied in 1986 worked even better in 1987. By the All-Star break he was batting .321, with 27 home runs and 68 RBIs, including three grand slams in May. Not surprisingly, he started in the All-Star Game for the first time, going 0-for-3. He started well in the second half; on August 2 he smacked his 30th home run of the season, making him the seventh player to join the 30-30 club (30 home runs and 30 stolen bases—he already had 37 steals). It seemed inevitable that Davis would become the first player ever to become a 40-40 man.[7] But he went through a second-half slump, due in part to a rib injury he suffered on September 4 crashing into the outfield wall at Wrigley Field while taking an extra-base hit away from Ryne Sandberg. The injury also forced Davis to miss 17 of the team's last 27 games. His numbers for the season were still very impressive:

37 home runs, 100 RBIs, and 50 stolen bases. After the season, Davis had to make room on the mantelpiece in his home because he won his first Gold Glove and Silver Slugger awards. There would be more to come.

Davis could kiss a 40-40 season goodbye early in 1988 as injuries and poor production led to a terrible start. After missing three games in mid-May with a hamstring injury, he entered the "can't-win-for-trying" society when some people thought he was hurting the team by coming back too soon from the injury, less than a year after facing accusations of malingering.

"Yes, I've heard both sides," he said. "I heard I don't play hurt, and now I hear I shouldn't play hurt. I know some of my teammates and the manager have said things, but not to me. They say it to the media."[8]

By May 31 Davis was hitting only .220 with 6 home runs, 23 RBIs, and 15 stolen bases. These numbers were so far below what he had reached the previous season that speculation as to why was inevitable. An article in the *Cincinnati Enquirer* on June 7 cited an unnamed National League executive as saying that rumors were going around that Davis was using drugs. Reds GM Murray Cook, who was said to be offering Davis as trade bait, flatly rejected the allegations.

"My official response is that I won't grace it with a reply," Cook said. "I'll say one thing, he's handled it [the adversity of the season] well and very maturely."[9]

That maturity manifested itself in a vastly improved performance spurred on, perhaps, by Davis's intention to disprove the drug allegations. His bat got hot just as the weather did, and he finished the year with a .273 batting average, 26 home runs, 93 RBIs, and 35 stolen bases. He also suffered the dings and bruises of outrageous fortune, as he sustained a number of freakish minor injuries that forced him to miss games on several occasions during the season. He sat out four games (and was only a pinch-runner in a fifth) with a swollen elbow after the Giants' Atlee Hammaker hit him with a pitch on June 17. He then celebrated Independence Day by bruising his knee after colliding with teammates Barry Larkin and Jeff Treadway while chasing a fly ball. He had to be carried off the field and missed three games.

After the season Davis met reporters for the first time since imposing a personal gag order on June 1. He explained that his bad start was more typical for him than the amazing start he had in 1987. "The way I started last year [1987], that doesn't happen often," said Davis. In a way, it was unfortunate, because that's what people are going to expect me to do all the time."[10]

Davis signed a one-year, $1.35 million contract, plus incentives, after stories in the media appeared about his wanting to be traded. Once the season started, he managed to avoid a visit from the boo-birds of unhappiness by getting off to a hot start By June 30 he already had 14 home runs, 49 RBIs, a .293 batting average, and a .919 OPS, but only four stolen bases. The numbers were particularly impressive considering he injured himself yet again, missing 14 games after tearing his hamstring in a 6-4 loss to the Expos in Montreal on May 2.

Davis continued to play well after returning from the injury, and was named to the National League All-Star team by manager Tom Lasorda. It was typical of Davis's emotional roller-coaster-type season that even that bit of good news became mired in controversy. Davis's contract called for a $55,000 bonus for being "elected" to the All-Star team, but he finished fourth in fan balloting with 810,744 votes. There seemed to be some confusion about the details, with his agent, Eric Goldschmidt, contending that Davis was entitled to the bonus regardless of how he made the team. The Reds eventually paid the bonus.

After the All-Star break, Davis was good until September 3, when he continued his habit of running into outfield walls, this time at Three Rivers Stadium in Pittsburgh, while catching a fly ball in foul territory. He missed four games with a strained wrist. None of these injuries prevented Davis from having an excellent season, with a .281 batting average, 34 home runs, 101 RBIs, and 21 stolen bases, earning him his second Silver Slugger award. He also stood out again defensively, winning his third straight Gold Glove.

The 1990 season was bittersweet for Davis. He signed a three-year, $9.3 million contract in the winter, then proceeded to have a horrible start to the season which included—you guessed it—yet another visit to the disabled list. He missed 23 games in April and May with a knee injury, and just never got on track. He finished the season with a .260 average, 24 home runs, a team-leading 86 RBIs, and 21 steals in 127 games. But this was a different year for the Reds, as new manager Lou Piniella led them all the way to a stunning four-game sweep of the Oakland A's in the World Series. Davis played well in the first three games, batting .286 with one home run and five RBIs. Disaster struck in Game Four, in Oakland.

Playing in his typical all-out way, Davis dove after and missed a Willie McGee fly ball in the first inning. After the trainer came out to have a look at him, he finished the inning, but collapsed on returning to the dugout. His teammates carried him to the clubhouse, and he was taken to the hospital after producing a blood-filled urine sample. He was diagnosed with a lacerated kidney, and spent 40 days in the hospital. A controversy erupted when he took a private plane home to Cincinnati, because Davis expected the Reds to pay for it.

"My agent talked to [then GM Bob] Quinn and asked him and he said, 'He's making $3 million, let him get his own plane,'" said Davis. "So I did. Then I sent them the bill."[11] The Reds eventually paid it.

Davis's doctor said he should take the entire 1991 season off, but he was on the field against the Astros on Opening Day at Riverfront Stadium. His 2-for-4 performance indicated that maybe his doctor was being overly cautious, but as the season progressed it was clear that Davis wasn't 100 percent. By July 20 he was hitting .252 with 10 home runs, 26 RBIs, 13 stolen bases, and a case of chronic fatigue that shelved him for 27 games in August—this was his second stint of the season on the disabled list, after he missed 14 games in June with a hamstring injury—and never did play up to his capabilities. He appeared in only 89 games all season, hitting only one home run and driving in five runs after returning from the DL.

Despite his valiant effort in 1991, Reds brass determined that Davis would never again be the player he once was or could be, and on November 27 he was traded with pitcher Kip Gross to the Los Angeles Dodgers for pitchers Tim Belcher and John Wetteland. For Davis it meant going home and playing with his childhood buddy Strawberry.

"The reality is they felt I couldn't perform any more," said Davis. "The No. 1 thing about how I performed last year was I had a kidney torn in three places. They held me accountable for that."[12]

It turns out the Reds were right. The much-ballyhooed reunion of the boyhood mates didn't result in a comeback for either player. Strawberry's personal problems and injuries limited him to 43 games in 1992, and Davis's hell-bent playing style led to more injuries, including a broken collarbone and a shoulder injury requiring surgery that ended his season in early September. Davis played in only 76 games.

Davis was a free agent after the season and, perhaps hoping there was still some of the 1987 player left in him, the Dodgers signed him to a one-year, $1million free-agent contract for 1993, plus $5,494.51 for every day he was on the active roster.[13] Well, as the saying goes, a million dollars doesn't buy what it used to. Dodgers general manager Fred Claire almost cut Davis in May when he was hitting .211, but he held on to him until August 31, when he traded Davis to the Detroit Tigers for a player to be named later.

That player was John DaSilva, who pitched in a total of six major-league games. For what the Tigers got from Davis, it was a pretty fair exchange. He played 23 games for them at the end of 1993. In 1994 he was batting .186 went on the disabled list on May 23 with a pinched nerve in his neck. He was out for 57 games, then left the first game he started upon his return (on July 26) in the seventh inning with a pulled groin.

The 1994 season was cut short due to the players' strike, but Davis would not have returned anyway. He underwent surgery for a herniated disc in his neck—his eighth operation in seven years—then called it a career at age 32 when doctors advised him of how extensive the damage was.

Davis spent 1995 in Los Angeles overseeing several businesses, including a PR firm, and working out. But along about October, when his two favorite teams, the Reds and Dodgers, met in the NLDS, the ol' competitive juices started flowing and visions of a comeback started dancing in his head. Finally, on January 2, 1996, Davis signed a minor-league contract with Cincinnati that promised him $500,000 if he made the team.

Davis had a great spring and did indeed make the team. The year off and a lot of work with hitting coach Hal McRae brought back some of the old Davis. Granted, he had his annual trip to the disabled list, when he missed 11 games with bruised his ribs he suffered making a diving catch in Denver on May 25, but notoriously stingy Reds owner Marge Schott really got her money's worth, as Davis went on to hit .287, with 26 home runs, 83 RBIs, and 23 stolen bases in 129 games. His homer and ribbie totals were second on the team behind Barry Larkin, and he was third in thefts. All in all it was a great season, culminating in Davis's winning the National League Comeback Player of the Year Award.

The Reds decided that even though Davis came back, he wasn't going forward, and didn't sign him for 1997. The Baltimore Orioles, on the other hand, were looking to replace Bobby Bonilla, who had left via free agency, and signed Davis to a one-year contract for $2.2 million with an option for 1998. He started the 1997 season off well, and was hitting .302 through May 25, when he had to stop paying due to a stomach ailment. That "ailment" turned out to be colon cancer, and he had a portion of his colon removed on Friday, June 13, at Johns Hopkins hospital in Baltimore.

There were some who thought that Davis was a malingerer because of all the playing time he missed due to injury. Most were no doubt impressed by his 1996 comeback after missing more than a year because of his neck problems; certainly no one would begrudge him if he decided the hell with it after undergoing cancer surgery. But on September 15 Davis returned to the Orioles' lineup, even while he was still getting weekly chemotherapy treatments, and helped them clinch the American League East title. He appeared in the NLDS victory over Seattle and the NLCS loss to the Cleveland Indians. Although he didn't get a second World Series ring, Davis won the Roberto Clemente Award for being the most inspirational player, and the Fred Hutchinson Award, which is given to the player who best exemplifies character, dedication, and competitive spirit.[14] In Boston in early 1968 he was also honored with the Tony Conigliaro Award, presented annually to a player who has overcome an obstacle and adversity with spirit, determination, and courage.

"I was able to get operated on four days after I was diagnosed," he said. "It was just a matter of getting this baseball-sized tumor out of me."[15]

Davis returned to the Orioles in 1998, and after that season dictionaries could have put his picture beside the words comeback, courage, or determination—take your pick. He spent a lot of time as DH and none on the DL, and had a magnificent season: a .327 average (fourth in the American League), 28 home runs, and 89 RBIs. He also led the team with a .970 OPS.

The 1998 season was Davis's last hurrah. He signed a two-year, $9 million deal with the St. Louis, but the Cardinals didn't get their money's worth. His 1999 campaign was cut short after 58 games due to surgery to repair a torn rotator cuff, and he appeared in 92 games as a part-time player in 2000. He retired after playing in 74 games with the Giants in 2001.

Davis got involved in a number of business and baseball activities. He served as a roving instructor for the Reds, dabbled in real estate, and produced two documentaries. The first, *Hitting From the Heart*, is a motivational DVD that shows how athletes can overcome any obstacle to achieve their goals. The second, *Harvard Park*, is about how the park where Davis and Strawberry played in as kids produced so many great athletes despite being in a crime-ridden neighbourhood.

But Davis's heart belonged to baseball. As of 2016, Davis was a special assistant to Reds general manager Dick Williams. He and his wife, Sherrie, had two daughters, Erica and Sacha.

SOURCES

In addition to the sources cited in the Notes, the author used the following:

Websites

Cincinnati.reds.mlb.com.

Fredhutch.org.

UPI.com.

Newspapers

Orlando Sentinel.

Santa Cruz Sentinel.

Seguin (Texas) *Gazette-Enterprise.*

Star-Democrat (Easton, Maryland).

Books

Swaine, Rick. *Baseball's Comeback Players: Forty Major Leaguers Who Fell and Rose Again* (Jefferson, North Carolina: McFarland & Company, 2014).

NOTES

1   Ralph Wiley, "These Are Red Letter Days," *Sports Illustrated*, May 25, 1887: 36.

2   Sam McManis, "South-Central L.A. Was Where It Began for Reds' Eric Davis—But Now, the Sky's the Limit," *Los Angeles Times*, February 2, 1987.

3   Ibid. That's a surprising statement because the school also produced major leaguers Chet Lemon, George Hendrick, Bobby Tolan, and Bob Watson.

4   Earl Lawson, "Davis' HR Binge Impresses Reds," *The Sporting News*, September 17, 1984: 22.

5   Hal McCoy, "Davis Job-Hunting Again With Reds," *The Sporting News*, April 7, 1986: 49.

6   Henderson was already in that elite group, having hit 24 homers with 80 steals in 1985. In 1986 he had 28 home runs and 87 stolen bases.

7   Jose Canseco of the Oakland A's achieved the feat in 1988 with 42 home runs and 40 stolen bases. By his own admission, Canseco used steroids while playing. Davis, whose playing weight was 165 pounds, was never suspected of using performance-enhancing drugs.

8   McCoy, "Is an Injured Davis Hurting Reds," *The Sporting News*, June 13, 1988: 25.

9   Michael Paolercio, "Davis: I Have No Drug Problem," *Cincinnati Enquirer*, June 7, 1988: C-1.

10   Greg Hoard, "Eric Davis Finally Has His Say," *Cincinnati Enquirer*, October 4, 1988: A-16.

11   Steve Dilbeck, "Davis Tells His Side of Incidents,'" *San Bernardino County Sun*, August 1, 1993: G5.

12   Joe Kay, *San Bernardino County Sun*, November 28, 1991: C7.

13   If the Dodgers were hoping that Davis would spend considerable time on the disabled list so they wouldn't have to pay this particular bonus, they were sorely disappointed. He was on the roster all season.

14   Called the Hutch Award, it was created to honor Hutchinson by Pirates broadcaster Bob Prince. Hutchinson was the Reds manager when he was diagnosed with cancer in December 1963 and was given less than one year to live. He came back to manage the Reds in 1964, but had to stop in midseason. He died on November 12 of that year.

15   "Baseball Star Eric Davis' Heroic Battle With Cancer an Inspiration On and Off the Field," *Jet*, Volume 94, Number 16, September 14, 1998: 52.

BRET SABERHAGEN

BY ALAN COHEN

"Times of adversity make you stronger. And sometimes those times make you so tired that when your son says to you, 'Dad, I want to be there at the last game you pitch,' you tell him, 'Kid, you might have been there already.'"[1]
— Bret Saberhagen — August 8, 2001 one day after his last major-league game.

SUCCESS CAME EARLY FOR Bret Saberhagen. In only his second major-league season, 1985, the 21-year-old won the Cy Young Award with a 20-6 record and was named the Most Valuable Player in the World Series. With his Kansas City team winless in its first two games against St. Louis, he pitched the Royals to a 6-1 win in Game Three and, with everything on the line, pitched an 11-0 shutout in Game Seven to give Kansas City its first World Championship in baseball. For his efforts in 1985, he had been paid $150,000. At season's end he was eligible for arbitration and won a third award, as the arbiter's decision yielded him $925,000 for the 1986 season.

He was on top of the world and was rated by writer Thomas Boswell as one of the three top pitchers in baseball (along with Dwight Gooden and John Tudor) going into the 1986 season. Saberhagen was heard to say, "I'm just going to do everything the same as last year. Take it one step at a time. Can't do too much too fast. I just have a feeling of confidence. Every time you go out there you have to think you're going to win or you won't. If I give the best Bret Saberhagen can give, then I'll be happy with it."[2]

However, in what was to become a pattern, the Saberhagen of the even-numbered years did not match up with the Saberhagen of the odd-numbered years.

He was born on April 11, 1964 in Chicago Heights, Illinois, but his formative years were spent in California. Bret is an only child. His parents Bob and Linda divorced when he was only 9 years old and, by then, the

Saberhagens had relocated to the West Coast. Linda took a position in the accounting department of a retail store. Bob remained in his son's life, relocating to Chatsworth, California, and taking a position with a computer leasing firm in Encino, California.[3] Bret starred as a sophomore at Grover Cleveland High School in Reseda, California, and was selected the MVP of the West Valley League in 1980. However, he had an off-year the following season, although he also played a good shortstop and was one of his team's leading batters with a .333 average. In his senior year, when the basketball season extended into early spring, he rushed himself into shape, developing tendonitis in his shoulder. Just after Easter, he resumed pitching and put together a 6-0 record in his team's regular season. On the eve of the high school playoffs, the major-league draft was held. At this point, most scouts felt that his velocity was still suspect and this reduced his chances at being a high draft pick. But Royals scout had seen Bret as he was rounding into form and Kansas City used its 19th round pick in the 1982 draft to select Saberhagen.[4]

Bret then went on to go 3-0 in the playoffs. His second playoff win came in the semifinals when he relieved in the first inning with none out and his team behind by five runs. Over the course of the remaining innings, he struck out 12 as his Cavaliers team came from behind to win, 7-6.[5] In the championship game, won by Cleveland 13-0, he pitched a no-hitter at Dodger Stadium to bring his overall high school record to 24-2, under the tutelage of coach Leo Castro. Were it not for a first-inning error by the Cleveland second baseman, Saberhagen, who struck out eight and retired the final 20 batters in a row, would have had a perfect game. After the game, he commented, "I didn't start thinking of it (the no-hitter) until the fifth inning (of the seven-inning contest). When I went out in the last inning, I was going for it."[6] His no-hitter was the first ever in the 44-year history of the city championship, and the last inning had its challenges. The first two of the final inning outs came on outstanding fielding plays by the first baseman and right fielder, respectively. After the final out, on a failed bunt attempt, Saberhagen said, "This is the best feeling I've ever had in my life. The rest of the team helped out and were with me all the way."[7]

Shortly thereafter, he was named City Player of the Year, and he signed with the Royals. Bret married his high school sweetheart, Janeane Inglett, in 1984. Their first child, Drew William Saberhagen was born on October 26, 1985, eight hours before the start of Game Six of the 1985 World Series, and Saberhagen celebrated with a 2-0 win in Game Seven. They had two more children, daughter Brittany Nicole (born September 5, 1986) and son Daulton, before separating in 1992. Their divorce became final in 1994.

Saberhagen's minor-league career was brief. His first exposure to professional baseball was in the Florida Instructional League in the fall of 1982, where he pitched to a 7-2 record with a 2.36 ERA. He began the 1983 season with Fort Myers in the Class-A Florida State League, going 10-5 with a 2.30 ERA. He was named to the Southern Division team for the league's All-Star game. He was promoted before the end of the season to Class-AA Jacksonville in the Southern League where he won six of eight decisions and lowered his ERA to 2.91. In the Florida Instructional League that fall, he allowed only one earned run and walked only three batters in 47 innings.

He made it to the majors in 1984, becoming the youngest Royal ever, and got off to one of the rockier starts in major-league history. In his first appearances, he was called in from the bullpen to replace Paul Splittoff, who had been ineffective. The score was 4-2 in favor of the Yankees, and Burch Wynegar was standing on first base with only one out. Manager Dick Howser said, "Don't worry about the runner on first. He's not very fast and I don't think he'll be stealing. Just concentrate on the batter." To Saberhagen's surprise, catcher Don Slaught then called for a pitchout. However, Saberhagen was focused on the batter and threw a curve that crossed up his catcher and rolled to the back stop. The wild pitch advanced the runner to

second base.[8] Saberhagen regained his composure and registered the next two outs. He went on to pitch 4 2/3 innings of scoreless ball that day, scattering three hits.

His first start came on April 19 against the Tigers, and resulted in his first career win. He went six innings, allowing only one run as the Royals defeated the Tigers 5-2, snapping a season opening nine-game winning streak by Detroit. He made a positive impression on Detroit pitching coach Roger Craig who said, "He's one of the best looking young pitchers I've seen. He's got as much poise as any young pitcher I've seen. I've seen guys with better stuff, but not many with as much poise."[9] In his first season, he went 10-11 with a 3.48 ERA.

In 1985, en route to a 20-6 record, becoming the fifth-youngest pitcher in major-league history to win 20 games, Saberhagen had a 2.87 ERA, third best in the league. He pitched with exceptional control and led the league with a 4.16 strikeout to walk ratio. He would go on to lead his league in that statistic two other times during his career, and his career ratio of 3.641 puts him at 18th place on the all-time list. He had gotten off to a slow start that year, but after May 12, he was 18-3 with a 2.54 ERA. His 20th win on September 30 put the Royals into a first-place tie with the Angels with six games left in the season. Five days later, they clinched the division and advanced to the League Championship Series. In the LCS, Saberhagen started Game Three but was knocked out of the box in the fifth inning. However, the Royals came back to win that game and Saberhagen was back on the mound in Game Seven. He bruised his thumb in the first inning and came out after three scoreless innings with the Royals leading 2-0. They went on to win the game and advanced to the World Series.

1986 was a disaster. As Peter Gammons wrong in *Sports Illustrated*, he went from "Cy Young to Die Young."[10] The season started out well for him. His second start and first decision of the season was at Fenway Park on the afternoon of April 16. It was not a typical Fenway game. Only 11,164 fans were in attendance, and if one dallied too long at the concession stand, he would miss an inning or two, as the game took only two hours and five minutes to complete.

Steve Balboni gave Saberhagen all the support he would need, leading off the second inning with a home run. Although the Royals could only muster five hits off Red Sox pitcher Al Nipper, Saberhagen, working quickly, limited the Red Sox singles by Tony Armas and Don Baylor in the early innings. He retired the last 15 batters in succession for a 1-0 shutout win.

After that, things did not pan out well for Saberhagen. His overindulgence on the banquet circuit after winning the Cy Young award caught up with him. He lost his next two starts in April before hurling his second and last shutout of the season, defeating Baltimore 5-0 at Kansas City on May 2. It was his only win of the month, and at the end of May, his record stood at 2-5. The season wore on and the losses continued to outnumber the wins. Arm troubles were such that he was on the shelf from August 10 through September 5, and his record for the season was 7-12 with an ERA of 4.15. Looking back on the season during a winter when the phone stopped ringing with invites, Saberhagen said, "I still don't have any answers. If I could figure out what I did wrong, I'd do something about it. It's tough to pinpoint. The big thing was the injuries. That didn't help for sure. I did so many different things (to improve); it's hard to say what went wrong. Who knows? I just know I was expected to win at least 20 last year and I was very, very upset at the year I had."[11]

His salary was cut to $740,000, but he went to spring training in 1987 determined to turn things around. After his first spring start he said, "I've been thing about this (his first spring start) for a long time, especially the last week. I was concerned because of what happened last year. But I know that if I can get through the spring like I did today, I should have nothing less than 17 wins this season."[12] But he came back with a good season in 1987 and was named the comeback-player-of-the year. He won each of his first six starts including a shutout of Cleveland on May 9 that brought his ERA down to 1.59. His 4-0 record in April garnered him Player of the Month honors. Over the course of the season, he won 18 games, losing only 10. He was second in the league in both shutouts (four) and complete games (15), and his ERA was 3.36. He

was named to his first All-Star team, and started the game on July 14 in Oakland, pitching three shutout innings marred only by a double off the bat of Andre Dawson. The Royals in a hotly contested West Division race (10 games separated the seven clubs) finished in second place, two games behind the Detroit Tigers.

At the beginning of the 1988 season Saberhagen had signed a lucrative three-year deal with the Royals. At the conclusion of the negotiations he said, "It turned out excellent for both sides. Now I don't have to keep going through this every year. It was driving me crazy."[13] He received $1.1 million in 1988, $1.25 million in 1989, and $1.375 million in 1990.

He was healthy in 1988, but his record fell to 14-16 with high numbers in all the wrong places. He led the league giving up hits (271) and allowed 110 earned runs as his ERA rose to 3.80. The only injury he sustained that year was when he tripped in his hotel room in New York in May and required 16 stitches to close the gash on his forehead and another five to sew up the laceration beneath his one of his eyes. More embarrassed than bruised, he did not miss a start.[14] It was a year of streaks for Saberhagen. In June, he was 4-1 with a 2.68 ERA, and at the end of June his record for the season stood at 10-6. After that, he was winless in his next five starts, in which he was charged with four losses. Over the last three months of the season was 4-10 with an ERA of 4.27. Even if Saberhagen had had a good season, the Royals would not have improved much on their third-place finish as the Athletics romped to the AL West title leading the pack by 13 games.

Saberhagen's second Cy Young Award season followed in 1989 when he went 23-6 with a league-leading ERA of 2.16. The durable Saberhagen pitched in at least 250 innings for the third year in a row, hurling a league high 262 1/3 innings. His first start of the season on April 10 was a harbinger of things to come. During the course of the season, he only lost successive games on one occasion, and that was in April. After April, he was 21-4 with a 1.93 ERA. He was left off the All-Star team, although his record at the All-Star break was 8-4. After the All-Star break his record bordered on the sensational, as he was 15-2 with a 1.74 ERA. His control during the season was exceptional as he walked only 43 batters while striking out 193. Although he committed a career high four errors during the season, he was awarded the only Golden Glove of his career. The Royals were in contention for most of the season, and on September first were 1 1/2 games out of first place. They finished at 92-70, but the Oakland A's distanced themselves from the pack in the late going. The Royals finished in second place, seven games behind the division champions.

By now you have guessed it - 1990 was a disaster. However, largely due to his record in the prior season when he had been snubbed, he was chosen to pitch in the All-Star Game on July 10. He pitched scoreless ball in the fifth and six innings, retiring each of the six batters he faced, and was awarded the win when the American League broke a scoreless tie in the top of the seventh inning and went on to win 2-0. His record was 5-7 when he had surgery in late July to have two loose bone chip fragments removed from his right elbow. He returned to the lineup later in the season and his record for the season was 5-9 with a 3.27 ERA. Not only was the season a disaster for Saberhagen, but the Royals hit the skids as well finishing in sixth

place. At the end of the season, general manager John Schuerholz resigned. He had assumed the role after the 1981 season and was at the helm during Kansas City's first World Championship in 1985.

Would Saberhagen return to his normal odd-year form in 1991? Not right away. He lost three of his first four decisions and after righting the ship winning each of his five decisions in May, his rollercoaster ride with the disabled list continued when he was placed on the D. L. in June due to tendonitis in his shoulder. He returned from the D. L. on July 13 and his record stood at 9-6 with a 3.10 ERA after he defeated the Yankees at Kansas City on August 21. He had recorded his first shutout of the season on August 2, defeating Cleveland 4-0.

Six weeks after coming off the DL he pitched the game of his career. On August 26, 1991, he pitched the first no-hitter of his major-league career, defeating the Chicago White Sox, 7-0. He received help from official scorer Del Black. Black had initially rule a line drive by Chicago's Dan Pasqua a double, much to the chagrin of the 25,164 fans in attendance. However, after viewing several replays, he ruled that left fielder Kirk Gibson had misplaced the fifth-inning line drive. When the H changed to E on the scoreboard, the crowd erupted and Saberhagen, who was looking towards home plate at the time, knew that his ho-hitter was still intact. "You can pretty well tell by the crowd's reaction. I heard the crowd and figured what happened." He settled down, got out of the inning and when Frank Thomas grounded to second base with two outs in the ninth inning, Saberhagen had the fourth no-hitter in Royals history. Reflecting on his achievement, he said, "This is terrific, but there will never be anything better than the (1985) World Series."[15]

For the season, his record was 13-8, and his record during eight seasons with the Royals was 110-78. He had been paid $2.95 million in 1991 and would be going into the second year of an expensive longterm contract with a "small-market" team. He was "on the block," and after the 1991 season, he was traded to the Mets along with Keith Miller and Bill Pecota for Kevin McReynolds and Greg Jefferies.

His first two seasons in New York were disappointing. Not only was his record disappointing but there were once again health issues. His first two starts in 1992 were a collective nightmare. In neither game did he make it past the fifth inning, and he allowed seven earned runs in each of those games. He was 0-2 and his ERA was18.00. In his third start, he allowed five runs in the third inning against the Expos and then turned things around. The Mets came from behind and take him off the hook as he pitched three innings of scoreless ball before leaving the game in the for a pinch-hitter in the seventh inning.

He then became the Saberhagen the Mets were expecting. On April 23, he pitched nine shutout innings in a game that the Mets went on to win in the 13th inning, and on April 29 he spun a three-hit shutout as the Mets defeated Houston 1-0. His streak of consecutive scoreless innings ended at 26 in his next start when the Astros tallied a single run in the sixth inning. By then the Mets had a 5-0 lead and they went on to win 5-1, evening Saberhagen's record at 2-2.

However, he would only win one more game in 1992. In his first season with the Mets, he was only 3-5 as tendonitis, this time in his right index finger, resulted in his being on the shelf from May 16 through July 20 and starting only 15 games over the course of the season, the lowest number in his career to date.

In his new baseball home, he found new love after the breakup of his marriage to Janeane. They separated at the end of 1992, and he soon met his second wife, Lynn Critelli, who he married in 1996. They subsequently divorced.

After the 1992 season, he was awarded a three-year contract extension by the Mets, estimated at $15.4 million, but 1993 turned into a year of frustration. The Mets of 1993 were most definitely not the Mets of 1986, and by season's end their record was an unenviable 59-103. Frank Cashen and Davey Johnson were gone and the new regime of General Manager Joe McIlvane and manager Dallas Green were not receptive when it came to Saberhagen's clubhouse pranks. Two pranks during July, 1993, one involving setting off a firecracker near reporters and another, involving spraying bleach, got him in trouble with management and in August

a tirade in the clubhouse made headlines. Eventually he was suspended for the bleach spraying incident, and he missed time at the beginning of the 1994 season. He also was fined $15,384, a day's pay, which was contributed to the Eye Research Foundation of Central New York. For the season, Saberhagen was 7-7 with an ERA of 3.29 in 19 starts.

That season was abbreviated when he underwent surgery on August 3 for a tear in the medial collateral ligament in his right knee. The knee injury was sustained when he inadvertently stepped on a ball when he was jogging in the outfield. In September, he once again had elbow surgery.

In 1994, there were many changes. The National League went from two divisions to three and the Mets found themselves in a restructured Eastern Division with the Phillies, Expos, Braves and Marlins. And the biggest change was Bret Saberhagen who reverted to his former self. He was still the prankster, but his actions showed a newfound maturity. "I've tried to change my habits around the clubhouse, not screw around so much. That's tough for me to do, because I've always been a practical joker. But now before I do something, I think of the ramifications."[16] In the early part of the season, Saberhagen was receiving good run support and through June 25, his record was7-4 with a 3.58 ERA. After that, it was lights out. He won each of his seven decisions and registered a 1.51 ERA in his final nine starts. During this time, he walked only five batters in 71 2/3 innings, and his strikeout to walk ratio was an eye-popping 11.00. For the season, which ended for him and everyone else in August, he was 14-4 with a 2.74 ERA with only 13 walks in 177 1/3 innings. He was third in the Cy Young Award voting and was named to his third All-Star team. This time around, he did not pitch as the game went into extra innings. He and José Rijo were the only pitchers left in the National League bullpen when the NL pushed across a run to win the game in the 10th inning. Oddly enough he was not named to the All-Star team in either of his Cy Young Award seasons.

The 1995 Mets went from bad to worse and by August of that year, Saberhagen was 5-5 on a team that was going nowhere. He and his big money contract were gone from New York on August 1 as he was traded along with Dave Swanson to the Colorado Rockies for Arnie Gooch and Juan Acevedo. With Colorado, he was 2-1 in nine starts and spent two weeks on the shelf from August 27 through September 9.

He missed the entire 1996 season, undergoing surgery on May 28 that involved a titanium anchor being drilled into the bone of his right shoulder to hold together his rotator cuff. He signed a minor-league contract with the Boston Red Sox for the 1997 season. He pitched his way back to the majors and was 0-1 with a 6.58 ERA in 26 innings at the end of the 1997 season. He returned to the Red Sox in 1998.

And return he did. However, the durability wouldn't be there. The man who had hurled 76 complete games in his first 12 major-league seasons would go no further than the seventh inning in any of his 31 starts. He put together a 15-8 record with a 3.96 ERA. The Red Sox finished in second place with a 92-70 record, and advanced to the Division Series against the Cleveland Indians.

Saberhagen pitched the third game of the series and allowed three runs on only four hits in his seven innings of work, walking one and striking out seven. He took a no-hitter into the fifth inning when Jim Thome led off the inning with a homer for Cleveland's first run of the game. It tied the score at 1-1. The next two Cleveland hits were also solo home runs—a sixth-inning blast by Kenny Lofton and a seventh-inning shot by Manny Ramirez. The Red Sox were unable to come from behind, losing 4-3, and Saberhagen was tagged with the loss. It was Saberhagen's last appearance in 1998. Cleveland won the best-of-five series in four games.

His success in 1998 led to his being awarded the Tony Conigliaro Award by the Boston chapter of the Baseball Writers' Association of America for overcoming adversity.

In 1999, Saberhagen was unable to duplicate the success of the prior season, but he wasn't far off, going 10-6 and cutting his ERA to 2.95. He only started 22 games and paid three visits to the disabled list. The Red Sox once again finished second in the AL East

and advanced to postseason play. Saberhagen started the second game of the Division Series against the Indians and had a rare bad day. His undoing came in the third inning and was initiated when Saberhagen's control abandoned him. He walked two batters and, with one out, gave up a triple to Omar Vizquel and a double to Roberto Alomar. Harold Baines, the eighth batter of the inning, came up with two on and two out and his three-run homer knocked Saberhagen out of the game. Cleveland won the game to take a 2-0 lead in the series, but the booming Boston bats won the next two games to force Game Five.

Saberhagen, given a chance to redeem himself, was once again ineffective. Given a two-run lead, he gave up three runs in the first inning and before an out was recorded in the second inning yielded two more. The knockout blow was a home run off the bat of Travis Fryman. But the booming Boston bats, which had generated 32 runs in Games Three and Four, were not about to be silenced. The Sox came back to win Game Five, 12-8, and it was on to the League Championship Series against the Yankees. The Yankees won two of the first three games and in Game Four, Saberhagen took the mound against Andy Pettitte. Saberhagen was effective in his six innings allowing three runs, only one of which (a Darryl Strawberry homer) was earned. However, he left the game on the wrong end of a 3-2 score. The Yankees broke the game open with six ninth-inning runs to take a commanding 3-1 lead in the series. The Red Sox were eliminated in five games.

But by 2000 Saberhagen was 36 years old and the pain had returned to his shoulder, causing him to miss the entire 2000 major-league season. He rehabbed that year, appearing in seven minor-league games, and also rehabbed in five games in 2001, returning to the mound at Fenway on July 27, 2001. He pitched six innings in a 9-5 defeat of the White Sox. It was his last major-league win. He followed up this outing with two losses and was placed on the disabled list one last time. He announced his retirement at the end of the 2001 season.

After baseball, Saberhagen retired to California. He coached son Drew at Calabasas High School.

SOURCES

In addition to the sources listed in the Notes, Baseball-Reference. com and the articles listed below were used by the author.

Antonen, Mel, "Unique Surgery Saves Saberhagen's Shoulder, Career," *USA Today*, April 29, 1998: 1C.

Attner, Paul. "Common Work Habits Mark Return to Royalty: Saberhagen Has His head, Body Back into the Game," *The Sporting News*, May 25, 1987: 4.

Durso, Joseph, "Saberhagen is Near Perfect in Cy Young Voting," *New York Times*, November 16, 1989.

Frey, Jennifer, "Saberhagen Sounds Off at Mets' Management," *New York Times* June 22, 1994.

Frey, Jennifer, "The Joke's Up for Bret Saberhagen," *New York Times* February 27, 1994.

Kravitz, Bob, "Saberhagen Decision Offers No Guarantees," *Rocky Mountain News*, January 18, 1996: 2B.

Martinez, Michael, "Saberhagen Still the Same Old Kid: '85 Success Has Not Led to '86 Excess," *New York Times* News Service, February 23, 1986.

Moran, Malcolm, "On a Rainy Day, Saberhagen Throws a Tantrum," *New York Times*, August 7, 1993: 31.

Nightengale, Bob, "Saberhagen Signs for 3 Years, Riches," *The Sporting News*, February 22, 1988.

Nightingale, Dave, "Even in Odd Year, Saberhagen's No. 1," *The Sporting News*, July 9, 1990: 8.

Ocker, Sheldon, "Royals Get Breaks to Slip by Indians and Post 5-4 Win," *Akron Beacon-Journal*, May 4, 1987: D4.

NOTES

1   Gordon Edes, "Towel May End Up as His Next Throw," *Boston Globe*, August 9, 2001

2   Thomas Boswell,= *The Heart of the Order* (New York, Doubleday, 1989), 278.

3   Lorenzo Benet. "Bret's Team — From the time he was 7, Baseball was Bret Saberhagen's Dream — His Parents helped make it Come True," *Daily News* (Los Angeles, California), November 6, 1985.

4   Vincent Bonsignore, *Daily News* (Los Angeles, California), May 7, 2002.

5   Joe Koenig, "Palisades Reaches the City Final Against Cleveland," *Los Angeles Times*, June 11, 1982: E15.

6   Randy Sparage, "Saberhagen's No Hitter Decides It," *Los Angeles Times*, June 15, 1982: D4.

7   Paul Vercammen, "Cavaliers Cradle City Baseball Crown After Hoping for a Lot Less," *Los Angeles Times*, June 17, 1982: V4

8   Bruce Nash and Allan Zullo, *The Baseball Hall of Shame 4* (New York, Simon and Schuster, 1990), 76-77.

9   "K. C. Rookie 1st to Tame Tigers," *Chicago Tribune*, April 20, 1984: C5

10 Peter Gammons, "Return of the Royal Nonesuch," *Sports Illustrated*, June 8, 1987.

11 Bob Nightengale, "Homework by Saberhagen gives him new Hope for 1987," *Kansas City Times*, January 14, 1987: 1-B.

12 Bob Nightengale, "Saberhagen Blots Out Past, Follows Plan in Spring Debut," *Kansas City Times*, March 11, 1987: E-1.

13 Bob Nightengale. *The Sporting News*, February 22, 1988.

14 *The Sporting News*, May 9, 1988: 17.

15 *The Pentagraph* (Bloomington, Illinois), August 27, 1991: B1.

16 *New York Post*, May 13, 1994.

MIKE LOWELL

BY BILL NOWLIN

MIKE LOWELL WAS A NEW York Yankees prospect who won a world championship with the 2003 Florida Marlins (beating the Yankees). He then became part of a salary dump that saw him sent to the Boston Red Sox, where he picked up a second world champion ring and was accorded the honor of being named Most Valuable Player in the 2007 World Series.

He drove in 100 or more runs in three seasons, twice for the Marlins and once for the Red Sox.

The third baseman set and still holds both the best single-season fielding percentage record and the best career fielding record in Red Sox franchise history.

He's a four-time All-Star and won a Silver Slugger and a Gold Glove.

Mike's father, Carl Lowell, was a ballplayer, too, "a right-handed pitcher who played on the Puerto Rican National Team in 1971. Though born in San Francisco, Carl Lowell was Cuban and remains the only Cuban pitcher to have beaten the Cuban national team. When he had the opportunity to meet the Cuban president, Carl Lowell chose to remain on the bus while the other Puerto Rican players had photographs taken with the Cuban leader. Mike's father-in-law, José Lopez, reportedly spent some 15 years as a political prisoner under Fidel Castro.[1]

They weren't the first in the family to experience political persecution. Carl Lowell's grandfather and great-grandfather had both been placed in anti-German internment camps on the Isle of Pines for more than two years.[2] In fact, grandfather Carl Vogt-Lowell was an American citizen, born in Chicago, apparently imprisoned because of his Germanic surname. After being released from the prison camp, he returned to the United States and became a paratrooper near the end of World War II.[3]

His son was born Carl Lowell, in California, but returned to the island with his father and was raised as a Cuban. He played baseball there, but his family elected to move to Puerto Rico when Carl was 11. There Carl (or Carlos, as he was called) attended San Ignacio High School and won an academic scholarship to St. Joseph's University in Philadelphia. He played baseball at St. Joe's, too, a pitcher who threw a no-hitter, and became MVP of the team, and—after returning to Puerto Rico for dental school—he was named to the Puerto Rican National Team. He was later inducted into the Puerto Rico Athletic Hall of Fame.[4] It was when the Puerto Rican team played in the 1970 World Series of Baseball that he declined to be presented to Fidel Castro. And then in 1972, the team traveled to Cuba for a Friendly Series and played and beat the Cuban National Team, 5-4. Carl had pitched, and left with a 5-1 lead, scoring that fifth (and ultimately deciding) run himself.

Mike was born in San Juan, Puerto Rico, on February 24, 1974. His mother, Beatriz, was Cubana. When Mike was 4, the family moved to the Miami area, where his father ultimately established a dental practice in Coral Gables. "My upbringing, my culture, my customs are all Latino," Mike said in a September 2006 interview.[5] English became the dominant language in the Lowell home, though for family gatherings at holiday time, Spanish was more commonly spoken. Mike felt his English was a little better than his Spanish, grammatically, but he clearly fit in well with the Spanish speakers in the three big-league clubhouses where he plied his trade.

Carl Lowell took a half-day off from work on Wednesdays each week to take Mike and his brother to batting practice, and he coached Little League as well. And yet, Mike said in 2007, "What I appreciated most about my dad was he didn't push baseball on me." That said, when Mike showed an interest, "He was big on the mental side of the game. I remember him telling me, 'If you want to drive in the run, you've got to be the guy who wants it.'"[6] When 8-year-old

Mike hit a game-winning homer one day in Little League, his father talked to him afterward, "Doesn't it feel great to get that hit? If you want to do that more often, you have to *want* to be the guy that's in that situation — because a lot of people say they want to be in that situation, but they don't want to be. … What's the worst that could happen? You make an out? Big deal. But if you *want* to be in that situation and you try your best, good things are going to happen."[7]

Mike graduated from Coral Gables High School, though he'd started high school at Christopher Columbus. He made the junior-varsity team there as a second baseman; one of his teammates was shortstop Alex Rodriguez. He began to sense he wasn't going to make the varsity, though, and so transferred to Coral Gables High.[8]

Mike had been drafted by the Chicago White Sox in the 48th round after high school, but elected not to sign. He became a freshman All-American at Florida International University, then played (and struggled) in a summer baseball league in Waynesboro, Virginia. The next summer he played for Chatham in the esteemed Cape Cod League. The FIU team, he said, was nationally ranked, at one point as high as eighth in the country. After he finished his junior year, he was drafted by the New York Yankees as their 20th-round pick in the June 1995 amateur draft. They settled on $20,000 plus the cost of tuition for his final two semesters of college. But they drafted him a catcher. He later said, "I had barely ever caught, and really had no desire to catch."[9] It is worthy of note that Lowell graduated summa cum laude from FIU.[10] His degree was in finance.

His first assignment was in Oneonta, New York, for the New York-Penn League Oneonta Yankees. He soon found himself playing third base, batting .260 in 72 games, with just one homer but with 18 doubles. He played in the instructional league, and then in 1996 played both for Greensboro and Tampa, batting .282 in both locations. Fielding was not always his forte; he committed 24 errors for Oneonta in 1995 and 34 for Greensboro and Tampa in 1996.

In 1997 Lowell broke out, batting .344 in 78 games for Double-A Norwich (Eastern League). Advanced to the Triple-A Columbus Clippers during the season, he didn't hit for as high an average (.276) but he hit 30 home runs for the season, 15 with Norwich and 15 with Columbus. He played in 126 games for Columbus in 1998, hitting 26 homers (and .304), earning himself a September call-up to the big leagues.

Lowell was right-handed, stood 6-feet-4, and weighed 195 pounds. The 1998 Yankees were on their way to a world championship, ultimately sweeping the San Diego Padres in four games in the World Series. It was a team that won 114 games. In September Lowell played in eight games. On September 13, his first at-bat produced a pop-fly single to center field at Yankee Stadium. A week later, he got into his second game and went 3-for-5, all singles. Those were his only four hits for the Yankees. He finished the tail end of the season 4-for-15 (.267) without a run batted in and with just one run scored. And he never played for the Yankees again. They had World Series MVP Scott Brosius and re-signed him for three more years.

On February 1, 1999, Lowell was traded to the Florida Marlins for three pitching prospects, Mark Johnson, Ed Yarnall, and minor-leaguer Todd Noel.

It was fortuitous. Lowell was pretty unlikely to break into the starting lineup for the Yankees at any time in the foreseeable future, whereas with Miami he was returning home and was positioned to earn a slot as a regular. Marlins GM Dave Dombrowski said, "He has a chance to be a premium third baseman for years to come."[11] And he had gotten married in the offseason, to Bertica Lopez.

Eighteen days after the trade, during a routine physical for spring training, Lowell was taken aside, given some more tests, and diagnosed with testicular cancer. Two days later, on February 21, he had surgery which removed one of his testicles. Fortunately the cancer had not spread, and he was made aware that both Mike Gallego and John Kruk had beaten testicular cancer and gone on to big-league careers.[12]

Mike and Bertica had met at Coral Gables High School. Oddly enough, after they had become engaged, she herself had an ovary removed due to a cyst which proved to be benign. They were able to joke that with

her having one ovary and Mike having one testicle, they were a "perfect fit."[13]

Mike's new father-in-law, José Lopez, had been a political prisoner in Cuba for 15 years. There were some allowances for family, however, and during one visit to his family, he met a remarkable woman who married him while he was in prison. Bertica was conceived during a conjugal visit, her father spending the first three years of her life behind bars before he was released to Venezuela. The Lopez family moved to Miami three years after that.[14]

The surgery was successful. Lowell underwent several radiation treatments as well; he lost 10 pounds in the first few weeks of treatment due to the associated vomiting. In just over five weeks, though, he was able to play in an exhibition game in Calgary, and hit two doubles and a home run.[15]

Lowell joined the Marlins, appearing in his first game on May 29. He was 0-for-4, but on May 30 was 2-for-3 with a single and a double and the first RBI of his career. That first base hit—the double to left-center off Cincinnati's Steve Parris and over the

center fielder's head—broke the ice: "Okay, it was just a simple double, but, believe me, few hits in my career have offered such a sense of relief. I was back in it. All that cancer, radiation weakness was behind me now."[16] He drove in one or more runs in each of the four games after that as well. Lowell was perhaps not at full strength but played in almost every game for the rest of the season—97 in all—batting .253 with 12 home runs and 47 runs batted in.

That winter, Lowell was presented the 1999 Tony Conigliaro Award "given annually to the major leaguer who overcomes adversity through spirit, determination and courage."[17]

Mike and Bertica had two children, Alexis and Anthony.

Lowell got off to a very strong start in the 2000 season and after the team's first 21 games was batting an even .300 with 19 RBIs. Then he declined to play the April 25 game, as part of a work stoppage to protest the handling of the Elián González case, that of a 6-year-old Cuban refugee who was taken from his great-uncle's home in America to be returned to Cuba. His absence was approved by the ballclub; it was announced that "the Marlins organization gave its OK for front-office workers, players and coaches to be absent without pay. The team will close its downtown merchandise store for the day."[18] Lowell quoted as saying, "I've got problems with them (the US government) saying they're concerned with the kid's welfare, and they go in there like it's World War III."[19] Field manager John Boles, GM Dave Dombrowski, and team owner John W. Henry all approved of the form of protest.

Over the long course of the 2000 season, Lowell saw his average dip to .249 in late June and was still just at .250 in mid-July, but he built it back up to .270 by season's end, with 22 homers and 91 RBIs.

He drove in an even 100 runs in 2001 (with 18 homers and a .283 average), and then 92 more in 2002, the year he was first accorded All-Star status. One highlight of 2002 was participating in the first triple play in team history. It came in the third inning of a 1-1 game against the Montreal Expos on July 28. There were runners on first and second and Vladimir

Guerrero at the plate. On a 3-and-2 pitch, Guerrero slashed one to third base. Lowell saw baserunner Brad Wilkerson break from second toward third, which prompted him to get closer to the bag at third. He snagged it at ankle height and then stepped on the bag. "It was part good reaction, part self-defense," Lowell said. "It was cool."[20] Wilkerson pulled up helplessly and Lowell tagged him, and then took his time throwing to first since the other runner, José Vidro, had been off with contact, too, and was simply standing on second base.

In 2003 Lowell enjoyed both strong individual stats (a career-high 32 homers, helping produce 105 RBIs, and a second All-Star nod), but also the ultimate in team success: the Florida Marlins won the World Series. He was hit in the hand by a Hector Almonte fastball on August 30, and the resulting fracture almost caused him to miss the opportunity to play in the postseason, but he was able to come back just in time to get into one more game, on September 28 (1-for-4, with a double), and continue from there.

Lowell only had three plate appearances in the Division Series, without reaching base.

In Game One of the NLCS, against the Cubs at Wrigley Field, after Sammy Sosa's two-run homer in the bottom of the ninth had tied it up, the score stood 8-8 after 10 innings. Marlins manager Jack McKeon had already used the team's primary pinch-hitter, Todd Hollandsworth. Reliever Ugueth Urbina was due to lead off for the Marlins in the top of the 11th. McKeon asked Lowell to pinch-hit. On the sixth pitch of the at-bat, Lowell homered to center field off Mark Guthrie, the game-winning hit. Father Carl Lowell said he had "cried like a baby, because I had seen him go through the personal suffering" of missing almost the entire final month of the season, which could have cost the team a shot at the playoffs and probably did prevent Mike from finishing higher than 11th in the MVP balloting.[21]

The Cubs won the next three games, but come Game Five, now an elimination game, Florida's Josh Beckett shut out the Cubs on just two hits. Lowell won the game with another home run, a two-run shot off Carlos Zambrano in the bottom of the fifth.

It looked as though the Cubs were wrapping it up in Game Six, with a 3-0 lead at home through seven innings. The Marlins had only three hits to that point, but then exploded with an eight-run eighth that pushed the Series to a seventh game. In that eighth inning—it embraced the notorious Steve Bartman incident which robbed the Cubs of an out on a foul ball—Lowell came up with the score tied, 3-3, and runners on second and third with one out. He was walked intentionally, scoring three batters later on Mike Mordecai's three-run double.

Lowell had hit only .200 in the NLCS (4-for-20), but two of the hits were game-winning homers, and he had scored five times.

In the 2003 World Series against the New York Yankees, he was 5-for-23 at the plate, with two RBIs (both in Game Five), thanks to a single to center in the bottom of the fifth that boosted a 4-1 lead to 6-1. The final score was 6-4, with Lowell's two runs driven in being the difference in the game. More than 55,000 fans saw the Marlins' Josh Beckett shut out the Yankees at Yankee Stadium in Game Seven, limiting them to five hits in a tight 2-0 win. Beckett was named Series MVP. Mike Lowell earned a world championship ring.

There had been a medical scare during the '03 season. Lowell had hit 28 of his homers by the Marlins' 95th game, but a hip tweak and playing for more than three weeks with a strained groin prompted him to get an MRI. The doctors found what they feared was a recurrence of cancer; fortunately it turned out to be fibrous dysplasia, and a huge relief to the Lowell family.[22]

With a certain irony, the home runs coming so often—but then dropping off in the second half of the 2003 season—prompted whispering that perhaps Lowell had been taking steroids. He himself had wondered back in 1999 if he would need to, after the removal of a testicle, but doctors had advised him "my body would adjust—and if I did take testosterone or anything related to steroids, it would raise my testosterone levels to a point where my healthy testicle was going to be fooled into shutting down. That's where any talk of supplements ceased for me."[23]

At the end of the 2003 season, owner Jeffrey Loria signed Lowell to a four-year deal for $32 million. "I'm embarrassed to answer when people who don't know baseball ask me how much I make. I can't justify the money they pay me. Every time I look at one of my checks, I can't believe it," he told Jeff Miller of the *Miami Herald*. He never flaunted his wealth, though, and the family stuck to its values; when Mike offered to pay for his younger brother's and sister's school, his father said thanks but no thanks.[24]

In 2004 the Marlins finished third, just four games over .500 (83-79). Lowell had another very good year, another All-Star year (.293, 27 HR, 85 RBIs). His biggest day was April 21, with a three-homer game with four RBIs in an 8-7 12-inning win in Philadelphia. Lowell was popular with other players, too. Before the 2004 All-Star Game, third baseman Scott Rolen of the Cardinals talked about Lowell's world championship ring, but said, "He plays the game right. He has a great knowledge of the game. He goes out and competes every day. He understands the importance of running out there and being accountable and being on the field. He's a fun guy to watch." Then, to keep from getting too carried away with compliments, he added a further assessment: "He's a [jerk]. I think his head is kind of disproportional to the rest of his body."[25]

Lowell had a discouraging year in 2005. The positive was his defense. In 150 games, he committed only six errors, a .983 fielding percentage, and he won a Gold Glove.[26] On offense, however, he put up what he himself called "grim numbers": a .236 batting average, with just eight home runs. He drove in only 58 runs. "That was the reality of my '05 season," he wrote. "And these grim numbers were all the more inexplicable given that I was coming off perhaps the best year of my career in '04."[27] He'd maybe tinkered too much with his swing. It was reported that in August a contact lens he wore on his lead eye broke and he never found a suitable replacement, but Lowell himself says he had no problems with contacts that year.[28]

Inexplicable was a good word. After the season, he turned for advice to Gary Denbo, who had been one of his minor-league hitting coaches in his early days with the Yankees. Denbo was coaching in Japan at the time, but he talked with Lowell and urged him to get back to fundamentals, even to start using a batting tee again. Denbo then looked at some video Mike sent him, and when Denbo returned to Tampa, they worked together simply focusing on hitting balls up the middle.

In the meantime, on November 24, Lowell changed organizations. As he put it, the Boston Red Sox were "forced to take me in a trade with the Florida Marlins if they were going to get the blessed arm of Josh Beckett."[29] The Red Sox wanted Beckett badly. He was 25 years old, coming off a 15-8 season with the Marlins, and had been the World Series MVP for them in 2003. The Marlins told the Red Sox that if they wanted Beckett, they had to take Lowell, too, saving them $18 million for the final two years of his four-year contract. The two were traded, with Guillermo Mota, in exchange for four young players with potential: Jesus Delgado, Harvey Garcia, Hanley Ramirez, and Anibal Sanchez. It was a trade that worked well for both parties—Beckett excelled for the Red Sox, a 20-game winner in 2007; Hanley Ramirez was Rookie of the Year in 2006, hit .300 in seven seasons in Miami, and won the NL batting crown in 2009. Though the Red Sox didn't know it at the time, they were not only acquiring the 2003 World Series MVP, but also—in Mike Lowell—the 2007 World Series MVP as well.

Lowell, of course, wanted to prove himself in 2006, and succeeded, starting with a home run on Opening Day in Texas. He put together a solid season, both on offense and defense, batting .284, hitting 20 home runs, and driving in 80 runs. His .987 fielding percentage in 2006 was (and remains) the best in Red Sox franchise history.

The short-season A ball minor-league affiliate Lowell Spinners scheduled a little fun during the year, changing their name for one night (July 28) to the Mike Lowell Spinners. They even tailored their jerseys for the game to read "Mike Lowell" on the front.[30]

The year 2007 was a magical year, though Lowell started shakily in the field with three errors in the second game of the season, and by the end of April he already had eight errors, two more than in the entire

2006 season. He committed 15 errors in all in 2007. By the end of April, though, he already had 20 RBIs.

There was no late-season injury this time to threaten his availability in the postseason. Lowell drove in 26 months in the month of September alone, helping the Sox seal the deal and clinch a playoff berth. He finished the season with 120 RBIs (a team record for a third baseman) and a .324 average.

The Red Sox swept the Division Series over the Angels, scoring 19 runs to their four. Lowell drove in one run in each of the three games. In the ALCS against the Cleveland Indians, it took seven games to win. Lowell drove in three runs in Game One (including the winning run) and three more in Game Two, a game lost when the Indians scored seven runs in the top of the 11th. Cleveland won three of the first four games, but then the Red Sox bounced back with three of wins of their own, lopsided ones at that. Lowell drove in one run in Game Six and one more in Game Seven, with a sacrifice fly that drove in the third run in an 11-2 win.

Then came the World Series against the Colorado Rockies. Josh Beckett won Game One with ease, 13-1, becoming 4-0 in the postseason. Curt Schilling won a 2-1 squeaker in Game Two, with Lowell's double in the bottom of the fifth breaking a 1-1 tie. In Game Three, in Denver, he drove in a pair in the top of the third. And in the final Game Four of the sweep, Lowell homered to lead off the top of the seventh, giving Boston a 3-0 lead at the time (the Red Sox won, 4-3.) "It was my third at-bat. ... I looked for a sinker in and there it was. ... I knew I hit it really well, with nice trajectory, but at that point I didn't take anything for granted because it was the World Series. I was looking at the left fielder and saw him running and subsequently slow down. That is a great feeling. But what I really, really enjoyed was that home-run trot." Harking back to the advice his father gave him when he was 8, he said, "This was the moment I had yearned for ever since that car ride with Dad. To be on the big stage at the big moment. It was also the culmination of years of what I call my visualizations."[31]

A number of players could have been awarded the MVP trophy, but it was presented to Mike Lowell.

The *Boston Globe's* Bob Ryan said he felt that Lowell merited it even before Game Four, then he scored the second run and then homered for the third run.[32] He'd hit .333 in the ALDS, .333 in the ALCS, and .400 in the World Series, with 15 postseason RBIs.

Lowell's contributions in the regular season earned him fifth in league MVP voting.

Three of the 2007 Red Sox won World Series MVPs — Beckett (with the Marlins) in 2003, Lowell in 2007, and David Ortiz in 2013.

Lowell's contract was up at the end of the year. Fan sentiment was vocal at postseason events. "Bring back Lowell!" was the cry. In the celebratory parade, someone handed Jason Varitek a sign reading "Re-sign Lowell" and he held it throughout. Manny Ramirez yelled it repeatedly to fans along the route. The sentiment was so strong that the team almost had no choice. The Red Sox didn't waste time, and in mid-November signed him to a three-year, $37.5 million deal. He probably could have gotten a fourth year elsewhere; Peter Gammons reported both the Phillies and Dodgers had offered it. "How cool is that?" asked Curt Schilling. "Leaving years and dollars on the table to come back here for three more years, good stuff."[33]

The 2008 season was a struggle. Lowell lost a few weeks in August and early September, and in October had to undergo surgery to repair a torn labrum in his right hip. He hit .274 with 73 RBIs, and put up very similar figures in 2009: .290, with 75 RBIs. He homered 17 times in each year.

Just before spring training began in 2010, the Red Sox tried to trade him to Texas, agreeing to pay 75 percent of his salary because a damaged ligament in his right thumb had caused him to fail a physical. In 2010, with Adrian Beltre at third base and Kevin Youkilis at first, Lowell had what became his final year, appearing in only 73 games, batting for a .239 average with 5 homers and 26 runs batted in. In early September he announced his retirement. "It's been 12 outstanding years and I don't regret anything in my career," he said. "I'm super happy to spend time with my family, but I'm super happy to say I played baseball as my job. I wanted to do it since I was 6 years old. To have that chance has really been unbelievable."[34]

On October 2, the Red Sox held a "Thanks, Mike Night" at Fenway Park.

In 2011 he began as a studio analyst on the MLB Network, and as of the close of 2016 continues to work for the network.

Having retired from the daily grind of baseball provides opportunities to make up for some of the inevitably "lost time" with family. In mid-November 2016, Lowell says, "I am enjoying plenty of family time. Specifically, coaching my son's 12u baseball team. I am also enjoying watching my daughter as she entered high school and played volleyball there as a ninth grader."[35]

SOURCES

In addition to the sources noted in this biography, the author also accessed Lowell's player file from the National Baseball Hall of Fame, the *Encyclopedia of Minor League Baseball*, Retrosheet.org, Baseball-Reference.com, and the SABR Minor Leagues Database, accessed online at Baseball-Reference.com. Most of the story regarding the political problems the family faced—and most of the information regarding Mike's upbringing in Cuba, Puerto Rico, and Florida come from his 2008 autobiography, *Deep Drive*.

NOTES

1   Bill Nowlin, "Hot Season at the Hot Corner," *Diehard*, October 2006.

2   Mike Lowell with Rob Bradford, *Deep Drive* (New York: Celebra, 2008), 39.

3   *Deep Drive*, 40.

4   *Deep Drive*, 81. Also see caption on photograph in the photo insert opposite page 146.

5   Author interview with Mike Lowell, September 2006.

6   Nick Cafardo, "A Firm Grasp at Third," *Boston Globe*, March 18, 2007.

7   *Deep Drive*, 5, 6.

8   *Deep Drive*, 98-103. Alex Rodriguez transferred, too, to Westminster Christian High School.

9   *Deep Drive*, 112, 113.

10   Clark Spencer, "Home Schooled," *Miami Herald*, February 29, 2004.

11   Rod Beaton, "Yankees Get Pitching, Marlins Finally Get Lowell," *USA Today*, February 3, 1999.

12   Joel Sherman, "Lowell Undergoes Testicular Surgery," *New York Post*, February 23, 1999.

13   *Deep Drive*, 139.

14   *Deep Drive*, 41-43.

15   Fred Tasker, "Mike Lowell Remembers Vividly the Day the Fort Lauderdale Oncologist Told Him He Had Testicular Cancer," *Miami Herald*, June 13, 2002.

16   *Deep Drive*, 145.

17   Bloomberg News, "Lowell Is Honored," *New York Times*, December 14, 1999.

18   Associated Press, "Marlins Join Cuban-American Protest," AOL News, April 25, 2000.

19   Ibid. The Marlins lost the game to the Giants, 6-4, in 11 innings.

20   Ted Hutton, "For Lowell, Triple Play 'Was Cool,'" *South Florida Sun Sentinel*, July 29, 2002: 3C.

21   "Home Schooled."

22   Any family that has experienced good news of a medical nature can relate to Lowell's talking about the family dancing around his brother Victor's apartment, joyfully chanting "fibrous dysplasia" over and over, when three doctors concurred in that diagnosis. See *Deep Drive*, 13, 14.

23   *Deep Drive*, 154.

24   Jeff Miller, "A Bargain, Even at $32 Million," *Miami Herald*, December 4, 2003.

25   Mike Berardino, "1st Class at 3rd; Lowell, Rolen," *Sun-Sentinel*, July 13, 2004.

26   Lowell did pull off the first two hidden ball tricks of the 21st century—on September 15, 2004, getting Montreal's Brian Schneider, and on August 10, 2005, tagging out Luis Terrero of the Diamondbacks.

27   *Deep Drive*, 21.

28   Chris Snow, "Lowell Offers His Spin," *Boston Globe*, November 26, 2005. Mike Lowell e-mail to author, November 14, 2016.

29   *Deep Drive*, 7.

30   "Name Game," *USA Today*, July 18, 2006.

31   *Deep Drive*, 205-207.

32   Bob Ryan, "Exclamation Point Added," *Boston Globe*, October 29, 2007: E4.

33   "Red Sox Keep World Series MVP Lowell with Three-Year Deal," ESPN.com, November 19, 2007.

34   John Tomase, "As End Nears, Mike Lowell Looks Back at Career," *Boston Herald*, September 13, 2010.

35   Mike Lowell e-mail to author, November 14, 2016.

KENT MERCKER

BY CLAYTON TRUTOR

A JOURNEYMAN IN THE BEST sense of the word, Kent Mercker made his name over the course of an 18-season career as a young, hard-throwing left-hander in the Atlanta Braves' bullpen before moving to the back end of the Braves' dream rotation in the mid-1990s that featured future Hall of Famers Greg Maddux, Tom Glavine, and John Smoltz as well as Steve Avery. Mercker's tenure with the Braves was highlighted by both team and individual accomplishments. He was a member of the Braves' 1991 and 1992 pennant-winning teams as well as the 1995 world championship team.

On September 11, 1991, Mercker pitched six hitless innings and got the win in a combined 1-0 no-hitter against the San Diego Padres with Mark Wohlers and Alejandro Pena. On April 8, 1994, Mercker pitched a no-hitter against the Los Angeles Dodgers.[1] His career was in turmoil through the late 1990s, as he bounced from club to club, unable to sustain the promise of his early career. Around the turn of the century, Mercker transitioned back to the bullpen, reinventing himself into a crafty set-up man who relied on his control, changeups, and breaking pitches to get hitters out instead of his heat. A steady presence in unsteady "steroid-era" bullpens, Mercker enjoyed some of his greatest success when he was well into his 30s.[2]

In the midst of his transition to the bullpen, Mercker suffered a life-threatening cerebral hemorrhage while on the mound for the Angels. On May 11, 2000, he was pitching at home against the Texas Rangers in a rare appearance as a starter. In the second inning Mercker began to feel dizzy on the mound before dropping to one knee. Angels medical staffers took him to the University of California-Irvine Hospital, where tests revealed that he had suffered a cerebral hemorrhage. Mercker spent days in the intensive-care unit. Hospital staff members prevented the bleeding on his brain from developing into an aneurysm, which likely would have

killed him. Mercker spent three months back home in Athens, Ohio, recovering before returning to the Angels bullpen in mid-August.[3]

For his courage and determination in a life-threatening situation, the Boston Chapter of the Baseball Writers Association of America named Mercker a co-recipient of the 2000 Tony Conigliaro Award, along with Tampa Bay's Tony Saunders, who recovered from a career-threatening broken arm the same season. Mercker and Saunders shared the award, which is given annually to the player who "best overcomes an obstacle and adversity through the attributes of spirit, determination, and courage that were the trademarks of Conigliaro."[4]

Kent Franklin Mercker was born on February 1, 1968, in Dublin, Ohio, a suburb of Columbus. The son of Franklin and Norma Mercker, he moved with his family several times during his childhood due to his father's job as a salesman. The family settled back in Dublin in 1980. Mercker was one of Ohio's finest high-school baseball players of the 1980s. Over four seasons he posted a 32-3 record pitching for the Dublin-Coffman High School Shamrocks. As a senior, the left-handed Mercker was clocked pitching as fast as 93 miles per hour. In 1983 he led the nearby Worthington American Legion baseball team to a third-place finish in the American Legion World Series.[5]

The Atlanta Braves selected the 6-foot-1, 175-pound pitcher Mercker in the first round of the June 1986 amateur draft. He proceeded quickly through the Braves organization, reaching Triple-A Richmond soon after his 21st birthday. The youngest player on the Richmond roster, Mercker went 9-12 for the 1989 International League champions, posting a 3.20 ERA in 27 starts. He received a September call-up with the sad-sack, 63-win 1989 Atlanta Braves. Mercker pitched in two games for the Braves that September. He was shelled in both outings, one of them a start, surrendering six earned runs and eight hits in 4⅓ innings.

Mercker began the 1990 season in Richmond and in late June was promoted to Atlanta. Aside from rehab assignments, he never again pitched in the minor leagues. He became a fixture in the Braves bullpen in the second half of the 1990 season, picking up seven saves in 36 appearances for yet another cellar-dwelling Braves team.

Mercker went 5-3 with a 2.58 ERA in the Braves' 1991 dream season, working primarily as a middle reliever and occasionally as a closer (six saves). He made four starts, including one on September 11 when he pitched the first six innings of a combined no-hitter against San Diego. Mercker made three appearances for the Braves in the postseason. He took the loss at home in Game Four of the NLCS, which tied the series with Pittsburgh at two games apiece. Mercker surrendered a 10th-inning walk to the Pirates' Andy Van Slyke, who wound up scoring the winning run when Mike Lavalliere singled him home off Mercker's replacement, Mark Wohlers. He made two brief appearances in the seven-game 1991 World Series, holding the Minnesota Twins scoreless both times.

Mercker remained a steady presence in his 53 appearances out of the Braves bullpen in 1992. He pitched well in the NLCS, a rematch between the Braves and Pirates. Mercker held the Pirates scoreless in three innings over two outings, one of which was a blowout victory for Pittsburgh (Game Five) and the other a decisive victory for Atlanta (Game Six). He suffered a rib injury during the Braves' victory celebration after Game Seven, and was not on the World Series roster.[6]

Mercker returned to top form in 1993, posting a 3-1 record and 2.86 ERA in 43 appearances. He started six games from late July through September, pitching effectively but never lasting more than six innings. Mercker made a career-high five postseason appearances in 1993, all in the Braves' defeat by the Philadelphia Phillies in six-games in the NLCS. In five innings of work, Mercker gave up just one run. He did not figure in any decisions.

In 1994 Braves manager Bobby Cox decided to make Mercker his fifth starter. The decision paid immediate dividends, as the 26-year-old lefty pitched a no-hitter and struck out 10 Los Angeles Dodgers on April 8, his first start of the season. In his first season as a regular starter, Mercker won nine of his 13 decisions and posted a 3.45 ERA during the strike-shortened season.[7] His record was second best among Braves starters, next to Greg Maddux, who posted a 16-6 record with a 1.56 ERA for the second-place Braves.

After the promise of 1994, Mercker's 1995 season proved disappointing. Though his performance was competitive with that of most fifth starters, Mercker did not develop into an ace. He went 7-8 with a 4.15 ERA. Mercker made two postseason appearances during the Braves' run to the 1995 World Series. In Game Three of the NLDS, he got Colorado Rockies catcher Joe Girardi to fly out to end the 10th inning in a 7-5 defeat. In Game Three of the World Series, he surrendered an earned run in two innings of relief work against the Cleveland Indians in a 7-6 defeat at Jacobs Field that narrowed the Braves' Series lead to two games to one.

In December 1995 the Braves traded Mercker to the Baltimore Orioles for right-handed reliever Joe Borowski and minor-league pitcher Chaad Stewart. Mercker struggled in Baltimore to a 3-6 record with a 7.76 ERA in 14 appearances, 12 of which were starts. In late July the Orioles sent Mercker to Cleveland for 39-year-old future Hall of Fame first baseman and designated hitter Eddie Murray. Mercker returned to a familiar role in Cleveland, posting a 3.09 ERA in 10 relief appearances, but the Indians left him off their playoff roster. (The Indians ended up losing the ALDS in four games to the wild-card Orioles. Eddie Murray, the man for whom Mercker was traded, batted .400 in the series and reached based in 9 of 18 plate appearances.)

On December 10, 1996, Mercker signed a one-year free-agent contract with the Cincinnati Reds. He was a hard-luck 8-11 as a starter for the 1997 Reds. His 3.92 ERA was well under the league-wide ERA of 4.24. His performance in Cincinnati impressed the St. Louis Cardinals enough for them to sign him to a two-year deal that ended up being worth $3.8 million. Mercker worked a career-high 161⅔ innings and won a career-high 11 games against 11 losses in 1998. His ERA ballooned to 5.07, but that mirrored a league-wide uptick in ERA to 4.31. Mercker's teammate Mark McGwire contributed significantly to the National League's skyrocketing ERAs with his record-breaking 70 home runs. Mercker posted a 6-5 record for the Cardinals in 1999, but his ERA remained over 5.00.

On August 24, 1999, the Cardinals dealt Mercker to the Red Sox for left-handed pitcher Mike Matthews and minor-league catcher Dave Benham. Mercker returned to form during his brief stint in Boston, going 2-0 in five starts with a 3.51 ERA for the wild-card-bound Red Sox. He made three postseason appearances for the Red Sox, who defeated the Indians in five games in the Division Series before losing to the Yankees in five games in the ALCS. Mercker started Game Four of the ALDS, lasting 1⅔ innings and surrendering two earned runs before being replaced by Rich Garces. Garces ended up with the win in Boston's wild 23-7 victory. Mercker started Game One of the ALCS and received a no-decision in a 4-3 loss at Yankee Stadium. He lasted four innings and gave up two earned runs. Mercker took the loss in Game Five of the ALCS, the victory that clinched the pennant for the Yankees. He surrendered two runs in 3⅔ innings in the 6-1 defeat.

In January 2000 the free-agent Mercker signed a one-year, $850,000 deal with Anaheim. In a season shortened by his life-threatening cerebral hemorrhage, he made 21 appearances, 14 as a reliever and 7 as a starter. The Angels declined to offer him a new contract after the season. His 6.52 ERA and 1-3 record in 2000, as well as his medical problems, tightened the market for his services. Mercker signed a free-agent deal with the Red Sox in January 2001, but Boston released him near the end of spring training.

Mercker signed a one-year, $500,000 deal with the Colorado Rockies on February 7, 2002. Playing his first full season since 1999, he went 3-1 with a 6.14 ERA for the Rockies in 58 appearances. Mercker signed with the Reds in January 2003 and turned his career around, becoming the set-up man he had been evolving

into over the previous few seasons. In 49 appearances, Mercker posted a 2.35 ERA. The Braves re-acquired Mercker down the stretch of their 2003 playoff run, and Mercker shined, surrendering just two earned runs in 17 innings of work for a 1.06 ERA. Mercker made one playoff appearance for the 2003 Braves, who lost in the Division Series to the Chicago Cubs. He pitched a scoreless eighth inning in the Braves' 4-2 home loss in Game One.

Mercker joined the Cubs in the offseason. At age 36, he made 71 relief appearances in 2004. After the season he signed a two-year, $2.75 million deal with the Reds. The seemingly ageless Mercker made a career-high 78 appearances for the 2005 Reds. Before season-ending elbow surgery in mid-August, he pitched in 37 games in 2006 and was released after the season. Mercker sat out the 2007 season to allow his elbow to heal. In 2008 Mercker, now 40, signed a one-year free-agent contract with the Reds. Forty-year-old Kent Mercker went 1-0 in 15 appearances, missing significant action with back trouble. He pitched his last game of the season on May 31, and he got a walk-off victory over his original team, the Braves. After the season, the Reds released him and he retired.

Mercker retired with a 74-67 career mark and a 4.16 ERA, strong considering that he spent much of his 18-year career pitching in one of the most explosive offensive eras in major-league history. The left-handed hitting Mercker had a career .113 batting average with 18 RBIs. Four of them came on Mercker's only home run, a fourth-inning grand-slam off the Florida Marlins' Jesus Sanchez on September 2, 1998.

As of 2015, Mercker resided in his hometown of Dublin with his wife, Julia, and three daughters. In 2009 he became an occasional broadcaster on Reds radio and television broadcasts. He also worked as a professional development adviser for athletes with Excel Sports Management, based in New York City.[8]

SOURCES

In addition to the sources cited in the Notes, the author also consulted Baseball-Reference.com and Baseball-Almanac.com

NOTES

1   Bob Nightengale, "A No-Hitter By Decision," *Los Angeles Times*, September 12, 1991. Accessed online on March 1, 2016: articles.latimes.com/1991-09-12/sports/sp-3120_1_kent_mercker; Maryann Hudson, "Dodgers No Hit; Mercker Big Hit," *Los Angeles Times*, April 9, 1994. Accessed online on March 1, 2016: articles.latimes.com/1994-04-09/sports/sp-43980_1_kent_mercker.

2   "Mercker Enjoying Home Life During Rehab," *Dublin Villager*, July 23, 2008. Accessed online on March 1, 2016: thisweeknews. com/content/stories/dublin/news/2008/07/23/0724dumercke rstory.html.

3   Ibid.; Chris Foster, "Angels' Mercker Recovers From Cerebral Hemorrhage to Pitch Again," *Los Angeles Times*, August 12, 2000. Accessed on March 1, 2016: articles.latimes.com/2000/aug/12/ sports/sp-3268.

4   United Press International, "Red Sox Sign Mercker," January 5, 2001. Accessed online on March 1, 2016: upi.com/Archives/2001/01/05/Red-Sox-sign-Kent-Mercker/5888978670800/; Christopher Smith, "St. Louis Cardinals' Mitch Harris, a Navy Lieutenant, Wins Tony Conigliaro Award Given by Boston Red Sox," *Masslive.com*, December 15, 2015. Accessed on March 1, 2016: masslive.com/ redsox/index.ssf/2015/12/st_louis_cardinals_mitch_harri.html.

5   Dejan Kovacevic, "Braves' Mercker Traces Pitching Career to Claridge," *Pittsburgh Post-Gazette*, August 1, 1991: E9.

6   Milton Kent, "World Series Notebook," *Baltimore Sun*, October 18, 1992. Accessed online on March 1, 2016: articles.baltimoresun. com/1992-10-18/sports/1992292143_1_blue-jays-league-champi-onship-series-rotation.

7   "Dodgers No Hit;Mercker Big Hit"; "No. 35, Kent Mercker," *Braves Journal*, October 19, 2006. Accessed online on March 1, 2016: bravesjournal.us/?p=2750.

8   "Linked-in Profile: Kent Mercker," Linkedin.com. Accessed online on March 1, 2016: linkedin.com/in/kent-mercker-95386b84; Tommy Poe, "Random Ex-Brave: Kent Mercker," *Walk Off Walk*. Accessed online on March 1, 2016: blog.walkoffwalk. net/2015/07/random-ex-brave-kent-mercker.html.

TONY SAUNDERS

By David E. Skelton

ON OPENING DAY 1998 THE reigning World Series champion Florida Marlins took the field minus a dozen of their 1997 teammates, many of whom were, as *The Sporting News* put it, "victims ... of a halved payroll," adding, "The roll call of departed comrades read like a Memorial Day remembrance of war casualties" with the loss of perennial All Stars such as Moises Alou, Kevin Brown, Jeff Conine, and Robb Nen.[1] The absent roster also included 23-year-old Tony Saunders who, despite a pedestrian 4-6, 4.61 record in his rookie season, had shown enough promise during the championship run to warrant angst over his loss. "My main concern is pitching," Marlins skipper Jim Leyland said going into the 1998 campaign. "Losing Brown, Nen, and Saunders, that's frustrating."[2]

Marlins pitching coach Larry Rothschild was no less impressed by the left-handed hurler. The first manager of the expansion Tampa Bay Devil Rays, Rothschild played a key role in the Devil Rays' selection of Saunders as the first player chosen in the 1997 major-league expansion draft. A seemingly bright future loomed for the youngster before a gruesome injury in 1999 ended his career.

Anthony Scott Saunders was born in Baltimore on April 29, 1974, the younger of two sons of William Frederick Saunders III and Joan (Lewis) Saunders. His paternal grandparents were from New England and William Frederick Jr. appears to have preceded his son in pursuit of a military career. Tony's father was born in Ohio in 1945 but settled in Maryland in the 1970s. Tony went to school in the Baltimore suburbs, attending Howard High School in Ellicott City before transferring to Glen Burnie High for his senior year. (His parents divorced when he was a child and one report suggests the transfer occurred because Tony moved from his mother's home into his father's.) Though he played baseball in the backyard of the Baltimore Orioles, Saunders grew up admiring

Atlanta Braves lefty Tom Glavine and patterned his pitching style after the future Hall of Famer, focusing on control and change of speed.[3] After graduating from high school in 1992 the All-County hurler spurned an athletic scholarship at George Mason University in Northern Virginia to pursue a professional career. Bypassed in the major-league amateur draft, Saunders attended an open tryout, where he was signed to a $1,000 bonus contract by Marlins scout Ty Brown.[4]

Saunders was assigned to Florida's Gulf Coast (Rookie) League team. Used exclusively in relief, the 18-year-old surrendered just 29 hits in 45⅔ innings while placing among the league leaders with 24 appearances in the short 60-game season. In 1993 Saunders was promoted to the Kane County (Illinois) Cougars in the Midwest League (Class A), where he continued his excellence with a record of 6-1, 2.27 in 23 appearances (10 starts). Elbow surgery limited him to just 23 starts (131 innings) over the next two seasons before Saunders rebounded with a record of 13-4, 2.63 in 1996 to pace the Portland (Maine) Sea Dogs to a first-place finish in the Double-A Eastern League. He led the league with 156 strikeouts while placing among the leaders in wins, starts (26), and innings (167⅔). The Marlins selected Saunders among the September call-ups though he did not make an appearance. Tabbed as the franchise's minor-league pitcher of the year, Saunders was sent to the Arizona Fall League, where his performance earned praise from Marlins GM Dave Dombrowski.

Except for the superb pitching of All-Stars Kevin Brown and Al Leiter, the Marlins' rotation was at best spotty and Saunders, who was added to the 40-man roster during the offseason, was eyed as a strong candidate to fill the club's fourth or fifth starter role. In his first spring-training start Saunders cemented his standing by striking out four over three shutout innings without a ball reaching the outfield en route to a strong Grapefruit League campaign. "He showed what he's

back against the defending NL champion Braves with six scoreless innings to earn his first major-league win (helping his own cause with a third-inning leadoff homer against Glavine for the game's first tally). Five days later he beat the Braves again after yielding only five hits and three runs over seven innings. On May 18 Saunders was lifted after carrying a 2-1 lead over the Pittsburgh Pirates through five innings. A double-play groundball from Pirates first baseman Kevin Young would prove to be Saunders last major-league pitch in nearly two months when a sprained right knee landed him on the disabled list.

After a minor-league rehab assignment Saunders returned to the Marlins in July stronger than ever—a 1.85 ERA over four starts. But he was 0-2 over this period as the Marlins managed just one run in three of the four games. On July 31 Saunders faced off against his favorite patsies, the Braves, to earn his third major-league win, all against Atlanta, as he combined with three relievers in a 1-0 nailbiter. Around this time the Marlins optioned Luis Castillo as the future All-Star second baseman struggled through an injury-plagued first half. Immersed in a three-way pennant race with the Braves and New York Mets, the Marlins dangled Saunders before the Philadelphia Phillies in an unsuccessful attempt to acquire second sacker Mickey Morandini.

But far less success awaited Saunders in the closing months of the 1997 season. Excluding a September 17 win against the Philadelphia Phillies—his last victory in the National League, he finished with a record of 0-3, 8.23 over nine appearances (eight starts). Saunders was unable to reach the third inning in two starts and, after watching videotape of one of these dismal appearances, he admitted, "That was the first time I've watched myself pitch (on tape), and I just look lethargic, like I was waiting for something [bad] to happen."[6] He finished the season with a record of 4-6, 4.61 in 111⅓ innings. Though Saunders placed among the club leaders with 102 strikeouts, this was countered by 64 walks. Control issues would plague him throughout his short career.

On September 23 the Marlins clinched the NL wild card—the franchise's first-ever postseason

shown every time we've seen him," Rothschild said. "He had a very, very good changeup, and he hit spots in and out with his fastball. He has good-enough command to go after people in tough spots."[5]

On April 5, 1997, Saunders made his major-league debut in Florida's Pro Player Stadium against the Cincinnati Reds. The Reds threatened in the first and scored in the second before Saunders settled down to retire the next 16 batters in a row. Lifted in the seventh after yielding a run-scoring double, Saunders did not figure in the decision in a 4-3 extra-inning win. Two weeks later, in San Francisco, he held the Giants to three hits with 10 strikeouts over 7⅓ innings (including striking out the side in the fourth) before a pair of eighth-inning singles led to a 3-2 Marlins loss (the tying and winning runs scored on a two-out double off relief pitcher Rick Helling).

Saunders struggled in two subsequent starts, yielding 12 runs (nine earned) over seven innings though he did not figure in either decision. On May 8 he bounced berth—with a 6-3 win over the Montreal Expos. Marlins manager Leyland planned a different rotation for each possible West Division foe and when that turned out to be the Giants, Leyland, who wanted two left-handed starters against a left-handed-leaning San Francisco lineup, announced his choice of Saunders over fellow rookie Livan Hernandez in the series. "This is a … surprise," Saunders confessed. "I didn't even think I would be on the roster in the first round [of the playoffs]. I thought they might put me on the roster if we played Atlanta. I haven't been pitching that well lately, and Livan has been pitching great."[7] As it turned out, the Marlins swept the best-of-five series and Saunders didn't pitch.

The club did not find it quite as easy against the Braves in the NLCS. On October 10 Saunders took the mound in Game Three with the series locked up at one game apiece. He and future HOF righty John Smoltz dueled to a 1-1 tie through five innings before Saunders was lifted in the sixth. The Marlins scored four runs in their half of the frame for a 5-2 win (Hernandez got the victory) and advanced to the World Series after capturing Games Five and Six.

Leyland reshuffled his rotation for the World Series against the Cleveland Indians by selecting Saunders and Hernandez as starters. (Eighteen years passed before another team—the 2015 Mets—used two rookie starters in the fall classic.) Tabbed as the starter in Game Four in Cleveland, Saunders said, ""I'm very excited. … This is something you never really think about because you don't believe it's going to happen your first year. There's a lot of players who play a long time and never get the opportunity (to play in the World Series), and I'm getting it my first year." Seemingly needing to defend his selection in the pressure-packed situation, Leyland said, "[Saunders is] on his way to becoming a very fine pitcher. I'm sure he'll have jitters; I'd worry if he didn't."[8]

The Indians countered with their own rookie starter, Jaret Wright, who had faced off against Saunders less than a year earlier in the Arizona Fall League. The Series "was a juxtaposition with respect to the weather. Four of the games were held in sunny, hot Miami, Florida, while the three others were held in freezing Cleveland, Ohio. Naturally, the games in Cleveland were going to be very cold, but no one expected" Game Four temperatures of 38 degrees. "[A]s the game progressed into the later innings, the media reported wind-chill readings as low as 18°F [to mark] the coldest game in fall classic history."[9] The frigid temperatures affected Saunders as he surrendered three runs in the first inning and another three in the third en route to a 10-3 Marlins loss. It proved to be the last postseason appearance of his career.

In what many considered a surprise move, the Marlins did not protect Saunders in the 1997 expansion draft. Meanwhile, the emphasis the Devil Rays placed on pitching was evident by the selection of nine consecutive hurlers in the middle rounds. But no one was more important to the new club than number-one selection Tony Saunders. Along with free agents Wilson Alvarez, Roberto Hernandez, and Dave Eiland, the left-handed hurler was looked upon to stabilize the staff in the club's inaugural season. On April 2, 1998, the franchise's third game, Saunders took the mound against the Detroit Tigers in Tropicana Field. He surrendered a game-opening homer to outfielder Brian Hunter before settling down to hold the Tigers to four hits and no runs through the sixth. Saunders was lifted in the seventh and did not figure in the decision in the 7-1 Devil Rays win.

As once-promising 1962 Mets hurlers Al Jackson and Jay Hook might have advised more than a generation beforehand, pitching for an expansion club was fraught with its own set of challenges. By July 4 the 20 losses Saunders and Devil Rays righty Dennis Springer compiled equaled that of the entire New York Yankees staff. After an April 16 win against the Anaheim Angels, Saunders compiled a major-league-high 16 starts without a win. Except for a particularly dreadful June in which he surrendered 24 runs in 29⅓ innings, many of the losses pinned on Saunders resulted from a lack of run support. In 15 of his 31 appearances he delivered a 2.59 ERA (league average: 4.65) that yielded eight losses and seven no-decisions. Throughout this dismal run, the 24-year-old remained remarkably stoic. "[The coaches have] been telling me … to stay with it, that things will turn around, that your luck will change," said an optimistic Saunders.[10] Control remained a problem as he surrendered a major-league-leading 111 walks while his seven hit batters contributed to the Devil Rays' 81 HBP (a mark that approached the record 85 by the Pittsburgh Pirates in 1895). Three days after the season ended, Saunders had arthroscopic surgery to remove a small bone chip from his left elbow. Throughout the offseason the Devil Rays fielded trade inquiries for the promising lefty but all offers were turned away. "[T]he team expects him to be part of the rotation for many years," Marc Topkin wrote in *The Sporting News*.[11]

But a spotty start in 1999 forced Topkin to admit that "Saunders continues to be equal parts astounding and confounding."[12] On April 22 the lefty's wildness—seven walks and a HBP—left hitters flatfooted as Saunders held the Orioles hitless through 7⅔ innings in a 1-0 win. But this near-gem—the closest he ever came to a major-league shutout—was sandwiched between four starts in which Saunders yielded 25 earned runs over 14⅓ innings. Briefly optioned to the Durham Bulls, he returned to the Devil Rays on May 15 and surrendered just three hits and one unearned run to beat the Angels in what proved to be his last major-league win.

Eleven days later, on May 26, Saunders appeared equally as strong against the Texas Rangers before a leadoff homer in the third was followed by three singles. Protecting a two-out, 3-2 lead he uncorked a full-count wild pitch to reigning AL MVP Juan Gonzalez that allowed the tying run to score. But little attention was paid to the tally as the focus of players and fans alike turned to the screaming pitcher writhing on the ground. The loud popping sound heard by all present was the breaking of Saunders' humerus, the long bone in the upper arm located between the elbow joint and shoulder. "You could hear it, plain as day," said teammate Wade Boggs, who was in the Devil Rays dugout. "That's about as bad as it gets." "Obviously, you're shocked," said Rothschild, who had rushed onto the field with the club's trainer and medical personnel after Saunders hit the ground. "[A break like this is] very rare."[13]

Rare perhaps, but hardly unheard of, because Saunders joined a list of four pitchers, all lefties, who had sustained similar injuries in the preceding 10 years (from Dave Dravecky in 1989 to Norm Charlton, Tom Browning, and John Smiley in the 1990s). Only Charlton—Saunders' teammate—was able to sustain a measure of success thereafter. Lying in a bed in St. Petersburg's Bayfront Medical Center that evening, Saunders vowed to break this trend. Six months later, after surgery to remove scar tissue from his left elbow (a procedure unrelated to the break) he announced his goal of being ready by Opening Day 2000. Though Jamie Reed, the Devil Rays trainer, felt the projected goal unrealistic, he worked closely with Saunders on a strenuous rehab program.

Saunders' goal was indeed overoptimistic: In July 2000 he threw 73 pitches with good velocity (approximately 85 mph) in the first of two simulated games. A month later he took the mound for the Charleston (South Carolina) River Dogs in the South Atlantic League, where he surrendered one hit and struck out two over two innings (27 pitches). Projected to join the Devil Rays in September, Saunders was moved to the St. Petersburg Devil Rays (Advanced Class A), where the parent team could closely monitor his progress. But all of his hard work went for naught on August 24 when Saunders suffered a second broken humerus in a game against the Clearwater Phillies. The break occurred just above the first, and this time Saunders knew it was the end. In a tearful press conference two days later the 26-year-old announced his retirement.[14] "I'd give anything if I could get back out there and play again," he said later. "You don't know how bad I want to say, 'You know what? Maybe I could try again.' But then reality sets in. And common sense sets in. There ain't no way I can go through that again."[15]

In the fall a panel of representatives from the office of the commissioner, the league offices, and Boston media selected Saunders as one of two recipients of the 2000 Tony Conigliaro Award. Named after the Boston Red Sox outfielder who returned to baseball in 1967 following a severe head injury only to succumb to cancer 23 years later, Saunders was recognized for his valiant attempt to overcome his ghastly injury.

Shortly thereafter, the Devil Rays established the Tony Saunders Courage Award to recognize high-school athletes in the Tampa-St. Petersburg region who overcame adversity.

In November 2000 Saunders joined the Devil Rays front office as an assistant for scouting and player development. Seeking to become a GM, he eventually resigned the job after tiring of writing reports on minor-league players whom he had once played alongside. Saunders dabbled in a number of ventures that included memorabilia sales, a partnership in a restaurant-bar near Tropicana Field called Bermuda Jake's, and a short stint as a broker with Morgan Stanley. Unable to stay away from baseball, in 2004 Saunders began coaching an AAU team in Tampa and discovered he could throw pain-free. The Devil Rays agreed to release him so he could solicit interest from other clubs. The Dodgers were interested, but on January 19, 2005, Saunders was signed by Orioles scout Ty Brown (the scout who originally signed him for the Marlins in 1992). Joining the Orioles in spring training as a nonroster invitee, Saunders was assigned to the Bowie (Maryland) Baysox in the Double-A Eastern League, but he never made an appearance. He briefly surfaced with the Mesa (Arizona) Miners in the independent Golden Baseball League before retiring for good.

In 2005 Saunders' former Devil Rays teammate José Canseco released his tell-all exposé on Major League players' steroid use entitled *Juiced: Wild times, Rampant 'Roids, Smash Hits and How Baseball Got Big*. In the book the slugger-turned-author claimed that Saunders' broken arm was likely the result of steroid abuse. The allegation sparked a public war of words as Saunders vehemently denied the claim. Emphasizing that he and Canseco were far from friends, he said, "If I don't have that injury, I'm nowhere near that book. He used my injury as a punch line. … Baseball was my livelihood. … It ain't right."[16]

Saunders moved back to Maryland, where the appeal of baseball remained strong. He was a pitching coach for a baseball school in Glen Burnie and on June 20, 2010, he traveled to Cooperstown, New York, to pitch one inning in the Hall of Fame Classic. Four years later he launched a short-lived business advisory venture called Strike 3 Consulting, LLC. On June 16, 2016, Saunders married Christine Jennings in the Annapolis suburb of Arnold, Maryland. It was his second marriage — 21 years earlier he had married his high-school sweetheart, Joyce Dickerson. That union produced a daughter, Samantha, and a son, Anthony, before dissolving in divorce around 2010.

Saunders' passion for baseball is represented by the tattoo on his left shoulder that says, "My World," the words written in script above a hand holding a baseball. His fervor for the sport is represented throughout his career from his valiant attempt to come back from a devastating injury to his vehement denial when he was accused of using steroids. Initially overlooked by major-league scouts in the 1992 amateur draft, Saunders fought his way through the minors to establish himself as one of the most promising pitchers during the last years of the twentieth century.

SOURCES

The author wishes to thank Dean Giampola and SABR members Bill Mortell and Rod Nelson (chair of the SABR Scouts Committee) for their valuable research.

In addition to the sources cited in the Notes, the author also consulted Ancestry.com and Baseball-Reference.com.

NOTES

1   "Breaking Up," *The Sporting News*, April 6, 1998: 42.

2   "Diaspora in South Florida," *The Sporting News*, January 5, 1998: 63.

3   In 1997 Saunders' first major-league win came at the expense of his idol.

4   Ty was the son of Pittsburgh Pirates executive Joe L. Brown, grandson of the comedian Joe E. Brown.

5   "Nen, Club Succumb to Giants' Hitting," *The Sporting News*, April 28, 1997: 22.

6   "It's All in the Family for Talented Alous," *The Sporting News*, September 8, 1997: 43.

7   "Playoff Rotation Set to Combat Lefties," *The Sporting News*, October 6, 1997: 44.

8   Steve Eby, "Eighteen Crazy Nights — Looking Back at the 1997 Cleveland Indians," October 22, 2014. Accessed September 3, 2016. (bit.ly/2bLzn1O).

9   Matt Nadel, "The Coldest Game in World Series History," January 5, 2014. Accessed September 3, 2016. (bit.ly/2bTkDsf).

10 "Saunders Pitches Past His Early Problems," *The Sporting News*, August 10, 1998: 27.

11 "Expansion Picks Provide Solid Footing for Future," *The Sporting News*, September 28, 1998: 68.

12 "Saunders Continues to Astound and Confound," *The Sporting News*, May 3, 1999: 22.

13 "Saunders Breaks Arm While Pitching," May 27, 1999. Accessed September 4, 2016. (bit.ly/2cbzovO).

14 "The Tampa Bay Devil Rays, Then and Now," April 24, 2014. Accessed September 4, 2016. (bit.ly/2cqlIvB).

15 "Career-ending Injury Puts Devil Rays Lefty in Front Office," *The Sporting News*, December 4, 2000: 63.

16 "Tony Saunders Denies Steroid Allegations," February 21, 2005. Accessed September 4, 2016. (bit.ly/2bOUpg2).

GRAEME LLOYD

BY RORY COSTELLO

LONG-LIMBED SOUTHPAW Graeme Lloyd became the first Australian to win a World Series ring. The 6'8"[1] reliever joined the New York Yankees bullpen late in the 1996 season and remained with the club for the 1998 championship too. Through the 2015 season, this distinction remained unique among Aussies. Just one other of Lloyd's countrymen, Grant Balfour, had made it into the World Series (Tampa Bay, 2008).[2]

Lloyd, the third Australian-trained major-leaguer, was also the first pitcher from Down Under to reach the majors (1993). By the end of 2015, 20 more hurlers had followed him.[3] None, however, had appeared in more games than Lloyd's 568. He pitched 533 innings, showing that he was used as a specialist for much of his career, but he did post 17 saves to go with his 30-36 won-lost record and 4.04 ERA. For middle relievers, perhaps the most telling statistic is the percentage of inherited runners allowed to score; over his career, Lloyd's mark was a respectable 141 out of 447 (32%). He also had a spotless 0.00 ERA in 13 postseason appearances, including a win in Game Four of the 1996 World Series.

Except for an unusual visa issue, Lloyd could have stayed in the majors beyond 2003—but he was then free to join the Australian national team as they won a silver medal in the 2004 Olympics. In late 2008, he became a coach in his native land.

Graeme John Lloyd was born on April 9, 1967 in Geelong. This small city (pronounced Juh-LONG) is about 60 kilometers southeast of Melbourne, the capital of the state of Victoria. His father, Noel, was a sheep rancher.[4] The ranch was in Gnarwarre, a little to the west of Geelong. Noel and his wife Pauline also had three daughters named Deborah, Sherryn, and Jennine.

At the age of 10, Lloyd picked up a baseball for the first time after one sister's boyfriend convinced him to try the game, which is not in the mainstream of Australian sports.[5] As the Associated Press reported in 1994, he was hooked. "It was sort of a fluke," Lloyd recalled. "The first day, I just grabbed the ball and started throwing it, never dreaming what it would lead to. And 17 years later, here I am. What if I hadn't gone that day? It's all pretty amazing."[6]

"I had a go at cricket in school and I played Australian Rules Football for a couple of years, but I always came back to baseball. It was what I was best at," he added.[7] That is significant because Victoria is the stronghold of Aussie rules football, and height is an asset in that game. Yet as a contributor to the Ultimate Mets website wrote in 2003, "I played baseball with Graeme Lloyd for about seven years. When he was ten years old everyone who saw him play knew that he was going to be something special. But apart from his obvious physical talent, 'Lloydy' had the one quality that I and none of his Australian contemporaries had: the mental toughness to make it to the top."

"My first team was the All Stars—they were a team in the Geelong baseball league," Lloyd recalled in 1989. "I spent two years playing with Essendon in the city [Melbourne], and then back to Geelong again before finally ending up at Sunshine." At age 19 in 1987, he made his debut in the Claxton Shield tournament, then Australia's top baseball competition. Amateur teams represented their states, and Lloyd was a utility player for Victoria. When his team faced Queensland in Brisbane, the crowd was rough. Lloyd said, "You watch the British soccer and you think, wow, you never see this in Australia, but I thought they were that close to coming over the fence."[8]

The Toronto Blue Jays signed Lloyd as an amateur free agent in January 1988. As he told the story the next year, "A few talent scouts came out from the American leagues to have a look around and see what talent was here. I think what happened with me was that someone said to one of these guys 'go and have a look at this guy.' So they came and had a bit of a look, and they decided to invite me to spring training."[9] In 2012, he said, "It's a whole different world now. . .The scouts now have the media in the palm of their hands. They see a kid on their iPhone and say 'wow, he has a great action' and think about coming to Australia to sign him. And we have a lot of scouts here now."[10]

The man who signed Lloyd was the Jays' director of international scouting, Wayne Morgan. He made an assessment that held true for Lloyd's pro career. "He doesn't throw real hard, but he might get a little faster. He's got good movement, a good delivery and can throw strikes. His curve is not bad and he's got the start of a pretty nice change-up."[11] A decade later, a *Sports Illustrated* scouting report ahead of the 1998 World Series described him at his big-league peak. "With his long arms LH Graeme Lloyd is tough on lefties: 'Wraparound' breaking ball gets them to flinch."[12]

Shortly after he signed, Lloyd appeared for Victoria in the Claxton Shield again in 1988. In addition to pitching, he played first base. In one game, he hit a three-run homer off Bob Nilsson (older brother of future big-league teammate Dave Nilsson) "with seemingly minimal effort. . .and casually strode around the bases."[13] The designated hitter was in effect for the bulk of Lloyd's pro career; in the majors, he came to the plate just seven times, going 0-for-6 with a walk. He did still occasionally appear at first base in Australian league play, though.

Lloyd pitched four seasons in the minors from 1988 through 1992. He did reasonably well in Class A his first year, but appeared in just three games in 1989 because of an elbow injury, which he attributed to bad mechanics. "I've pulled tendons off the bone," he said that December, "and that was caused by the seemingly simple thing of lowering my elbow and in effect slinging the pitch."[14]

However, he had a backup plan behind baseball. "You need something else playing the minors. See, I'm an electrician by trade." (He had gone to high school at Geelong Technical College.[15]) He added, "I've noticed as a sales rep for Pony [the athletic shoe company], so I know I won't be at a loss if I don't make it. I've been diverse in my interests so I know I'm going to be okay either way."[16]

Lloyd was speaking as the brand-new professional Australian Baseball League began operations in the winter (summer, in the Southern Hemisphere) of 1989-90. He was a member of the Melbourne Monarchs — but played mainly first base in 18 games. He was 14 for 51 (.275) with a homer and five RBIs, even stealing three bases. He appeared just once on the mound, retiring one batter and picking up a save.

Returning to Myrtle Beach of the South Atlantic League (Class A) in 1990, Lloyd still wasn't ready for a heavy pitching load. He appeared in just 19 games. Yet he began to show promise, going 5-2 with a 2.72 ERA. Another point of interest was that he started six games — from then on, he appeared exclusively out of the bullpen in the U.S., though not in Australia. In fact, during the 1990-91 season, he was the starter in all nine of his outings for his new team, the Perth Heat. He completed four (but pitched just 55 innings total), posting a 6-1 record with a 2.62 ERA. Perth won the ABL championship.

In 1991, Lloyd moved up to Dunedin in the Florida State League (high Class A). He had a fine season as the closer, saving 24 games in 52 appearances (2-5, 2.18). That broke the club record set the previous year by Mike Timlin. Lloyd then followed up with another strong season for Perth: 6-2, 2.70 in 60 innings pitched across 11 games.

Climbing to Double A in 1992, Lloyd notched 14 more saves for Knoxville in the Southern League (4-8, 1.96). Perhaps his most salient stat as a minor-leaguer was that he allowed just 10 home runs in 271 innings pitched.

On December 7, 1992, the Philadelphia Phillies selected Lloyd in the Rule 5 draft — but the very next day, they traded him to the Milwaukee Brewers for a minor-league pitcher named John Trisler who never got beyond Double A. Meanwhile, Lloyd went on to have his strongest season yet at home: 8-1, 1.48 for Perth in 10 games. In 61 innings pitched, he struck out 57 and walked just four.

Lloyd never pitched a day in Triple A. He jumped right to the majors based on his performance in spring training 1993. On April 11 in the Oakland Coliseum, announcer Roy Steele made public note that the first Australian pitcher was making his debut. The Brewers were trailing 6-0 when the rookie entered in the eighth inning with two outs. He retired the first man he faced, Eric Fox, but gave up a two-run homer in the ninth to Rickey Henderson. Manager Phil Garner thought it was a good low pitch, but "(Bleep) happens," said Lloyd. "It didn't exactly put icing on the cake. I was disappointed in that. Apart from that, it was good to get out there."[17]

Three days later, on April 14, he became half of the first Australian battery in the majors as Dave Nilsson returned from an injury rehab assignment—but a 6-2 California Angels lead turned into a 12-2 blowout. As Nilsson said, "It wasn't a real great moment, was it? I'm just ashamed that it happened in a game like that. I just wished it would have happened in a better game."[18] Over time, the pair would hear more than their share of kangaroo and koala jokes.

After Lloyd and the whole Milwaukee bullpen got off to a shaky start, pitching coach Don Rowe issued a vote of confidence, saying, "They're trying as hard as they can. As long as they don't give up, I'm not going to give up on them. We're going to give these guys every chance to succeed."[19]

Lloyd went on to have a solid rookie year: 3-4, 2.83 ERA, WHIP of 1.2 in 55 games. He did not appear in a game after September 19, though. Phil Garner said, "I just think he needs a long rest," and the club indicated that Lloyd would not pitch in Australia that winter.[20] As it turned out, he did see limited duty with Perth (0-1, 4.66 with four saves in nine relief outings).

The following two big-league seasons were no great shakes, with an aggregate record of 2-8 and a 4.90 ERA in 76 games (79 innings pitched), though he did pick up seven saves. Milwaukee's closer in those years was Mike Fetters. Of course, 1994 was cut short by the major-league strike. Once the ABL season opened, Lloyd returned to form. He was 5-2 with a 2.27 ERA in 10 games (47 2/3 innings pitched).

In 1995, Lloyd strained a tendon on the middle finger of his pitching hand and did not appear after late July. He pitched his last 10 games at home in 1995-96

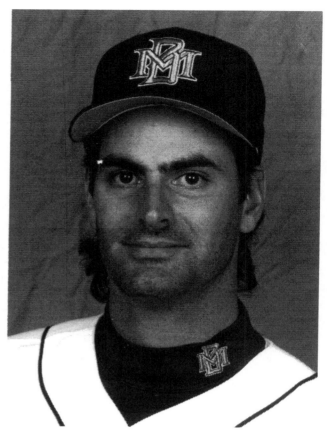

with a new team, the Brisbane Bandits. Pitching only out of the bullpen, he was 2-2, 2.20 with three saves in 16 1/3 innings. That brought his lifetime ERA in Australia to 2.34, the best in the league's history, to go with his winning percentage of .701 (36-15).

Lloyd was pitching well for the Brewers in 1996, but the club had a mediocre 61-68 record as of August 23. He then got an exciting change of scenery. The New York Yankees, leading the American League East, traded reliever Bob Wickman and outfielder Gerald Williams to Milwaukee. In return, they received Pat Listach, a player to be named later, and Lloyd. "Yankees General Manager Bob Watson had been trying all season to land a proven left-hander for his bullpen," wrote the *New York Times*.[21]

However, Lloyd had a bad time of it over the remainder of the season. He allowed 12 hits and 5 walks in just 5 2/3 innings, and as a result he was 0-2 with a frightening 17.47 ERA. It emerged that he not only had a bone spur in his elbow (which prevented him from throwing his bread-and-butter pitch, the curveball) but also that his shoulder had required a cortisone shot not long before the trade. The Yankees filed a formal complaint with the American League office.[22]

Nonetheless, New York kept him on the postseason roster. Said manager Joe Torre, "When you make a deal, you make a commitment. . .To make up your mind about a guy after just one, two or three games when he's hurt is a mistake. Wanting Lloyd to succeed is more than just a Joe Torre-Bob Watson thing. The whole organization was involved in wanting him over here and I felt that once he was okay physically we owed it to him to give him the opportunity to help us."[23]

Their faith was rewarded. Lloyd pitched twice in both the division series against Texas and the league championship against Baltimore, facing eight batters and allowing just one hit. Then in the World Series, he kept his ERA at 0.00. In Game Three, he got two important outs in the eighth inning. After replacing Mariano Rivera, who was then still a setup man, he retired lefties Ryan Klesko and Fred McGriff. In Game Four, with the game tied and runners on first and second in the ninth inning, he got McGriff to hit into a double play. The Yankees then scored two in the tenth, and Lloyd got the win.

After the bone spur was removed in November 1996, Lloyd remained a useful member of the Yankees' pen for the next two seasons. In 1998, after returning from double hernia surgery the previous December,[24] he was especially effective—it was likely his best season in the majors. Although he pitched just 37 2/3 innings in 50 games, he was 3-0 with a 1.67 ERA and his WHIP was just 0.85. His 1998 performance was intriguing because it defied his reputation as a Lefty One-Out Guy. Even though he held lefties to a .200 average (16 for 80, three home runs allowed), he was even tougher on righties that year: .179 (10 for 56, and no homers).

One colorful episode in 1998—albeit somewhat out of character for the easygoing Australian—came in a game against Baltimore on May 19. After Orioles reliever Armando Benítez served up a three-run homer to Bernie Williams, he drilled Tino Martinez in the back with a pitch, and a brawl erupted. "Lloyd, who was the first to attack Benítez after sprinting from the bullpen, and [Darryl] Strawberry received three-game

suspensions for what [AL President Gene] Budig described as 'overly aggressive behavior, fighting and prolonging the violent incident.'"[25]

Cleveland knocked the Yankees out in the AL Division Series in 1997, but it wasn't Lloyd's fault, as he retired all five men who faced him in two outings. During the 1998 postseason, as New York won 11 games and lost just two, the specialist saw very little action. He appeared just once in each series against Texas, Cleveland, and San Diego, facing just four batters and giving up one hit.

Lloyd also got married in 1998.[26] He had met Cindy Lee Barak in Tampa—the spring training home of the Yankees—and their wedding took place in Australia.[27]

Not long after the newlywed returned for spring training in 1999, on February 18, New York acquired Roger Clemens from the Toronto Blue Jays. They sent David Wells, Homer Bush, and Lloyd in return. Lloyd had hoped to get a shot as the closer, a role for which Toronto had penciled in Robert Person.[28] He got some save opportunities in the early going, but rookie Billy Koch emerged as the closer. Returning to setup duties, Lloyd had an active and generally good year for the Jays in 1999, appearing in 74 games and going 5-3, 3.63 with three saves.

After the season, Lloyd rejected an arbitration offer from Toronto, became a free agent, and signed in December with the Montreal Expos. He signed a three-year deal worth $9 million (including a $3 million signing bonus) to become setup man for Ugueth Urbina. A new owner, Jeffrey Loria, had just taken control of the Montreal club a couple of weeks earlier. The signings of Lloyd and Hideki Irabu were a sign that Loria was willing to spend after the Expos had tightened their purse strings in previous years.

The year 2000 brought professional and personal crises to Graeme Lloyd. It was a series of events right out of the Book of Job. First, in spring training, he went on the disabled list with tendinitis in his pitching shoulder. While he was sidelined, on April 3, his wife Cindy died. The young woman was just 26. She had been battling Crohn's Disease, the inflammatory bowel disorder, for 14 years.

Lloyd felt continued shoulder pain in late April, and after an MRI, he underwent arthroscopic surgery in May for a partially torn rotator cuff. The initial estimates called for him to be out three to four months, and though he was able to test his arm on the sidelines in early August, he was not able to return.[29] On top of that, in August, a tornado destroyed his home in Palm Harbor, Florida.[30]

Lloyd worked hard to rehabilitate his shoulder. As his friend Keith Zlomsowitch said, "He did it for her. Cindy was so proud of him. He made it his mission after surgery to get back for her."[31] Lloyd has apparently also done charitable work on behalf of Crohn's Disease, although press citations are not visible, suggesting a low-key effort.

Reminiscing about that period in 2004, Lloyd said, "I suppose you can either go one way or the other. The other way wasn't an option for me. I just went through deciding what I wanted to go on with in life and how I wanted to do it. I came back the next year after the surgery and after I lost Cindy, and I had probably one of the best years I had in my career. We all go through tough times, and I thought, 'This is what they talk about, you either move on or get stuck.' I decided to see what I could do. I think my focus was a little different after that."[32]

Indeed, the comeback effort was successful: Lloyd appeared in a career-high 84 games for Montreal in 2001. He also won nine games, a personal best, while losing five and posting a 4.35 ERA with one save. He won the Tony Conigliaro Award for battling back from his adversities. "The Conigliaro Award. . .yeah, it is special to me," he said in 2012.[33]

An amusing moment with Lloyd came in a Nike commercial presented during the 2001 World Series. The spot celebrated the international character of Major League Baseball, with 10 players from various nations singing "Take Me Out to the Ballgame" in different languages. Lloyd delivered the line "And it's root, root, root for the home team." The creative people at the ad agency, Wieden & Kennedy, must have had a subversive streak — "root" in Australian slang means "have sex." Judging by Graeme's mischievous smile, he was a willing co-conspirator in the inside joke.

Lloyd picked up a career-high five saves in 41 games for Montreal before the All-Star break in 2002. On July 11, the Expos — in salary-cutting mode again — included him in an eight-player deal with the Florida Marlins. The book *Clubhouse Lawyer: Law in the World of Sports* told how it came about, entirely against Lloyd's wishes.

"Lloyd's contract with Montreal allowed him to name twelve teams to which he could not be traded. Florida was one of the no-trade teams that Lloyd had identified. . .To his dismay, Lloyd later learned that, under the terms of his contract, he was required to submit his list. . .by November 1, 2001. Lloyd and his agent did not submit the list until after that date, negating the benefit of the no-trade provision."[34]

One reason the pitcher was unhappy was because Florida had come to be owned by Jeffrey Loria. "Lloyd reacted to the trade by saying that Loria had lied to him when Loria owned the Expos. Appalled by the prospect of playing for Loria again, Lloyd filed a grievance in an attempt to reverse the deal."[35] But after arbitrator Shyam Das upheld the trade, Lloyd took it like a pro. "Now I'm here. I'm going to be a Florida Marlin. I do resolve things with people I had problems with, and I don't hold grudges. . .I'm the type of person that likes to get along with everybody."[36]

Lloyd finished out the season with the Marlins, became a free agent once more, and signed a minor-league deal in January 2003 with the New York Mets. "I know that I'll be battling for a job," he said. "I have to show what I have, and hopefully that's good enough to go north with the team. . . I have a lot left in baseball and I want to redeem myself."[37]

He did a creditable job in 36 outings for the Mets (1-2, 3.31, 1.3 WHIP). New York was having a dreadful season, and as part of what the *New York Times* called a "purge," the Mets traded the veteran on July 28 to the Kansas City Royals — who at the time were leading the AL Central.[38] The last 16 appearances of his big-league career came in 2003, and he allowed runs in 10 of them. That left Lloyd with a 10.95 ERA for Kansas City, which faded and finished third.

Yet again, he became a free agent that October. The Boston Red Sox — where fellow Australian Craig

Shipley was in the front office—were interested in bringing the lefty on board for the 2004 season. But as the *Sydney Morning Herald* wrote, "That's when the U.S. Government stepped in. Just two weeks before Lloyd was to apply for his new working visa—a hurdle all Australian sportspeople must clear before playing professionally in the U.S.—the immigration department announced its annual quota had been reached. All of which left Lloyd without a U.S. club for the season, although, in a timely turn of fortune, it paved the way for his entry into the Australian Olympic squad for Athens."[39]

Lloyd was excited about going to the Olympics at age 37, saying, "It might be karma."[40] Australia upset Japan 1-0 to reach the finals against Cuba, but lost a tough game and wound up taking silver. Lloyd pitched one inning in that game, after having appeared in three others during the initial round-robin phase of the tournament.

At least one story indicated that Lloyd hoped to resume his big-league career after the Games ended.[41] However, he did not resurface in baseball until 2008, when he rejoined the Perth Heat for Claxton Shield competition, which had resumed several years previously after the Australian pro circuit had become defunct. There was some talk that at age 41, the new pitching coach might also toe the rubber again, but he put those thoughts aside after a couple of setbacks during training. Yet there was tangible excitement about his presence, among the media as well as the team. Geoff Hooker, managing director of baseball for Western Australia, said, "He has a certain aura about him and not just his physical size either. To have Graeme, who current and former players have had to look up to for years, is a major coup."[42]

The Australian Baseball League was revived for the 2010-11 season, and Perth won the first championship in the league's new incarnation. The Heat repeated as champions in the 2011-12 season, and Lloyd remained the team's pitching coach, "instilling [his] work ethic into many of the young players on their roster."[43] The notion arose that he might become manager at some point.[44] Geoff Hooker, also Chief Executive Officer of the Heat, said, "I am so pleased for getting him. I think he brought a confidence and calmness to the clubhouse that gave us a real edge in the tight games."[45] Lloyd was still the Heat's pitching coach as of the 2015-16 season. In 2016, one of the Aussie hurlers he instructed, Warwick Saupold, made it to the majors.

In February 2012, Graeme Lloyd looked back on what baseball has meant to him and favorite memories from his career. "Baseball has given me the most amazing experiences of my life, from the depths of despair to the absolute euphoria of reaching the pinnacle of sport. It has opened my life up to the different cultures of the USA, Mexico, the Czech Republic and pretty much everywhere else in between. The dynamics of the game do not change, it's still you against a hitter and the competitiveness that goes with it.

"I've been lucky enough to play for a few big league teams, and with each team, I met an amazing cross-section of people from throughout the USA and Canada—from the incredibly harsh environment in New York to the relative kindness in Kansas City. I've been booed by 50,000 and cheered by 50,000. Baseball gave me more experiences in three weeks than you'd expect in an entire career."[46]

In memory of Cindy Lloyd (1974–2000). The Crohn's and Colitis Foundation of America website (www.ccfa.org) provides information and notes how you can help if you wish.

Grateful acknowledgment to Graeme Lloyd for his memories and to Geoff Hooker for obtaining Graeme's input over lunch on February 20, 2012. Continued thanks to Nicholas R.W. Henning in Australia for his input. Graeme Lloyd is frequently mentioned in the second novel by Nicholas, Boomerang Baseball.

SOURCES

In addition to the sources in the Notes, the author also consulted Baseball-Reference.com, Retrosheet.org, ultimatemets.com, and:

http://www.sports-reference.com/olympics/athletes/ll/graeme-lloyd-1.html (Olympics information)

Peter Flintoff, & Adrian Dunn, *Australian Major League Baseball: The First Ten Years* (Self-published and printed independently, 2000). (Used as a source for Australian Baseball League statistics only.)

NOTES

1   Many sources (for example, assorted U.S. baseball cards) show Lloyd's height as 6'7". However, Australian sources show him as either 203 or 204 centimeters tall, which translates into 6'8".

2   Balfour also appeared in postseason play in 2004, 2010, 2012, and 2013. Other Australians who had gotten into playoff games: Damian Moss (2002), Peter Moylan (2010), and Liam Hendriks (2015).

3   This excludes infielder Trent Durrington, who faced one batter in 2004.

4   Vic Ziegel, "Lloyd No Longer Sheepish Over Trade," *New York Daily News*, March 28, 1997. Various other citations are available.

5   Peter Curran, "An unsung hero touches home base in the big time," *The Age* (Melbourne, Australia), December 17, 1989: 25.

6   "Aussie in love with baseball," Associated Press, March 29, 1994.

7   Ibid.

8   Harvey Silver, "Vic rookies still stunned by their violent welcome," *The Age*, February 3, 1987: 44.

9   Curran, "An unsung hero touches home base in the big time"

10   Brad Elborough, "Pitching great Graeme Lloyd warns Perth Heat not to let chance slip," *Perth Times*, February 9, 2012.

11   "Jays sign Australian lefty who 'can throw strikes,'" *Toronto Star*, January 30, 1988: B5.

12   "1998 World Series—The Scout's View: Yankees." SI.com. (http://sportsillustrated.cnn.com/features/1998/weekly/981012/yankee.html)

13   Harvey Silver, "Vics in 11-0 Claxton Shield Rout," *The Age*, February 2, 1988: 44.

14   Curran, "An unsung hero touches home base in the big time."

15   Ziegel, "Lloyd No Longer Sheepish Over Trade."

16   Curran, "An unsung hero touches home base in the big time,"

17   Tom Haudricourt, "Lloyd makes Brewers debut," *Milwaukee Sentinel*, April 12, 1993: 1B.

18   Bob Berghaus, "Nilsson, Doran return after rehabilitation stints," *Milwaukee Journal*, April 15, 1993: C6.

19   Bob Berghaus, "Cause for concern," *The Sporting News*, May 3, 1993: 27.

20   Bob Berghaus, "Early finish," *The Sporting News*, October 4, 1993: 29.

21   Jason Diamos, "Yanks, Seeking Relief, Trade for a Left-Hander," *New York Times*, August 24, 1996.

22   John Giannone, "Cracking Up: Watson Tells AL to Void Graeme," *New York Daily News*, September 25, 1996.

23   Bill Madden, "Graeme Rewards Lloyalty," *New York Daily News*, October 23, 1996.

24   "Around the Bases," *Sarasota Herald-Tribune*, February 24, 1998: 6C.

25   David Lennon, "Brawl Comes with a Price," *Newsday* (Long Island, New York), May 21, 1998.

26   "Griffey Fenced In," *Hartford Courant*, April 9, 2000.

27   Eileen Schulte, "Storm adds to troubled year," *St. Petersburg Times*, August 20, 2000.

28   "Lloyd covets closer's role," *Toronto Star*, February 19, 1999: Sports-1.

29   "Rockies Report," *The Gazette* (Colorado Springs, Colorado), April 27, 2000. Associated Press, April 29, 2000. "National League Notes," *Atlanta Journal-Constitution*, May 9, 2000. *St. Petersburg Times*, August 6, 2000.

30   Schulte, "Storm adds to troubled year."

31   Ibid.

32   Alex Brown, "After major diversions, Lloyd is now a pitcher of success," *Sydney Morning Herald*, August 14, 2004.

33   Elborough, "Pitching great Graeme Lloyd warns Perth Heat not to let chance slip."

34   Frederick J. Day, *Clubhouse Lawyer: Law in the World of Sports* (Lincoln, Nebraska: iUniverse, 2002), 191-192.

35   Jim Fream, "Marlins' Lloyd a Real Pro," *Lakeland* (Florida) *Ledger*, July 28, 2002: C8.

36   Mark Long, "Arbitrator upholds Lloyd trade," Associated Press, July 24, 2002.

37   Adam Rubin, "Ex-Yank Lloyd Gets Crack at Mets Pen," *New York Daily News*, January 25, 2003.

38   Rafael Hermoso, "Mets' Purge Continues as Royals Take Lloyd," *New York Times*, July 29, 2003.

39   Alex Brown, "Red Sox fiasco puts stamp in Lloyd's Olympic passport," *Sydney Morning Herald*, June 17, 2004.

40   Ibid.

41   Mike Dodd, "Cuba, less than intimidating, takes gold," *USA Today*, August 26, 2004: D10.

42   Gene Stephan, "Lloyd eyes home base," *The West Australian*, November 7, 2008, 57. Brad Elborough, "Perth Heat marquee signing Graeme Lloyd arrives in Perth," *Perth Times*, November 5, 2008.

43   Elborough, "Pitching great Graeme Lloyd warns Perth Heat not to let chance slip"

44   Gene Stephan, "Lloyd to pitch in and help with Heat," *The West Australian*, September 26, 2011.

45   E-mail from Geoff Hooker to Rory Costello, March 3, 2012.

46   Ibid.

JASON JOHNSON

By Ryan Brecker

RIGHT-HANDED PITCHER Jason Johnson overcame a diagnosis of insulin-dependent diabetes mellitus as a youth to forge an 11-year major-league career during which he became the first ballplayer to wear an insulin pump on the field of play.

Jason Michael Johnson was born on October 27, 1973, in Santa Barbara, California, to John and Deanna Johnson. The family moved to Elk Ridge, Utah for a stretch of five years where John Johnson opened and operated a photography store and studio for five years. They later moved to Kentucky when John Johnson got a job offer to work as a district manager at CPI Photo Finishing. John Johnson later in life designed and sold sculptures. Deanna Johnson worked as a respiratory therapist for 20 years before becoming a flight attendant for the final 14 years of her career. The second of five children, Jason had an older brother who died in a car accident at age 16 and three younger sisters. Growing up sports-crazed, he was 11 years old when he developed typical diabetic symptoms including chronic dehydration and fatigue, leading to a diagnosis of insulin-dependent diabetes mellitus. Regarding his diagnosis, Johnson noted in 2006, "My first fear was that I couldn't play baseball anymore. Baseball and basketball were my two favorite things to do. That was tough, as a kid."[1]

Having had an aunt who died as a result of diabetes, Johnson and his family were somewhat familiar with the disease. His father in particular provided encouragement that helped as Johnson recalled in 2006: "My dad said, 'Don't let this stop you from doing anything you want to. If you love to play sports, keep doing it. You're not going to be any different than anyone else when it comes to that.' That always stuck with me."[2] He grew into a 6-foot-6 baseball and basketball star at Conner High School in Hebron, Kentucky. His major-league playing weight is listed at 225 pounds.[3] He was talented enough in basketball to earn a scholar-ship offers from multiple Division 1 schools including Morehead State and Richmond. Johnson's first love, however, was baseball, and he turned down the scholarships. He fell out of the MLB draft after a high-profile outing in which he topped out at only 78 mph, more than 10 mph below his normal velocity after having stayed out most of the night before.

After high school Johnson joined an amateur youth travel team in Ohio, the Midland Redskins, where he was quickly offered a tryout with the Pittsburgh Pirates after bird-dog scout Buck Buchanan saw him throw only one pitch. At the tryout he showed a velocity return to the low 90s and was quickly signed by Pirates scout Steve Demeter as a nondrafted free agent in July of 1992.

Once joining the Pirates system, Johnson made his professional debut in Bradenton and advanced slowly, pitching at the Class-A level for his first five seasons while compiling a 15-38 record. Johnson had to carefully monitor his blood sugar during games, virtually between every inning, and related this anecdote in a 2005 interview: "One time when I was pitching in Single-A for the Pirates, the pitching coach realized I was a little shaky. He hid a Coke under his jacket, walked to the mound like he was going to give me a talk and whole infield gathered around so no one could see me bend down and drink the Coke. Everyone acted like we were just talking and, sure enough, in a couple of minutes I was fine and continued to pitch."[4]

Johnson's career and life nearly came to abrupt end in December of 1996 when he was involved in a serious car accident after his Jeep hydroplaned. Johnson wasn't breathing when found by first responders, but was revived and later found to have a fractured skull, clavicle, and mandible. Johnson made a remarkable recovery and made great strides during the 1997 season, that he credited entirely to gaining better control of his diabetes.[5] While starting back with Class-A Lynchburg, he earned a July call-up to Double-A

Carolina and a subsequent big-league call-up in late August on the strength of his first winning record as a professional (11-7, and a 3.85 earned-run average, with 155 strikeouts in 156⅔ innings between the two levels).

In his major-league debut, on August 27, 1997, Johnson relieved Steve Cooke in the top of the second inning at Pittsburgh's Three Rivers Stadium. Johnson inherited two baserunners and was rudely greeted by Mike Piazza, giving up a three-run home run to the future Hall of Famer on his first pitch in the majors. He pitched three innings of relief on September 1 and two more innings on September 27, for a total of three appearances for the Pirates late in the 1997 season.

Expansion came to baseball for the 1998 season and Johnson's overall success in 1997 made him attractive in the expansion draft, in which he was taken by the Tampa Bay Devil Rays with their seventh pick. Johnson started the season at Triple-A Durham, but was recalled after only two starts when an injury opened a spot in the big-league rotation. He made 13 starts before being sidelined himself by a stress fracture in his lower back sustained while taking batting practice; the injury kept him out the rest of the regular season. He was 2-5 for Tampa Bay. Johnson was recovered enough to participate in the Arizona Fall League, where he was named AFL Pitcher of the Year and one of the top two right-handed pitching prospects in the circuit on the strength of his league record-tying seven wins for the Grand Canyon Rafters. Highlighting the eventful year, Jason and his wife, Stacey, were married over the All-Star break.

Another change of address was in store for the 1999 season as Johnson was traded to the Baltimore Orioles at the end of spring training for outfielder Danny Clyburn and a player to be named later (Bolivar Volquez). Optioned to Triple-A Rochester, Johnson made eight starts for the Red Wings before being recalled for the remainder of the 1999 season. Over 22 games and 21 starts, he went 8-7, finishing strong on a five-game win streak over his last seven starts. The injury bug bit again as he had to miss his last start of the year due to a broken toe.

Johnson was a favorite to make the Orioles rotation in 2000, but a poor spring training resulted in a return

to Rochester. He quickly made his way back to the majors after being named the International League Pitcher of the Week for April 17-23 on the strength of a five-hit shutout. He was unable to build on this success in the majors as he started the year 0-8, despite lasting into at least the fifth inning in 12 of his 13 starts. Returned to Triple-A, he continued to show he had little to prove in the minors with a 1.80 ERA over his five starts and returned to the Baltimore bullpen for the remainder of the 2000 campaign, finishing the year 1-10 with a 7.02 ERA.

That winter brought two significant changes for Johnson that furthered his career. First, believing he was too easily distracted on the mound, he enrolled in focus training at the suggestion of the Orioles vice president of baseball operations, Syd Thrift. Johnson noted that after this training, "I'm able to get in a zone out there where I only see my catcher."[6] Second, after meeting with an insulin-pump manufacturer, Johnson

started wearing an insulin pump on days he wasn't pitching. This led to tighter control over his blood sugars along with an increase in energy. These changes allowed Johnson to spend all of 2001 in the Orioles starting rotation, leading the team with 10 wins and 15 quality starts over his 32 games.

This success was noticed by the Boston Baseball Writers Association and Johnson was awarded the Tony Conigliaro Award for spirit and determination in overcoming obstacles, in Johnson's case his diabetes. (He shared the award with Graeme Lloyd.) The Orioles also noticed his success, and bought out his first two arbitration years with a two-year, $4.7 million contract. Additional off-field success included being named the Baltimore Orioles representative to the Major League Baseball Players Association.

Johnson was a rotation mainstay for the Orioles in 2002; although two separate DL stints—one for a broken finger and one for shoulder tendinitis—limited him to 22 starts and a dismal 5-14 record. During spring training in 2003, Johnson suffered a hypoglycemic seizure, but did not require hospitalization. He was able to remain healthy for the full season in 2003; Johnson made 32 starts for the Orioles, finishing with a 10-10 record. With his two-year contract expiring, and the Orioles fearing a significant raise in arbitration, he was nontendered and released in December of 2003.

Johnson was not unemployed long, as the Detroit Tigers signed him less than 10 days later to a two-year, $7 million pact. On the advice of Kevin Rand, the Tigers trainer, Johnson sought approval from Major League Baseball to start wearing his insulin pump during games. "When I first got the insulin pump, I figured they'd never let me wear this on my belt," he said. "No one else in the league had ever worn one during a game, and I thought hitters would complain about it being different and that it would throw them off."[7] MLB did grant approval, and Johnson started wearing the pump during games; moving it to his lower right back to stay out of the way of batted balls.

A strong spring training resulted in Johnson making the 2004 Opening Day start for the Tigers. He experienced some success over his two seasons with the Tigers—highlighted by winning the July 11, 2004,

AL Player of the Week Award. He also became the first Tigers pitcher to hit a home run in the DH era, connecting off the Los Angeles Dodgers' Jeff Weaver on June 8, 2005. Over his two seasons with the Tigers he was an innings-eater, tossing 406⅔ innings over 66 starts, but with an overall record of 16-28 for the second-division club.

Another change of address was in store for 2006 as Johnson signed an incentive-laden contract with the Cleveland Indians worth a guaranteed $4 million for one year; but worth up to $11.5 million over two years. The honeymoon was short-lived however, as he was designated for assignment after going 3-8 in only 14 starts for the Tribe. Claimed by the Boston Red Sox on June 21, he started six games without any more success (he was 0-4), was released, and finished the year with four appearances in the Cincinnati Reds bullpen.

An opportunity across the Pacific presented itself for the 2007 season and Johnson signed with the Seibu Lions of Japan's Pacific League. Shoulder injuries limited him to a 1-4 record over seven games. Returning stateside in 2008; he pitched most of the year at Triple-A Las Vegas, a Dodgers farm team, but did make it back to the big leagues for 16 games with the Dodgers; including a start of six scoreless innings in his first appearance back.

Signing a minor-league contract with the Yankees for the 2009 season, Johnson hoped to make the big-league club out of spring training, but was diagnosed with choroidal melanoma, a cancerous growth behind his right eye that required surgery and implantation of a radiation plaque. He did pitch in nine minor-league games, but was unable to make it back to the major leagues. He married his second wife, Ember Blueggel, in November of 2009.

After missing the 2010 season with shoulder surgery, Johnson attempted comebacks in the independent leagues with the Camden Riversharks in 2011 and the Amarillo Sox in 2013 but was unable to make a full recovery from the shoulder surgery.

After retiring from baseball, Johnson remained active, living in the Tampa area with his wife and two daughters. He became a certified scuba diver in 2007 and began giving pitching lessons. He became very active in fundraising and education with the Juvenile Diabetes Research Foundation, and has served as an ambassador for MiniMed, a company that manufactures insulin pumps. A role model for those with diabetes, Johnson noted in 2005, "Some people might think it's a bad break to have diabetes, but I think the disease has affected my career in a positive way. I'm succeeding in life at my chosen profession, and I get a chance to help people too. I tell kids all the time to never give up. Never let anyone tell you that you can't do something."[8]

SOURCES

In addition to the sources cited in the Notes, the author also consulted Jason Johnson's player file at the National Baseball Hall of Fame Library, the *2003 Baltimore Orioles Media Guide*, and the following articles:

Carig, Marc. "New York Yankees' Jason Johnson Battling Eye Cancer While Trying to Make Final Roster," nj.com/yankees/index.ssf/2009/03/new_york_yankees_jason_johnson.html, March 19, 2009, accessed August 6, 2016.

Hawbaker, Karrie. "Behind The Photo: Jason Johnson," loop-blog.com/minimed-ambassador-jason-johnson/, accessed August 6, 2016.

Nadel, John. "Jason Johnson Pitches Dodgers Past Giants 2-0," *USA Today*, usatoday30.usatoday.com/sports/baseball/2008-07-30-2989047442_x.htm, July 30, 2008, accessed August 6, 2016.

Strauss, Joe. "Pumped-Up Johnson Adds Tony C. Award to 10 Wins," *Baltimore Sun*, articles.baltimoresun.com/2001-12-12/sports/0112120268_1_johnson-conigliaro-tony-saunders, December 12, 2001, accessed August 6, 2016.

"Jason Johnson Biography," dlife.com/diabetes/famous_people/sports/jason_johnson_biography, November 28, 2012, accessed August 6, 2016.

NOTES

1   Anthony Castrovince, "Diabetes Doesn't Have Johnson Down," mlb.com, m.mlb.com/news/article/138303//, April 5, 2006, accessed August 6, 2016.

2   Ibid.

3   According to baseball-reference.com. Retrosheet.org lists him at 220 pounds.

4   Jason Johnson with Dennis Tuttle, "It's Always a Roller-Coaster Ride," espn.com/espn/print?id=2112188&type=Story&imagesPrint=off, July 20, 2005, accessed August 8, 2016.

5   Jason Johnson, telephone interview with author, August 26, 2016.

6   *The Sporting News*, June 25, 2001.

7   Bill Finley, "BASEBALL; Belt Pump Helps Pitcher With Diabetes," *New York Times*, nytimes.com/2004/07/06/sports/baseball-belt-pump-helps-pitcher-with-diabetes.html?_r=0, July 6, 2004, accessed August 6, 2016.

8   "It's Always a Roller-Coaster Ride."

JOSE RIJO

By Charles F. Faber

FEW, IF ANY, BASEBALL PLAYERS have ever had as many peaks and valleys in their careers or in their lives as José Rijo. Raised in poverty in the Dominican Republic, he signed a contract with the New York Yankees at age 15. After three years in the minor leagues, he made it to the majors at the age of 18. Battling injuries, he was unable to win consistently and was traded twice in four years. He married the daughter of his country's most celebrated pitcher, and sued her for divorce. Although he missed part of the 1990 season due to injuries, he recovered in time to help pitch the Cincinnati Reds to a world championship, and was named the Most Valuable Player of the 1990 World Series. He became a hero to his countrymen. In 1995 Rijo was sidelined with a serious elbow injury and was out of baseball for five years. In 2001 he attempted a comeback, but was again struck by injuries. He twice won an award for exemplary conduct on and off the field. He won the Tony Conigliaro Award for his spirit, determination, and courage in overcoming adversity. After retiring as a player he became an assistant to the general manager of the Washington Nationals. He was fired amid allegations of improprieties in a baseball academy he operated in the Dominican Republic. His academy was closed. He was investigated for his association with a person accused of drug trafficking and money laundering. He was not found guilty of any wrongdoing. As of 2015 Rijo was once again helping young Dominicans with baseball aspirations. Once again he is a hero in his native land.

José Antonio Rijo Abreu was born on May 13, 1965, in the municipality of San Cristobal, in San Cristobal Province, Dominican Republic, on the Caribbean coast about 20 miles east of Santo Domingo in the sugar-cane producing area of the island. He was the son of Glady Abreu, a nurse, and Reynardo Rijo, a taxi driver, the 10th of the elder Rijo's 13 children. José's father left the family when the boy was 4 years old. José then shared cramped quarters in an aluminum-roofed four-bedroom house with his mother, grandparents, aunts, uncles, and many of his brothers, sisters, and half-siblings. "We were so poor," José said, "I had to play ball in a friend's shoes, which were too small. The shoes were so tight and worn out I had blisters on each of my toes."[1] He didn't see his father again for 19 years.[2]

Very little is known about José's early childhood. He was called Chago in his homeland, but the nickname never caught on in the United States. Like many Dominican boys he probably learned baseball in the streets of his impoverished hometown. His first baseball may have been homemade, with a small pebble in the center and strips of cloth wound tightly around the core. Bats may have been broomsticks or tree branches. When he was 12 José was playing on an organized club equipped with real balls and real bats. He was very good, a *jugador de beisbol estrella* (star baseball player).

After Jackie Robinson broke the color barrier, the Dominican Republic became a prime source of major-league baseball players. By the time José was a teenager, scouts were flocking to the Dominican Republic in search of talented players. On August 1, 1980, scout Willie Calvino signed 15-year-old José Rijo to a contract with the New York Yankees for $3,500. The youngster quit school in the ninth grade. "I signed because I hated school, and my family needed the money," he explained. "I knew leaving school was a big gamble. If I didn't succeed in baseball, I didn't know what I would do."[3]

Rijo never said so publicly, but it must have been quite a thrill for a poor 15-year-old Dominican boy to sign a contract with the New York Yankees, who often were regarded as the most prominent baseball club in the entire world.

Major League Baseball now prohibits the signing of Caribbean players under the age of 16, but that rule was not in effect in 1980. Anyway, Rijo turned 16 before he started his professional career in 1981 in the Yankees farm system at $600 per month. In his first year, he was used sparingly for the Yankees team in the Rookie-level Gulf Coast League, winning three and losing the same number. In 1982 he was promoted to Paintsville, Kentucky, in the Advanced Rookie Appalachian League, where he posted an 8-4 record. Rijo later said that he had had pain in his elbow ever since he was 17 years old. An x-ray taken of his elbow in 1982 showed a bone abnormality, possibly a bone spur. But he kept pitching. Sometimes the pain got worse; sometimes it got better.

In 1983 Rijo was assigned to the Fort Lauderdale Yankees of the Class-A Florida State League. He was a skinny 18-year-old who still didn't speak English. He resolved to try to learn three English words every day.[4] He found lodging in a street near the beach that was home to drug users and hoods. Homesick, he spent most of his money on phone calls back to his family in the Dominican. Luckily, he heard about a local family that was known to take in an occasional Latin player. John Cummings was a computer programmer and his wife had come from Mexico. They weren't eager to take in another ballplayer. Caring for players was very demanding on their schedule. They had to take them to and from the ballpark, but they decided to take José in. "He was just like our baby," Cummings said. "He was the only one we got really close to, to the point where he was like a member of the family. He was one of those guys you could never stay mad at. He did what he did because he didn't want anything to mess up his chance at a career in baseball. When he came back for spring training in '84 … there was a major-league rule that players had to stay at the team hotel. Rijo refused to, because he wanted to stay with us."[5]

Rijo had his best minor-league season in 1983, going 15-5 with an ERA of 1.68 for Fort Lauderdale before being promoted to the Nashville Sounds of the Double-A Southern League (3-2). He led the Florida State League in wins, complete games, and earned-run average. He was named the league's Most Valuable Player. This performance earned Rijo a promotion to "The Show." At age 18 he was on top of the baseball world.

In 1984 Rijo won the James P. Dawson Award as the best rookie in the Yankees' spring-training camp. He achieved his goal of reaching the major leagues. George Steinbrenner, owner of the Yankees, hoped Rijo could compete with Dwight Gooden, the sensational teenage pitcher of the New York Mets, for the affection of Gotham's fans. On April 5, 1984, the 6-foot-1, 200-pound right-hander made his major-league debut. Rijo entered the game against Kansas City at the Royals Stadium in the third inning, with two on, two out, and the Yankees trailing, 14-0. He struck out Greg Pryor, the very first major-league hitter he ever faced. He finished the game, giving up only one earned run on four hits and two walks, while striking out five in 5⅓ innings. It appeared to be an excellent start to a stellar major-league career. However, Rijo's high hopes for a great rookie season soon came crashing down. He won only two games and lost eight that year. He could not match the flamboyant Gooden either on the mound or in the hearts of fandom. On December 5, 1984, he was traded along with Tim Birtsas, Jay Howell, Stan Javier, and Eric Plunk to the Oakland Athletics for Bert Bradley, Rickey Henderson, and cash.

Rijo was pleased about the trade. "I think I had the Yankees mixed up in my head last year," he said. "I had a lot of pitching coaches in New York. One told me to do things one way. One told me to do things that way, and I was kind of confused. … I'm really happy to be here. I hope I play here the rest of my life. There is less pressure here. It is a better place for a young player to play."[6]

Rijo was disgruntled with the way the Yankees handled him. "I came in as a reliever," he said. "Then two days later they told me I was going to be a starter. People don't know about that feeling."[7]

When Rijo reported to the A's he was tired from playing winter ball. He told teammate Jay Howell that his arm and shoulder were bothering him and that made him throw everything up. He had no breaking ball. He claimed that he had lost it in New York

nocently admits to counting his strikeouts as the game goes along."[10] Cohn concluded that Rijo's apparent arrogance was not a character flaw, but a prerequisite to greatness. In order to be successful, Cohn wrote, a pitcher must believe in his abilities, must cultivate the sin of pride.[11]

When he was healthy Rijo showed flashes of brilliance. On April 19, 1986, he struck out 16 Seattle Mariners at the Kingdome for a club record. Five days later, in a game at the Oakland-Alameda County Stadium against the same Mariners, he pitched a two-hitter while striking out 14. Once again he appeared on the brink of stardom. He was on top of the world. But once again the euphoria didn't last.

Shortly after his outstanding performance against Seattle, Rijo developed a problem with his left leg. At times he had no feeling in the leg. Unable to throw his fastball, he had to rely on his slider. In June he told a writer for the *Kansas City Times*, "Last night was bad, I couldn't get any sleep. I've got to forget about my leg, but it's a little tough. Right now I'm just running around. I haven't thrown a good fastball yet. I don't feel it yet. … My leg is dancing all over the place when I plant it. I have no control."[12]

The A's tried Rijo in the bullpen, but that didn't work. They moved him back into the rotation, to no avail. He won nine games for the A's in 1986, and only two in 1987. Before the '87 season was over, he was sent back down to Tacoma.

During the season Rijo was dating Rosie Marichal, a student at San Francisco State University and the daughter of Hall of Fame pitcher Juan Marichal, the most celebrated pitcher ever to come out of the Dominican Republic. Marichal did not know the two were dating, and when the couple announced wedding plans he was furious. "Maybe because he knows how ballplayers are, the lifestyle of the guys," Rijo said. "I don't blame him. I had the reputation of going out a lot. … The hunt was on every day."[13] Rosie and José were married in September. It was José's second marriage. Very little is known about his marriage to Alma Rijo, his first wife.

On December 8, 1987, Rijo was traded along with pitcher Tim Birtsas to the Cincinnati Reds for aging

when they were flip-flopping him between starting and relieving.[8]

Rijo's stay in Oakland was marked by injuries. In 1985 he split the season between Oakland and the Tacoma Tigers, the A's farm club in the Triple-A Pacific Coast League. While in Tacoma he developed a changeup to go with his fastball and slider. In 1986 he was brought back up to Oakland. During spring training he missed a couple of days of practice because he had an infection on his right toe. Manager Jackie Moore blamed the infection on Rijo trying to be trendy and not wearing socks.[9]

In the spring of 1986 Rijo was still chafing from comparisons with Gooden. He told Bay Area sportswriter Lowell Cohn that he could have matched Gooden's 24 victories the previous season if he had been given the chance. Was Rijo a cocky kid who should shut up until he gets a respectable season under his belt? Cohn wrote that Rijo knew he had a rare talent, was not bragging but only stating what he believed to be facts. "When you talk to him, he is pleasant enough. He tends to wear loud clothes like flaming red slacks with white shoes and no socks, but he speaks softly, shakes hands with reporters, in-

slugger Dave Parker. In three years with the A's he had won only 17 games.

Rijo began his Cincinnati career as a middle reliever. His first appearance for the Reds came on Opening Day. He pitched the sixth and seventh innings at Riverfront Stadium as the Reds downed the St. Louis Cardinals, 5-4. His next appearance came in the 16th inning of a game in Cincinnati five days later. He was hit hard, gave up five runs, and was charged with the loss as the Reds fell, 8-3, to Houston. It was the only game Rijo was to lose in relief all season. Over the next several weeks he was dominant in the sixth, seventh, and eighth innings. He credited his success to manager Pete Rose's faith in his judgment. "At Oakland I wasn't smart enough to call my own pitches. They called all of them. I went through hell but I learned," he said.[14]

By early June Rijo had won six games against only one loss. He was happy as a reliever. However, the Reds traded away starting pitcher Dennis Rasmussen on June 8, and they needed another starter. That very night Rose pressed Rijo to fill that role. In his first start he defeated the San Diego Padres, 7-1, giving up only one run on two hits in six innings and striking out eight Padres. Instead of basking in his success, Rijo was conflicted. "I consider myself a relief pitcher, and I don't want to ruin it by starting over. Tonight I help the team as best I can. Now I hope I can go back to my bullpen. I hope somebody else can do the starts"[15]

Rose responded by saying, "He wants to go back to the bullpen? Tell him he can go back to the bullpen — until Tuesday night against Houston, his next start. … I have him penciled in for 21 more starts between now and the end of the season. He's a real horse, and he going to win a lot of games — as a starter."[16] As it turned out, Rijo made 19 starts and won 7 of 14 decisions as a starter, giving him a 13-8 record for the year. In August he experienced pain and weakness in his shoulder and was placed on the 21-day disabled list on August 18, the first of 10 times he was put on the DL during his career in Cincinnati. He was reinstated on September 8 and pitched well the remainder of the season.

The Reds were counting on Rijo to be one of their top pitchers and perhaps help them win a pennant in 1989. After finishing second in the National League West for four consecutive seasons, the Reds had reasonable expectations for a championship in '89. They got off to a great start, leading the division in April and much of May. Then the injury bug hit. Player after player went down, and the Reds plunged all the way to fifth place. The Reds had counted on Rijo being a big winner. He had a record of 7-6 with a 2.84 ERA on July 17 when he suffered a stress fracture in his lower back, which sidelined him for the remainder of the season.

After the 1989 season ended Rosie and José became parents of a baby boy, José Jr., called Josie. But their marriage was already beginning to come apart. "She didn't want me to visit my friends, go out and have a drink, whatever. She wanted me to let her know everything I do, where I spend my money and what I spend it on. … It's tough having someone trying to control you," he said. "When the woman wants to take control, you know, it ain't going to work. You know a man is a man. And I wear the pants in the house. I bring the food into the house, so I should have control"[17] Despite marital discord, the union endured throughout the 1990 season.

How Cincinnati would fare in 1990 depended, among other things, on how the wounded troops recovered from their injuries and how the players responded to their new manager, Lou Piniella. The results were positive on both fronts. Most of the players recovered from their injuries, and most of them responded well to Piniella's fiery leadership. The Reds got off to a terrific start, winning nine consecutive games to start the season, and were never headed, leading their division wire-to-wire. Although Rijo had been expected to be the club's ace, he was unable to contribute to the streak, suffering from tendinitis in his throwing shoulder. However, other pitchers picked up the slack. When Rijo won his first game of the season, on the last day of April, Cincinnati's record was 13-3. Of course, they couldn't keep winning at that pace, but they held onto first place. On June 29 Rijo went on the disabled list with a muscle strain in his right shoulder. The Reds were 45-26 at that point, and Rijo was 5-3. When Rijo returned on July 21 the

Reds were 57-32. Rijo won his first game back after being reinstated, but lost three of next five decisions.

During the dog days of August the Reds were losing more often than winning. They lost five in a row from August 17 to 20. On August 21 pitching coach Stan Williams lit a fire under Rijo. He called the starting pitchers together and told them he was thinking about going to a four-man rotation. "Awesome," Rijo said.[18] "Well, good, José, because you're not one of them," replied the coach.[19] Piniella said the rotation would include Tom Browning, Danny Jackson, Norm Charlton, and either José Rijo or Jack Armstrong—"whoever is pitching well."[20]

In fact, Williams and Piniella did not go to a four-man rotation. If the gambit was intended as a motivational ploy, it worked. Over his next nine starts, Rijo went 6-2 with a 1.27 ERA. Sportswriters John Erardi and Joel Luckhaupt wrote that Rijo put the Reds on his back and carried them to the finish line.[21]

The Reds won the division and faced the favored Pittsburgh Pirates in the National League Championship Series. As the ace of the staff, Rijo drew the assignment to start the first game of the NLCS at Riverfront Stadium. He pitched 5⅓ innings, being relieved by Norm Charlton with two on and one out and the score tied, 3-3, in the top of the sixth inning. Charlton escaped the jam, but lost the game, 4-3, on a double by Andy Van Slyke in the seventh inning. After the series moved to Pittsburgh, Rijo started Game Four at Three Rivers Stadium. He picked up the victory this time, pitching seven innings in a 5-3 Cincinnati win. The Reds won the NLCS in six games for their first National League pennant since 1976.

The Reds faced the defending world champion Oakland Athletics in the 1990 World Series. Led by the "Bash Brothers," Mark McGwire and José Canseco, and featuring an outstanding pitching staff, the A's were overwhelming favorites. Manager Lou Piniella chose Rijo to start Game One, and Rijo was masterful, pitching seven shutout innings before turning the game over to Nasty Boys Rob Dibble and Randy Myers to nail down the 7-0 win. The Reds won Game Two, 5-4, and took Game Three, 8-3. It was Rijo's turn again in Game Four and he wrapped up the world championship for Cincinnati with another outstanding performance, pitching 8⅓ innings and giving up only one run. Myers came in to shut the door and the Reds claimed the game, 2-1. Rijo was named the Most Valuable Player of the World Series.

In the Series Rijo had twice defeated Dave Stewart, the ace of the Oakland staff. Stewart was not a gracious loser. He implied the Reds win was a fluke. "It's not always the best team that wins. It's the team that plays the best," he said. "I didn't take anything away from Cincinnati. I just wouldn't admit they were a better team than we were. I don't feel they were. I don't feel that now. They were just better than us in four games. It wasn't me that made the odds for the World Series. Someone else said we were going to win, we were the better team. Even the Cincinnati fans thought the Reds were going to lose."[22]

Less than two months after the end of the World Series, Rijo filed for divorce from his wife, Rosie. He alleged in the suit, filed in the Hamilton County (Ohio) Court of Common Pleas, that he and Rosie were incompatible and that Rosie was guilty of gross neglect of duty. Rosie denied the charges. "My husband, José, is a wonderful baseball player and a world-class athlete, but he has a lot to learn about marriage. José does not understand that a successful marriage, like a winning ballclub, requires the efforts of more than one player."[23] Rosie claimed that José never told her he was planning to sue for divorce. She said she learned about the divorce proceedings from news reports. "I'm in shock," she said. "We just came back from a cruise, and I'm pregnant."[24] (The Rijos' daughter, Sasha, was born the following summer.)

"I did tell her," José said, "but I think she always thought I was joking. She never thought I was going to do it. … I love Rosie. I love my wife. I don't think I'm ever going to find anyone better than her. She's a beautiful wife. She's the best cook I've ever seen. I treasure her a lot. She's a very reliable person. I just think her attitude was a little tough to deal with. She thought she was boss."[25]

Marge Schott, owner of the Reds, had tried to save the marriage. "There has been a problem that I worked very hard on with Rijo and his wife. … I got into their thing about a year ago. They've got a child, she's pregnant again. There's nothing I want more than Rijo and his wife to stay together."[26]

For his part, José resented Schott's interference. When her efforts to bring about a reconciliation failed, Schott provided a lawyer to look out for Rosie's financial interests. "She recommended her a lawyer," Rijo said. "That's personal life. Nobody should interfere with my personal life. But she tried to talk to me about getting back together. She didn't want me to get a divorce."[27]

"I don't want to be changing wives liked I've changed uniforms," Rijo said. "But a man's got to do what he's got to do."[28]

With divorce proceedings under way, it appeared the marriage was irretrievably doomed. Then, surprisingly, the couple quietly reconciled. Many pages had been written about the pending divorce, but no newspaper articles heralded the reconciliation. It was mentioned briefly in *USA Today Baseball Weekly*,[29] but otherwise ignored by the press. Apparently, news sources considered it a nonstory. Anyway, José and Rosie were back together again.

After his stellar performance in the 1990 World Series, Rijo had good reason to believe he deserved a large pay raise. In order to avoid arbitration, the Reds signed him to a three-year, $9 million contract. Dave Stewart, perhaps still smarting from his World Series losses, had some comments. "The money has gotten ridiculous in the game for mediocre players. I'm not saying he's not worth $3 million. I'm saying I don't think his statistics right now indicate he should be paid that kind of money. Maybe they're paying him on potential. You look at his statistics the last two, three years and I don't see $3 million worth. ... If you can get it, that's great. I can appreciate that. But a lot of guys are getting a lot of money when they haven't quite earned it yet. But if the owners want to give it, O.K. It works out good for players like myself who have earned it.[30]

Schott was asked if she thought Rijo was worth $3 million a year. Even though she was the one who authorized his salary, she replied. "He only had one really good year—last year. No, I don't, but I'm as guilty as the rest of the owners. I mean, who's worth that kind of money anyway? A person who runs General Motors doesn't get that kind of money. The president of the United States doesn't get that kind of money. Plus (pitchers) only play part-time."[31] Rijo, of course, thought he was worth every cent he was paid.

During the offseason Rijo spread some of his money around in the Dominican Republic. The World Series star was accorded a new status in his homeland. "I became a king," he said. "I was like some kind of hero, which I'm not. I'm just a very lucky person."[32] "I had 30 people a day asking me for money," he said. "And people started calling me El Millonario. Even my friends started looking at me differently, which made me feel sad."[33]

"People weren't just asking me for $100," he said. I had people asking me for 2 million pesos to make a business. One person wanted to sell me a hotel. Everybody had a different problem. Some people said, 'I need medicine for my baby.' Other people said, "I need some money to buy rum. ... It's sad. I like to help people who really need help. But people were trying to use me. And I hate to be used."[34] He built a fence around his mother's house to keep solicitors out.

In some ways Rijo was generous with his new-found wealth. When he returned to the Dominican, he took a load of gloves, bats, T-shirts, and tennis shoes to give to children. He spent about $60,000 for two ambulances, one for the police department, one for his hometown's hospital. "They deserve it," he said. "They need it. They suffer a lot. I've seen a lot of people die there because they didn't have transportation to a hospital. I figure as long as I've got the money, I can help them."[35]

Rijo didn't give all his money away. He spent plenty on his passion for classic automobiles. In 1989 he had purchased a cherry-red Porsche 960 Turbo from Pete Rose. By 1991 he was proudly driving a white BMW 750IL, one of seven cars he kept in his three residences in Florida, Ohio, and the Dominican Republic.[36]

During spring training in 1991 Rijo discussed his prospects for the future. "I'm capable of doing a lot of things if I can stay healthy for a full season," he said. "That's what I'm praying for, to be healthy for one full year and see what I can do. I've got one goal in mind, being in the All-Star Game and being the Cy Young winner."[37]

When asked about his inability to stay healthy, he replied: "It bothers me big time. It's happened the last three years and now you wonder if it's going to happen again."[38]

Rijo couldn't stay healthy. Shortly before Opening Day, he had some wisdom teeth removed, which contributed to manager Lou Piniella's decision to start Tom Browning rather than Rijo in the season's first game. Rijo was irate about the manager's action. "I don't think it's fair," he said.[39]

Injuries continued to haunt Rijo. In a game against the Montreal Expos at Riverfront Stadium on June 20, he broke an ankle while trying to steal second base. He missed six weeks, not returning to action until August 5. Meanwhile, dissension disrupted the clubhouse. The togetherness and camaraderie that had marked the championship season of 1990 was gone. Rijo contributed to the rancor. After a 13-0 loss in San Diego on August 11, he said, "It's hard to comprehend the situation, but when you see it, you believe it. I see a losing team. I see a team giving up with two months to go. Look at the game today. If you'd said we'd play like that, I'd have said 'No way.'"[40]

Four days later Rijo was pitching a shutout in the early innings of a game at San Francisco's Candlestick Park until Reds third baseman Chris Sabo committee an error that led to two unearned runs. After the Reds lost the game, 4-1, Rijo confronted Sabo in the dugout and took a swing at him. It took the efforts of six players to separate the two and prevent a real knockdown fight.[41]

His problems with his teammates were soon patched over. Around the first of September his elbow started hurting again, Rijo pitched through the pain and pitched some of the best baseball of his life. Seven shutout innings against Houston on September 15 earned him his sixth win in a row and brought his season record to 14-4. There was talk about Rijo as a candidate for the Cy Young Award. Piniella said, "José is developing into the best pitcher in the National League, pure and simple. He's really got it all together

out there. … As far as the best pitcher in the league, he's got my vote."[42]

José said, "I'm right at the top in almost every category. I don't know if they're going to take that (broken ankle) into consideration, but if they do, I'll have a fair shot. … I think I'm quickly developing into the luckiest pitcher in the league, the way my elbow feels."[43]

Alas, Rijo lost two of his last three starts and came in fourth in Cy Young voting. Nevertheless, he had a great season. Despite missing six weeks with a broken ankle, he won 15 games for the first time in his major-league career. He led the league in won-lost percentage and WHIP (walks plus hits per innings pitched), and was second in earned-run average and strikeouts per innings pitched.

In 1992 Rijo won 15 games again, despite another stint on the disabled list. He was on the DL from April 18 to May 3 because of an inflammation of his right elbow. When he returned, Piniella, with the advice of Dr. Frank Jobe and Dr. James Andrews, placed him on a pitch count of 65-70 pitches for the next six or seven starts. He was afraid Rijo would break down again if he tried to come back too quickly. When Rijo protested the pitch count, Piniella advised him to keep his mouth shut. "He's being paid to pitch. He'll do what we tell him. We're doing what's best for him."[44] According to Retrosheet, over the next seven games Rijo pitched, his lowest pitch count was 83; three times he exceeded 100 pitches.

While he was on the DL, Rijo was taking four capsules of a powerful anti-inflammatory drug daily. Because of possible dire effects, the drug, Butazolidin, commonly called Bute, was given only in cases of severe pain. Dr. Mark Siegel of the Cincinnati Sportsmedicine and Orthopaedic Center said, "It's kind of a drug of last resort. It's usually used in cases where you need a good response quickly because it's usually this or possibly surgery.[45]

Rijo hedged his bets on which religion could help him most. For a long time he kept a voodoo doll and a bottle of snake oil in his locker. In 1991 he looked for a new source of help. He started carrying a picture of Pope John Paul II in his shaving kit. Before a start in

Pittsburgh, he removed the picture from the case and propped it on a hook in his locker. He told himself, "If he falls off the hook, we lose. And if he hangs in there, we win."[46] Perhaps papal intervention paid off. At any rate, on July 2 Rijo pitched seven innings of six-hit ball, and the Reds beat Pittsburgh, 2-1, to end a three-game losing streak.

Rijo made it through the 1992 season without recourse to surgery, but it was extremely difficult. In July he didn't know if he could make it. His sore elbow was a major concern. "All I know is it's not getting any better. I'm trying to take it like a man. But I'm not having any fun even though we're winning. ... I'm trying. I'm doing my best. It's bad, but I've been able to swallow my pain and go out and pitch. ... but it's getting harder and harder."[47]

Somehow Rijo made it through the season. It may have been the Bute, or voodoo, or snake oil, or the pope, or just sheer determination on his part. His numbers weren't quite as good as they had been in '91, but they were still good. His strikeouts-to-walks ratio was second best in the National League.

The Cincinnati chapter of the Baseball Writers Association of America yearly presents the Joe Nuxhall Good Guy Award to a player who shows exemplary conduct on and off the field. The 1992 recipient was José Rijo. (Ten years later he won the award again, the first Red to be so honored twice.)

For the first time in six seasons with the Reds, Rijo avoided a stay on the DL in 1993. He won 14 games again. He could have won several more had he received a little more help from his teammates. Five potential victories were blown by the bullpen in the ninth inning and three more were lost by relievers in the eighth. In eight of his losses the Reds had scored a total of seven runs. He had good reason for his claim. "Given the lineup (Atlanta) had last year, and I probably would have won 25. It definitely would have been at least 20."[48]

Rijo led the league in strikeouts in 1993. He ranked second in ERA and third in WHIP. He led the league in games started and ranked second in innings pitched. Rijo finished fifth in balloting for the Cy Young Award in 1993. Despite those stellar numbers, Rijo was not

a happy camper in 1993. He and Rosie had marital problems and broke up again. (This breakup appeared to be permanent.) The Reds were beset with troubles. Owner Marge Schott was suspended from Organized Baseball for a year because of inappropriate remarks. Manager Tony Perez was fired. Rijo clashed with some of his teammates, including one expletive-filled tirade when he thought they were not supporting Perez. "To me he is the best manager we've ever had here. He lets us have fun, and he lets us know when we've done something wrong. He's been great.[49] After Perez was fired, Rijo said, "We've definitely reached the highest level of embarrassivity."[50]

The Reds lost 89 games, the most they had lost in a season since 1984. "There was no happiness," Rijo said. "There were no good times at all. It was all aggravation, irritation. To lose every day is not fun. Even though you're throwing the ball good, it's no consolation because you're supposed to do that. You've got to win. That's the most important thing."[51]

The Reds turned things around in 1994. They got off to a good start and led their division almost every day until the season came to an abrupt halt. Rijo's slider was one of the principal reasons for the Reds' success. While José was still a teenager, Pascual Perez taught him how to throw the pitch. The slider is typically so hard on the elbow that some clubs refuse to teach it to their young hurlers. Perhaps overuse of the slider is partially responsible for the elbow and shoulder injuries that plagued Rijo throughout much of his career. He refrained from throwing sliders between starts and in early exhibition games, but when the season started he was willing to throw sliders at any time. By 1994 he was throwing the slider 50 percent of the time. In a poll conducted by *The Sporting News*, Rijo's slider was voted best in the National League by an overwhelming margin. He received 43 votes; John Smoltz and Larry Andersen tied for second with four votes each.[52]

Rijo achieved one of his goals by being selected for the 1994 All-Star Game, although he did not pitch in the game. His record was 8-4 at the time. He won only one more game after the break. His hopes of competing in another World Series were thwarted when the baseball season was ended by a strike on August 12. Although the Reds were in first place at the time, there was no postseason for them or any other team. Rijo had a record of 9-6, with an ERA of 3.08. He led the league in games started and was second in strikeouts.

The work stoppage ended when US District Judge Sonia Sotomayor issued a preliminary injunction against the owners on March 31, 1995. After an abbreviated spring training, the season began in late April. The Reds were again expected to win the National League Central. Sportswriter Bob Nightengale foresaw Rijo winning the Cy Young Award that he had coveted for so long.[53] Instead Rijo's world came crashing down on him again.

On June 2 Rijo was placed on the DL with tendinitis in his right elbow. He came off the DL on June 17 and attempted to pitch again, but even with the help of cortisone shots the pain was too much. The bone spurs that had troubled him for years were getting worse. By 1995 the bone spurs were 2½ times larger than when he was 17. On July 19 he was put on the DL again in the hope that rest would relieve the pain and enable him to pitch effectively again. It didn't work. Magnetic resonance imaging (MRI) showed a partially torn ulnar collateral ligament (UCL) as well as some bone formation within the ligament. Some bleeding was detected.

On August 22, 1995, Tommy John surgery was performed on Rijo's right elbow by Dr. James Andrews in Birmingham, Alabama. The surgery consisted of removing a UCL and replacing it with a tendon from elsewhere in the body. Andrews estimated Rijo would be able to pitch again in about one year. He thought there was an 80 percent probability that Rijo would regain his full pitching capability. He cautioned that physical recovery after surgery is but a fraction of the recovery process. "What we're really talking about here is mind over matter," Andrews said. "We're talking about six months to a year or even more in recovery, and a player has to prepare for that mentally even more than what he has to endure physically. Surgery is just the first step in a long journey."[54]

Rijo was soon ready mentally to pitch, but the surgery did not end his physical problems. Rijo has been cited as one of the greatest failures of Tommy John surgery.[55]

Rijo was expected to miss most, if not all, of the 1996 season, but in early spring he appeared to be making great progress and was already throwing sliders in addition to fastballs. The Reds were not eager to reactivate him; not only did they not want to jeopardize his recovery by rushing him back too soon, but it was also to their financial advantage to keep him on the DL. Their insurance company was picking up all of his $5.9 million salary. They were right. Rijo did push himself too soon. During spring training he developed excruciating pain. He had to undergo a second surgery on his right shoulder on April 4, 1996. It was an arthroscopic procedure to remove elbow calcification, bone formation in his elbow and scar tissue. He started throwing again in late May, but he couldn't handle the strain. He had to undergo surgery again on November 20 to repair a ruptured flexor tendon, his third time under the knife in 15 months. There seemed no chance that he could pitch in 1997. By early March of that year, it seemed likely that Rijo would never pitch in the majors again.[56] On April 7 Dr. Andrews removed some sutures and scar tissue. However, Rijo kept trying. In August he severely injured the flexor tendon in his right elbow. The tendon was torn completely off the bone. The result was a fourth elbow surgery by Dr. Andrews on August 27. The Reds

granted Rijo free agency on October 29. On January 8, 1998, they signed him to a minor-league contract for 1998, but it was doubtful that he could pitch.

Rijo reported to the Reds' 1998 spring-training camp in Sarasota able to throw, but was told to wait a few weeks before pitching off a mound. He agreed to stay with the club as a scout if his comeback failed. He was told that the position of scout could lead to a role in management or as a pitching coach.[57] Nothing came of this agreement. He was granted free agency again on October 15, 1998.

In the spring of 1999, Rijo opened a baseball academy he built on a hillside on the southern coast of the Dominican Republic, near his hometown of

San Cristobal. *Lomo del Sueno,* he called it, Hill of Dreams. "I know a lot of dreams are going to come true there," he said.[58] The complex included seven baseball fields, 10 indoor batting cages, a track, two weight rooms, two dining rooms, four locker rooms, and housing for 600 youngsters. "This is my biggest pitch of my whole life. I can pass on all the knowledge that I learned about the game to those kids," he said.[59] In its first two years, his academy helped nearly 100 youths sign minor-league contracts.

For five years Rijo worked very hard at rehabilitation. He kept trying to come back but met setback after setback. In 2000 he said, "I'm going to lay off for a whole year, start traveling, eat steak, drink wine, have fun and forget about baseball for a year. … I was resting my mind and my arm both."[60] To keep himself in shape, the 35-year-old Rijo played basketball with the youngsters at his academy.

As he had so many times in the past, Rijo tried to make a comeback in 2001. His slider had lost some of its bite, but he had developed a forkball that dropped almost straight down, and he still had an effective fastball. In May he traveled to Cincinnati for medical exams to see if his rehabilitation had been complete enough for him to resume pitching. He passed the tests; On July 1 Rijo signed a free-agent contract with Cincinnati. The Reds sent him to Dayton of the Class-A Midwest League. He started one game for the Dragons, pitched three innings in which he allowed only one run, and was ready to move on. His next stop was at Chattanooga in the Double-A Southern League. He pitched three innings for the Lookouts, struck out three, walked one, and allowed one hit, but no runs. "Those were three good innings," he said. "My arm feels outstanding. My mechanics were good. … I feel ready (for the major leagues.)"[61]

In order to prove that he was indeed ready for the big leagues, Rijo needed to be tested at the highest minor-league level. He made four starts and two relief appearances for the Louisville Riverbats of the Triple-A International League before Jim Bowden, Cincinnati's general manager, pronounced him ready for prime time. He was called up on August 17. He pitched the eighth and ninth innings of a loss to the Milwaukee Brewers that evening. In two innings he gave up two hits, walked two, and struck out two. It was his first major-league appearance since 1997. Rijo became the first pitcher to return to the majors after having been out of Organized Baseball for five seasons.

Rijo's joy at returning to the majors was almost more than he could express. "I cannot describe with words how I feel right now. It's beyond anything in my life that I ever accomplished," Rijo said. "No moment could beat this moment today, until I die and go to heaven and meet Jesus. This feeling is that close. … I never thought it would take this long. Nobody has any idea how hard it was to be here today."[62]

After posting a 2.12 ERA in 13 appearances with the Reds in 2001, Rijo joined the Florida Instructional League to stay in shape so he could pitch in the Dominican Winter League. In January Rijo signed a minor-league contract for 2002, but he fully expected to pitch in the majors. That expectation was fulfilled. In March he was added to the Reds' 40-man roster and given a one-year contract for $500,000. "I feel like I'm a walking miracle right now," he said.[63]

Rijo started the 2002 season as a long reliever, but moved into the starting rotation on April 21. He went 4-3 in eight starts until his shoulder began giving him trouble. He went on the DL on June 7. He returned to action as a reliever on July 13. During the season he made nine starts and relieved 22 times, while compiling a 5-4 record. He didn't know it at the time, but his last major-league appearance came on September 28, 2002. The 37-year-old right-hander pitched the seventh inning of a 6-0 loss at Montreal, giving up one earned run on two hits and a walk.

Rijo received two well-deserved awards at the end of the season. Cincinnati baseball writers presented him with his second Joe Nuxhall Good Guy Award. The Boston Red Sox honored him with the Tony Conigliaro Award, given annually to the major-league baseball player who best overcomes adversity through spirit, determination, and courage.

Rijo was looking forward to another good year in 2003, but again adversity struck. During spring training his elbow began giving him trouble. On March 11 he flew to Birmingham, where Dr. Andrews performed an arthroscopic procedure to remove a bone spur, the sixth surgery on Rijo's elbow. Rijo expected to be back in action in a few weeks, but it didn't happen. By June he was feeling pain in a different part of the elbow. Dr. Andrews told him another operation was not an option. He had two choices—to pitch with the pain or to retire.[64]

Rijo could pitch through pain. He had done it before, and he was willing to do it again. But he couldn't pitch if he couldn't get the ball over the plate. Rijo admitted he couldn't handle any more surgeries.[65] So he really had no choice. He never threw another pitch in Organized Baseball. The Reds granted him free agency on October 15, 2003; his playing career was over at the age of 38.

For the next few years Rijo worked mainly at his baseball academy in the Dominican Republic. On November 1, 2004, Jim Bowden, Cincinnati's general manager, became general manager of the Washington Nationals. He hired Rijo as a special assistant, primarily to increase the organization's ability to attract Latin ballplayers, especially Dominicans. The Nationals developed a special relationship with Rijo's academy. Rijo also spent time in Washington during the season, working with the club's pitchers. "I have a lot of knowledge of the game," he said, "and it means a lot to me to share that knowledge with the young pitchers to help them get better."[66]

Rijo was credited with saving six young Cuban players from deportation. "They had left (Cuba) to look for a better life. They came over in a boat and were caught by the police.

They were very scared. When they learned they were going to be sent back to Cuba, they almost started crying. They said they would rather be shot in the Dominican," Rijo said. "They did not want to go back to receive the punishment they were going to receive."[67]

Rijo appealed to Dominican officials and got the players released so they could live and play at his academy.

Meanwhile, Rijo's career in Cincinnati was not forgotten. On June 11, 2005, he and Eric Davis were inducted into the Cincinnati Reds Hall of Fame. They were the first two players from the world champion 1990 Reds to be so honored. Rijo came back to the Queen City for the ceremony. "There were so many people I was looking forward to seeing here. It reminds you of some people who have left the game. It reminds you of the World Series. It reminds you of how far you've come and how much you can help other people. There are a lot of memories for me here; it has a place in my heart."[68]

Rijo reflected on Dominican baseball. "I think when you play the game in the Dominican, a Dominican kid does a lot with a little, doing the only thing he knows how to do, and that's playing ball. ... The desire to become a major-league player is unbelievable. You know that's the only way you're going to make a difference in your country. If I'm healthy, I'm happy. Every day when I wake up, I feel good, and I feel motivated. When I wake up in the morning, I think about the kids in the Dominican. There, 70 percent of the kids don't really have education; they help provide for their families. Some of them don't even know what they're going to eat in the morning."[69]

When asked about his responsibilities with the Nationals, Rijo replied: "Responsibilities? I have too many. I'm assistant GM, I'm a scout, and I'm also a part-time coach at the major-league level. But I'm going to do everything I can to stay around the game."[70]

Those were heady days for José Rijo. He zipped around the Dominican in his fire-engine-red Mercedes convertible, basking in the adoration of his countrymen. Rijo's relationship with the Washington Nationals lasted for more than four years. It came to an unhappy conclusion in February 2009. The Nationals fired Rijo and ended its association with his academy less than a week after it was revealed that prized prospect Esmailyn Gonzalez, who had trained at Rijo's academy before receiving a $1.4 million signing bonus in 2006, had lied about both his name and his age. Rijo denied any knowledge of wrongdoing.[71]

Rijo defended the lengths to which Dominican players will go, including identity fraud, to gain a foothold in North American baseball. Sociologist Alan Klein reported Rijo as saying, "We used to have a factory with 3,000 jobs. It's gone. We used to have a gun factory. Gone. Duty-free, gone. We used to have a hotel in this town. We don't have one anymore. We used to have three movie theaters. We don't have movies anymore. All the job opportunities here are gone. What's people going to do? Be honest? And get a job where?"[72]

Supply and demand outweighed some other considerations. The Dominican has a seemingly inexhaustible supply of young men seeking baseball careers. The major leagues have a demand for more and more talented players. Baseball academies are thriving on the island. Every major-league club now operates an academy. Other academies are operated by entrepreneurs, called *buscones,* who furnish room and board, baseball training, and sometimes English-language instruction to 13- to 15-year-olds, In the expectation of receiving 15 percent of the player's signing bonus, if he is offered a professional contract at age 16.

Soon after Rijo was cleared of any wrongdoing in the Gonzales case, Rijo was back working in an academy as a *buscon.* In 2009 he was still indulging in his passion for automobiles, driving a white Lexus SC430 convertible. But he couldn't avoid suspicion. In December 2011 he was subpoenaed for questioning about his possible involvement in money-laundering for drug traffickers. No concrete evidence was found, and the case was dropped.

Once again Rijo was back in the good graces of his countrymen. How long that would continue remained to be seen.

NOTES

1   *Washington Post,* April 11, 1991.

2   Ibid.

3   *Washington Post,* April 11, 1991.

4   *USA Today,* February 28, 1991.

5   Clipping in Rijo's Hall of Fame File, no date.

6   HOF file, April 3, 1985.

7   HOF file, no date.

8   HOF file, no date.

9   *The Sporting News,* March 10, 1986.

10   HOF file, no date.

11   Ibid.

12   *Kansas City Times.,* June 24, 1986.

13   *Washington Post,* April 11, 1991.

14   *The Sporting News,* May 9, 1988.

15   *The Sporting News,* June 20, 1988.

16   Ibid.

17   *Washington Post,* April 11, 1991

18   John Erardi and Joel Luckhaupt, *The Wire-to-Wire Reds.* (Cincinnati: Clerisy Press, 2010), 164.

19   Ibid.

20   Ibid.

21   Ibid.

22   *New York Times,* March 1, 1991.

23   *Washington Post,* April 11, 1991.

24   HOF file, December 14, 1990.

25   *The National Sports Daily,* no date.

26   *USA Today,* February 28, 1991.

27   *New York Times,* March 13, 1991.

28   *USA Today,* February 28, 1991.

29   *USA Today Baseball Weekly,* March 4-10, 1992.

30   *New York Times,* March 1, 1991.

31   *Washington Post,* April 11, 1991.

32   *New York Times,* March 13, 1991.

33   *Washington Post,* April 11, 1991.

34   Ibid.

35   *USA Today Baseball Weekly,* March 4-10, 1992.

36   *Washington Post,* April 11, 1991.

37   *New York Times,* March 13, 1991.

38   Ibid.

39   HOF file, March 22, 1991.

40   *The Sporting News,* August 19, 1991.

41   *The Sporting News,* August 26, 1991.

42   HOF file, no date.

43   Ibid.

44   *The Sporting News,* May 18, 1982.

45   HOF file, June 28, 1992.

46   Ibid., July 13, 1992.

47   *USA Today,* July 26, 1992.

48   HOF file, April 4, 1994.

49   *The Sporting News,* May 3, 1993.

50   *The Sporting News,* June 7, 1993.

51   *The Sporting News,* May 4, 1994.

52 *The Sporting News,* July 11, 1994.

53 *The Sporting News,* May 1, 1995.

54 *The Sporting News,* March 20, 1996.

55 W. Laurence Coker, *Baseball Injuries: Case Studies by Types in the Major Leagues* (Jefferson, North Carolina: McFarland, 2002), 69.

56 *The Sporting News,* March 3, 1997.

57 *The Sporting News,* March 2, 1998.

58 *The Sporting News,* January 5, 2001.

59 Ibid.

60 *USA Today,* March 25, 2002.

61 *Cincinnati Post,* July 10, 2001.

62 *New York Post,* August 18, 2001.

63 *USA Today,* March 25, 2002.

64 Associated Press, June 11, 2003.

65 *Cincinnati Enquirer,* June 11, 2003.

66 *Washington Post,* March 4, 2005.

67 *Washington Times,* March 4, 2005.

68 *Dayton Daily News,* June 9, 2005.

69 Ibid.

70 Ibid.

71 Espn.go.com, February 26, 2009.

72 Alan Klein, *Dominican Baseball: New Pride, Old Prejudice* (Philadelphia: Temple University Press, 2014), 4.

JIM MECIR

By Rick Swaine

JIM MECIR PITCHED PROFES-
sionally for 15 years, from 1991 to 2005,
including all or part of 11 seasons in the
major leagues, with a permanent disability that would
have kept most people on the sidelines. Mecir (pronounced Mah-sear) was born with a ~~pair of~~ club foot
~~feet~~, a condition that was only partially corrected
by medical procedures in common use when he
was an infant. He defied the opinions of doctors
and coaches by successfully competing in sports at
all levels, culminating with his successful career in
major-league baseball as a top relief specialist.

Club foot (also known as CTEV for Congenital
Talipes Equinovarus) is a malformation of the bones,
joints, muscles, and blood vessels in the foot caused by
abnormal development of the fetus during pregnancy.
In appearance a clubfoot is usually somewhat kidney
shaped with a high mid-foot arch. The condition is
characterized by the inward rotation of the back part
of the foot at the ankle and the turning under of the
forefoot. In addition, the heel is drawn up due to the
strain on the Achilles tendon, resulting in an inability
to bring the foot to a flat standing position.[1]

Club foot is a relatively common birth defect,
occurring in approximately one out of 735 births.
The affliction is ancient—Egyptian mummies have
been discovered with club feet. The disfigurement
occurs roughly twice as often in boys as in girls and
affects both feet (bilateral clubfoot) about half the
time. Although the condition appears to be genetic,
it often seems to be repressed and can skip many
generations. The severity of the condition varies widely.
Several world-class athletes have been born with the
deformity including Olympic figure skater Kristi
Yamaguchi, Pro Bowl quarterback Troy Aikman, and
women's professional soccer star Mia Hamm. Former
major-league infielder Freddy Sanchez was also born
with a club foot.[2]

Thanks to advances in the treatment of club foot in
the latter part of the twentieth century, most patients
getting treatment in early infancy now recover completely during early childhood and are eventually able
to walk and run normally. That was not Jim Mecir's
situation. When he was an infant an attempt was made
to straighten his disfigured right foot and then by a
surgical procedure involving the temporary insertion
of a bar between his feet. Another operation at the
age of 8 was required which left the His calf muscle
atrophied after the procedure, resulting in his right
leg being an inch shorter than the left and causing
him to walk with a pronounced limp.[3]

It has generally been reported that Mecir was
born with two club feet, but in a recent telephone
interview he disclosed that only his right foot was
deformed—his left foot was normal.[4]

Despite his condition, Mecir developed into an
outstanding high-school athlete playing basketball and
even running track in addition to starring in baseball
for East Smithtown (New York) High. When Mecir
first joined the Oakland A's during the 2000 season,
his new teammate Jason Giambi, recalled playing with
him in the 1994 Arizona Fall League. "I guarantee
you he's one of the fastest guys on this team," Giambi
stated. "He can fly."[5]

James Mason Mecir was born on May 16, 1970 in
Bayside, a neighborhood in the New York City borough
of Queens. He grew up in Smithtown on Long Island.
Long Island, of course, is Carl Yastrzemski territory
and as an 18-year-old, Jim won the award bearing the
Red Sox legend's name that goes to the outstanding
high-school baseball player in Suffolk County. Previous
winners included major leaguers Tom Veryzer and
Neal Heaton, and National Football League quarterback Boomer Esiason, while former major-league
pitcher Bill Koch and infielder Tony Graffanino as
well as current big leaguers Steven Matz and Marcus
Stroman were subsequently honored.[6]

Scouting reports tabbed Mecir as a prospect worth following. He was described as intelligent with good stuff, a loose arm, and a strong upper body. His clubfoot and resulting limp were mentioned, but didn't seem to be considered a major issue. Of some concern were his mechanics. A tendency to sling the ball, opening up too soon, and throwing with his arm only were the observations of at least two scouts, though they apparently did see a connection between these flaws in his delivery and his foot condition.[7]

After high school, Mecir attended Eckerd College, a small private school in St. Petersburg, Florida. Eckerd, a Division II school, was not exactly a baseball powerhouse, although two of its alumnae, Jim Lefebvre and Steve Balboni, had made the major leagues. The Eckerd pitching coach was former major leaguer Rich Folkers, who was initially dubious about Mecir's ability to play with his condition, but was quickly impressed with Jim's all-around athletic ability once he saw him in action. While at Eckerd, Mecir learned to throw a screwball by watching the left-handed Folkers work with a lefty teammate. The screwball is an unusual pitch that breaks in the opposite direction from the arm movement. The pitch requires pronating the arm so that the palm of the pitching hand actually ends up facing away from the body at the completion of the delivery. Not only is the pitch difficult to master, it's also considered very hard on the arm and has largely fallen out of favor for that reason. In fact, according to the pitch tracking system PitchF/X, Hector Santiago of the Los Angeles Angels was the only pitcher to throw the pitch in the majors during the 2015 season. But the pitch has an illustrious history. Legendary right-hander Christy Mathewson threw it in the early years of the twentieth century, although it was called a fadeaway in those days. Probably the most renowned screwballer was former New York Giants left-hander Carl Hubbell, who used it almost exclusively to win 253 games from 1928 to 1943. Longtime Braves ace Warren Spahn won 363 National League games with the aid of the "scroogie." Of more recent vintage is Fernando Valenzuela, who rode his screwball to Rookie of the Year and Cy Young Award honors in 1981. And of course there's righty relief ace Mike Marshall, a master

of the pitch and doctor of kinesiology (the scientific study of body movement). Marshall, who set all-time records by appearing in 106 games and pitching 208 innings in relief in 1974, maintains that the screwball motion is actually easier on the arm.[8]

Mecir, whose pitches had a natural tendency to tail away, struggled with traditional breaking pitches, but seemed to pick the screwball up quickly. With Folkers's guidance and encouragement, he incorporated it into his arsenal to complement his fastball.

By his junior year Mecir was gaining attention as a big-league prospect. A 1991 preseason scouting report tabbed him as a "definite prospect" worth a bonus in the $50,000 range. The report mirrored previous ones in mentioning his strong, well-developed upper body, but also noted his "thinnish" legs. It predicted that he had the "stuff to be front-line ML starter." As for his clubfoot, the report stated, "[He] walks with a slight limp," then added, "no other effects." The observation "will at times sling the ball" was again noted, but was dismissed as "correctible," indicating that a link between Mecir's physical disability and his resulting unorthodox pitching motion was still not recognized.[9]

In the third round of the 1991 amateur draft, Mecir was selected by the Seattle Mariners, foregoing his senior year at Eckerd, although he did go back to earn a degree in Economics. He began his professional career as a starting pitcher with San Bernardino in the California League that year. After three mediocre seasons as a starter, he switched to relief in 1994 with Jacksonville in the Southern League and enjoyed outstanding results. He posted an excellent 2.69 earned-run average along with 13 saves, signaling that his days as a starter were over. He never started another game except for a few short stints on minor-league rehab assignments. After another fine performance in relief for Tacoma of the Pacific Coast League in 1995, Mecir was called up to the Mariners for a late-season audition. His September 4 debut saw him pitch 3⅔ innings at Yankee Stadium, allowing only one unearned run. His only other appearance was on October 1, with one inning of scoreless ball in Texas against the Rangers.

That offseason, Mecir was traded to the New York Yankees along with first baseman Tino Martinez and reliever Jeff Nelson for pitcher Sterling Hitchcock and third baseman Russ Davis. He spent the 1996 and 1997 seasons bouncing between the Yankees and their Columbus International League affiliate, pitching well in the minors but failing to establish himself in the big time.

At the end of the 1997 campaign, Mecir was sent to the Boston Red Sox to complete an earlier deal. He caught a break six weeks later when he was selected by the newly formed Tampa Bay Devil Rays in the 1998 expansion draft. Finally getting an opportunity to pitch regularly, he won seven games while losing only two for a team that lost 99 times to finish with the worst record in the American League. He posted a fine 3.11 earned-run average, and struck out 77 batters in 84 innings. He got off to a great start in 1999, appearing in 17 of Tampa Bay's first 33 games, but fractured his right elbow in a freak collision with a teammate shagging flies during pregame batting practice—ending his season prematurely.[10]

Mecir recovered from the broken elbow to win seven of nine decisions for the Devil Rays before being swapped to Oakland in July 2000 for fellow reliever Jesus Colome. Although it was exciting to move from a cellar-dwelling club to a contender, the Tampa Bay area had become Mecir's adopted home. It's where he attended college and where he'd met his wife, Pamela, a Tampa native. Jim was drafted by Tampa Bay while the couple was honeymooning and they'd set up housekeeping in nearby Gulfport. It was difficult to leave.[11]

But Mecir quickly became an integral part of the A's bullpen corps, setting up for closer Jason Isringhausen. He even closed some games himself and racked up four saves when Isringhausen hit a rough spell. For the season, Mecir's combined won-lost record for Tampa Bay and Oakland was 10 wins against 3 losses with a tidy 2.96 ERA to help the A's make it to the Division Series as the wild-card entry. They lost to the Yankees, but Mecir was outstanding, pitching 5⅓ scoreless innings in three appearances, yielding only one hit.

Mecir also pitched well in 2001 as the A's again captured the wild-card berth. But the year was not without some disconcerting physical problems. His

disfigured right leg started to give him trouble, and for the first time complications from his clubfoot put him on the disabled list.

Throughout his career, Mecir had steadfastly followed the universal mantra of athletes with disabilities—claiming that his condition didn't really put him at a disadvantage. He had always stubbornly maintained that his limp was the sole manifestation of his disfigurement and that it affected only his walking. The reality, however, was that his whole pitching motion was unconventional because of his damaged foot. He wasn't able to keep his left shoulder closed the way pitchers are generally taught. As the scouts noted when he was a prospect, his left shoulder would fly open when he delivered the ball and he was largely dependent on the torque generated from his upper body for velocity. What they failed to discern was that his weakened right leg made it impossible for him to properly drive off the mound. Of course, Mecir claimed that this actually helped him by making his pitches more difficult for the batter to pick up. In addition, he contended that his upper-body mechanics allowed him to throw his vaunted screwball more naturally.[12]

Inevitably Mecir had to accept the fact that his condition was having an adverse impact on his body. He is a big man, packing 230 pounds on a 6-foot-1 frame in his prime (according to his 2002 SI.com player page). Over the years the constant wear and tear, which was intensified by the misalignment of his right leg, destroyed the cartilage in his knee. Complicating the problem was that in addition to a club foot, Mecir was born without an anterior cruciate ligament. Consequently, with almost no cartilage left, the bone grinding on bone caused muscle problems as well.[13]

In August 2001 Mecir's knee became so painfully inflamed that he had to undergo arthroscopic surgery. During the procedure, a jelly-like material harvested from the back of a rooster's head was injected into the knee to lubricate the joint and rebuild the damaged meniscus or fibrous cartilage. Mecir made it back to the mound in early September and posted a sensational 1.46 earned-run average over his final 12 appearances. But he was not as effective in the Division Series; the A's were again eliminated by the Yankees. For the entire regular season he posted a fine 3.43 ERA.[14]

This all played out against the backdrop of 9/11's horrific occurrence that narrowly missed engulfing Mecir's family. His father, James Sr., was a New York City firefighter. He and Jim's mother, Carole were on vacation when the World Trade Center was attacked. Upon hearing of the catastrophe, he rushed to the site to help out. Several friends and co-workers were missing. "It's definitely hard on him," Jim said. "It's not good there. Luckily, he was on vacation. My parents called me pretty quickly and told me they were fine."[15]

Mecir's 2002 season was similar to the previous campaign. He pitched well, but as the season wore on, his knee wore out. He ended up with a 6-4 won-lost mark in 61 games and ranked sixth in the league with 21 holds, but his ERA rose to 4.26 and his workload was greatly reduced in the closing months of the season because of soreness in his right knee. The damaged joint was simply making it impossible for him to plant his foot and deliver the ball with the same velocity he once had. In the past, his fastball approached the mid-90s, but now he struggled to reach the 90-mph mark.[16]

"There's no question this could affect my career," Mecir admitted in a *Baseball Weekly* column. "Over the years all the grinding has destroyed the cartilage and now I'm getting muscle problems. I'm just not throwing the way I felt I could before."[17]

The A's captured the 2002 division title outright, but they were once again eliminated in the first round, this time by the California Angels. Mecir pitched only a single scoreless inning in the Division Series.

Mecir's leg problems were compounded when he injured his left knee in the offseason while playing with his children. In November he underwent surgery to repair a torn patella tendon and was expected to miss the first two months of the 2003 season.[18]

The veteran workhorse returned to the mound ahead of schedule, making his first appearance three weeks into the season. He may have rushed it as the 2003 campaign turned out to be the worst of his career. His ERA soared to an unsightly 5.59, although his FIP (Fielding Independent Pitching) indicated that he actually pitched somewhat better than that. Later in the season his balky knee sent him back to the disabled list. All told, he appeared in only 41 contests and pitched only 37 innings. The A's finished first in the American League West again and were again eliminated in the first round. Mecir pitched only two-thirds of an inning in the five-game series loss to the Boston Red Sox.

One of the few bright spots of that difficult season occurred when Mecir was named the winner of the Tony Conigliaro Award, which goes annually to "the player who most effectively overcomes adversity to succeed in baseball."[19]

The 2004 season was the final year of a four-year pact Mecir signed with Oakland. Considering his 2003 performance, his roster spot was in jeopardy, but he made the squad and rewarded the A's with a workmanlike 3.59 ERA in 65 games—the most appearances he had made since 1998, despite starting the season on the disabled list—and ranked third in the league with 21 holds. But for the first time in

Mecir's tenure with Oakland, the club failed to make the postseason.

After the 2004 campaign the A's cut ties with Mecir. He considered retirement, but eventually filed for free agency and signed with the Florida Marlins. Mecir pitched in 46 of the Marlins' first 109 games with a fine ERA of 3.00, but the heavy workload took its toll on the 35-year-old hurler's troublesome shoulder. He landed on the disabled list in early August and pitched only sparingly when he returned on September 4. For the year he appeared in 52 games and finished with a 3.12 ERA for a little over 43 innings of work. At the end of the season, he announced his retirement as a player.

Throughout his career Mecir's affliction had garnered little attention, but in his final season it caused a bit of a flap. On Sunday, May 15, 2005, he endured his worst outing of the season. Entering the game in San Diego in the bottom of the seventh with the Marlins up 4-3, no outs, and the bases loaded, he yielded eight runs (five of which were charged to him) before finally retiring the Padres.

ESPN *Baseball Tonight* analyst John Kruk, noting Mecir's limp when he took the mound and unaware of his deformity, criticized the Marlins on the air for bringing in an injured hurler. When advised of the pitcher's condition, Kruk publicly apologized. Mecir did not take offense, quietly defusing the situation by shrugging it off.[20]

Mecir retired from baseball with a lifetime 29-35 won-lost record and an ERA of 3.77 for 527 innings of relief over 474 appearances. He boasted a sparkling 1.74 ERA for seven postseason appearances.

As of 2016 Mecir, his wife, Pamela, and their three children lived in the village of Kildeer, Illinois, a suburb of Chicago. He worked as a motivational speaker, using his baseball experiences to teach communication and teamwork skills to businesses, and he kept his hand in baseball by providing private pitching instruction to youngsters. In 2016 he was inducted into the New York State Baseball Hall of Fame.[21]

In his heyday, Jim Mecir was considered one of the best set-up men in the game. A rare talent, with a screwball that made the right-hander as effective against lefty hitters as righties, thereby minimizing the need for additional pitching changes for lefty/righty match-ups when he was on the mound. He was also excellent at stranding baserunners.

While Mecir was with Tampa Bay, his pitching coach, Rick Williams, summed up the man and the pitcher with these words. "Courage is the first word that comes to mind. Guts … Perseverance … Not listening to anyone tell him what he could not do and proving that he can. … It's just not a factor with him. It really isn't a limitation. He's turned it into a nonfactor."[22]

NOTES

1   "Facts About Clubfoot: Clubfoot Information and Parental Support," Clubfoot Support Group, Seekonk, Massachusetts, xprss.com/clubfoot/credentials.asp (accessed 9/4/2002).

2   "Facts About Club Foot: Clubfoot Information and Parental Support"; Mayo Clinic Staff, "Clubfoot Overview," Mayo Clinic, mayoclinic.org/diseases-conditions/clubfoot/home/ovc-20198067 (accessed 11/2016); "Famous People with Club Feet or Foot," *Disabled World*, disabled-world.com/artman/publish/famous-clubfoot.shtml (accessed 11/2016).

3   "Facts About Club Foot: Clubfoot Information and Parental Support"; Susan Slusser, OO"Oakland's New Reliever Has Overcome Skeptics,"n Francisco Chronicle, August 4, 2000, sfgate.com/cgi-bin/article.cgi?file=/chronicle/archive/2000/08/04/SP55783.DTL (accessed 3/2/2003). Susan Slusser, "Oakland's New Reliever Has Overcome Skeptics," *San Francisco Chronicle*, August 4, 2000, sfgate.com/cgi-bin/article.cgi?file=/chronicle/archive/2000/08/04/SP55783.DTL (accessed 3/2/2003).

4   Author telephone interview with Jim Mecir (12/7/2016)

5   Susan Slusser.

6   "Yastrzemski Award," *Newsday*-High School Sports, newsday.com/sports/high-school/yastrzemski-award-1.1277008 (accessed 11/2016).

7   MLB scouting reports supplied by Bill Nowlin.

8   Susan Slusser; Ted Berg, "Major League Baseball's Last Screwball Pitcher," *USA Today* Sports-For the Win, March 16, 2016, ftw.usatoday.com/2016/03/hector-santiago-los-angeles-angels-screwball-fip-era-outlier-mlb (accessed 11/2016).

9   MLB scouting report.

10 *The Sporting News*, May 24, 1999: 25.

11 Marc Topkin, "Mecir Finds a Pennant Race, if Not Good Eats," *St. Petersburg Times*, September 12, 2000, sptimes.com/News/091200/Sports/Mecir_finds_a_pennant.shtml (accessed 3/2/2003).

12 Susan Slusser.

13 CNNSI.com, Sports Illustrated-Baseball Jim Mecir player page,CNNSI.com, Sports Illustrated-Baseball. sportsillustrated .cnn.com/baseball/mlb/players/3328/ (accessed 3/2/2003); *USA Today Baseball Weekly*, August 28-September 3, 2002: 13.

14 CNNSI.com, Sports Illustrated-Baseball.

15 sptimes.com/News/091701/Sports/Baseball_briefs.shtml.

16 *USA Today Baseball Weekly*, August 28-September 3, 2002.

17 Ibid.

18 *The Sporting News*, December 2, 2002: 64, and January 6, 2003: 57.

19 "Jim Mecir Voted 2003 Tony Conigliaro Award Winner," MLB Official Info-Press Release, December 12, 2003, oakland.athletics.mlb.com/news/press_releases/press_release. jsp?ymd=20031212&content_id=615923&vkey=pr_oak&fext=. jsp&c_id=oak (accessed 11/2016).

20 Bill Center, "Shoulder Surgery Bagwell's Only Hope," *San Diego Union-Tribune*, May 25, 2005, legacy.sandiegouniontribune.com/ uniontrib/20050522/news_1s22bbhorn.html.

21 Andrew Martin, "An Interview with Former Relief Pitcher Jim Mecir," Seamheads.com, December 13, 2015. seamheads.com/ blog/2015/12/13/an-interview-with-former-relief-pitcher-jim-mecir/ (accessed 11/2016); Jim Mecir Facebook page, accessed December 2, 2016.

22 "Athletes with Clubfoot—Jim Mecir, Major League Baseball Relief Pitcher, Oakland Athletics," Clubfoot Support Group, Seekonk, Massachusetts, xprss.com/clubfoot/credetials. asp (accessed 9/4/2002). Rick Williams quote taken from Marc Topkin, "Devil Rays Day by Day," *St. Petersburg Times*, March 3, 1998.

DEWON BRAZELTON

BY RICHARD BOGOVICH

IF THE 2009 MOVIE *THE BLIND Side*, for which Sandra Bullock received a Best Actress Academy Award, had been released about five years earlier, it might have been called the football version of Dewon Brazelton's story. The true saga of offensive lineman Michael Oher bears many similarities to Brazelton's life experiences: Both are African Americans from Tennessee who were born into difficult circumstances, and as their mothers each dealt with substance abuse, other families stepped in to give the young men a better chance at success — with each ultimately becoming a first-round draft choice and a pro athlete. Of course, the stories differ in several key respects, including an aspect of personal tragedy in Brazelton's life from day one.

Dewon Cortez Brazelton was the first of twin brothers born on June 16, 1980, in Tullahoma, Tennessee. They were born about four weeks prematurely. At the time their mother, Monalisa, became pregnant, she was a star on the women's basketball team of Tullahoma High School. According to a *Washington Post* profile in 2005, Monalisa was shunned by the father, Limuel Tilford, and calls to his home phone number for their story were unanswered.

"My whole life changed in three weeks," Monalisa told the *Post*, referring to her milestone 18th birthday on May 25, 1980, her high-school graduation the following weekend, and giving birth.[1]

Monalisa Brazelton only found out from her doctor that she was carrying twins three days before the delivery. Dewon was energetic, but his twin brother, Fewon, didn't seem well. "He wasn't breathing, so they had to help him," Monalisa said of Fewon in a *Sports Illustrated* profile of the older twin. "He had trouble from the beginning." He had cerebral palsy, never developed the ability to speak, and couldn't control his limbs.

"I've told Dewon that he was given so much power and personality because it was all made for two, not one," she added. "That's the only explanation. He has always been a special child. A lot of that comes from Fewon."[2]

In 2005, when Dewon was named Opening Day starter for the Tampa Bay Devil Rays and he quickly broke the news to his mom, he linked that achievement to a decision Monalisa made when he was just a few years old. "I thanked her for signing me up for that first T-ball game," Dewon said. "She could have signed me up for something else like soccer."[3]

Monalisa recalled Dewon at 7 years old testing her patience by constantly banging a tennis ball against a wall outside of where they lived. She also remembered him digging holes in the yard to create golf courses. He would welcome friends over to play baseball games in which they would pretend to be major leaguers.[4]

Monalisa often worked 70-hour weeks to support the twins. Meanwhile, Dewon developed relationships that would stand the test of time, and draw admiration from across Tullahoma (population of about 18,000). For example, little more than a month before that 2001 major-league draft, a college classmate of his, a softball player named Wendy Pollack, looked back on their time during middle and high school as well. "He's still that same goofy guy I rode on the bus with to middle-school basketball games," she told a campus newspaper after having declared, "Dewon's an exceptional human being in every aspect."[5]

For a time Monalisa worked days in a factory and nights at a Krystal sliders restaurant. That meant Dewon was often his twin's caretaker, which was a tall order. Dewon has said that life in the small city's housing projects sometimes meant encounters with drug dealers and swindlers.

"I was an adult at 13 years old," he recalled about a decade later. "I drove myself to Little League practice when I was 12. If I had to pick up my brother, I'd go

pick him up. I had to do a lot of things a lot of kids couldn't handle. … And that was my life every day. Not twice a week, but every day."[6]

When the twins were 12 years old, Monalisa cracked under the pressure of their situation and left them with her mother, though that arrangement would prove to be temporary. Fewon ended up in the Bedford County Nursing Home, where he would see Monalisa frequently after she became a nurse's aide there. However, during Dewon's early teen years, the popular kid bounced from family to family across town.[7]

The main reason Monalisa had cut Dewon loose was that she was trying to overcome substance abuse. At least early on, Dewon didn't seem to show signs of anxiety in the new situation. As reported by *Sports Illustrated*, during eighth grade he would regularly be seen walking around his neighborhood, happy and joking, keeping an eye out for a chance to shoot hoops in someone's driveway or play Wiffle ball. He'd spend a few hours with one family, and when a parent or older kid drove him home, his mother was never there. "They'd notice my mom wasn't around, and they'd say, 'Why don't you stay over?'" Dewon recalled. "That's

how it started." Four other households eventually took him in with regularity.[8]

Dewon had contact from time to time with his father, Lim Tilford, and perhaps because Monalisa had relocated to Shelbyville, about a 30-minute drive to the west, Dewon and Lim spent more time together. In fact, Dewon moved in with his father at one point.

"But it wasn't really a healthy situation," he told the *Washington Post*. "My daddy smoked a lot of pot — he used to do it right in front of me. He'd do it in the car with me there. I've never touched drugs — partly because of him and partly because of my mama. I was always trying to do what's right, and it always bothered me that he would roll a joint up right in front of me.

"I stayed with him for a pretty good while. But I knew it just wasn't right. He'd beat up my step-mama. It wasn't a good situation." One day it came to a boiling point.

"I don't know what happened. He had to have been high on something, or something," Dewon said. "I don't know. But my daddy took me out in the yard and he beat the [expletive] out of me. Beat the [expletive] out of me. Simple as that. I went to school and called my mama in Shelbyville and told her what happened."

Monalisa phoned Cheryl Frazier, a friend from high school who happened to be white, and asked a huge favor. The Fraziers became the first family in Tullahoma to take Dewon in for an extended period of time, which ended up being two months.[9]

The Tuggle family was the next to welcome Dewon, and later there were the Barnetts, the Robisons, and the Darlingtons. Dewon met Dianne and Scott Darlington in 1995 at Grace Baptist Church, and two years later the couple gave him a key to their house. "We said, 'Dewon, this is your home. You always have a place to stay, and you don't have to call and ask,'" Dianne said. "He is, in many ways, our third child." As a result, Dewon frequently calls Dianne "Mom," as he does Deby Barnett, in addition to Monalisa.[10]

Dewon had one persistent challenge at school, and it often caused other kids to make fun of him: "I had a speech impediment and went to speech class," he told a group of teens in the Transition Program of the Watson Center for the Blind and Visually Impaired, in Largo, Florida, in 2003. "I still can't say some words now. Anyway, I had the speech problem and I was not what everybody thought was cool."[11]

Over time, though, Dewon's athletic success made him increasingly popular during high school. He excelled in three sports, one of which, not surprisingly, was baseball. The pinnacle may have been in 1997, during his junior year, when he helped lead Tullahoma High's Wildcats to the finals in the state baseball tournament, though they lost the championship game 3-0 to Christian Brothers High School of Memphis.[12]

Dewon was the winning pitcher by the same score a year later when Tullahoma defeated Florida's Crestview High School to win the USA Classic tournament in Millington, Tennessee. The pressure was heightened for Dewon, who at the time stood 6-feet-4 and weighed 160 pounds, because his team wasn't able to score until the seventh inning. In the end, Tullahoma outperformed the nation's top-ranked school, Florida's Miami Southridge, as well as the tournament's defending champs, Murfreesboro Oakland.[13] Dewon was named MVP of the tournament. Under coach Jerry Mathis he was consistently a dominant pitcher in high school, with a career earned-run average of 1.75, and his overall batting average was .350. He was named to the All-District and All-Midstate baseball teams. The other two sports in which he lettered were basketball and football.[14]

This success was almost derailed permanently before Dewon was halfway through high school. He was the school's starting quarterback by his sophomore year, but early in the season he tore the anterior cruciate ligament in his right knee. He somehow managed to recover by baseball season, only to blow out the ulnar collateral ligament in his right elbow and undergo reconstructive Tommy John surgery. It's assumed that these events made major-league teams reluctant to draft Dewon during high school.[15] He himself soon became suspicious of his durability. As a college student he admitted, "I am terrified of getting hurt, terrified. I use the railing when I go down the stairs now, like I'm an old man. I used to drive fast but not now."[16]

At some point during Dewon's high school years his mother's situation improved a bit, and Monalisa Brazelton returned to Tullahoma. She moved into the Carver Homes housing project. She gave Dewon space in her apartment for his possessions, but he preferred to stay with the other families regularly. Shortly before his first semester of college, he found that his key to Mona's apartment wouldn't work. He learned nothing from many frantic phone calls to people who knew her, but a long time later he learned that his mother had gone to Nashville and asked to be admitted to a rehab clinic.[17]

Somewhat ironically, Brazelton had declined an offer of partial scholarship offer from the University of Tennessee, about three hours away in Knoxville by car, and accepted a full ride from Middle Tennessee State in Murfreesboro, which is only 35 miles from Tullahoma.[18] "Since I'm a momma's boy, I didn't want to go too far away. I also wanted my family to be able to come see me play."[19]

Baseball success continued for Brazelton at Middle Tennessee. During his first two seasons with the Blue Raiders his pitching record was 15-8, though with a 4.82 ERA. He wasn't satisfied with the latter and concluded, "I got beat up a lot by throwing my curveball too much. "He decided to rely more on his fastball, which was sometimes clocked up to 97 miles per hour. He also perceived a need to make a mental adjustment, saying, "I wore my emotions on my sleeve. You could tell if I won or lost by just looking at me." Brazelton started gaining nationwide attention in August of 2000, when he starred for the US national team that beat Cuba to win the Honkbal Baseball Week tournament in The Netherlands. His record was a perfect 6-0, and no prior Team USA starter had achieved his 0.65 ERA.[20]

In the next month Brazelton was in experts' top 10 lists. Philadelphia sportswriter Jim Salisbury noted that with the worst record in the NL, the Phillies would have the second pick in Major League Baseball's June 2001 amateur draft. "The cream of the 2001 draft crop includes right-handed pitchers Josh Karp (UCLA) and Dewon Brazelton (Middle Tennessee State) and third baseman Mark Teixeira (Georgia Tech.)," he wrote.[21] Similarly, Marc Topkin in the Tampa Bay area identified "early front-runners" in that draft as Teixeira "and a slew of right-handed pitchers," specifically Mark Prior of USC, Karp, and Brazelton, plus high schoolers Gavin Floyd in Maryland and Mike Jones in Arizona.[22]

In 2001 the honors started piling up. At the beginning of the year, Brazelton was named a baseball All-American; in March he was one of four players selected Louisville Slugger National Players of the Week; and shortly after that he was named national pitcher of the week by the National Collegiate Baseball Writers Association. He was named the Sun Belt Conference's pitcher of the year after going 13-2 with a 1.42 ERA, limiting opponents to a .178 batting average and piling up 154 strikeouts in 127 innings.[23]

Brazelton's time at Middle Tennessee was also successful academically. He carried a 3.2 grade-point average into his junior year.[24] As his time there was winding down, Deby Barnett seemed as proud of the fact that Dewon had made the honor roll every semester except for one, and he missed it by a whisker then.[25]

On the eve of the June 2001 draft, Brazelton publicly thanked Middle Tennessee alumnus Jason Maxwell of the Minnesota Twins, who had been a late-round draft pick of the Cubs in 1993. Maxwell worked out at the campus during the offseason. "He's really helped me a lot," Brazelton said. "He helped me with a lot of little things and taught me how to carry myself better." Maxwell returned the praise. "He's willing to work hard," he said of Brazelton, "and he knows how to avoid all of the distractions."[26]

In the amateur draft, it didn't take very long at all for Brazelton to be selected. After the Twins chose Joe Mauer and the Cubs selected Mark Prior, the Tampa Bay Devil Rays made Brazelton the third pick overall. "This is what I wanted," Brazelton said. "There was a rumor going around that I'd be the number-1 pick, but I didn't want it. I wanted to be a Devil Ray. I don't want to be in the minor leagues forever."[27]

Brazelton signed with Tampa Bay on August 25, and spent the last month of the season with the big leaguers, though with no plans by anyone for him to make his major-league debut. "I've always been good about learning by watching," he said. "You never know what you might pick up being around the team, listening to how they talk, how they think." His first thrill was reportedly meeting hitting coach Wade Boggs.[28]

In 2002 Brazelton played in his first pro game for the Double-A Orlando Rays. In 26 games, all starts, his record was just 5-9 but his ERA was a respectable 3.33, so he was given a brief promotion to the Triple-A Durham Bulls, and helped them in an International League playoff game. In his last eight minor-league starts, including two for the Bulls, he was 6-0 with a 1.06 ERA. Soon enough, though, Brazelton was called up to the parent club, and made his major-league debut on September 13, 2002, in Toronto. Despite his defense backing him with a triple play, he gave up five earned runs on five hits and three walks in six innings and was tagged with a loss. He started a second game for the Devil Rays, on the 19th at home against the New York Yankees, and gave up only two runs in seven innings. He left with his team down 2-1 but the Rays tied it in the eighth and won it in the 10th. His ERA was 4.85 ERA over the 13 innings.

Less than three months after his first major-league game, the offseason took on a very somber tone for Brazelton and his loved ones. His twin, Fewon, died on December 2 of pneumonia, which he had suffered in previous winters. He weighed just 90 pounds, in contrast to Brazelton's usual MLB-listed weight of 215. "He was a part of me. We had a bond better than anyone could know," Brazelton said. "He's always in my heart, regardless of whether he's here or not." Writing in the *St. Petersburg Times*, Marc Topkin noted that Fewon's death was "the latest development in what has been a lifetime of sorrow and success [and] an inspirational story that is sure to make its way to Hollywood."[29]

As the Devil Rays were deciding their Opening Day roster for 2003, right knee and left groin injuries undercut Brazelton's chances of being included. He took the setback in stride. "I'm here to compete, and I don't want anything handed to me," he said. "I have to earn it."[30]

Brazelton started the season with Triple-A Durham, and after five starts, he was recalled by the Devil Rays before the end of April. He pitched in 10 games for Tampa Bay, all starts, from May 3 to June 24. His record in the first five was 0-4 but on May 30 he picked up his first major-league victory, at home against Anaheim. Over the 10 games he had a 6.89 ERA.

It was no surprise that Brazelton was demoted to the minors on June 25, but it was unusual that he was sent all the way down to a Single-A team, Bakersfield. "The scariest part of what we're going through right now concerning our young players is that we know we rushed a lot of them to the major leagues and we know that there's risk involved," said Chuck LaMar, Tampa Bay's general manager. Topkin noted that although the move seemed harsh, a similar demotion helped Toronto's Roy Halladay (the 2003 AL Cy Young Award winner) two years earlier. Topkin observed reasons for applying the same to Dewon. "Brazelton had an unorthodox delivery in college, kicking his left leg higher and dropping his right arm lower, similar to Satchel Paige," he wrote. "Rays coaches changed Brazelton's mechanics in the minor leagues, but with his fastball down about 5 mph, they will at least let him experiment with his old delivery."[31]

Brazelton pitched in nine games for Bakersfield, all starts. His record was 1-5 with a 5.26 ERA, but in mid-August he threw seven shutout innings in the last of those starts and was promoted to Double-A Orlando. He won both of his starts for Orlando, with a satisfying 2.53 ERA. The Rays next assigned him to the Arizona Fall League. His teammates on the Mesa Solar Bears included Delmon Young, Tampa Bay's first-round pick a few months earlier, and outfielder Jonny Gomes. Brazelton was named the league's top right-handed pitcher by virtue of a 4-0 record and 3.27 ERA in seven starts, with a league-leading 36 strikeouts in 33 innings. He was the winning pitcher in the AFL championship game, in which he scattered two hits and two walks in six innings.[32]

In 2004 Brazelton started the season with Triple-A Durham. From April 9 to May 29 he made 10 starts for the Bulls and had a 4-4 record with a 4.71 ERA. In early June the Rays released starting pitcher Paul

Abbott and called up Brazelton. He turned 24 years old on June 16 and less than 10 days later came within four outs of making history at home against Florida, the previous season's World Series champion.

Brazelton and Florida starter A.J. Burnett held each other's opposing batters scoreless through the fifth inning. Dewon continued that through the top of the sixth, though more significantly, he had also kept the Marlins hitless. He started cramping in his right hip around then, but he toughed it out. The Rays scored twice in the bottom of the sixth, and Brazelton retired two more Marlins in the top of the seventh. That brought up Mike Lowell with the bases empty.

Brazelton got ahead of Lowell in the count before the veteran Marlin worked it to three balls and two strikes. Lowell fouled off the next three pitches. "When I got 3-2 on him, chances are, no-hitter or not, if I walked this guy, Lou's going to bring somebody else in," said Dewon, referring to manager Lou Piniella. "So I went right after him. I made three or four quality pitches that he fouled off. The next one, I threw right down the middle." Lowell lined a ground-rule double between outfielders Carl Crawford and Joey Gathright. After his 125th pitch — a new career high — Brazelton was removed to a standing ovation from the 25,000 fans at Tropicana Field. The score remained unchanged after he left, and he earned only his second major-league win. It happened almost exactly a year after the shortest start of his major-league career, the one against the Yankees after which he was quickly demoted to Class A. Tampa Bay wouldn't have a pitcher throw the franchise's first no-hitter until July 26, 2010, when Matt Garza shut down the Detroit Tigers.

The win was an important one for the franchise's psyche, because their record improved to 35-35 and in their previous six seasons of existence it had never reached the .500 mark that late in a season, beating the old mark by a month. In their second season, 1999, they were 22-22 on May 23 before it all went downhill. What's more, the near no-hitter meant that the Rays had come back completely from a horrible start and in a short span recovered from 18 games below .500 to break-even. No team had managed that from the year 1900 until then.[33] The Rays couldn't sustain their surge past Independence Day, and finished 2004 at 70-91. Brazelton, by contrast, maintained his momentum longer. Before he was shelled by the Boston Red Sox on August 11, his record stood at 4-3 with a 2.56 ERA. He stayed with the Rays through the end of the season, and in what was his longest major-league stint he had a 6-8 record with a 4.77 ERA in 22 games. In December of 2004 Brazelton was named winner of the Tony Conigliaro Award, presented to a player who had overcome adversity "through the attributes of spirit, determination, and courage."

Brazelton had a good spring training in 2005, and in mid-March Lou Piniella named him the Opening Day starter at home against Toronto on April 4. To some extent Piniella was playing percentages: All of the young pitcher's career wins had been at Tropicana Field, and two were over Toronto in 2004. "I'm honored to be the Opening Day starter, but it lets me know I have to step it up more to stay at that level," he said.[34] Brazelton retired the first nine Blue Jays but faltered in the fourth and gave up three runs. Still, he held Toronto there until he left with one out in the seventh inning. Meanwhile, Tampa Bay batters didn't accomplish much against 2003 Cy Young Award winner Roy Halladay, and the final score was Jays 7, Rays 2.

Brazelton lost two more starts before beating Texas, again at Tropicana Field, on April 21. It proved to be the final victory of his major-league career. Three days after that, he was one of six players ejected during a game against the Red Sox. Presumably in response to Boston pitcher Bronson Arroyo having beaned Aubrey Huff, in the top of the seventh Tampa Bay pitcher Lance Carter threw high-and-tight pitches to Manny Ramirez and David Ortiz. A bench-clearing scuffle broke out, and Piniella, Carter, and Brazelton were thrown out, along with Boston's Trot Nixon. In the bottom of the inning, Arroyo plunked Chris Singleton in the leg, causing the benches to empty again. Arroyo and Boston manager Terry Francona were ejected. A few days later Arroyo was suspended for six games, Carter and Brazelton five, managers Francona and Piniella three, and Nixon two. Ortiz and Singleton were both fined for charging the mound.

Before mid-May, Brazelton had already lost seven games, with a 6.43 ERA, and was demoted to Durham. On May 16 he was put on the league's restricted list for failing to report within the required 72 hours. Though his agent, Bo McKinnis, released brief statements, Brazelton's whereabouts remained a mystery until early June, when he requested and received reinstatement by the league, and immediately went to Tampa Bay's minor-league complex to work out. Afterward he spoke to a few reporters briefly but didn't shed much light on his absence. McKinnis released a statement saying that Brazelton "dealt with a personal matter" and asked people to respect his privacy.[35] Brazelton started a game on June 21 for the Double-A Montgomery Biscuits and had a good three innings, giving up no runs and two hits while striking out six. He returned to the majors as a reliever, and got into games for the Rays from June 25 to August 7. He then made five starts for Durham from August 14 to September 3, going 2-2 with a 3.72 ERA. He finished up with two more relief outings for Tampa Bay on September 13 and 20. His ERA for the Rays ended up at 7.61.

On December 7, 2005, Tampa Bay traded Brazelton to the San Diego Padres for third baseman Sean Burroughs, another former first-round pick. Brazelton played for Mayaguez in Puerto Rican Winter League before starting the 2006 season on the Padres' roster. He lost both of his starts with San Diego, on April 8 and 13, then made seven more appearances in relief. His final major-league game was in San Diego against Milwaukee on May 11, 2006. His career major-league record was 8-25 with a 6.38 ERA.

Brazelton started 16 games for the Padres' Triple-A team in Portland during the remainder of 2006 and did okay, with a 4.53 ERA. On October 15 he was granted free agency, and on December 5 the Kansas City Royals signed him. He pitched poorly for their Omaha team in early 2007 and was released on April 26. The Pittsburgh Pirates signed him on May 31 and he pitched decently for Double-A Altoona, with a 3.53 ERA, but was granted free agency again on October 29. One month later the St. Louis Cardinals signed him to a minor-league contract, but he didn't play during 2008. In his six minor-league seasons,

Brazelton compiled a record of 27-38 with a 4.02 ERA. His only other pro teams were independent ones, the Camden Riversharks in 2009 and the Kansas City (Kansas) T-Bones in 2010. His lone decision for the latter was a win.

Brazelton was back in the news briefly in mid-2011, and for a reason nobody desires. He was jailed briefly for striking his fiancée in public, in St. Petersburg's International Plaza. "A witness told police the couple got into an argument and he hit her in the head as she pushed away from him," said the *St. Petersburg Times*. "The woman, who was not identified, has been living with Brazelton for six years and the two are engaged, the police report said."[36]

Fast-forward five years, and before Tampa Bay hosted the Red Sox in mid-2016, superstar Evan Longoria tossed a ball to a 12-year-old Little League pitcher named D.J., who snared it with his mitt. Smiling with great approval was his father, Dewon Brazelton, even though D.J.'s favorite player was on the other team: David Ortiz. At the time, Brazelton was sharing custody of Dewon, Junior, with his son's mother, Elizabeth Boyce, in Orlando. Their early — and ugly — custody battle was the reason for Brazelton's mysterious disappearance in May of 2005. The battle took years, but ultimately D.J.'s parents grew friendly again.

Brazelton expressed regret to Roger Mooney of the *Tampa Bay Times* for missing much of D.J.'s life earlier. "Now I enjoy being a part of my son's day-to-day life. I looooove going to parent-teacher conferences," he enthused. "I check his schoolwork. 'Why did you get a frowny face?' I looooove being a part of that."

Brazelton was selling commercial and residential real estate while also managing a gas station and tire shop in the Bay area, but also found time for golf. In 2013 he was enshrined in the Middle Tennessee State athletic hall of fame, and has donated $250,000 for the baseball stadium's renovation. He proudly showed a photo on his phone of himself with D.J. inside the ballpark, standing at the entrance to the Dewon Brazelton Alumni Suite.[37]

NOTES

1   Dave Sheinin, "Making His Mothers Proud," *Washington Post*, April 29, 2005: D1.

2   Jeff Pearlman, "From Afterthought to Ace," *Sports Illustrated*, May 14, 2001: 76.

3   *Damian Cristodero, "Brazelton Gets Opening Assignment," St. Petersburg* (Florida) *Times, March 17 2005: 1C.*

4   Pearlman: 79.

5   Courtney Huckabay, "Brazelton Throwing for His Future," *Sidelines* (Murfreesboro, Tennessee), April 30, 2001: 4B.

6   Marc Topkin, "Sensitive Subject," *St. Petersburg Times*, March 2, 2003: 1C.

7   Huckabay: 6B.

8   Pearlman: 76.

9   Sheinin: D1.

10   Pearlman: 79.

11   "Close-Up," *Tampa Tribune*, June 16, 2003: sports section, 2.

12   Ryan Simmons, "Player Profiles," *Middle Tennessee 2000 Baseball Media Guide* (Middle Tennessee State University), 9.

13   Kevin Gorman, "Tullahoma Earns USA Classic Title," *Memphis Commercial Appeal*, April 11, 1998: D3.

14   Simmons, 9.

15   Pearlman: 79.

16   Huckabay: 4B.

17   Sheinin: D1.

18   Pearlman: 79.

19   Huckabay: 4B.

20   Joel Rippel, "2001 Amateur Draft Spotlight: Dewon Brazelton," *Minneapolis Star Tribune*, June 3, 2001: 16C.

21   Jim Salisbury, "Clemens Shows He's Back in the Game," *Philadelphia Inquirer*, September 16, 2000: E5.

22   Marc Topkin, "Questions Abound for Next Year's Club," *St. Petersburg Times*, September 24, 2000: 5C.

23   Rippel: 16C.

24   Pearlman: 76.

25   Tony Stinnett, "Long, Hard Road: MTSU Pitching Phenom Dewon Brazelton Has Traveled a Tough Path," *Murfreesboro Daily News Journal*, April 22, 2001.

26   Rippel: 16C.

27   Chris Anderson, "Brazelton Eyes Bigs in 3-4 Months," *Sarasota* (Florida) *Herald Tribune*, June 6, 2001: C1.

28   Marc Topkin, "Brazelton: Let Learning Begin," *St. Petersburg Times*, September 1, 2001: 3C. Topkin indicated early on that Brazelton's surname is pronounced with the emphasis on the

second syllable, "Brah-ZEL-ton," though baseball-reference.com shows it as "BRAZ-el-ton."

29 Marc Topkin, "Sensitive Subject," *St. Petersburg Times*, March 2, 2003: 1C.

30 Carter Gaddis, "Injuries Actually May Benefit Brazelton," *Tampa Tribune*, March 23, 2003: 20.

31 Marc Topkin, "Rays Get Brazelton out of Fire," *St. Petersburg Times*, June 29, 2003: 9C.

32 Dennis Maffezzoli, "Rays Coach Finalist for Reds Job," *Sarasota Herald Tribune*, November 23, 2003: C3.

33 Dennis Maffezzoli, "Devil Rays at .500; They Shut Out World Champs on a Two-Hitter," *Sarasota Herald Tribune*, June 26, 2004: C1.

34 *Cristodero: 1C.*

35 Dave Scheiber, "Brazelton's Few Words Reveal Almost Nothing," *St. Petersburg Times*, June 4, 2005: 3C.

36 Robbyn Mitchell, "Ex-Ray Brazelton Charged With Hitting Fiancee," *St. Petersburg Times*, June 5, 2011: 3C.

37 Roger Mooney, "His New Career: Being 'Daddy,'" *Tampa Bay Times*, July 22, 2016: 1C.

AARON COOK

By Joy Hackenmueller and Bill Nowlin

SOMETIMES, LET'S SAY MOST of the time, knowing exactly what we want out of life is the key to making it happen. Aaron Lane Cook, born February 8, 1979, at Fort Campbell, Kentucky, was asked in the eighth grade to fill out a questionnaire on what he wanted to do when he grew up.

"My teacher didn't understand," Cook recalled. "She said, 'You can't do that, you have to do something serious.' I said, 'I want to be a professional baseball player.'"[1]

Cook grew up in Hamilton, Ohio, where his father worked in the local paper mill. Garry Cook, Aaron's father, offered support to his son by coaching his teams as often as he could. Garry mentioned a pivotal moment when young Aaron was one out away from defeating the New England Mariners at a national AAU tournament in Des Moines, Iowa, "Aaron motioned for me to come out to the mound. Keep in mind he was just 13. I thought he wanted me to take him out. Instead, he said 'I just need a minute here to calm down.' On the way back to the dugout, I thought, 'He's actually got a chance to do something big with baseball.'"[2] Aaron added, appreciatively, "He was always there for me. He never missed a tournament or anything until I was 16. He helped me chase my dreams."[3]

Aaron's mother, Veronica, left when he was 15, after a divorce. Aaron's best friend growing up was Curtus Moak. As Patrick Saunders wrote, "Cook and Moak competed against each other in Little League before becoming best friends the summer before their sophomore year at Hamilton High. Because Cook's house was far out of town, he often spent the night at Moak's house. 'We'd sleep in these bunk beds and we'd talk for hours,' Moak recalled. 'We became like brothers. My mom became his second mom.'"[4]

The two Hamilton High teammates helped lead the team to two statewide baseball titles. Moak, a left-handed pitcher, later played for the University of Cincinnati and in 2001 was drafted in the 25th round by the Cincinnati Reds. He played four years in the minors, but never rose as high as Double A.

As a young teenager, Cook threw a fastball in the low 80s. By the time he was 18 years old he had harnessed a 90-mph fastball with exceptional control. On June 3, 1997, the high-school senior was drafted by the Colorado Rockies in the second round of the amateur draft. He grew to 6-feet-3 and was listed at 215 pounds.

The Rockies placed Cook in Mesa, pitching Rookie-league ball in the Arizona League; he was 1-3 in 46 innings of work, with a 3.13 earned-run average. He devoted five years to development before rising as high as Double A. In 1998 he was with the Portland Rockies (Northwest League), and in 1999 he pitched ball for the Asheville Tourists in the Class-A South Atlantic League. There he might have felt discouraged, winning only four games against 12 losses and with an ERA of 6.44. Asheville finished in last place in the six-team league. But Cook kept working, trying to hone his craft.

In 2000, his second year with Asheville, he began to turn things around and, though the Tourists still had a losing record at 66-69, Cook improved dramatically in his control, converting his 1.74 strikeouts/walks ratio to 5.13, halving his walks to 23 while striking out 118. His ERA dropped to 2.96 and he was 10-7 in wins and losses. He spent part of the season in high A ball, pitching for Salem (Virginia) Avalanche in the Carolina League. He was overmatched (1-6, 5.44), but once more he improved with experience, and in 2001 he started 27 games for Salem and worked to a 3.08 ERA. He was 11-11 for the 70-68 Avalanche.

In 2002 Cook climbed the ladder rapidly. First, in Raleigh with the Double-A Southern League's Carolina Mudcats, he was 7-2 (1.42); and then in Triple

A with the Pacific Coast League Colorado Springs Sky Sox, he held his own (4-4, 3.78).

Cook got the call to come to the big leagues. On August 10, 2002, at age 23, he made his debut for the Rockies against the Chicago Cubs. After five innings, the Cubs were winning 14-1, and manager Clint Hurdle called on Cook as the third of five Rockies pitchers that day. The first batter he faced was Cubs left fielder Moises Alou, who homered to make it 15-1, but Cook retired the next three batters. He also worked the top of the seventh, giving up a leadoff single but then getting the next three batters. On August 26 he was given his first start, against the visiting San Francisco Giants, and acquitted himself well enough, working six innings while giving up three runs, in a game the Rockies ultimately lost. Cook gave up three runs again, working seven innings in San Diego in his second start, but lost his first decision; the Rockies were shut out, 3-0. Cook then won back-to-back starts, against the Padres in Denver and the Astros in Houston. He finished the season appearing in nine games, five of them starts, with a record of 2-1 and a 4.54 ERA in 35⅔ innings.[5]

In both 2003 and 2004, Cook spent some time on Interstate 25 traveling the hour or so between Colorado Springs and Denver and working for both teams, though the lion's share of his time was with the big-league club in 2003, when he pitched in 43 games, 16 of them starts. Cook's ERA was a disappointing 6.02 and his final record 4-6, but the Rockies kept the faith.

By the 2004 season, Cook had developed full trust in his sinkerball, one he worked diligently to develop with Rockies minor-league pitching coach Bryn Smith.[6] His sinker developed from his straight fastball. Eventually, a conventional grip of two fingers on both seams was tweaked and became one finger across one seam to become his signature sinkerball.

Bob McClure of the Rockies' minor-league pitching staff taught Cook that contact was OK. "One thing I give Bob McClure credit for is teaching me how to pitch to contact and trusting that I can get guys out with groundballs," said Cook. "Swings and misses, for me, are more of a timely thing—certain situations with guys on, less than two outs, less than one out,

that's the time I really try to go for the strikeouts. But other than that, I really try to make guys mis-hit the ball, hit pitches that I'm trying to make."[7] Once Cook trusted contact, he went from throwing 110-115 pitches per game to around 80. His sinkerball technique in combination with a pitch flying at upward of 90 mph made his pitches unhittable.

After beating the Diamondbacks with a complete-game 10-2 win on August 1, 2004, Cook was feeling good about himself; he was 25 years old and seeing the fruits of his technique training. Six days later, on August 7, Cook took the mound against the Cincinnati Reds at Coors Field. After three innings, 10 batters and five hits, Cook complained of dizziness and short-ness of breath. He left the mound and was taken to Rose Medical Center, where he was diagnosed with pulmonary embolisms, a sudden blockage of the arter-ies, in both lungs. Doctors, medics, and the Rockies medical team all told Cook later that it was a miracle he was alive. Indeed, he told the *Boston Globe*'s Nick Cafardo several years later, "I had the paramedic and doctor telling me as I was lying on the stretcher that I should be dead," Cook recalled. "At that point, I'm fighting for my life. I wasn't thinking about baseball. I was thinking about my family and my health and whether I was going to make it."[8]

Cook had essentially gone from the peak of his young career to a debilitating condition. "I had experi-enced trouble breathing for a couple of days before that start," Cook said. "I don't think I could have thrown another pitch in the game."[9] The clots originated near his first rib, constricting flow against his collarbone. He had two surgeries; his top rib was removed to correct the problem that was causing the clots. After rehabilitation lasting the better part of a year, Cook got back to baseball.

It was a bit of a slog to get back in the big leagues after recovery, and in 2005, Cook pitched for four minor-league teams. First he pitched in two games for the Tri-City Dust Devils (Pasco, Washington) of the Northwest League. Then he advanced to the Modesto Nuts (Class-A California League) for one game, then on to the Double-A Tulsa Drillers for one game, then to the Triple-A Sky Sox in Colorado

Springs for three games. In late July he was deemed ready for the Rockies.

Cook was activated from the disabled list in time to start on July 30 at Coors Field against the visiting Phillies. It did not go well; he was hit for seven runs, all earned, in 4⅓ innings. But he had made his way back to big-league baseball and was pitching from a major-league mound. Next time out, on August 5, he yielded only one run in six innings. Then he won six games in a row. He took one more loss, and then added another win. By the end of his half-season, Cook was 7-2 with an ERA of 3.67. It was a remarkable recovery after a near-fatal illness.

Bob Apodaca, the Rockies' pitching coach, commented on Cook's dedication after his surgeries: "I think that changed him. … Any success he is getting now is the result of pure hard work. Before, I think he did rely on pure ability. I think that's why we would scratch our head and wonder, what kind of pitcher he would be? Now we don't have to wonder any more. He's shown us."[10]

In January 2006 Cook was given the Tony Conigliaro Award for his quick comeback and dedication to the game. The day after receiving the award, he signed a two- year, $4.55 million contract with the Rockies.

Cook had 32 starts in 2006, winning nine and losing 15 with a 4.23 ERA. That he had worked 212⅔ innings was a testament to his having regained full health.

In 2007 Cook worked a full load through August 10, when he suffered an oblique injury that kept him out for the rest of the regular season. He was 8-7, 4.12. That was the year the Rockies caught fire and won 14 of their last 15 games, earning them a wild-card slot in the postseason. Cook was not on the postseason roster for either the Division Series, which they swept in three games from the Phillies, or for the NLCS, which they swept in four from the Arizona Diamondbacks. With the back-to-back sweeps, the team had now won 21 of its last 22 games and was headed to the World Series against the Boston Red Sox. Cook was with the team in Phoenix and enjoyed the champagne the Rockies sprayed on one another.

Cook was activated for the World Series, and he started

Game Four at Coors Field. The pendulum of sweeps had started to go the other way, with Boston taking the first three games of the World Series and on the brink of a sweep if Cook couldn't stop them. It could hardly have been a more emotional time for a return. Rockies manager Clint Hurdle said, "The opportunity to tell him, 'You're going to get the ball in Game Four' was very special. And it was meaningful, but again, for all the right reasons. If it was about sentiment, he would have pitched in the NLCS, and he understood that." For his part, Cook said, "I feel ready to go. I feel as strong as ever."[11]

Game Four was, as the *New York Times* observed, "a duel of survivors. [Red Sox pitcher Jon] Lester fought his way back after offseason treatment for lymphoma, and Colorado's Aaron Cook once missed almost a year with blood clots in both lungs."[12]

Both pitched good games. Cook gave up a leadoff double to Jacoby Ellsbury, who moved to third base on a grounder by Dustin Pedroia, then scored when David

Ortiz singled to right field. In the top of the fifth, the score still 1-0, Mike Lowell doubled to lead off and Jason Varitek singled him in. Lowell homered leading off the seventh, making it 3-0 Red Sox, and Hurdle brought in Jeffrey Affeldt to take over from Cook. Lester had departed after 5⅔ innings. The Rockies came back with a run in the bottom of the seventh. Boston's Bobby Kielty pinch-hit for Mike Timlin in the top of the eighth and homered, so when the Rockies got two more in the bottom of the eighth, they still trailed, 4-3, and that was the final score. Cook bore the loss.

Cook had his winningest season in 2008. He was 11-5 through July 1, and had won six consecutive starts from April 13 to May 9. Cook was named to the National League All-Star team. He pitched three scoreless innings, the 10th, 11th, and 12th. In the 10th he faced a bases-loaded situation with no outs after second baseman Dan Uggla made back-to-back errors, and Carlos Guillen was walked intentionally. Cook worked his way out of the jam, inducing three ground-outs, the first two resulting in forces at home. It was said that he could have been named the game's MVP had the National League won,[13] but AL prevailed in 15 innings, 4-3.

Cook finished the 2008 season 16-9 (3.96). In 2009 he was 11-6 in 27 starts with a 4.16 ERA. He had also enjoyed the day on May 29 when he attended the dedication of a "Field of Dreams" baseball complex in Windsor, Colorado, a facility for which he had been a major donor.[14]

In 2009 Cook had another opportunity to play postseason baseball. The Rockies were the wild-card team again after Clint Hurdle (18-28) was replaced as manager by Jim Tracy (74-42). They faced the Phillies in the Division Series, and Cook started and won Game Two, 5-4, giving up three runs in five-plus innings of work. All three runs scored in the top of the sixth, when he allowed two singles and a double without securing an out. The two runners inherited by reliever Jose Contreras both scored, but then the bleeding was stopped and Cook got the win, the only game Colorado won in the NLDS.

In 2010 Cook started 23 games and was 6-8 (5.08), while in 2011 he had another subpar year (3-10, 6.03), his most disappointing year, after accidentally breaking his index finger in a screen door during spring training. He said, "I couldn't pick up a baseball for four weeks after I broke my finger."[15]

The Rockies granted Cook free agency after the season. With the Rockies he had been 72-68 over the course of 10 seasons, as of 2016 second only to Jorge de la Rosa in wins among Rockies pitchers.

The Red Sox took a chance on Cook, signing him to a minor-league deal in early January 2012. The incoming Red Sox pitching coach was Bob McClure, who had tutored Cook as Cook was ascending through the minors.

After arriving in Boston, he spoke about receiving the Tony Conigliaro Award. "It was an honor to be recognized for what had happened to me and that I was able to overcome what happened to me to resume my career," Cook said. "I grew up in church, and what happened to me renewed my faith in the Lord. He got me through a challenging time in my life, and the whole experience made me stronger as a person. It's allowed me to put everything in perspective. I know what's important. I know better what things I need to worry about and what things I have no control over. But it's made me stronger. No doubt about that."[16]

With the Red Sox Cook was 4-11, 5.65, pitching in only three games before July 4. He was 3-0 in Triple-A Pawtucket, but working in the majors in what proved to be his last season in the big leagues was difficult. In his four wins combined, he allowed a total of only four earned runs, but the rest of the time he was challenged.

A free agent after the season, Cook signed with the Phillies for 2013, but was released in spring training and later signed a minor-league contract with the Rockies. With Colorado Springs he added a cutter to his repertoire, but finished 0-5 with an 8.15 ERA.

In 2014, as a free agent, Cook decided to put a hold on his career, recuperate from repeated instances of severe inflammation in his elbow, and focus on getting himself in front of major-league teams for the 2015 season. He was unable to find a team willing to take a chance.

Longtime friendships and strong faith have supported Cook. A longtime member of the Hamilton Christian Center,[17] he met his wife, Holly there, and counted as one of his best friends Curtus Moak, youth pastor at the church.[18]

Cook and Holly have three children—daughter Alexis and sons Elijah and Colton. When he realized in 2013 that retirement might be in his future, he said, "I'd be a better dad with my summers open."[19]

SOURCES

In addition to the sources mentioned in the Notes, the authors also consulted baseball-almanac.com and baseball-reference.com.

Joy dedicates this article to her father, Gary, born with cerebral palsy in the 1940s, long before he could benefit from the Americans with Disabilities Act; the ADA specifies that students with disabilities must have the same opportunities to participate in sports and activities as anyone else.

NOTES

1   Patrick Saunders, "Aaron Cook: Midwestern Success Story," *Denver Post*, July 12, 2008.

2   Ibid.

3   Ibid.

4   Ibid.

5   Baseball-almanac.com, Aaron Cook 2002 Game-by-Game Pitching Logs.

6   Alex Speier, "Outlier: Why Aaron Cook Is a Pitcher Like Few Others," WEEI.com, May 5, 2012. weei.com/sports/boston/baseball/red-sox/alex-speier/2012/05/05/outlier-why-aaron-cook-pitcher-few-others.

7   Ibid.

8   Nick Cafardo, "Cook's Story Is Stirring," *Boston Globe*, March 1, 2012: C1.

9   Irv Moss, "Colorado Classics: Aaron Cook, Colorado Rockies' Winningest Pitcher," *Denver Post*, May 28, 2013.

10   Saunders.

11   John Powers, "Game 4 Is on Cook's Menu," *Boston Globe*, October 28, 2007: F7.

12   Tyler Kepner. "Red Sox Coronation," *New York Times*, October 29, 2007: D1.

13   "National League All-Stars vs. American League All-Stars," ESPN, July 15, 2008.

14   Colorado Rockies press release, May 27, 2009.

15   Cafardo.

16   Ibid.

17   Associated Press, "Blood Clots Unable to Block Cook's Faith," ESPN, July 29, 2005. espn.com/espn/wire/_/section/mlb/id/2119671

18   Ibid.

19   Moss.

FREDDY SANCHEZ

BY RICHARD BOGOVICH

THE **AMERICAN DREAM OF** being a well-known baseball player was firmly established years before Babe Ruth's major-league debut in 1914. For instance, in 1910 a *New York Times* article on recreation centers and urban parks asked, rhetorically, "What youngster nowadays dreams of being President of the country when it is just as easy to conjure up a vision of one's self as a pitcher in the National League?"[1] If Fred and Michelle Sanchez of Hollywood, California, had any such visions when their son Freddy was born shortly before Christmas 1977, they must have been deflated when a doctor first explained how unusual their son's feet were. Envisioning the boy ever being able to walk would be dream enough.

Frederick Phillip Sánchez Jr. was born in the Hollywood Presbyterian Medical Center on December 21, 1977, with a club right foot and a left foot that was severely pigeon-toed. The clubfoot was the more significant medical challenge, and one for which treatment was attempted without delay. Casts were put on both legs on his second day of life. One covered his entire leg, and the other went up to his knee. The casts were replaced weekly, so on Tuesday nights the infant's legs would be soaked in water long enough to make removing the casts easy, and new casts were put on the next morning.[2]

As a hospital magazine explained after he won the 2006 Tony Conigliaro Award, "Freddy had to wear a cast on his right leg in an attempt to correct his clubfoot, which was twisted in and down. A clubfoot is the most common birth defect, occurring in one to two per 1,000 live births nationwide. In Freddy's case, the correction didn't take, and at age 13 months he came to Children's Hospital Los Angeles for surgery by orthopaedic surgeon Saul M. Bernstein, MD." Michelle Sanchez recalled pulling Freddy in a Radio Flyer wagon made available for transporting little ones through the hospital's hallways. In the surgery,

a pin was inserted in his right foot in addition to yet another cast up to his thigh, and a smaller cast was placed on his left foot. A permanent outcome was a shortened calf muscle diminished range of motion in his ankle. Still, just one day after this first surgery Freddy climbed out of the wagon unassisted and started to walk. "'Can't' was not in our vocabulary as a family," Mrs. Sanchez said.[3]

"I couldn't believe what I was seeing," she recalled in another interview. "From that moment, he has never stopped being a miracle." However, not everything was cured miraculously with that one surgery; as an infant Freddy had also been diagnosed with hearing loss in his right ear.[4]

Years of physical therapy were in Freddy's future. Around the time the first of his own sons was 13 months old, Freddy said he didn't really recall the daily trips with his mother to the hospital, his dependence on a walker, or the special shoes with metal bars that he needed to wear. Nevertheless, by kindergarten he was scampering all over like other kids, and before he was a teenager he had decided on baseball as his career. In fact, his mother reported that in his sixth-grade yearbook, Freddy wrote that his dream was to "be drafted into pro baseball right out of high school."[5]

Michelle Sanchez recalled that Freddy was playing catch with his father as early as age 2. She remembered watching one afternoon when the tennis ball they were using was veering away from the boy. Instead of being content to give chase, little Freddy sprang horizontally toward it. "Even then, he preferred to dive rather than catch a ball straight on," she observed.[6]

Freddy credited his father and uncle with teaching him baseball before he was old enough for kindergarten, and soon enough he wanted to play on teams. "But in the LA area it's tough to find parks and rec leagues so I would always go play with the local guys who were way older," Freddy recalled. "I was 6 or 7 and they were 13 or 14 years old."[7] So Freddy wasn't only fitting in, he was putting himself in a position to be challenged.

By the time Freddy was in his early school days, Fred and Michelle Sanchez were seeing more frequent signs of the normalcy that they had lived before he was born. They were both born in the Los Angeles area, and met through friends. Fred served two tours of duty with the US Army in Vietnam right after high school, a common enough experience for young men of that generation. Gradually, their experience as parents included more everyday activities, such as watching young Freddy play T-ball. When Freddy was a sixth grader the family moved to Burbank, and he spent the rest of his youth living across the street from the high school.[8]

Freddy told a *Los Angeles Times* reporter that he didn't consider his childhood to have been unusual "because I didn't know any better when I was younger. I didn't know about any limitations. My parents didn't treat me any different than anybody else."[9]

ESPN writer Jerry Crasnick called the Burbank of Sanchez's youth "a town of mixed incomes and races and big dreams." Freddy's father made a living as a truck driver, and one job that his mother had was with a janitorial services company. Despite this middle-class description, living so close to Hollywood meant brushes with celebrities, and as a high schooler Sanchez played pickup basketball games with actor Will Smith and R&B singer-songwriter Brian McKnight. Sanchez used sports to sidestep superficial socializing on weekends. He told Crasnick his friend Jeff Atkinson would spend time with him on a tennis court next to the high school's baseball diamond until the lights were extinguished at 11 P.M. They would wield baseball bats, mark a strike zone, and whip tennis balls at each other from 25 to 30 feet apart.[10]

In or around his freshman year of high school, Freddy had surgery for the hearing deficiency that had been diagnosed in his right ear when he was an infant. His mother said that for a short time he wore a hearing aid but it was more hindrance than help; it would make nearby traffic or other background noises louder and thus drown out conversations.[11]

In his second year Freddy began to be recognized for his athleticism. In March of 1994, a preview of high-school baseball teams in the *Los Angeles Times* named Freddy, a shortstop, as one of the top three newcomers for Burbank's squad.[12] The following season, the *Times* singled him out for igniting a big rally during a playoff game with a home run (albeit in a losing cause).[13]

As so often happens, everything seemed to fall into place for him as graduation day grew near. "Sanchez, who was batting .250 less than a month ago, has been on a tear," reported the *Times* toward the end of April 1996. "He has raised his average to .419, with 18 of his 25 RBIs coming in the past three weeks."[14] About a month later, after finishing with a .425 batting average, he was named the Foothill League Player of the Year despite the fact that his Bulldogs didn't qualify for the playoffs.[15] Then on June 4 the Atlanta Braves drafted Sanchez in the 30th round of the annual amateur draft. In mid-June he received the Most Valuable Player trophy at the conclusion of an all-star game.

"You don't see many people get it for playing defense," Sanchez noted at the time. "It's usually an offensive player." Still, he had contributed at the bat in the top of the eighth inning, singling home a run to increase his team's lead to 3-1. Nevertheless, he felt that two subsequent plays on defense earned him the trophy. In the bottom of the eighth he slid to snare a groundball and threw home to nail a runner who was trying to score. And with two runners on in the ninth Sanchez fielded a difficult ball behind second base and fired a fastball to first to end the contest. "I practice every day," he said. "I work hard on my defense and my offense. I just see the ball and react. That's just me."[16] When Burbank High School retired Sanchez's number 21 years later, former coach Steve Wilson recalled that the three-sport athlete had been given a key to the ballfield so he could cross the street to practice whenever he chose.[17]

Sanchez chose not to sign with the Braves and instead enrolled at nearby Glendale Community College. As a sophomore in the spring of 1998 he had a .407 batting average, with 10 home runs and 33 RBIs. He was named the Western State Conference

South Division player of the year, and the Vaqueros became playoff co-champions in their first trip to the postseason in 17 years.[18]

After junior college, Sanchez recalled, "The only other offer I had was Chico State, and I didn't get drafted. My [Glendale] coach talked to [Dallas Baptist University's] coach, and I never even visited the school. I just went out there. Sanchez played shortstop for Dallas Baptist's 1999 National Association of Intercollegiate Athletics (NAIA) World Series team. However, the head coach soon left the program, and Sanchez transferred to Oklahoma City University for the 1999-2000 school year.[19]

Though Sanchez played only one season for Oklahoma City University, results and recognition came as quickly as at Dallas Baptist. He batted .434 with 13 home runs and 59 RBIs. He was named an NAIA All-American shortstop. "Everything I learned baseball-wise pretty much came from OCU. That's the best baseball program I've been around," Sanchez said a few years later. "I learned how to be a smart baseball player and do all the little things right."[20]

On June 5, 2000, Sanchez was drafted by the Boston Red Sox in the 11th round. He signed on the 14th and made his professional debut on the 20th about 30 miles northwest of Boston, in the season opener for the short-season Lowell Spinners in a 2-1 loss at home to the Pittsfield Mets before 5,000 fans. Sanchez batted second and was hitless in three at-bats with a stolen base, though he was singled out in the local newspaper for "flashy defense" at shortstop.[21]

After 34 games Sanchez was hitting .288 when in early August he was promoted to the low Class-A GreenJackets of the South Atlantic League. There he hit for an even higher average, .303, in 30 games. For the start of 2001 he climbed another rung at the Class-A level, with Sarasota in the Florida State League. After 69 games he was hitting .339 and was promoted to Double-A Trenton. He finished the season there with 44 more games and hit .326.

Lowell Sun sportswriter Chaz Scoggins had been following Sanchez's progress carefully. "After spending millions and millions of dollars on free agents, many of whom weren't worth 40 cents on the dollar, the day may come soon when the Red Sox consider Freddy Sanchez the best thousand bucks they ever spent," Scoggins wrote after Sanchez finished at Trenton. "Signed by the Red Sox for a paltry $1,000 bonus … the slick-fielding shortstop led all organization players in hitting this past summer." Scoggins noted that after starting his pro career with only two hits in his first 20 at-bats (which Sanchez attributed to using a wood bat for the first time), he not only became Lowell's Player of the Year but was named that at Sarasota as well.

Scoggins mentioned a highlight from Sanchez's first major-league spring training, in 2001. The Red Sox called him up for a day and used him late in a game against the New York Yankees. Besides making an impressive play on defense, he homered in his lone plate appearance. "I never thought I would get into that game. I had been called up a couple times before and didn't get into one," he said. "Just to get in there and play would have been enough of a thrill. But when I batted I just wanted to put the ball in play and instead got good wood on it."[22]

Sanchez started the 2002 season with Trenton, where he hit .328 in 80 games, had a 27-game hitting streak, and homered in the Double-A All-Star Game.

That all earned him a promotion on July 16 to Triple-A Pawtucket (International League). The buzz was building about a promising future as a major leaguer. However, the speculation was that it couldn't be at shortstop for Boston, where Nomar Garciaparra was entrenched, so Sanchez was seeing some time at second base for Pawtucket. "I'm willing to play any position to get to Boston," Sanchez said, but acknowledged that there might not be room for him at second base, either. "I want to be part of the Red Sox' tradition," he said, "but if they have other plans for me then so be it. That goes along with this job."[23]

Sanchez had a wonderful reason not to overthink his baseball future: He married his high-school sweetheart, Alissa Dowdy, on August 8, 2002. During high school she had done some acting, and earned credits in 1995 for TV appearances on *The Nanny* and *The Fresh Prince of Bel-Air*.[24] Over the years Freddy's family had grown with the additions of younger siblings Joseph and Sarah, in addition to older half-sister Tina, and now he and Alissa were poised to start their own family.

In the end, Sanchez ended up hitting .301 for Pawtucket in 45 games, and couldn't have been very surprised when he was summoned by Boston. In Florida on September 10 the Red Sox were pounding the Devil Rays, and Sanchez was sent to the plate in the seventh inning to make his major-league debut. He singled home two runs in what ended up a 12-1 Boston win. *Boston Globe* sportswriter Gordon Edes tracked down Fred Cook, Burbank High's athletic director, for a reaction. "He could have played basketball for me, he was that good an athlete," Cook said, but he soon changed from praise to poking fun. "A good kid, a good all-around athlete. The last time I saw him, we played golf. His golf game stinks. And tell him his younger brother Joe is driving around in his car."[25]

Sanchez collected only two more hits in 11 more games for Boston, ending up with a .188 batting average. He started 2003 back with Pawtucket, but he played in 20 more games for Boston, hitting .235 from June 4 to July 11. He was back with Pawtucket in late July, and hit .341 in 58 games overall, when the major-league trading deadline arrived. On July 31 Boston traded Sanchez, Mike Gonzalez, and some cash, to the Pittsburgh Pirates for three pitchers, Jeff Suppan, Brandon Lyon, and Anastacio Martínez. (Suppan was a disappointment during Boston's stretch run, compiling a 5.57 earned-run average and giving up 12 home runs in 11 games, but Lyon had nine saves and a 4.12 ERA in 49 games.)

Sanchez thus switched to Triple-A Nashville but an ankle injury ended his season after one game. In the offseason he had a bone spur in his right foot removed surgically to alleviate a diagnosis of ankle tendinitis. A full recovery was anticipated by spring training of 2004.[26]

The first half of 2004 did not go as expected. Sanchez wasn't able to play for Nashville until June 20 and got into only 44 games through September 6, hitting a modest .264. He did get back to the major leagues, making his debut for the Pirates on September 9, though he hit only .158 in nine games. A friend of his from a summer league during high school, Jack Wilson, happened to already be on the Pirates, so during those few weeks Jack and his wife, Julie, took in Freddy and Alissa as houseguests.[27]

Sanchez's circumstances improved before 2004 ended. Assigned to the Peoria Saguaros in the Arizona Fall League, he played well enough that in mid-November the Pirates decided to cut loose their top pinch-hitter and utility player, Abraham Núñez. "We're seeing a healthy Freddy, the kind of player we thought we were getting when we traded for him in 2003," said Pirates general manager Dave Littlefield.[28]

On April 19, 2005, Freddy and Alissa had their first child, Evan. Sanchez then enjoyed his first full season in the major leagues, and didn't sit on the bench much. He started 100 games and subbed in 32 other games. He started at his natural shortstop position just six times; most of his duty was at third and second. He finished with a .291 batting average, thanks in part to a hitting streak over the season's last 17 games. Sanchez experienced a very personal thrill on September 23 when the Pirates began a series in Los Angeles. His father had taken him to Dodgers games but this was his first visit as a major leaguer. "I've played at Yankee Stadium, I've played at Fenway Park, and I've played at Wrigley Field," he said. "This is the first stadium that I'm at where I still get butterflies."

Any nervousness Sanchez felt upon arrival didn't undercut his performance: In the third inning, he hit his fourth home run of the week, with a man on, to give Pittsburgh a 2-1 lead. The Dodgers won, 4-3, and that certainly countered Sanchez's personal excitement. "I hate losing more than I like winning," he said a couple of days later.[29]

During the offseason it wasn't clear that Sanchez would begin 2006 as a starter. He didn't demonstrate the power hitting that is often expected from third basemen, his .336 on-base percentage reflected few bases on balls, and there were ongoing concerns about a pattern of injuries. "Hey, I can improve but, in my eyes, I know I will," he said in mid-December. "To me, the key last season was getting all those reps near the end. I was showing up at the park every day knowing I'd be in the lineup, and my confidence took off."[30] Early in 2006 he had an opportunity to gauge his support among Pirates fans by taking part in the second leg of the team's Winter Caravan. He traveled to 10 area communities, including Wheeling, West Virginia, and Punxsutawney, Pennsylvania, with Jack Wilson, Mike Gonzalez, pitching coach Jim Colborn, broadcasters Lanny Frattare and John Wehner, and others.[31]

For 2006 the Pirates ended up signing third baseman Joe Randa to a $4 million contract and Sanchez began the season as an extra infielder. When Randa injured his foot on May 1, Sanchez had another chance to make a strong impression. By the time fan voting for the All-Star Game concluded, Sanchez was hitting well over .300. He received more than 856,000 write-in votes, the most of any player, but that was only good enough for fifth place among third basemen. Nevertheless, that turned out to be enough to persuade NL manager Phil Garner to add Sanchez to the All-Star roster. Sanchez celebrated immediately with a 3-for-4, four-RBI game that raised his batting average to .363. "It's an unbelievable feeling, coming from spring training and not even knowing how many at-bats I'd get and knowing my role as a utility player," Sanchez said after Garner chose him. "I can't even describe it."[32]

The 2006 All-Star Game was played on July 11 at PNC Park in Pittsburgh. Because the Pirates had the worst record in the majors, local fans needed something that exciting. It probably wasn't much of a surprise that Sanchez got to play the last five innings of the NL's 3-2 loss, first at shortstop, then switching to second base. He grounded out in both of his plate appearances. Right from the start he made a strong impression. "Garner's take-it-to-them attitude was evident in the field" when NL pitcher Bronson Arroyo got the best of slugger Vladimir Guerrero to start the fifth inning, "with Pirates spark plug Freddy Sanchez actually shoving third baseman David Wright out of the way to catch a foul popup," the Associated Press reported. "Sanchez, playing shortstop, also went high into the air to make an excellent catch of Mark Loretta's liner to end the fifth."[33]

Because the Pirates continued to struggle, and ended the season with a record of 67-95, the main attraction for their fans during the final weeks of the season was Sanchez battling for the NL batting crown. It came down to October 1, the last day of the regular season. Sanchez led Miguel Cabrera of the Florida Marlins every day during the final week, but his lead narrowed from 11 percentage points to just 3 when the last games began. Sanchez singled in the first and fourth innings that day, and wound up winning the title by 5 points. Sanchez's .344 average was the highest by a Pittsburgh batting champ since Roberto Clemente's .357 in 1967. His 53 doubles also led the NL and he reached the 200-hit mark. That hit in the fourth was the one that got him there, two years after teammate and high-school friend Jack Wilson had reached the same milestone. Jack hugged Freddy when they took the field in the next inning. "I'm proud of you," Jack told him. "We're in the history books with the 200 hits. Pretty cool from where we've come."[34]

If anyone was worried that Sanchez might've developed an unlikable ego as a result of his success, a few weeks after the season pitching coach Colborn helped allay such fears with a touch of humor. Colborn was asked about the supposition in some circles that during games teams might try to read the lips of opposing players and coaches. "When I go to the mound and I'm saying something, I try to keep my lips from moving. In other words, I do ventriloquism coaching," he asserted. "And when I have to chew the pitcher out, what I do is, I do it in Freddy Sanchez's voice, and then they won't get mad at me—and they won't get mad at Freddy, either, because everyone likes Freddy."[35]

On November 4 Sanchez was inducted into the Athletics Hall of Fame at Oklahoma City University. By that time he was able to articulate more about the final day of the season. "It was pressure packed, but it wasn't like being up with the bases loaded in the ninth. It was a hundred times more than that," he stated. "That was probably the most pressure I've had at the plate. Two hundred hits were there. The batting title was there."[36]

About a month later came another honor: receiving the 17th annual Tony Conigliaro Award. Sanchez received one more vote than Boston outfielder Gabe Kapler and four more than San Diego pitcher Doug Brocail. Other players receiving votes were Rocco Baldelli, Mike Cameron, Brian Roberts, Jermaine Dye, and Joe Borowski.[37]

Sanchez was a little nicked up at the start of the 2007 season, and on April 5 he played one game for the Triple-A Indianapolis on a rehab assignment. Back with the Pirates, early on he became a fixture at second base. In fact, for the rest of his major-league career that was the only infield position at which he started. The Pirates fared as poorly as they had in 2006, so one of the few bright spots was when Sanchez was named to the NL All-Star team again, this time as the only Pirate. His batting average at the end of the season was .304, and his 81 RBIs were just four shy of his career best the previous season. He hit 11 homers, the only time he reached double figures in his professional career.

On January 26, 2008, Freddy and Alissa celebrated the birth of their second son, Ryan. As for the 2008 season, his .271 batting average was his lowest as a major-league regular, and for his fourth consecutive year as a starter he played on a team that couldn't win 70 games.

Things were brighter during the first half of the 2009 season. On May 29 Sanchez had one of the most noteworthy batting performances of his life, after he was almost given the night off in Chicago. Not long before, he had been mired in a 5-for-34 slump, but on the 29th he went 6-for-6 with four runs scored and three driven in, two of which were on a homer. The previous Pirate to have a six-hit game was Wally Backman 19 years earlier. Sanchez didn't have any sophisticated insights about this achievement. "I was striking out too much before," he explained. "I shortened my swing and put the ball in play."[38]

In July Sanchez was picked for the All-Star Game for the third time in four years (though this time he didn't get to play). As the game approached, there was speculation that the 32-year-old wouldn't be a Pirate much longer. The team, once again last in its division, had made major trades in June, and other clubs reportedly interested in acquiring Sanchez included Minnesota, Colorado, and San Francisco,[39] the latter two teams neck and neck in the NL wild-card race. On July 29 Sanchez was dealt to the San Francisco Giants for minor-league pitcher Tim Alderson, the Giants' first-round draft choice two years earlier. His batting average at the time of the trade was .296, so his performance was back to normal after his off-year of 2008.

Jack Wilson was traded the same day, to Seattle. Both had said they wanted to end their careers as Pirates, though both had also turned down two-year contract extensions two weeks earlier. "It's tough because I lost more than a teammate in Jack but someone who is like a brother to me," Sanchez said. "It's a very emotional day."[40] He experienced physical issues during the remainder of the season, and on August 26 he was placed on the 15-day disabled list because of a strained left shoulder. Sanchez got into only 25 games for the Giants, who lost the wild-card battle to Colorado but finished with a record of 88-74, which had to make for a much more optimistic offseason for Sanchez than usual.

Before suiting up for the Giants in 2010 Sanchez spent the week of May 11-18 in minor-league rehab stints. Rejoining the Giants, he played in 111 games and hit .292. Finally he was able to enjoy being in a pennant race. The Giants' 92-70 record gave them the Western Division title by two games over San Diego. It was a battle until the season's end. "We always felt if we got to the playoffs, we would have a chance to win," Sanchez commented. "But you know, we weren't sure we were going to get there until that last weekend."[41]

Sanchez's first postseason appearance was against the Atlanta Braves in the best-of-five Division Series. He was only 2-for-18 but made a major contribution at a key moment. After the teams split the first two contests, the Braves led Game Three 2-1 in the top of the ninth at Atlanta. When Sanchez stepped up to face rookie right-hander Craig Kimbrel in the top of the ninth, the Giants had the tying run on first but were down to their last out. Soon enough Sanchez and the Giants were down to their last strike, but he grounded a single to center to keep the game alive. Aubrey Huff followed with a single off Michael Dunn to tie the game and Sanchez gave the Giants the lead on the next play by scoring on an error. The Giants hung on in the bottom of the ninth to win, 3-2. They then won the fourth game to advance to the NL Championship Series.

Against the Phillies, who had won the NL's previous two pennants, Sanchez hit a much more characteristic .320 as the Giants won the series in six games to take the pennant. In the World Series they faced the Texas Rangers.

In Game One, in San Francisco, Sanchez doubled off Cliff Lee in the first inning but was doubled off second on a popup. He atoned in the third inning with another double to drive in the Giants' first run. In the fifth he hit another double to put the Giants ahead for good. He added a third RBI in the eighth with a hit that was first ruled a double, then changed to a single plus an error by the right fielder. Sanchez became the first player to hit three doubles in his first three World Series plate appearances. If that fourth hit had remained a double, he would have tied the record for the most two-baggers in a World Series game, held by Frank Isbell of the 1906 White Sox.[42] The Giants were 11-7 winners.

Sanchez was 0-for-5 as the Giants' Matt Cain blanked Texas 9-0 in Game Two. The Rangers won Game Three, 4-2 (Sanchez was 1-for-4) but the Giants shut them out again, 4-0, in Game Four (Sanchez was 0-for-4 Janie McCauley of the Associated Press wrote that it was defense that put the Giants on the verge of winning the World Series, and she credited Sanchez foremost. In the 4-0 shutout, he started two double plays but also made what she called a "gutsy grab" of a line drive to end the second inning with a Ranger on first base. His leap sent him onto his back, and he barely kept the ball in his mitt. "That was all Freddy," first baseman Travis Ishikawa told her. "He was tremendous out there, going left, going right. He definitely made a lot of key plays for us tonight."[43]

The Giants won Game Five, 3-1, and were World Series champions. Sanchez heaped praise on the strong starts by pitchers Madison Bumgarner and Tim Lincecum in the last two games. "I was fortunate to stand out there behind two pitchers who threw two of the best games in World Series history," he gushed. "I can't even say enough good things about those two performances."[44]

Sanchez continued with the Giants in 2011. He was hitting .292 in his 60th game of the season on June 10 when he dislocated his shoulder diving for a grounder. That game against the Reds turned out to be his last as a major leaguer. He tried to come back in early 2012, and played in three games for the San Jose Giants in a rehab assignment from April 23 to 26. He batted 4-for-10 in what were his final games as a pro ballplayer. On July 5 it was announced that back surgery would end his season. He was granted free agency on October 29. He didn't officially retire until December 21, 2015, on his 38th birthday. Sanchez accumulated 1,012 hits as a major leaguer and finished with a batting average of .297.

In June of 2016 Sanchez and Jason Bay represented the Pittsburgh Pirates at the annual draft, and in that capacity announced the team's first-day choices following the first round. Otherwise, he spent time with his family, one result of which is coaching elementary-school students in baseball tournaments.[45]

NOTES

1   "Personally Directed Sports Are Popular With Children," *New York Times*, July 24, 1910: 12.

2   Telephone interview with Michelle Sanchez, September 11, 2016.

3   Candace Pearson, "A Dream Life," *Imagine* (Children's Hospital Los Angeles), Fall 2007: 20.

4   Lee Jenkins, "The Pirates' Stealth Swinger Is Rewriting the Script," *New York Times*, September 12, 2006: D1.

5   Gretchen McKay, "Home Base," *Pittsburgh Post-Gazette*, July 15, 2006: D1.

6   Pearson.

7   Matt Patterson, "Batting Champ Inducted into OCU Hall," *The Oklahoman* (Oklahoma City), November 5, 2006: 5B.

8   Michelle Sanchez interview.

9   Tim Brown, "Sanchez's Time Finally Comes," *Los Angeles Times*, July 12, 2006: D5.

10 Jerry Crasnick, "Pirates' Sanchez Defying the Odds," espn.com/mlb/columns/story?id=2549356, August 15, 2006.

11 Michelle Sanchez interview.

12 "High School Baseball Season Preview: Foothill League," *Los Angeles Times* (Valley Edition), March 5, 1994: 20. Freddy was incorrectly identified as a senior rather than as a sophomore.

13 "High School Baseball Roundup," *Los Angeles Times* (Valley Edition), May 17, 1995: 9.

14 "Midweek Report/High School Sports Update," *Los Angeles Times* (Valley Edition), April 25, 1996: 7.

15 "Local Notes: Burbank's Sanchez Tops in League," *Los Angeles Daily News* (Valley Edition), May 29, 1996: S6.

16 Vince Kowalick, "Sanchez Comes to East's Defense," *Los Angeles Times* (Valley Edition), June 16, 1996: 10.

17 Heather Gripp, "It's No Average Ceremony: Burbank High Honors Sanchez," *Los Angeles Daily News* (Valley Edition), January 13, 2007: S1.

18 "Valley/Venture County Sports," *Los Angeles Times* (Valley Edition), May 14, 1998: 13.

19 "Giants Update," *Contra Costa Times* (Walnut Creek, California), June 11, 2011: B5.

20 Bob Hersom, "Ex-OCU Star a Big Hit in Majors," *The Oklahoman* (Oklahoma City), June 24, 2006: 1C.

21 David Pevear, "For Openers, It Was (Almost) Perfect," *The Sun* (Lowell, Massachusetts), June 21, 2000: 27.

22 Chaz Scoggins, "Sanchez May Prove to Be Bargain for Boston," *The Sun* (Lowell, Massachusetts), October 7, 2001: 29.

23 Carmine Frongillo, "Future May Not Be at Shortstop for Sanchez," *The Sun* (Lowell, Massachusetts), August 11, 2002: 25. Freddy was quoted extensively after the article jumped to page 29.

24 imdb.com/name/nm0235725/.

25 Gordon Edes, "Major Raves for Sanchez," *Boston Globe*, September 11, 2002: D5.

26 Robert Dvorchak, "Stairs Rejects Offer, Decides on Free Agency," *Pittsburgh Post-Gazette*, October 31, 2003: B-11.

27 McKay, D1. Sanchez was born eight days before Wilson.

28 Robert Dvorchak, "Pirates Release Davis Among Four Dropped as Roster Is Set at 40," *Pittsburgh Post-Gazette*, November 20, 2004: D-1.

29 Edgar Melik-Stepanyan, "This Is What I live for," *Burbank* (California) *Leader*, October 1, 2005: B1.

30 Dejan Kovacevic, "Who's on Third? After Losing Mueller, Is Sanchez the Man?" *Pittsburgh Post-Gazette*, December 18, 2005: D-17.

31 Dejan Kovacevic, "McCutchen Gets Pleasant Surprise," *Pittsburgh Post-Gazette*, January 22, 2006: C-13.

32 John Mehno, "Sanchez Becomes All-Star Surprise," *Altoona* (Pennsylvania) *Mirror*, July 3, 2006: B3.

33 Alan Robinson, Associated Press, "Aggressive Garner Can't Steal Victory," *Daily News* (Bowling Green, Kentucky), July 12, 2006: 4C.

34 Paul Meyer, ".344, 200 Hits, 1 Title," *Pittsburgh Post-Gazette*, October 2, 2006: A-1. Jack Wilson was quoted extensively after the article jumped to page A-6.

35 Mark Roth, "Most Agree That There's No Lip Reading in Baseball," *Pittsburgh Post-Gazette*, October 21, 2006: A-1.

36 Patterson.

37 "Sanchez Wins Tony Conigliaro Award," *The Progress* (Clearfield, Pennsylvania), December 7, 2006: 9.

38 "Ready, Freddy," *New Castle* (Pennsylvania) *News*, May 26, 2009: B1.

39 For example, see John Perrotto, "More Roster Changes Are Likely in 2nd Half," *Johnstown* (Pennsylvania) *Tribune-Democrat*, July 12, 2009: B1.

40 John Perrotto, "Wilson, Sanchez Saddened by Deals," *Johnstown* (Pennsylvania) *Tribune-Democrat*, July 30, 2009: B2.

41 Mark Purdy, "Improbable Comes True for Eclectic Clubhouse," *Appeal-Democrat* (Marysville-Yuba City, California), November 3, 2010: B1.

42 Josh Dubow, "Sanchez Leads Giants to Game 1 Win Vs. Rangers," *Herald Zeitung* (New Braunfels, Texas), October 28, 2010: 6.

43 Janie McCauley, Associated Press, "Closing in: Defense Carries SF to Cusp of Series Win," *Indiana* (Pennsylvania) *Gazette*, November 1, 2010: 13. Travis Ishikawa was quoted after the article jumped to page 17.

44 Purdy.

45 Telephone interview with Michelle Sanchez, November 7, 2016.

JON LESTER

BY SAUL WISNIA

THE LATTER STAGES OF A potential no-hitter are always cause for excitement, but as Red Sox left-hander Jon Lester moved into the final innings of his May 19, 2008, start against the Kansas City Royals, even more emotion than usual was building at Fenway Park.

Boston manager Terry Francona later admitted that he was on the verge of breaking down in the first-base dugout as the last out neared and Kansas City remained hitless.[1] Second baseman Dustin Pedroia, who had played in Clay Buchholz's no-hitter the previous September, recalled knowing this one would feel different given the special circumstances.[2] It was far too early in the season to be worried about the standings, but the contest had the energy and intensity of a playoff game—with fans yelling even louder than they had in the previous October's World Series.

What made this chilly Monday evening at the ballpark so powerful for those experiencing it went far beyond the zeros lining the visitor's column of Fenway's left-field scoreboard. Just 20 months before, in late August of 2006, Lester, then a rookie, had been diagnosed at age 22 with a rare blood cancer known as large-cell non-Hodgkin's lymphoma. After chemotherapy and other treatment cost him the remainder of that season, he spent nearly a year regaining his strength. It was a great story when Lester returned to win the clinching game of the 2007 World Series for Boston with five-plus gutsy innings, but he was still honing his craft; entering this start against the Royals, the lefty's career earned-run average was 4.47.[3]

Part of the challenge was pitch counts. Because of his youth, and health challenges, Lester had thrown more than 110 pitches only twice in his 35 previous career starts. He was usually well below 100, but Francona was likely to keep him in this one as long as Kansas City failed to hit safely.

The Royals had a few chances early on. Shaky Boston shortstop Julio Lugo fielded a tough grounder by Tony Peña and threw him out in the third inning, and center fielder Jacoby Ellsbury made a great running catch of a liner hit by Jose Guillen in the fourth. By that time, the Red Sox had scored five runs in their half of the third on four hits, three walks, and an error, giving Lester a major cushion.

By the ninth inning it was 7-0, and the only drama was whether Lester could do it. He walked Esteban German leading off the frame—Kansas City's second walk, and first baserunner, since the second inning—but then Peña and David DeJesus grounded out. All of Fenway was now on its feet cheering wildly, and when he struck out Alberto Callaspo with a rising fastball on his 130th and final pitch of the night, it was a signal to the baseball world: Jon Lester was fully recovered from his cancer, and ready to make his mark as an elite pitcher.[4]

"He's a wonderful kid, not just because he threw the no-hitter," Francona said after the game. "To watch him do that tonight is beyond words. What a story. You feel like a proud parent."[5]

The manager's reaction—including an on-field hug with Lester during which Francona finally let his tears flow—was due as much to what he and his young pitcher had gone through together during the past two years as to the no-hitter itself.[6] Lester was nearly the same age as one of Francona's sons, and they had stayed in contact regularly during his year spent recovering away from the team.

"It's something I'll remember for a long time," Lester said of the hug with Francona, which was caught by photographers and TV cameramen and broadcast repeatedly. "He has been like a second dad to me. He cares a lot about his players. It's not just about what you do on the field."[7]

In Lester's case, that's a lot. His accomplishments since the no-hitter—more than 130 regular-season wins, four All-Star selections, additional postseason heroics, and status as an ace for three different big-league clubs—are a testament to Lester's talent, toughness, and durability. These traits, along with his soft-spoken demeanor off the mound and bulldog style on it, have made him an immensely popular player. For cancer patients and their families, many of whom he has met through his outreach efforts with Boston's Dana-Farber Cancer Institute and other organizations, he has also become an inspiration.

Born in Tacoma, Washington, on January 7, 1984, Jonathan Tyler Lester is the only child of John Lester, a sergeant in the Pierce County Sheriff's Department, and Kathi Lester, an employee of the public works department. He grew up playing baseball, football, basketball, and soccer, but his future dreams lay on the diamond. Helping fuel them were the Seattle Mariners, who played about a half-hour from his home and were on the rise in the mid-1990s behind future Hall of Famers Ken Griffey Jr. and Randy Johnson. Like Johnson, Lester was a tall left-hander who could throw fast, and he made the varsity team as a freshman at Bellarmine Prep, a Catholic high school of about 1,000 in nearby Puyallup.[8]

The poise and maturity that would one day help Lester reach the majors were already on display, as was a fastball clocked at 93 mph. He was named Bellarmine's MVP in his freshman year and Gatorade Player of the Year for all of Washington State as a sophomore. Professional scouts started showing up at his high-school games—including, it was reported, some from his beloved Mariners. In one season he had 86 strikeouts in 42 innings; in one game he threw a seven-inning no-hitter with 18 strikeouts. College recruiters, hoping the 6-foot-4, 200-pound hurler would choose to further his education rather than sign a pro contract, regularly called the Lester home. (They were not allowed at the games.)[9]

Lester was very close with his parents, and newspaper accounts at the time noted that he sought their insights on whether to choose college or professional baseball after graduation. Possessing no experience in the latter area, Lester's father reportedly used a connection at Safeco Field in Seattle to secure a meeting for Jon with Mariners pitcher Jamie Moyer. The fellow left-hander recommended that Lester go to college

and continue developing as a ballplayer rather than go for the easy payday.[10]

It made for a good story, but despite the advice Moyer may have given him, Lester denied any trepidation about his decision.

"You know, I've never really known where that came from," he told writer David Laurila in 2004. "My dream has always been to play pro ball, and I wasn't a big school guy, anyway. I felt I made that clear at the time. I think I was real honest with everyone about my plans and expectations coming into the draft."[11]

Expressing surprise that Lester was still on the board for them to grab, the Red Sox made the 18-year-old their first selection (57th overall) in the June 2002 amateur draft. He received a $1 million signing bonus, and even though Lester didn't last long in his professional debut that summer—allowing six runs on five hits and a walk in just two-thirds of an inning for Boston's Gulf Coast League rookie team—Red Sox assistant general manager Theo Epstein expressed confidence that the team had made a sound investment.[12]

Due to his late signing (in August), that was Lester's only pro appearance in 2002. He pitched in the Instructional League during the offseason, and then the next year compiled a fine ERA of 3.65 that overshadowed his 6-9 record at Class-A Augusta. Highly regarded by the Boston organization, he was coveted by other clubs as well—leading to his role as a footnote in the biggest baseball story of the 2003-04 offseason.

By this point Epstein had taken over as Red Sox GM. Worried that fan favorite Nomar Garciaparra was slipping defensively at shortstop, the young executive put together a three-team trade in which Texas Rangers superstar and reigning American League MVP Alex Rodriguez would come to Boston to take Garciaparra's place at short. Lester would go to Texas in the deal, along with cash and Red Sox left fielder Manny Ramirez—whose big bat would offset the loss of Rodriguez's power in the Rangers lineup. Garciaparra, meanwhile, would go to the Chicago White Sox with reliever Scott Williamson in exchange for pitching prospect Brandon McCarthy and outfielder Magglio Ordonez—replacements for Lester and Ramirez.

The only hang-up to the deal was Rodriguez's huge contract, which still had seven years and $179 million remaining. Epstein felt Boston could not afford to take on all that salary, and Rodriguez was willing to restructure the deal at about $4 million less per season. But the latest Collective Bargaining Agreement between the players union and owners stated that any player restructuring his contract for less money must be given something of equal value in return; to compensate, the Red Sox agreed to give Rodriguez the option to become a free agent after just two years—and every year thereafter—versus a post-fourth-year free-agent clause in the existing contract.

Rodriguez gave his OK to the terms on December 16, 2003. News reports of the trade made it into print and TV broadcasts, but before a press conference to give Rodriguez a Boston uniform could be held, associate general counsel Gene Orza of the players union voided the trade out of concern it would set a precedent for similar risky restructuring by players to come.[13]

A few weeks shy of his 20th birthday, Jon Lester was still a Red Sox. And in the spring of 2004 he reported to Class-A Sarasota—where he met another left-hander who would have a huge impact on his development. Al Nipper had been a regular member of the Red Sox rotation as a rookie during the team's 1986 drive to the World Series, but soon broke down due to multiple arm injuries. Now, as Boston's minor-league pitching coordinator, he wanted to help Lester avoid a similar fate by reworking his windup and giving him better command of his pitches.[14]

"He just wasn't quite synched up," Nipper explained at the time. "He was throwing across his body, which was stressing his arm and the back of his shoulder. It was twofold, a health issue long term, and a command issue." Nipper used his laptop computer to remedy the problem; he put video of Lester on one side of a split screen, and synchronized it with footage of top pitchers Greg Maddux and Roger Clemens on the other. In Clemens' case, he inverted the video so that the former Red Sox ace right-hander (then with the Astros) looked like a lefty. Watching his motion side-by-side with these two Cy Young Award winners, Lester could see which parts of his delivery needed tinkering with.[15]

Nipper and Lester both credited the process for a major improvement in Lester's pitching. By putting more emphasis on a full windup in which he brought his hands up over the head, as well as a longer stride, the pupil threw with better control and velocity. Whereas Lester once reached 93 miles per hour with his fastball, he could now go as high as 96 or 97.[16]

The benefits were not immediate—Lester went 7-6 with a 4.28 ERA at Sarasota that summer—but after an offseason spent continuing to work on what Nipper taught him, Lester flourished for the Double-A Portland Sea Dogs in 2005. Named Pitcher of the Year in the highly competitive Eastern League, he had a circuit-leading 2.61 ERA and 163 strikeouts for Portland in 148⅓ innings. This got Lester a serious look from the big-league club during the next spring training, and when he was dispatched to Triple-A Pawtucket it was understood that a promotion to Boston would soon come.

Injuries to several Boston starters, coupled with a solid first two months by Lester at Pawtucket, resulted in a call-up for his first major-league start on June 10. It was at Fenway Park, against the same heavy-hitting Rangers team to which he had nearly been traded two years before, and he got a no-decision, allowing three runs on five hits and four walks in 4⅓ innings. The first of his four strikeouts came to the first man he faced, Gary Matthews Jr., and he struck out the side in the second inning.[17] Among the fans cheering this feat were Lester's mother and father, who had come from Tacoma for the game.[18]

It was an encouraging start, but what came next was truly impressive. Lester earned his first major-league win at Atlanta on June 16 with six innings of five-hit, one-run pitching, and five days later he captured his first home victory while striking out 10 in six innings against Washington at Fenway Park. By the time he beat the Royals with eight innings of one-hit pitching at Fenway on July 18, Lester had a 2.38 ERA and had become the first left-handed rookie to ever start his Red Sox career with a 5-0 record.

Then the roof caved in.

First a few shaky outings caused his ERA to rise, but Lester kept his spot in the rotation. He was involved in a minor car accident on Boston's Storrow Drive while coming to the ballpark before a start against the Yankees on August 18, and was shelled for seven runs in less than four innings while fighting back pain he assumed was a result of the crash. He managed to win at Anaheim on August 23 to improve to 7-2, breaking a six-game Boston losing streak in the process, but by now was dealing with night sweats and a persistent cold in addition to his bad back.[19] Lester was also losing weight, and his parents insisted he visit his uncle Paul, a Seattle-area internist, when the Red Sox flew there from California.[20]

"My parents and I went to the hospital early in the morning, not thinking much of it, but we were there until four in the afternoon," Lester later recalled. "The emergency room doctor came out and told me I either had testicular cancer or lymphoma."[21]

After going to the ballpark and telling Francona, Lester flew with his parents and Uncle Paul back to Boston on Red Sox owner John Henry's private jet for more tests. Francona, whose own paternal relationship with Lester extended to calling him Junior, told the young pitcher's parents, "We will take care of your son."[22]

Additional tests confirmed Lester's diagnosis: large-cell lymphoma. Lymphomas are cancers of the lymph nodes, an essential part of the immune system, and Dr. Robert Soiffer of the Dana-Farber Cancer Institute stated that while the disease is fast-growing, it is also often curable. "It's responsive to chemotherapy," said Soiffer, "and it is hopefully curable with chemotherapy." Adding that "being young is in his favor," Soiffer said that he hoped Lester would be able to resume pitching after four to six months of chemotherapy.[23]

Lester began treatment immediately, with chemotherapy every three weeks. Other than his initial diagnosis, details of his health and progress were kept out of the media, in large part at Francona's insistence. Although he received care at Dana-Farber and Massachusetts General Hospital in Boston, most of Lester's treatment took place back home at Seattle's Fred Hutchinson Cancer Center.[24] After each chemo session, Lester texted his manager to check in.[25]

In December he chose instead to call Francona. "I'm cancer-free," he said. "You're my first call."[26] Francona told him to get ready for spring training, but things wouldn't be that easy. Lester reported to Florida for workouts still 10 pounds underweight, and although he was anxious to return the big leagues, Francona told him he would have to work his way back slowly. He spent the bulk of the 2007 season in Greenville, Portland, and Pawtucket before being called up. In his first start with Boston, at Cleveland on July 23, he pitched six innings and got the win.

Lester wound up 4-0 in 12 games, with Boston winning 9 of his 11 starts. He never went beyond the seventh inning, however, and experienced elbow pain that required another short rehab stint. When the Red Sox made the postseason, he was kept off the roster for the Division Series but was activated for the American League Championship Series against Cleveland, pitching 3⅔ innings (over two relief outings) as Boston prevailed in seven games.

For the World Series, against Colorado, Lester was chosen by Francona to start Game Four after Boston won the first three contests. He delivered five shutout innings, and after walking a man with two outs in the sixth and the Red Sox up, 2-0, was removed by Francona for a reliever. In his autobiography, Francona said he resisted the urge to hug Lester right there on the mound.

"It was like he had climbed Mount Everest," said Francona. "I know the game wasn't over, but you have to appreciate a moment like that. I knew his mom and dad were there. It was emotional. Having him be a part of that game meant as much to me as anything else."[27]

At the Boston Baseball Writers Association dinner in January 2008, Lester was named winner of the annual Tony Conigliaro Award, which honors the memory of the late Red Sox outfielder and is given each season to a big-league player who has "overcome adversity through the attributes of sprit, determination, and courage that were trademarks of Tony C."[28] Fresh off this accolade, Lester promptly took his comeback to another level in the 2008 season when he pitched his no-hitter and compiled a 16-6 record with a 3.21 ERA and 152 strikeouts in 210⅓ innings. In online fan balloting after the season, his no-hitter was overwhelmingly voted the MLB "Performance of the Year."[29]

While Lester's emergence as a top-flight pitcher had an especially meaningful impact on Francona due to their father-son-like relationship, it also made a big impression on those facing similar health challenges. The day after his no-hitter, patients undergoing chemotherapy infusions at Dana-Farber said they felt a special pride in the young athlete's accomplishment.[30]

"It's hard to describe; even when the treatment is over, it's really tough to get back to where you were before," said one patient, who had been a sports star himself in high school and college. "To see him pitching in the World Series just a year after starting treatment, and now pitching a no-hitter, it's incredible. It definitely gives you inspiration and more hope."[31]

At that moment, an elderly man arrived for treatment with a surprise for his fellow infusion patients. "I look at this guy and say, 'He's come a long way in a short time,'" the man said, taking off his jacket to reveal an authentic Jon Lester jersey. " 'If he can do it, I can do it.'"[32]

Lester kept doing it deep into October, but there was no repeat of the previous year's magic for Boston. The Red Sox lost a seven-game ALCS to Tampa Bay,

with Lester suffering a tough 3-1 defeat to Matt Garza in Game Seven. Still, Lester's overall numbers in four starts that postseason—a 2.36 ERA, 26 strikeouts, and just five walks in 26⅔ innings—made it clear that his World Series heroics of 2007 were more a function of grace under pressure than adrenaline and luck.

And any concerns the Red Sox had about whether Lester's past cancer treatment would impact his future health or durability were soon dismissed. In the next three years (2009-2011) he averaged 31 starts, 201 innings, a 16-9 record, 3.37 ERA, 1.29 WHIP, and 211 strikeouts per season. He was an All-Star in both 2010—when he finished fourth in AL Cy Young Award voting with a 19-9 mark—and 2011, when he started Boston's season opener for the first of three straight years.

Despite his best efforts, however, the Red Sox made the postseason only once during the stretch, and were swept in the 2009 ALDS by the California Angels (including a Game One loss by Lester to future teammate John Lackey). The 2011 season was particularly jarring for how it ended; Boston had the best record in the American League entering September, and then went 7-20 to blow what had seemed like a sure playoff spot—one of the worst September collapses in major-league history.

Making matters even worse for the Red Sox and their fans was what happened next. Widely popular manager Terry Francona resigned, and within two weeks the *Boston Globe* published a story which claimed Francona had lost control of the team.

To illustrate this point, *Globe* writer Bob Hohler cited sources who claimed Francona's three top starting pitchers—Josh Beckett, Lackey, and Lester—had spent games they were not scheduled to pitch bonding in the clubhouse over fried chicken, beer, and video games while their teammates were on the diamond blowing their big playoff lead.[33] General manager Theo Epstein, who like Francona was beloved in Boston as the architect of two World Series champions, resigned shortly thereafter and took over a leadership role with the Chicago Cubs.

As would be expected, the three pitchers at the center of the controversy were all lambasted by fans in the days after the story broke. Lester, the youngest of the three, was the first forgiven in the court of public opinion. His previous popularity as a hard-working athlete who triumphed over cancer, along with his quick and sincere apology for his actions, no doubt helped. Even as the team spiraled into last place in 2012 and Lester slumped to a 9-14, 4.82 season, the loudest booing was reserved for Lackey, Beckett, and others.

Among those in uniform who felt the most heat that year was new Boston manager Bobby Valentine, of whom Lester was definitely not a fan. In one July game against Toronto at Fenway Park, Valentine left Lester in the contest to absorb an 11-run beating, and the pitcher never forgot it. When Valentine was fired as manager after the season and replaced by John Farrell, Francona's former Boston pitching coach, Lester was thrilled with the change; the pair had a strong relationship, and having Farrell in charge led to a tremendous comeback for the pitcher and the team.

Lester went 15-8 with a 3.75 ERA in 2013, and the Red Sox went "worst to first" in winning the AL East.[34] "I take my job serious. Every year, my expectations are higher," Lester had said that spring training. "I don't think anybody wants to be in the position we were in last year. We want to be on top."[35]

During the playoffs, just as in 2007, Lester took things up two notches with a 1.56 ERA and four victories in five starts (including Game One of the ALDS, NLCS, and World Series). When he won both his World Series starts against the St. Louis Cardinals, it gave him a lifetime 3-0 record and 0.43 ERA in the fall classic.[36] The Red Sox beat the Cardinals in six, and catcher David Ross summed things up perfectly: "Jonny, he's just a stud."[37]

As he entered the last year of his contract in 2014, Lester anticipated a big payday. Then the Red Sox front office made what ultimately may go down as one of the worst management decisions in the team's history. Gambling that at just 29, after averaging more than 200 innings for the past six seasons, Lester's best days were behind him, they offered their World Series hero a four-year, $70 million extension proposal that was way below market value. Lester balked at the

offer, cut off all discussion on the topic, and went out to prove his value.[38]

He had a tremendous first half, with a 2.52 ERA through July 25, and was named to his third AL All-Star team. But reversing their one-year revival, the Red Sox fell back to the AL East basement and stayed there. As the July 31 trade deadline neared it was clear that Boston had no realistic chance of making the playoffs, so management decided to cut its losses and trade off several top players—including Jon Lester.

The second-winningest left-hander in franchise history[39] went to the wild-card-hopeful Oakland A's with outfielder Jonny Gomes in a swap for young slugger Yoenis Cesepedes and a draft pick—a move that spurred a massive outcry from Boston fans. Lester ended his Red Sox career with a 110-63 record, and through 2016 still ranked fifth in franchise history with a .636 winning percentage and fourth with 1,386 strikeouts.[40]

"He's one of the best pitchers in the game. No question about it," said Red Sox DH and longtime teammate David Ortiz. "I don't know, man. It's frustrating to see him going somewhere else. It's just the situation that we're facing right now."[41]

Lester did what his new team hoped he would, stringing together several strong outings that helped propel the A's into the playoffs. Manager Bob Melvin gave his new ace the start in the winner-take-all wild-card contest, and after seven innings he had a 7-3 lead and appeared in total command. Then suddenly the Royals rallied behind a series of lightly-hit singles, errors, and stolen bases, chasing Lester and rallying for a 9-8 victory.

Rumors that the Red Sox might be able to re-sign Lester as a free agent that winter were dismissed by fans throughout New England as unrealistic given how the team had already slighted its homegrown star. The diehards were right; although Boston offered a six-year, $135 million contract, Lester signed with Epstein and the Cubs for $155 million over six years (including a $30 million signing bonus).[42] Among the moves Theo and Co. made to win him over was a recruiting video that showed the Cubs celebrating a future World Series title at Wrigley Field—a bit of a stretch since the franchise was coming off a last-place season and had not such championship since 1908.

But Jon Lester had made a career out of proving he has what it takes. He had a strong year adapting to the National League, with a 1.22 WHIP that ranked ninth in the circuit, and helped the Cubs reach the playoffs for the first time in seven years. When he started Game One of both the NLDS and NLCS in 2015, it marked the third straight year he had pitched in the postseason — each time for a different franchise. He lost both contests, however, and Wrigley fans were once again denied a World Series on Chicago's North Side.[43]

There was no stopping the Cubs or Lester during the 2016 season. Epstein picked up several proven veterans, including Lackey, to bolster his club's strong core of young talent. This led many media experts and fans to pick the Cubs to win their first National League championship since 1945, and Chicago exploded out of the gate and never looked back — finishing with a major-league-best 103-59 record. Lester had a career year with a 19-5 record good for an NL-high .792 winning percentage, a 2.44 ERA (second in the league), 1.016 WHIP (third), and 197 strikeouts (seventh). He even won a 12-inning game for Chicago on July 31 as a pinch-hitter, dropping down a perfect squeeze bunt to bring in the winning run.

Down the stretch of 2016, there was no better pitcher in baseball. Although a loss in his last regular-season appearance denied Lester his first 20-win season, he was 10-0 with a 1.34 ERA in 13 previous starts dating to mid-July. The Cubs rotation was the NL's finest with Jake Arietta, Kyle Hendricks, Jason Hammel, and Lackey, but it was once again Lester who started Game One for his team in both the NLDS and NLCS — helping Chicago to its first World Series berth in 71 years with an 0.86 ERA over three starts and 21 innings during those two playoff rounds.

By the time Lester toed the mound at Cleveland in Game One of the 2016 World Series, the Cubs were the biggest story in sports as they sought to end a 108-year world championship drought. Watching on from the home dugout at Progressive Field was Indians manager Francona, who had been like a father to Lester during their years together in Boston and was now trying to beat him. Perhaps the pressure of it all was a bit much for the usually unflappable left-hander; Lester allowed two hits and two walks, and hit a batter during a brutal first inning, and, although he recovered well, left in the sixth trailing 3-0. Chicago went on to lose, 6-0.

Lester's chance at redemption came in Game Five at Wrigley Field, with Chicago now down three games to one and facing elimination. Again he fell behind early, this time on a solo home run by José Ramirez in the second, but moments like this were what had compelled Theo Epstein to sign Lester to his huge deal. The big left-hander retired 10 of 11 in the middle innings, and after the Cubs scored three in the fourth he kept the lead. He left after six on top, 3-2, and that was the final score.

After Chicago won Game Six as well, the World Series came down to a winner-take-all finale at Cleveland's Progressive Field on November 2. Hendricks got the start for Chicago, but Cubs manager Joe Maddon made it clear that it would be all hands on deck if he faltered. Both teams had been relying heavily on their bullpens during the Series, but Maddon still raised many eyebrows when he pulled Hendricks after a two-out walk in the bottom of the fifth. Chicago had a 5-1 lead, and the National League ERA champ had been pitching well up to that point. But the skipper saw something he didn't like, so in came Jon Lester — making just the fourth relief appearance of his 339-game career (regular and postseason combined), and the first since 2007.

Initially it appeared Maddon had outsmarted himself; Lester seemed flustered by the unfamiliar role, and allowed a single and wild pitch to plate two runs. But he struck out Francisco Lindor to end the inning, and then held Cleveland scoreless over the next two frames. When he left with two outs in the eighth to a standing ovation by the many Chicago fans in the visiting ballpark, the Cubs had a 6-3 advantage and Lester was in line for the franchise's most historic victory in more than a century. Ace closer Aroldis Chapman denied Lester that glory by quickly allowing three runs — two on a game-tying homer by

Rajai Davis—but Chicago eventually prevailed, 8-7, in a 10-inning thriller to earn Lester his third World Series ring.

Where Jon Lester would end up ranking all-time among pitchers was still unclear entering the 2017 season. At 33 years old he had a career regular-season record of 146-84, good for a .635 winning percentage. That plus his 1,861 strikeouts and 1.234 WHIP placed him among the top hurlers of his generation; were he to stay at or near his current level for five more years (not an unreasonable expectation), he would have close to 250 victories and 2,800 strikeouts—and that coupled with his role in helping two storied franchises to the top would make him a borderline candidate for the Baseball Hall of Fame. Certainly a 4-1 record and 1.77 ERA in 35⅔ World Series innings through 2016 was another huge plus in support of his candidacy, but winning a first Cy Young Award –he finished second in the 2016 voting—would be a big help.

Off the field, Lester already had the type of credentials that tend to attract Cooperstown votes. He has been a longtime spokesman for the National Pediatric Cancer Research Foundation through its NVRQT fundraising campaign (for "never quit"), in addition to his work through the years with Dana-Farber. His wife, Farrah, has been active in his charity work as well, and the couple's son and daughter have been seen hanging around their dad at work.

If he does reach the Hall of Fame, it's a pretty safe bet Lester will be wearing a Boston cap on his plaque—a nod to the team on which he developed as a pitcher, reached the majors, became a star, and captured his first two World Series titles. And while he may have won far more important games than he did for the Red Sox on May 20, 2008, and likely would win a few more, no contest will ever have quite the same special meaning as the day he no-hit the Royals and showed the world he was a survivor.

"Obviously you don't want to go back and redo any of the sickness or treatment, but I wouldn't trade my journey for anything," Lester said in 2014. "It's been a heck of a ride, and hopefully I can continue on the good health side of it and keep rolling along."[44]

SOURCES

In addition to the sources cited in the Notes, the author also consulted Baseball-Reference.com, the *2014 Boston Red Sox Media Guide*, the Pediatric Cancer Research Foundation's NVRQT website, the online archives of the *Boston Globe*, *New York Times*, and *Chicago Tribune*, MLB.com, Redsox.com, Cubs.com, and the SABR Minor League Database (accessed online at Baseball-Reference.com)

NOTES

1 Ian Browne, "Lester Completes No-Hit Feat," *MLB.com*, *m.mlb.com/news/article/2731480/*, May 20, 2008.

2 Dustin Pedroia with Edward Delaney, *Born to Play* (New York: Simon Spotlight Entertainment, 2008), 233-234.

3 Browne.

4 In his autobiography, *Born to Play*, Dustin Pedroia wrote that "after this game [Lester] took himself from being a good major-league pitcher to being one of the best in the game. And I think everybody in the whole stadium knew that, and were watching it happen. He grew up right in front of us." See p. 234.

5 Dan Shaughnessy, "Lester Adds a Historic Chapter," *Boston Globe*, May 20, 2008.

6 Francona wrote in his autobiography that a framed photograph of his hugging Lester after his no-hitter hung in the den of his home.

7 Ibid.

8 Chris Snow, "Superlatives Tossed Around When Lester Is the Subject," *Boston Globe*, March 31, 2006.

9 Ibid.

10 Jon Lester bio on *JockBio.com*, *jockbio.com/Bios/J_Lester/J_Lester_bio.html*. The Chris Snow *Globe* article of March 31, 2006 (see Note 8), also mentions that Moyer was a Lester family confidant.

11 David Laurila, *Interviews from Red Sox Nation* (Hanover, Massachusetts: Maple Street Press, 2008), 29-30.

12 Bob Hohler, "Silver Lining to Lester Debut," *Boston Globe*, August 25, 2002. Hohler wrote that only one of the runs against Lester had been earned: "Most of the hits were bleeders or broken-bat singles."

13 In addition to being a great "What If?" to ponder later, the near-swap had an interesting twist; as a teenage a decade earlier, Lester had rooted for Rodriguez when A-Rod first came up with the Mariners. Gordon Edes, "How the A-Rod Negotiations Ended with Red Sox Shut Out," *Boston Globe*, December 31, 2003.

14 Chris Snow, *Boston Globe*, March 31, 2006.

15 Ibid.

16 Ibid.

17   Prior to his debut, Lester told the *Boston Globe's* Chris Snow, he had thrown just 10 pitches to Red Sox catcher Jason Varitek, all during warm-ups.

18   Chris Snow, "Lester Lays Low on Eve of Debut," *Boston Globe*, June 10, 2006.

19   Lester's August 23, 2006, start was the second major-league game for Dustin Pedroia, who had gone 1-for-3 in his debut the day before. In Lester's debut he went 0-for-4, batting second.

20   Gordon Edes and Liz Kowalczyk, "Lester Diagnosed with Cancer," *Boston Globe*, September 2, 2006.

21   Terry Francona and Dan Shaughnessy, *Francona: The Red Sox Years* (Boston: Houghton Mifflin Harcourt, 2013), 168.

22   Ibid.

23   Gordon Edes and Nick Cafardo, "Lester Said to Be Making Progress," *Boston Globe*, December 5, 2006.

24   Like the Dana-Farber Cancer Institute in Boston, whose Jimmy Fund charity has been affiliated with the Red Sox since 1953, the Hutchinson Cancer Center has deep baseball ties; it is named for former big-league player and manager Fred Hutchinson, a Seattle native who died of cancer in 1963. His brother Bill was a renowned surgeon in Seattle, and established the center in Fred's memory.

25   Francona, 178-179.

26   Ibid.

27   Francona, 194.

28   Lester's Red Sox teammate in 2006-2010, third baseball Mike Lowell, had won the Conigliaro Award while with the Florida Marlins in 1999. Lowell was a testicular cancer survivor who came back to the majors three months after his February 1999 surgery, and hit 12 home runs that year.

29   "This Year in Baseball Awards—2008," archived on MLB.com at *mlb.mlb.com/mlb/awards/y2008/tyib/index.jsp*.

30   Saul Wisnia, "Lester's No-hitter Gives Fellow Cancer Fighters A Lift," from Dana-Farber staff Intranet site, archived on author's "Fenway Reflections" blog at saulwisnia.blogspot.com/2014/12/for-some-fans-jon-lester-was-more.html.

31   Ibid.

32   Ibid.

33   Bob Hohler, "Inside the Collapse of the 2011 Red Sox," *Boston Globe*, December 31, 2003.

34   Lester's 100th career win, over Toronto at Fenway Park on September 20, 2013, clinched the AL East title for Boston.

35   Dan Shaughnessy, "Ace Jon Lester," from *For Boston, From Worst to First, the Impossible Dream Season of the 2013 Boston Red Sox* (Chicago: Triumph Books, 2013), 110.

36   Lester was just the fifth pitcher, and the first since 1946, to allow one or fewer runs in his first three career World Series starts. Only Christy Mathewson, with four straight from 1905-1911, had a longer streak.

37   Ben Reiter, "Closing Strong," from *Sports Illustrated* special commemorative issue, *Boston Red Sox: A Splendid Season*, (New York: Sports Illustrated, 2013), 46.

38   In July 2014 Red Sox beat reporter Peter Abraham of the *Boston Globe* estimated that "the market value for a pitcher of Lester's experience and accomplishments would be approximately $22 million-$24 million a year over five or six years."

39   The only left-hander in Red Sox history with more wins than Lester through 2016 was Mel Parnell, who won his last of 123 games in 1956.

40   Only Roger Clemens, Cy Young, Luis Tiant, and Lester have started 31 or more games for six straight seasons in a Red Sox uniform, and only Clemens, Young, Pedro Martinez, and Lester had at least 150 strikeouts six times consecutively for Boston.

41   Peter Abraham, "Jon Lester Traded to Oakland," *Boston Globe*, July 31, 2014.

42   Peter Abraham, "Red Sox Made Curious Strategy Change in Jon Lester Pursuit," *Boston Globe*, December 11, 2014.

43   The most "offensive" incident of Lester's 2015 season came on July 6, when an infield single that caromed off the leg of past (and future) teammate John Lackey became his first major-league hit after 66 fruitless at-bats. It was the longest stretch of ineptitude to begin a career in big-league history.

44   Jon Lester, "Through the Eyes of Jon Lester," first-person account (as told to MLB.com's Ian Browne), *Red Sox Magazine*, fifth edition, 2014.

ROCCO BALDELLI

By Eric Frost

WHEN ROCCO BALDELLI emerged as a young star in the minor-league system of the Tampa Bay Devil Rays, he drew comparisons to Joe DiMaggio. Though that association was almost certainly setting him up for failure, the speedy outfielder had been more earnestly compared to a young Andre Dawson or Dale Murphy. Within a few years, however, Baldelli's story underscored the fickle nature of baseball and illustrated the ups and downs faced by elite athletes on the cusp of stardom.

Baldelli was born on September 25, 1981, in Woonsocket, Rhode Island. As of 2016, only 76 players from the Ocean State have made it to the major leagues. Nevertheless, Woonsocket has been well represented: It is the birthplace of Hall of Famers Nap Lajoie and Gabby Hartnett. While most youngsters in Rhode Island passionately support either the Boston Red Sox or the New York Yankees, Baldelli said he never developed an allegiance to any one team.[1]

The son of Dan and Michelle Baldelli, Rocco Dan Baldelli has two brothers, Nicholas and Dante. The family is primarily of Italian and French ancestry. Dan Baldelli, a retired Woonsocket firefighter, was as of 2016 a small-business man of many parts; his enterprises included a coffee shop and a pawn shop/ check-cashing store in Woonsocket. He coached the Little League teams of each of his sons. Michelle Baldelli seemed destined to be involved in baseball, as she was named after Mickey Mantle.[2]

The cold, snowy Rhode Island winters prevented Rocco from getting outside and playing as frequently as his peers from the Sunbelt. So he took his game inside, to the basement of his father's Hava Java Coffee House. The basement, with its 13-foot ceiling, featured a homemade batting cage. The Dungeon, as the basement became known to scouts, allowed Baldelli to take hits cuts even as the temperature outside dipped below freezing. Karl Allaire, an Astros second-round

pick out of Rhode Island College in 1984 who worked for Dan Baldelli, would throw Rocco all the batting practice he wanted.

As a 12-year-old, Baldelli played AAU baseball, and his team went to the national finals. In a basketball game at age 13, Rocco suffered a serious injury. He shattered his tibia, severely injuring the tendons in his leg. Doctors thought that the injury looked as if he had been in a car accident, and they encouraged Baldelli to focus on his schoolwork because his injury might prevent further participation in basketball.[3] He later said, "I wasn't really worried about sports. I wanted to concentrate on rehab so I could walk again and maybe even run someday."[4]

He skipped playing baseball in both his freshman and sophomore years of high school, but his father urged him to try out for the local American Legion team. "I hadn't touched a baseball in two years," Baldelli said. "Rusty was an understatement. I was pretty awful. Even shagging balls in the outfield—it wasn't happening."

"He looked so bad," Dan said. "He missed everything. I was sitting in the car wondering why I had asked him do this. He came back to the car and gave me a look like, 'Are you happy now?'" The family was surprised when they learned that Baldelli's return to baseball had not been a short-lived experiment. He had made the team.[5]

Baldelli ended up playing baseball, basketball, and volleyball for Bishop Hendricken High School in Warwick, about 25 miles from home.[6] In high school, Baldelli had his sights set on attending an academically strong college, hoping that he could play both basketball and baseball.[7] An honor student at Bishop Hendricken, Baldelli was considering schools like Wake Forest and Princeton.[8]

In the summer before his senior year, Baldelli attended a major-league scouting event at Holy Cross College in nearby Worcester, Massachusetts, which put

him on the radar of professional baseball organizations. He had received a nearly-unbelievable 50 scholarship offers from various colleges after impressing observers at the 1999 East Coast Showcase in Wilmington, North Carolina. Though he didn't have the typical baseball pedigree, pro scouts weren't always looking for in-game records. "We fell in love with his athletic abilities," said Dan Jennings, Tampa Bay's scouting director at the time. "He showed every tool you want to see. His arm was the only thing that wasn't above average. We made sure we jumped on him right away."[9]

In addition to the attention he received for his baseball skills, Baldelli received a scholarship offer to play volleyball at UCLA.[10] Baldelli was an elite volleyball player known across the nation for his skills, and when he sent video footage to major-league clubs, the tape included 20 minutes of his play on the volleyball court and only two minutes of action on the baseball field.[11]

Skipping basketball in his senior season, Baldelli devoted his free time to taking batting practice in the family's batting cage. Partway through his senior baseball season, Baldelli pulled an oblique muscle and was unable to play for a month. Though he returned in time to play one game before the 2000 major-league baseball draft, Dan Baldelli said that he didn't know what to expect from the draft. The family had heard

that Baldelli might be drafted somewhere between the 5th and 15th rounds, and they decided that he would go to college unless he was taken in the first round.[12]

Just before the draft, Peter Gammons of ESPN wrote that Baldelli could be the top prospect available. He noted that because of Baldelli's injury and the Rhode Island weather, not many teams had seen him play in person. Baldelli worked out for the Devil Rays only four days before the draft, and the Cleveland Indians found out about him after former Cleveland Browns head football coach Bill Belichick called Indians executives and told them that Baldelli might be the best athlete he had ever seen.[13]

The Devil Rays drafted Baldelli with their first pick; he was the sixth pick overall. Mike Arbuckle, the head of scouting for the Philadelphia Phillies, said that if Baldelli had been available in the draft at the 15th pick of the first round, the Phillies might have selected him instead of taking Chase Utley, the player who became their longtime second baseman.[14]

Shortly after the draft, Baldelli worked out at Tropicana Field before a Devil Rays game. He showed humility in the comments he made after an impressive batting practice. "There's nothing I do well enough to be a major-league player," Baldelli said. "This is great, coming to St. Petersburg, getting a little taste of baseball at its highest level, but I am excited about getting on to the Rookie League, where I can learn."[15]

Baldelli struggled with the Rookie-level Princeton Devil Rays that year. He hit just .216 with three home runs in 251 plate appearances over 60 games. He said that he had always tried to pull the ball for a home run in high school, and he had to spend much of his first two professional seasons learning to hit the ball to all fields.[16]

In 2001, playing for the South Atlantic League's Charleston (South Carolina) River Dogs of the low Class-A South Atlantic League, Baldelli improved his batting average to .249 and homered eight times in 113 games. In 2002 he had his breakout season. He played at three levels, promoted from High-A to Double A to Triple A, and was named the Minor League Player of the Year by *Baseball America*.[17] "That's just an honor," Baldelli said. "Those kind of honors don't come around too often. It's a credit to so many who put in so much time to help me out."[18]

In 77 games with the Bakersfield Blaze (California League), Baldelli hit .333 with 14 home runs. For the Double-A Orlando Rays (Southern League), he hit .371 in 17 games, and in Triple A, he hit .292 for the Durham Bulls.

In 2003 Baldelli spent all season in the major leagues with the Devil Rays. The child with the seriously injured leg had grown into a 6-foot-4 baseball star listed at 190 pounds. The right-handed center fielder would play in over 500 big-league games. Based on speed and the name of his hometown, he came to be known as the "Woonsocket Rocket," a nickname that Baldelli said he remembered first hearing on television sports programming.[19]

Baldelli started his major-league career with a 13-game hitting streak, the second longest streak to begin a career between 1990 and 2003. The streak also set a rookie record for the Devil Rays, and only four Tampa Bay players had ever hit longer consecutive-game hitting streaks. Baldelli was hitting second in the batting order, and he was expected to see a high number of fastballs because Tampa Bay's leadoff hitter, Carl Crawford, was an accomplished basestealer. Baldelli had 64 major-league plate appearances before he walked.[20]

By late May 2003, Albert Chen of *Sports Illustrated* had written about Baldelli's aggressive approach to hitting in his first couple of months as a major leaguer. He had struck out 37 times at that point in the season, and his strikeout-to-walk ratio was 6.2 to 1; only two players had a higher ratio. However, Baldelli was hitting .353, which was also third in the league. He had set a record among rookies by getting 40 hits by the end of April. Chen pointed out that only four major leaguers had ever hit .300 in a season with a strikeout-to-walk ratio greater than 5 to 1.[21]

Baldelli's hitting philosophy seemed to correlate with a generally restless personality. He said that he often found himself pacing around before games to pass the time, and though he had tried reading and completing crossword puzzles to occupy his time during the season, he found that he lacked the patience to finish those activities. Coach Chuck LaMar noted Baldelli's uniqueness. "Some players have a magnetism that you can't measure or explain. It's something that fans, teammates, even opponents respect. Rocco has it," he said.[22]

By early July Baldelli was hitting .309 with 5 home runs and 40 runs batted in. No Devil Rays player was voted onto the American League All-Star Team by the fans, but each team would have an All-Star Game representative chosen by AL manager Mike Scioscia. Baldelli and Rays teammate Aubrey Huff were thought to be the likely candidates. However, Scioscia had only five picks and four of those needed to be pitchers, so reliever Lance Carter (4.17 ERA, 14 saves in 20 opportunities) emerged as the surprise selection from Tampa Bay.[23]

Appearing in 156 games in his rookie season, Baldelli batted .289 with 11 home runs and 78 runs batted in. He showed impressive speed, finishing the season with 27 stolen bases, and he came in third in the AL Rookie of the Year voting, behind Angel Berroa of the Kansas City Royals and Hideki Matsui of the New York Yankees. In a year of controversy over whether Matsui should be considered a rookie because of his playing experience in Japan, Berroa received 12 first-place votes compared with Matsui's 10 and Baldelli's 5.[24]

In his second season, Baldelli got off to a difficult start. A few weeks into the season, when he was hitting below .200, Baldelli remembered, he was called into manager Lou Piniella's office, thinking he might be demoted to the minor leagues. Instead of a demotion, Piniella reaffirmed the team's commitment to him as the starter in center field. Baldelli later said that the affirmation helped him to relax and improve his hitting mechanics.[25] A hamstring strain limited Baldelli to 136 games that year, but he hit .280 and his home run total increased to 16.

After the 2004 season, no one knew that Baldelli had already played the two most complete seasons of his major-league career. He tore a ligament in his knee while he was playing in the yard at the family home in Rhode Island in October 2004; the injury sidelined him for several months. He was playing in the minor leagues on a rehab assignment in June when he injured his elbow. Baldelli tried to ignore the injury and he played in a couple of games after that, but he realized that the pain was not getting better. Team physicians diagnosed a torn ulnar collateral ligament. He required Tommy John surgery.[26]

Though he missed the entire 2005 season, the Devil Rays signed Baldelli to a three-year contract with team options for an additional three years. He would receive $9 million over the first three years, and the full six years could have been worth as much as $32 million. Fellow outfielder Carl Crawford, who had also signed a six-year deal for similar compensation, expressed surprise that Baldelli had commanded that much money despite his injuries.[27]

In 2006 injuries struck Baldelli again. He missed the opening two months of the season with a strained hamstring he had suffered in spring training.[28] He hit .302 with 16 home runs in 92 games that year. Baldelli's name surfaced in trade rumors after the season when Devil Rays manager Joe Maddon noted that the team had outfield depth but could use veteran pitching.[29]

No trade materialized, and in 2007 Baldelli played in 35 games. Though he had recovered from a spring-training hamstring injury in time for the season opener, his regular-season misfortune began when he crashed into a wall in late April and missed a couple of games. Then, mired in a 1-for-40 slump, Baldelli left a mid-May game with another hamstring injury.[30] He missed the rest of the season as the hamstring continued to bother him.

By that point in his career, Baldelli was experiencing frequent muscle cramping and severe fatigue that would set in after even light exercise. Before the 2008 season, he announced that his baseball career was indefinitely on hold. Though he was not retiring, he said that the fatigue rendered him unable to perform the basic baseball functions like running, throwing, and hitting. Baldelli drew an analogy between his condition and a cell phone that would not hold a charge.[31]

"I feel like I've done a serious workout after a very short period of time, and it's a very odd feeling. I try not to be too dramatic when I explain what's going on, but it's not easy when you're out on the field for a very short period of time and you're done, and you're not really worth anything else out there. That's a tough thing to handle because you wonder why," Baldelli said at the time.[32]

Baldelli resolved to continue to seek answers for his condition, and he said he would try to find any solution that could get him back to playing baseball. The Rays were supportive, and executive vice president Andrew Friedman said he was optimistic that Baldelli could play again. He said the team would probably decline the 2009 option on his contract, but that he hoped Baldelli would stay within the organization.[33]

Baldelli was sent to several physicians, who evaluated him for conditions like Lou Gehrig's disease and multiple sclerosis. His symptoms were not consistent with those diagnoses, and doctors began to suspect that he had a mitochondrial disorder, a defect in the energy-producing part of the body's cells. With medications, nutritional supplements, rest, and dietary changes, his condition seemed to improve.[34]

Missing most of the 2008 season, Baldelli returned to play 28 regular-season games in August and September. He hit two home runs in postseason play, including a three-run homer in the ALCS victory that help propel the Rays to the World Series. Alan Schwarz of the *New York Times* said that the ALCS home run was "as medically remarkable as Kirk Gibson's wobbly-kneed shot 20 Octobers ago." Baldelli had returned to action, but he was having to carefully conserve his energy, sometimes skipping batting practice or sitting down on the field when his team brought new pitchers in from the bullpen.[35]

In November the Boston chapter of the Baseball Writers' Association of America recognized Baldelli's determination to get back on the baseball field, presenting him with the 2008 Tony Conigliaro Award. Pitchers Doug Davis and Brad Ziegler finished in second and third place in the award voting.[36]

Baldelli was a free agent after that season, and he was pursued seriously by four teams: the Boston Red Sox, Pittsburgh Pirates, Cincinnati Reds, and Philadelphia Phillies. A source told the *Pittsburgh Post-Gazette* that Baldelli was leaning toward Boston, at least in part because playing in the American League would leave the door open for a role as the team's designated hitter. Ultimately, the Red Sox prevailed in negotiations with Baldelli.[37]

By the time he joined the Red Sox, Baldelli's diagnosis had been revised to a channelopathy, a protein abnormality that interferes with muscular function.[38] That news was thought to be very positive; though channelopathies represent a wide range of conditions, Baldelli's father said that the new diagnosis meant that his son did not have a progressive and life-threatening disease. (In 2009 Rocco said he did not like talking about his medical condition.)[39] The Red Sox had signed Baldelli with the understanding that his medical condition would limit his use. The team planned to utilize him as their fourth outfielder, and he was expected to appear primarily against left-handed pitching.

Baldelli was tiring of answering questions about his health by the time he arrived in Boston. "I was going to make a sign that says, 'Feeling good, thanks for asking,' and tack it to my locker, so I don't have to answer that anymore," Baldelli said. "I've been disappointed a lot at times, but as far as self-pity, no one really wants to hear any excuses. No one feels that bad for you, no matter what you're going through. I'll be fine. I'll manage no matter what's going on."[40]

Though he joined a crowded Red Sox outfield, Baldelli became immediately popular among Boston fans, who gave him a standing ovation the first time he came to the plate in April. Former Tampa Bay teammate Scott Kazmir noted that it was fitting that Baldelli ended up in Boston because he had always had a large fan following when the Rays visited Fenway Park.[41]

Baldelli played in 62 games for Boston in 2009. He had a .253 batting average in those games and hit 7 home runs. After the season, three or four teams expressed interest in signing him, but he did not sign a contract. Just before the 2010 season, the Rays hired Baldelli as a special instructor while he continued to work on rehabbing from a shoulder injury. There were no promises that Baldelli would play professionally, but he said he was not officially retiring as a player.[42]

After returning to the field with a rehab stint in the minor leagues, Baldelli was called back up to the Rays in September. In his first major-league at-bat of the 2010 season, Baldelli hit a pinch-hit home run.[43] Teammate Evan Longoria expressed how happy he was to see Baldelli's home run. "I feel great for the guy," Longoria said. "He's a professional in every respect. Just the pure persistence of his journey through the big leagues and back down and back up again—I can't do anything but commend him."[44]

Before the American League Division Series that year, Baldelli was named to the postseason roster. Willy Aybar had been left off the postseason roster, with the team opting to include Desmond Jennings, who brought defense and speed to the team.[45] When Baldelli's play was curtailed by severe muscle cramping, he was replaced on the roster by Aybar before the second game of the ALDS.[46]

When Baldelli saw that he was no longer contributing as a player during the 2010 postseason, he realized that he needed to retire as a player. He officially announced his retirement in January 2011, having spent the previous three months thinking over the decision at the request of Tampa Bay executives. The Rays kept him in the organization as a special adviser for scouting and player development. Baldelli said he was sad that he had not been able to play more during his career, but that he chose not to focus on the negatives in his life.[47]

"I don't regret anything," he said. "You know what's sad is that I love to play, and I really didn't get a chance to do it as much as I wanted to. But I don't live angrily; I live kind of happy. Why would I look at the negative aspects of everything that I've been through and live the rest of my life talking about those things that aren't the important things to me? The important things to me were all the wonderful things I got to do. It's tough, because you almost never put playing and being an athlete behind you. But in my mind, I already feel like it's a step behind me."[48]

Though Baldelli had not identified a particular interest for a post-baseball career, the Rays were impressed by his intelligence and his character, so they invited him to stay with the organization in a role that he would help to delineate. In spring training before the 2011 season, Baldelli met with general manager Andrew Friedman, and they decided that he would work in scouting and player development for the Rays.

In his new role, Baldelli specialized in scouting hitters, and he noted that travel was a significant part of the new job. "I'm a Southwest A-List preferred member now and I just became a Marriot Silver member this spring. I think I'm teetering on Gold status already," Baldelli joked. The Rays, who were preparing to make 12 picks out of the first 89 slots in the 2011 draft, said that Baldelli would have a key role in the team's "war room" during the draft.[49]

Before the 2015 season, the Rays were dealing with significant personnel changes, including a new general manager, Matt Silverman, and a new manager, Kevin Cash. They moved Baldelli back onto the field as a first-base coach. The 33-year-old became the youngest coach in the major leagues.[50]

When Baldelli was not coaching, he ran a small thoroughbred-horse breeding operation. His family has never owned horses, but former teammate Dan Dement, manager Lou Piniella, coach Don Zimmer, and baseball executive Gerry Hunsicker all liked horse racing, furthering Baldelli's interest in it. Baldelli bought his first mare in 2011. In 2014 he sold a colt for $400,000 at auction.[51]

Baldelli's younger brother Dante also played center field for Bishop Hendricken High School. Dante said he appreciated learning from Rocco's major-league experience. Before the 2016 season, MaxPreps named Dante the number-one high-school prospect in Rhode Island.[52] He was selected by the Philadelphia Phillies in the 39th round of the June 2016 Draft, but he elected to play baseball at Boston College.

SOURCES

In addition to the sources listed below, the author utilized statistics, game logs, and player information available from Baseball-Reference.com.

NOTES

1   Hubert Mizell, "Baldelli Gives Glimpse of Talent," *St. Petersburg Times*, June 19, 2000.

2   "Rocco Comes Home," *Rhode Island Monthly*, October 2009.

3   Will Kimmey, "2002 Minor League Player of the Year," baseballamerica.com/online/minors/poybaldelli.html.

4   Ibid.

5   Ibid.

6   Mike Scandura, "Pedigree Aside, Bishop Hendricken's Dante Baldelli Truly His Own Man," ESPN.com, espn.com/blog/boston/high-school/post/_/id/41743/pedigree-aside-bishop-hendrickens-dante-baldelli-truly-his-own-man, April 14, 2016.

7   Kimmey.

8   "Rocco Baldelli in 'Comfortable' Place," *Fall River* (Massachusetts) *Herald News*, January 28, 2012.

9   Kimmey.

10   Mizell.

11   Peter Gammons, "This Year's Draft as Uncertain as Ever," ESPN.com, espn.go.com/gammons/s/0603.html, June 3, 2011.

12   Tim Britton, "MLB Draft: R.I.'s Rocco Baldelli Recalls His Roller-Coaster Ride in 2000," *Providence Journal*, June 7, 2015.

13   Gammons.

14   Tyler Kepner, "For Scouts, Consolation Prizes Are Often the Best Kind," *New York Times*, October 17, 2008.

15   Mizell.

16   Hudson Belinsky, "Baldelli Offers Unique Perspective as Coach," *Baseball America*, March 20, 2015, baseballamerica.com/majors/baldelli-offers-unique-perspective-coach/#d5KcKMTvtsxXrlYm.97.

17   Ibid.

18   Kimmey.

19   Daniel Russell, "Rocco Baldelli on Data Analytics and Joining the Rays Coaching Staff," Draysbay.com, January 20,, 2015. draysbay.com/2015/1/20/7854487/rocco-baldelli-interview-rays-baseball-analytics.

20   "Baldelli Built for Streaks," *Sarasota Herald-Tribune*, April 20, 2003.

21   Albert Chen, "Five At-Bats, 18 Pitches, 10 Swings, Two Hits, Two Runs ... and No Walks: Rocco Baldelli, the Devil Rays' Free-swinging Rookie Centerfielder, Isn't About to Let a Hittable Pitch—or His Shot at Stardom—Go By," *Sports Illustrated*, May 26, 2003. As mentioned, Baldelli finished the season at 2.89.

22   Ibid.

23   Marc Topkin, "Carter Surprise All-Star," *St. Petersburg Times*, July 7, 2003.

24   Dom Amore, "Close Call, Berroa Wins," *Hartford Courant*, November 11, 2003.

25   Russell.

26   Bill Chastain, "Baldelli Faces Tommy John Surgery," MLB.com, June 15, 2005. mlb.mlb.com/news/print.

jsp?ymd=20050615&content_id=1090726&vkey=news_mlb&c_id=mlb&fext=.jsp.

27   Marc Topkin, "Rocco's Deal Too Like Crawford's for Carl," *St. Petersburg Times*, December 5, 2005.

28   Eduardo Encina, "Hamstring Forces Baldelli Out," *Tampa Bay Times*, May 16, 2007.

29   "Trade Talk Finally Trickling for Sox," *Chicago Tribune*, December 6, 2006.

30   Encina.

31   Marc Topkin, "Baldelli's Prognosis Unclear," *Tampa Bay Times*, March 13, 2008.

32   Ibid.

33   Ibid.

34   Alan Schwarz, "Getting Back in the Game," *New York Times*, August 6, 2008.

35   Alan Schwarz, "Baldelli Lifts Rays and the Spirits of Youngsters," *New York Times*, October 16, 2008.

36   "Rocco Baldelli Wins 2008 Tony Conigliaro Award," MLB.com, November 25, 2008. mlb.mlb.com/content/printer_friendly/bos/y2008/m11/d25/c3692672.jsp.

37   Dejan Kovacevic, "Pirates Lose Baldelli to Boston," *Pittsburgh Post-Gazette*, January 8, 2009.

38   Glen Farley, "Baldelli's Boston Debut on Deck?" *The Patriot Ledger* (Quincy, Massachusetts), April 8, 2009.

39   Amalie Benjamin, "Baldelli Adjusts to Ordeal," *Boston Globe*, February 8, 2009.

40   Jeff Goldberg, "Rocco Ready to Join the Fray," *Hartford Courant*, February 22, 2009.

41   Alan Schwarz, "Red Sox' Baldelli Revels in (and Braces for) His Homecoming," *New York Times*, April 8, 2009.

42   Joe McDonald, "Rocco Baldelli: 'Not Ready to Retire,'" ESPN.com, March 2, 2010. espn.com/boston/mlb/news/story?id=4959387.

43   Tony Fabrizio, "Baldelli HR in Return a Nice Moment for Rays," *Tampa Tribune*, September 5, 2010.

44   Marc Topkin, "Rocco Baldelli Homers on First Swing in Return to Tampa Bay Rays," *Tampa Bay Times*, September 5, 2010.

45   Associated Press, "Rays add Rocco Baldelli to ALDS roster," October 6, 2010.

46   "Rays Get Permission to Add Willy Aybar," ESPN.com, October 7, 2010. espn.com/boston/mlb/news/story?id=5658547.

47   Marc Topkin, "Illness Forces Tampa Bay Rays Outfielder Rocco Baldelli to Retire," *Tampa Bay Times*, January 25, 2011.

48   Ibid.

49   Jerry Crasnick, "Rocco Baldelli's New Role," ESPN.com, June 2, 2011. espn.com/mlb/draft/2011/columns/story?id=6615468&columnist=crasnick_jerry.

50   Belinsky.

51   Mike Hogan, "Baldelli Breaks Into Breeding Biz," ESPN.com, February 22, 2016. espn.com/horse-racing/story/_/id/14823587/ex-major-league-ballplayer-baldelli-now-breeder.

52   Mike Scandura, "Pedigree Aside, Bishop Hendricken's Dante Baldelli Truly His Own Man," ESPN.com, April 14, 2016. espn.com/blog/boston/high-school/post/_/id/41743/pedigree-aside-bishop-hendrickens-dante-baldelli-truly-his-own-man.

CHRIS CARPENTER

By Donna L. Halper

CHRIS CARPENTER SPENT 15 seasons in major-league baseball, first with the Toronto Blue Jays and then with the St. Louis Cardinals .His won-lost record was 144-94 with an earned-run average of 3.76, and in 2005, his 21-5 season and 2.83 ERA won him the National League's Cy Young Award. But statistics alone don't tell the story of Carpenter's career. His determination to play, despite serious injuries that nearly ended his career on several occasions, impressed both the fans and the writers who covered him. As one columnist said of the right-hander, he was "the epitome of persistence — he won three separate Comeback Player of the Year awards in two seasons — as he missed nearly five full seasons with major arm injuries. He had three surgeries on his elbow and two on his shoulder, and had a rib removed in hopes of making a return from thoracic outlet syndrome, which caused weakness in his pitching shoulder."[1] Few pitchers overcame as many obstacles as Carpenter, and yet there was a time in 2003 when he doubted he'd ever throw a baseball again.[2]

Christopher John Carpenter was born on April 27, 1975, in Exeter, New Hampshire, the son of Bob and Penny Carpenter.[3] Raised in nearby Raymond, he developed a love of sports at a young age: Mentored by his father, whom he credited with teaching him the fundamentals of baseball, he began playing that sport before he was 8, getting involved in Little League and then Babe Ruth League.[4] (He also followed the Boston Red Sox faithfully; his favorite players were Roger Clemens and Carlton Fisk.)[5] Carpenter attended Trinity High School in Manchester, where he continued to excel at baseball. But he also enjoyed playing hockey: despite being 6-feet-6 (or 6-feet-9 on skates, as his dad jokingly recalled), he was a three-time all-state defenseman, and both the Chicago Blackhawks and Boston Bruins scouted him for a possible professional career.[6]

However, Carpenter's first choice was baseball. A versatile athlete who could both play the outfield and pitch, he was one of the star players on the Trinity High Pioneers team. By his senior year, baseball scouts rated him in the top 10 among high-school pitchers,[7] and local newspapers were predicting that he would be drafted.[8] But taking nothing for granted, Chris had signed a letter of intent to attend Creighton University in Omaha, Nebraska, on a baseball scholarship. As it turned out, going to Nebraska would not be necessary: The Blue Jays drafted him in the first round, as the 15th overall pick. Local sports reporters who had followed his high-school career noted that Carpenter was the first New Hampshire baseball player ever selected in the first round of the amateur draft.[9]

The 18-year-old right-hander received a signing bonus of more than $500,000 from the Jays, and the team also promised to pay for his education if he decided to go to college.[10] As he prepared to report to Dunedin, Florida, home of Toronto's rookie and Class-A teams, his future looked bright. Ted Lekas, the Jays' scouting supervisor, said he believed Carpenter had all the tools to be on a major-league team, and the young pitcher agreed with that assessment; in fact, he predicted he'd be in the majors within four years.[11]

In 1994 Carpenter made his professional debut, pitching for the Medicine Hat (Alberta) Blue Jays in the rookie-level Pioneer League; he won six and lost three, with a 2.76 earned-run average. The following year, he began the season with the Dunedin Blue Jays in the Florida State League; he went 3-5, with an ERA of 2.17, and opposing teams batted only .229 against him. This earned Carpenter a midseason promotion to the Knoxville Smokies of the Double-A Southern League.[12] His record there was just 3-7, with a 5.18 ERA. When he returned to Knoxville for the 1996 season, Carpenter was determined to improve, and he did. His record was 7-9 with a 3.94 ERA.

In 1997 Carpenter was in Triple A, pitching for the Syracuse SkyChiefs. But prior to reporting, he had the chance to meet one of his childhood heroes, Roger Clemens, who was now with the Blue Jays; when Carpenter arrived early at the Jays training camp in Dunedin in early February, there was Clemens, the man he had emulated even as a Little Leaguer. Carpenter was just 11 when Clemens won his first Cy Young Award in 1986, and he wanted to be as good a pitcher as the Red Sox ace. "When I thought of baseball, I thought of Roger Clemens," Carpenter recalled. He also remembered how he would pretend to be Clemens when pitching in an important Little League game.[13] Now, more than a decade later, the two were at spring training together; and in the future, they might be major-league teammates.

But there was no plan to hurry Carpenter along: the Blue Jays, while impressed with his potential, felt he still needed more time in the minor leagues. At Syracuse, Carpenter's fastball continued to impress, but he was still learning to improve command of his curveball and changeup. He was only 1-4, with a 3.88 ERA in early May, when something unexpected happened: Toronto pitcher Erik Hanson developed shoulder trouble, and after his replacement, Robert Person, also got a sore shoulder,[14] Carpenter was suddenly on his way to Toronto to make his major-league debut.[15]

It did not go well. Pitching against the Minnesota Twins on May 12, 1997, he lasted only three innings, giving up seven runs (five earned) and eight hits, as the Jays lost to the Twins 12-2. Carpenter was the losing pitcher.[16] In his brief time with the Jays, he was 0-2, with a less-than-impressive 12.71 ERA.[17] When Person was able to come off the disabled list, Carpenter was optioned back to Syracuse.[18] On the other hand, reporters observed that the 21-year-old pitcher had good stuff, and with some more experience, he would undoubtedly do much better the next time he was called up.

In late July Carpenter's record with Syracuse was 4-9, with a 4.50 ERA, but local baseball writers noted that his record was deceptive—the SkyChiefs' poor defense and lack of timely hitting had cost him several

games, yet despite that, he had shown steady improvement.[19] The writers believed Carpenter would get called up again soon, and Chris was confident that this time things would go better.

On July 29 Carpenter was recalled by the Blue Jays, but it would take a few more starts (and several more losses) before he finally got his first major-league win, on August 19, when the Jays defeated the Chicago White Sox 6-5. Carpenter gave up four runs in six innings, but a win was a win, and he was happy to get one. As the season progressed, he used every available moment to soak up additional information about the art of pitching from the team's veterans,[20] and gradually he began to show improvement. On September 9 he gave his best major-league performance, beating the Anaheim Angels, 2-0. It was his first shutout and his first complete game, and he gave up just three hits; only two runners reached second base.[21]

Carpenter finished the season with an overall record of 3-7 and an ERA of 5.09, much of that the result of his early outings. When the Jays began the 1998 season, he was in the starting rotation, eager to build on what he had learned during his rookie year. He made 24 starts that year, compiling a record of 12-7, with a 4.37 ERA. Most of those wins came in the second half of the year; he went 6-1 over a period from July through September. His manager, Tim Johnson, stated that Carpenter was showing an ability to use all of his pitches consistently; Johnson also stated with certainty, "He'll be a quality pitcher for years."[22]

As the 1999 season approached, Carpenter seemed poised to have a breakout season. He was about to be part of a rotation that featured Roy Halladay, Kelvim Escobar, Pat Hentgen, and David Wells. Although Chris had a couple of minor health problems in 1998 (including several weeks during spring training when he had some tightness in his shoulder,[23] and a time in the late summer when he saw an asthma specialist after experiencing some breathing problems),[24] neither situation caused any lasting effects. During April and May of 1999, Carpenter led all Jays pitchers in innings pitched and complete games, and was the only starter with an ERA under five—his was 3.63.[25] Then, without warning, in early June he suddenly began to experience soreness in his elbow. He ended up on the 15-day disabled list, then did a rehab start at Class-A St. Catharine's (Ontario), and prepared to rejoin the Jays.[26]

But although he said he felt good, his pitching was once again inconsistent, and he was having problems with control.[27] As it turned out, his elbow was not 100 percent after all. He decided to see a specialist to find out why he continued to experience recurring pain. The Jays' trainer thought it might be a bone spur, and that meant surgery would be needed.[28] Carpenter finished 1999 with a record of 9-8 and a 4.38 ERA. In the offseason, he had elbow surgery, after which he worked on strengthening his arm, and said he would be ready for the 2000 season.[29] But just like before, he pitched inconsistently; in early May, he was 3-3 with a 4.50 ERA. He insisted he was fine, but some players who knew him suspected he was in more pain than he wanted to admit.[30] Carpenter soldiered on throughout 2000, but he rarely was the dominant pitcher everyone hoped for. He was in and out of the starting rotation, and he finished up with a losing record, 10-12 with an unimpressive 6.26 ERA. By this point, fans and baseball writers alike were wondering why he continued to underachieve. Said one reporter, Carpenter was one of several pitchers on the Jays who were "long on potential but short on performance."[31] No one, including Chris Carpenter himself, had a good explanation.

In fairness, Carpenter was playing for a team that had endured quite a bit of management turmoil. By spring training of 2001, the Jays were on their fourth manager and coaching staff since Carpenter's major-league debut, and along the way, several of the coaches insisted on changing his mechanics in hopes of addressing his inconsistency.[32] But Carpenter refused to make excuses. He was now 25, had plenty of major-league experience under his belt, and he wanted to step up and become the team's ace. At times during the early part of the season, he seemed ready to do just that, like when he overpowered the White Sox in late May, pitching a six-hit shutout and boosting his record to 5-2.[33] But then the inconsistency and loss of control recurred and he began losing (and giving up too many runs). In early August, Carpenter's record was 7-9 with a 4.33 ERA, he hadn't won a game since late June, and he admitted he had lost command of his curveball.[34] Carpenter was unable to turn things around until late August, when he finally won a game, pitching seven shutout innings in the Jays' 5-0 victory over Baltimore—his first win in 11 starts. For the remainder of the season, Carpenter once again pitched well, and brought his record up to 11-11, with a 4.09 ERA; he also pitched a career-high 215⅔ innings.

In the offseason, with his three-year contract up, Carpenter found that the Jays' new management (general manager Gord Ash was gone, replaced by J.P. Ricciardi) was not as accommodating as the previous management had been. The Jays refused to give him a multiyear deal, nor did they offer him the kind of money he had hoped to make. In fact, his agent believed Carpenter's days with Toronto were numbered.[35] In the end, the Jays and Carpenter avoided salary arbitration, but he was signed to only a one-year contract, worth $3.45 million, less than the $4.5 million he wanted.[36]

And yet again, it was a difficult year for Carpenter. In early April, after a game in which he gave up four home runs in less than three innings, he was put on the disabled list with shoulder tendinitis (which he admitted had begun during spring training).[37] He returned, but ended up on the DL again—in fact, he was on it a total of three times, as his shoulder continued to bother him throughout the season. By early September, Chris had a record of 4-5 and a 5.28 ERA, and he had pitched only 73⅓ innings for the Jays. The team announced that the hard-luck pitcher would need surgery to repair a torn labrum in his right shoulder, and even if everything went well, he would not be able to pitch for at least nine months. But few of the beat reporters in Toronto expected to see Carpenter in a Jays uniform again. With his contract up again, the consensus was that Carpenter's time with the Blue Jays was over.[38] In his six years with the Jays, he had compiled a record of 49-50, with a 4.83 ERA. Few people thought that was all he was capable of. Perhaps a new start would be for the best.

As it turned out, those who predicted Carpenter's time with Toronto had ended were correct. When the Jays wanted to assign him to Triple-A Syracuse, Carpenter instead decided to test the free-agent market. It was a good decision: The day after he severed ties with the Jays, the St. Louis Cardinals made him an offer. Even though he would be unable to pitch till at least July of 2003, the Cardinals guaranteed $300,000, which would grow to $500,000 as soon as he was put on the active roster that year.[39] There was also a $2 million option for 2004.[40] Best of all, he would not have to go to the minors and work his way back to the big leagues. Carpenter expressed frustration at the previous couple of seasons, and especially at his inability to improve his won-lost record. And while he and his wife loved Toronto, he agreed that it was time for a change.

Things did not go the way either Carpenter or his new team planned. Instead of being able to come back to the Cardinals in July, there were unexpected complications. The team had sent him to do a quick rehab stint in late June, first for the Class-A Palm Beach Cardinals, and then at the Triple-A Memphis Redbirds. When he took the mound for the Redbirds, Carpenter gave up three runs and four hits in the first inning, and he definitely did not look ready for the majors. Rather than rush him, it was decided he needed more time in the minors.[41] But when Carpenter did not pitch any better in a subsequent rehab appearance, the Cardinals grew concerned. They had good reason. Not only was he giving up a lot of runs, he was once again feeling discomfort in his surgically repaired shoulder. He was sent to St. Louis to get an MRI, and Cardinals manager Tony La Russa acknowledged that it was unlikely Carpenter would pitch for the team in 2003.[42]

The test results confirmed La Russa's assessment. Carpenter needed additional surgery, this time to remove scar tissue from his shoulder. The operation took place in late July, and the Cardinals said that once this was taken care of, he would be ready for spring training in 2004.[43] Of course, this was not what St. Louis fans had hoped for. The Cardinals needed pitching, and Carpenter had been expected to help the team in 2003. Now, everyone would have to wait and see, and some fans were skeptical about whether the team had made the right decision to sign him. But showing they still believed Carpenter would come back and contribute positively, the Cardinals gave him another one-year contract, with terms similar to the last year's, and additional incentives once he had reached 10 starts. GM Walt Jocketty expressed confidence that in 2004 Carpenter would be one of the team's starters.[44]

And after living through so many disappointments and setbacks, Carpenter was eager to get some results. He was also confident that this surgery had worked: Back home in New Hampshire, he was pitching to some college players, and noticed that his pitches had the kind of movement they used to have before his arm trouble. His location was back, and he could even throw his changeup for strikes.[45] Before this most recent surgery, he had considered retiring, concerned that the constant pain would never go away and he would never be able to pitch effectively again.[46] It was his wife, Alyson, who encouraged him and persuaded him not to quit,[47] and now, finally, he was pain-free.

He was optimistic again, and he couldn't wait to get to spring training. And when Cardinals players saw how good Carpenter's stuff was, they were optimistic too.

In fact, 2004 turned out to be the kind of year people had long believed Carpenter was capable of. His velocity and command were back, and he pitched 182 innings, going 15-5, with a 3.46 ERA. The Cardinals were heading for the playoffs, and everyone was excited to see what Carpenter would do. But once again there was a roadblock. In late September Carpenter began feeling pain in the biceps in his throwing arm. Resting it did not help; there was some kind of nerve irritation in the arm, and neither the team doctor nor the specialist could predict when it would get better.[48] The Cardinals waited to see if Carpenter would be available during the playoffs, but he never was. The team subsequently lost the World Series to the Red Sox, much to the frustration of the fans, who had been excited by Carpenter's 2004 comeback and disappointed that he couldn't pitch in the postseason.

No one was more frustrated and disappointed than Carpenter. While Red Sox fans rejoiced in their first World Series win in 86 years, Cardinals fans wondered if he would ever stay healthy for a full season. Meanwhile, Carpenter won *The Sporting News'* Comeback Player of the Year award for 2004, a year before a similar award was given by Major League Baseball.[49] But better than winning an award was the fact that resting his arm had allowed the nerve disorder to heal; Carpenter returned to the Cardinals once again able to throw without pain.[50] He looked so good in spring training that manager LaRussa named him the Cardinals' Opening Day starter. He did not disappoint, pitching seven innings of four-hit, one-run baseball in a 7-3 victory over Houston.[51]

It was a preview of things to come. By the All-Star break Carpenter had 128 strikeouts and 13 wins, one of which was against his former team, the Blue Jays; he overpowered them, throwing a one-hitter in an interleague game the Cardinals won 7-0.[52] When players were named for the All-Star Game, Carpenter was selected It was his first time, and La Russa chose him as the National League's starting pitcher. He gave up two hits, induced a double play, and pitched a scoreless inning.

Throughout the rest of 2005, Carpenter's pitching was outstanding; no one used words like "mediocre" or "underachiever" any more. Now, he was "brilliant" and "dominant and his teammates praised his focus, his intensity, and his desire to win. He was so overpowering that he did not lose a game in 16 starts from June 14 to September 8; during that period, he went 13-0 with a 1.36 earned-run average.[53] His final four outings were subpar, but he still ended the season with a record of 21-5 and a personal best 2.83 ERA. Carpenter's peers voted him the winner of a Players Choice Award, as the National League's Outstanding Pitcher.[54] Carpenter also won the Cy Young Award; he beat out Florida Marlins left-hander Dontrelle Willis in a close vote. His career had totally turned around—from a time in 2003 when he thought he would never play again to being honored as the National League's best pitcher in 2005. He was now making $13 million (a far cry from the $500,000 he had signed for), but many reporters noted that compared with some other star pitchers, he was quite underpaid. Carpenter said he didn't mind; he was healthy, he was winning, and he felt he was with the right team.[55]

In May 2006 Carpenter made another sudden trip to the disabled list, but this time it wasn't his arm. He had experienced back spasms in April, and they had never improved; he now had some stiffness in the shoulder area, and was finally diagnosed with bursitis. It was affecting his mechanics, and some time on the DL seemed prudent, given his history.[56] When he returned in June, he felt better, and he gave the Cardinals some quality starts; but at several points during the season, he had to leave games with painful cramping in his arms or legs, said to be caused by dehydration.[57] And while he didn't put up Cy Young numbers, he still finished with a solid record: 15-8 and a 3.09 ERA in 221⅔ innings; more importantly, whenever the Cardinals needed a big win from him, he usually produced, including during the playoffs. For example, although the Cards barely made it into the postseason, Carpenter gave them 6⅓ innings of clutch pitching in Game One of the NLDS versus

San Diego; he was the winning pitcher, allowing five hits and one run in the Cardinals' 5-1 victory. That win improved Carpenter's lifetime playoff record to 3-0, with an ERA of 1.98. Meanwhile, the Cardinals began to play like champs, defeating the Detroit Tigers in five games in the World Series. And one of the Cardinals' wins came from Chris Carpenter, who pitched eight shutout innings in Game Three, giving up only three hits as the Cardinals won 5-0.

But nothing ever was simple in Chris Carpenter's career. When he came to spring training in 2007, he soon began to experience elbow stiffness, soreness, and inflammation. He was diagnosed with arthritis and an MRI showed bone spurs. It was hoped that a cortisone shot and some rest would be all that was needed.[58] But the elbow did not improve, and by May it became obvious that Carpenter would need surgery to remove the bone spurs. The hope was that he would return to the Cardinals in about three months.[59] But in July management admitted that its original optimistic report was inaccurate. In fact, not only was Carpenter not coming back in August; he needed additional elbow surgery, to replace his medial collateral ligament, better known as Tommy John surgery. He would probably miss much of 2008.[60] This was a major disappointment for the fans, the team, and of course, for Carpenter, who had hoped his arm troubles were behind him.

By mid-July of 2008 Carpenter was far enough along in his recovery to begin an injury rehab assignment; he pitched four pain-free innings for the Double-A Springfield (Missouri) Cardinals, and while he did not have his command back yet, the outing was encouraging. In fact, Cardinals said he would return to the team at the end of the month. He made several appearances with the Cardinals, and all seemed to be going well; but then, in mid-August, Carpenter experienced soreness in his triceps area. Again he had to go see the specialists. Everyone breathed a sigh of relief when the diagnosis was just a mild muscle strain on the back side of his right shoulder. But it still meant another trip to the DL, certainly not what Carpenter had hoped. And there was worse news: Tests showed nerve irritation in his shoulder, and he was told not to pitch any more in 2008.[61] He also required one more surgery, to reduce pressure on a compressed nerve in his shoulder. It was becoming increasingly difficult for Carpenter to remain positive. All he wanted to do was pitch, but it seemed there was one obstacle after another.

Still, Carpenter persevered. He was back at spring training in 2009, and early indications were that his velocity had returned. He returned to the Cardinals' rotation, determined to win games and not worry about his arm. The season brought him some much-needed good news: he threw well, and looked like the dominant pitcher everyone saw in 2005. In fact, from early July through mid-August of 2009, he was 7-0 in eight starts, with an ERA of 1.67.[62] And at season's end, he had an impressive 17-4 record, with a league-leading ERA of 2.24. And there was one other interesting note: In early October, on the last day of the season, Carpenter (a .105 lifetime hitter as of 2009) hit a grand slam and knocked in six runs in a game the Cardinals won 13-0 against the Cincinnati Reds.[63] In early October Carpenter was voted the National League's Comeback Player of the Year. Some of the baseball writers also expected Chris to win another Cy Young, but he lost out to San Francisco Giants ace Tim Lincecum. The vote was very close, and not everyone agreed with the decision.[64] But Carpenter's amazing season also earned him other accolades: In January 2010 the Boston chapter of the Baseball Writers Association of America announced it had unanimously chosen him for the 20th annual Tony Conigliaro Award, given to "a Major League player who has overcome adversity through the attributes of spirit, determination and courage."[65]

The 2010 season saw Carpenter continuing to put up good numbers. He was 35 now, but just as his injuries hadn't stopped him, neither did his age. He made a league-leading 35 starts, finishing at 16-9 and a 3.22 ERA. But he pitched one complete game, and said that at times he felt uncomfortable with his mechanics.[66] In 2011 he was once again the Cardinals' Opening Day pitcher, the fifth time he had been chosen.[67] During the season, he was sometimes inconsistent, but he came up big when the Cardinals needed him to. And he was still a workhorse: Carpenter led the National League with 237⅓ innings pitched. His record was 11-9, with a 3.45 earned-run average. But he was especially dominant during the Cardinals' pennant drive late in the season. Then, in Game Five of the NLDS, Carpenter outpitched his friend and former Blue Jays teammate Roy Halladay, throwing a three-hitter and winning, 1-0. Throughout the playoffs, he continued to win big games, including giving the Cards six-plus innings on only three days' rest in Game Seven of the World Series, helping his team to defeat the Texas Rangers and win the Series again. Carpenter's hometown newspaper, the *Manchester* (New Hampshire) *Union Leader*, editorialized that he was the epitome of good sportsmanship, competitiveness, and character, someone that every young athlete could emulate.[68]

In 2012, however, Carpenter was injured again, this time with a nerve problem that affected his rotator cuff. Determined to continue pitching, he agreed to another surgical procedure, but he made only three starts that year, and was winless. Things did not improve for him in 2013, when he experienced periods of numbness in his pitching hand. He was unsuccessful in completing a rehab assignment. Finally, Carpenter decided there was no point in living with continued pain that made it impossible for him to be effective. In November 2013 he announced his retirement. In spite of all the injuries, he compiled an impressive record during his major-league career: 144 wins and 94 losses (he went 95-44 with the Cardinals), with an ERA of 3.76 and 1,697 strikeouts. He had won a Cy Young Award, been named Comeback Player of the Year, played on three All-Star teams, and was on two championship World Series teams.[69] Not bad for a young man from Raymond, New Hampshire, who almost became a hockey player. After his playing days ended, the popular Carpenter was given a job in the Cardinals' front office, but he left that position after only a year; he told reporters he had been going through some personal changes (including getting divorced, and ultimately remarrying), and did not feel he was able to focus on what the organization needed. He hoped to come back to the Cardinals in some capacity in the future.[70] In 2016 he was voted into the St. Louis Cardinals Hall of Fame.

NOTES

1   Jim Connell, "Carpenter at Home on the Sidelines," *Springfield* (Missouri) *News-Leader*, January 24, 2015:D1.

2   Lori Shontz, "Pitching on Wife Support." *St. Louis Post-Dispatch*, July 30, 2004: D1.

3   Joe Strauss, "That's a Winner," *St. Louis Post-Dispatch*, August 16, 2005: D1.

4   Ronald Blum, "American League Stars Shine Bright in Detroit," *Portsmouth* (New Hampshire) *Herald*, July 13, 2005: B1-2.

5   "Chris Carpenter, Toronto Blue Jays Pitcher," *Hamilton* (Ontario) *Spectator*, July 2, 1999: E6.

6   Joe Strauss, "That's a Winner," *St. Louis Post-Dispatch*, August 16, 2005: D1.

7   Tom King, "Welch Now a Met," *Nashua* (New Hampshire) *Telegraph*, June 4, 1993: 23.

8   "Area High Schools: Baseball," *Nashua Telegraph*, April 17, 1993: 18.

9   "Trinity's Carpenter Signs With the Jays," *Nashua Telegraph*, August 12, 1993: 27.

10 Ibid.

11 "Jays Come to Terms With NH Prospect," *Lowell* (Massachusetts) *Sun*, August 12, 1993: 26.

12 "A Walk Through the Parks," *Toronto Globe and Mail*, June 27, 1995: C4.

13 Matt Michael, "SkyChief Prospect Idolizes Clemens," *Syracuse* (New York) *Post-Standard*, March 27, 1997: C1.

14 S.P. Services, "Expos Mighty Pleased with 5-4 Coast Record," *Saskatoon* (Saskatchewan) *Star-Phoenix*, May 12, 1997: C4.

15 John Benson, "New Faces Offer Rotisserie Risks and Opportunities," *Stamford* (Connecticut) *Daily Advocate*, May 18, 1997: C2.

16 "Twins Get Back on Victory Lane," *Aberdeen* (South Dakota) *Daily News*, May 13, 1997: 4C.

17 Matt Michael, "Struggling Syracuse Gets Help," *Syracuse Herald-Journal*, May 28, 1997: C3.

18 "Transactions," *Stamford Daily Advocate*, May 28, 1997: C5.

19 Matt Michael, "Carpenter Twirls a Dandy, But SkyChiefs Fall," *Syracuse Herald-American*, July 13, 1997: C8.

20 Richard Griffin, "Rookie Pitcher Carpenter Could Be the Real Deal," *Toronto Star*, August 21, 1997: D6.

21 "Toronto Led by Young Lineup," *Lawrence* (Kansas) *Journal-World*, September 10, 1997: 4C.

22 Scot Gregor, "Blue Jays Carpenter Silences Belle, Rest of White Sox," *Daily Herald* (Arlington Heights Illinois), July 17, 1998: Section 2, p. 3.

23 Tom Maloney, "Guzman's the Wild Card in Jays' Rotation," *Kitchener* (Ontario) *Record*, February 18, 1998: E5.

24 "Carpenter Works on Control—Of His Mind," *Toronto Star*, August 12, 1998: 1.

25 "Baseball: Hurting Jays Lose Top Starter," *Kingston* (Ontario) *Whig-Standard*, June 7, 1999: 19.

26 Chris Jones, "It Was Only Class-A, but It Was a Game Worth Catching," *The National Post* (Don Mills, Ontario), June 24, 1999: B16.

27 Robert MacLeod, "Texas Hitters Hammer Carpenter," *Toronto Globe and Mail*, August 28, 1999: A21.

28 "Carpenter Sees Specialist," *Toronto Star*, September 14, 1999: 1.

29 "Blue Jays Starting Rotation on the Mend," *Alaska Highway News* (Fort St. John, British Columbia), February 21, 2000: 8.

30 Geoff Baker, "Walking Wounded Straddle a Fine Line," *Toronto Star*, May 30, 2000: C7.

31 Bob Matthews, "Indians Will Return to Prominence," *Rockford* (Illinois) *Register Star*, March 31, 2001: 6C.

32 Mark Zwolinski, "Carpenter Out to Rebuild Reputation," *Guelph* (Ontario) *Daily Mercury*, February 27, 2001: B4.

33 "Carpenter Whitewashes Sox," *Chatham* (Ontario) *Daily News*, May 30, 2001: 11.

34 "Carpenter Needs Work," *Timmins* (Ontario) *Daily Press*, August 3, 2001: 9.

35 Allan Ryan, "Blue Jays' Carpenter Feels Chill in Post-Ash Era," *Toronto Star*, January 19, 2002: E4.

36 Richard Griffin, "Who Loves Ya, Chris? Not the Blue Jays," *Toronto Star*, February 14, 2002: C18.

37 "Blue Jays: Carpenter Placed on Disabled List," *Kingston Whig-Standard*, April 8, 2002: 18.

38 Richard Griffin, "Carpenter's Cut Leaves Jays in a Quandary," *Toronto Star*, September 5, 2002: D2.

39 "Carpenter Signs With Cardinals," *Barrie* (Ontario) *Examiner*, December 14, 2002: B1.

40 Drew Olson, "Job One: Keeping Your Own," *Milwaukee Journal Sentinel*, December 14, 2002: 6C.

41 Joe Strauss, "Knee Pain Again Gives Drew Cause for Concern," *St. Louis Post-Dispatch*, July 6, 2003: F9.

42 Joe Strauss, "Jocketty Won't Deal for Pitcher Right Now," *St. Louis Post-Dispatch*, July 24, 2003: D5.

43 "Cards Pitcher Carpenter's Season Is Over Following More Surgery," *St. Louis Post-Dispatch*, August 6, 2003: D5.

44 Joe Strauss, "Cards Still Like Carpenter's Tools," *St. Louis Post-Dispatch*, December 2, 2003: D2.

45 Dan O'Neill. "Cards Hitters Say This Carpenter Is Electric," *St. Louis Post-Dispatch*, February 28, 2004:OT5.

46 Tom D'Angelo, "Carpenter Retools," *Palm Beach Post*, March 2, 2004: 8C.

47 Lori Shontz, "Pitching on Wife Support," *St. Louis Post-Dispatch*, July 30, 2004: D1.

48 Derrick Goold, "Pitchers' Injuries Strike Raw Nerve," *St. Louis Post-Dispatch*, October 8, 2004: C4.

49 Gary Gillette and Pete Palmer, eds., *ESPN Baseball Encyclopedia* (New York: Sterling Publishing, 2007), 1769.

50 Joe Strauss, "Carpenter Bounces Back," *St. Louis Post-Dispatch*, February 21, 2005: D1.

51 Derrick Goold, "Carpenter's Opening Effort Draws Accolades," *St. Louis Post-Dispatch*, April 6, 2005: B5.

52 "Carpenter, the Ace That Got Away, Rips Apart Blue Jays," *Peace River Daily News* (Dawson Creek, British Columbia), June 15, 2005: 6.

53 Pat Borzi, "Cardinals' Top Starters Not Strong to Finish," *New York Times*, October 4, 2005: D4.

54 Derrick Goold, "Players Honor Cards' Carpenter," *St. Louis Post-Dispatch*, November 4, 2005: D3.

55 Joe Strauss, "No-Brainer for Carpenter," *St. Louis Post-Dispatch*, March 19, 2006: D1.

56 Joe Strauss, "Cards Will Put Carpenter on DL," *St. Louis Post-Dispatch*, May 29, 2006: D5.

57 Derrick Goold, "Muscles Cramp Carpenter's Style," *St. Louis Post-Dispatch*, August 27, 2006: D5.

58 Derrick Goold, "To Help Heal His Aching Elbow, Carpenter Must Rest," *St. Louis Post-Dispatch*, April 14, 2007: B7.

59 "Cards' Ace May Be Out Until August," *Deseret News* (Salt Lake City), May 6, 2007: D12.

60 Joe Strauss, "Season Ends for Cards Pitcher," *St. Louis Post-Dispatch*, July 20, 2007: D1.

61 "Cards Drop in Wild-Card Race," *Toronto Globe and Mail*, September 13, 2008: S3.

62 "Pujols, Holliday Back Carpenter to Topple Reds," *Fort Wayne* (Indiana) *Journal-Gazette*, August 13, 2009: B4.

63 Rick Hummel, "Carp Uses His Hammer" *St. Louis Post-Dispatch*, October 2, 2009, C1.

64 Joe Strauss, "Sigh! It's Lincecum's Cy; Chris Carpenter and Adam Wainwright Finish Second and Third in Cy Young Voting," *St. Louis Post-Dispatch*, November 20, 2009: C1.

65 Neil Keefe, "Chris Carpenter Wins 2009 Tony Conigliaro Award," Online at nesn.com/2010/01/chris-carpenter-wins-2009-tony-conigliaro-award/.

66 Joe Strauss, "Mad on the Mound," *St Louis Post-Dispatch*, March 13, 2011: C1.

67   Derrick Goold, "Carpenter Set to Go First," *St. Louis Post-Dispatch*, March 31, 2011: C5.

68   "Cheering Carpenter: Elite Talent, Elite Ethic," *Manchester Union Leader*, October 23, 2011. Online at unionleader.com/article/20111023/OPINION01/710239971/0/.

69   Derrick Goold, "End of an Era as Carpenter Retires," *St. Louis Post-Dispatch*, November 21, 2013. Online at stltoday.com/

sports/baseball/professional/end-of-an-era-as-carpenter-retires/article_fa898878-d869-59d8-9207-94b978f26642.html.

70   Rich Hummel, "Hall of Fame Induction Special for Carpenter," *St. Louis Post-Dispatch*, August 28, 2016: C9.

JOAQUIN BENOIT

By Mark Brunke

FOR MANY PITCHERS, THE pathway to the major leagues is a trail marked with the challenges and opportunities of injury. Joaquín Benoit is among those for whom injury presented both a challenge and opportunity. The perseverance that led him to win the 2010 Tony Conigliaro Award was a character trait present even at the outset of his career. Benoit found himself on the disabled list with regularity and always managed to rise to meet the ever-increasing challenge of injury. As is the case with many pitchers, injuries to others provided his early opportunities to move up from the minors, while at the same time being the test he would need to face in remaining. Along the way, Benoit found a role that would allow him to stay in the majors and enjoy a lengthy career.

A native of the Dominican Republic, Joaquín Antonio Benoit Peña was born on July 26, 1977. His home city of Santiago was founded in 1504. One of the oldest continuously occupied colonial settlements in the Western Hemisphere, Santiago is the second largest city in the Dominican Republic and the fourth largest city in the Caribbean. In a country with a tradition of producing the greatest number of foreign-born players in major-league baseball, Santiago has its own great tradition. Represented in the Dominican Winter League since 1937 by the Cibao Eagles, Santiago has produced 11 players who have made a major-league roster as of Opening Day 2016. On May 20, 1996, Joaquin Benoit joined that list after being signed as a nondrafted free agent by Texas Rangers scouts Omar Minaya and Cornelio Peña.[1]

Benoit spent his first summer as a professional with the Rangers' 1996 Dominican Summer League team in Santo Domingo. He finished that short summer season with a 2.28 ERA, earning his way to the Rangers' Florida Rookie League the next year. Benoit then spent 1997 with the Port Charlotte Rangers of the Gulf Coast League. This was a city Benoit would see

a lot of as the Rangers operated both their Gulf Coast League team and their Class-A Florida State League teams out of Port Charlotte from 1996 to 2002.

The 6-foot-4, 250-pound right-hander was initially thought of as a starting pitcher. He made his way through the minor leagues being developed for a starting role. Benoit started 10 games in Port Charlotte in 1997. He ended the year with a 3-3 record, pitching 44 innings and compiling a 2.05 ERA with 10 earned runs surrendered. Benoit closed out the season by pitching eight shutout innings against the Kansas City Royals' GCL affiliate in the semifinals of the league playoffs.

The Texas Rangers added the A-level Savannah Sand Gnats of the South Atlantic League to their minor-league system in 1998. Benoit started 15 games before his season ended early due to a strain to an ulnar collateral ligament in his right elbow. The determination was to heal with rehabilitation instead of surgery.[2] This was the first of several interruptions to Benoit's career by injury. Before being shut down on August 4, Benoit had

put together a record of four wins and three losses. Nearly doubling his innings, Benoit increased his workload to 80 innings, giving up 79 hits and 18 walks. His 3.82 ERA was the best among Sand Gnats starters with 15 or more starts.

Benoit was back in Port Charlotte for 1999. His return trip to the city this time was a move up to the Florida State League Port Charlotte Rangers, the Rangers' high-A affiliate. Benoit started 22 games, going 7-4 with a 5.31 ERA while surpassing 100 innings for the first time. In 105 innings he gave up 117 hits and 50 walks.

Benoit was promoted to Tulsa of the Double-A Texas League for 2000 and was the Opening Day starter.[3] Early in the season he injured his right shoulder.[4] Limited to 82 innings in 16 starts, Benoit went 4-4 and improved his ERA to 3.83. After the season Benoit pitched in the Arizona Fall League. Going

Joaquin Benoit, holding the Tony Conigliaro Award

2-2 with a 1.91 ERA in 33 innings, he was voted the league's best right-handed starter for that season.[5] Benoit returned to Tulsa in 2001 to be the Opening Day starter there for the second year in a row.

After going 1-0 in four starts for Tulsa, Benoit was promoted to the Rangers' Triple-A team, Oklahoma City RedHawks of the Pacific Coast League.[6] There he had control problems.

On May 1 he gave up six runs and six walks in two-thirds of an inning. On May 23 against New Orleans, he walked eight in 3⅔ innings. In spite of this, batters were batting only .188 against him at that point. Manager DeMarlo Hale said of Benoit that even though he had walked five batters in a row on the May 23 game, "[H]e has a bright future. He's a very good pitcher. He has three pitches that are major-league stuff in his fastball, slider, and changeup, and he mixes in his curveball."[7]

Benoit's 24 starts tied for the team lead with R.A. Dickey, and he finished second to Dickey in innings pitched with 131. On August 8 Benoit was called up to the Rangers for a spot start against Detroit. Making

his major-league debut, Benoit lasted five innings in a no-decision, giving up six earned runs

During the 2001-2002 offseason Benoit pitched for his hometown Santiago team, Águilas Cibaeñas (Cibao Eagles), and was named the Dominican Winter League's Pitcher of the Year.[8] Benoit put up a 5-0 record with a 2.37 ERA.[9]

Heading into the 2002 season Benoit was rated by *Baseball America* as the seventh best prospect in the Rangers' farm system.[10] He spent most of the season going back and forth between Oklahoma City and the Texas Rangers. This was the year the Rangers began exploring using Benoit out of the bullpen, a decision that resulted in a permanent change in his career path. In the process Benoit set a major-league record while recording his first save. For Oklahoma City Benoit was 8-4 in 16 starts with a 3.56 ERA, striking out 103 batters in 98⅔ innings. He fell into the situation of being a spot starter who is called back and forth as needed between Triple A affiliate and the major-league club, often because of player injuries. Such was the case for Benoit, who was called up for the first time to make a start on May 9.

Called up because pitcher Ismael Valdes was bothered by stiffness in his back, Benoit flew to Arlington overnight and started against the Chicago White Sox on only three hours' sleep. Benoit pitched six innings in a 4-1 win. After the game he said, "In the first couple of innings, I was trying to do too much, but those last three innings, I was getting my energy back."[11] Two days later he was back pitching for Oklahoma City.[12]

Benoit got another opportunity to pitch for the Rangers when Rudy Saenz was placed on the disabled list with shoulder tendinitis.[13] This time, Benoit was used in long relief, pitching from the second into the sixth inning of a 13-7 loss to the Atlanta Braves on June 7. He walked five, gave up five hits, and surrendered two earned runs. After the game, he was optioned back to Oklahoma City. On June 24 outfielder Gabe Kapler went on the disabled list with tendinitis in his left wrist. Benoit was recalled and struck out two and walked three in five innings in an 8-5 win over the Anaheim Angels. After the game, in which Benoit picked up his second win, he was optioned back to

Oklahoma City. After another callup and a start on July 15, a loss to the Kansas City Royals, Benoit came up for the rest of the major-league season at the end of July. He threw 84⅔ innings for the Rangers in 2002, with 13 starts in his 17 appearances with a 5.31 ERA.33

Though still used primarily as a starter, Benoit set a record on September 3, 2002, for the longest save in major-league history. It happened in a contentious meeting with the Baltimore Orioles that had its genesis a few days earlier when Orioles pitcher Travis Driskill hit Rangers star Rafael Palmeiro and Rangers pitcher Aaron Myette threw behind the Orioles' Chris Richard.14

On the 3rd, Orioles starter John Stephens hit Alex Rodriguez in the first inning. In the bottom of the first, Rangers starter Myette threw the first two pitches behind the Orioles' leadoff hitter Melvin Mora, and was ejected by home-plate umpire Mark Hirschbeck. Todd Van Poppel then pitched two innings in relief and Benoit entered the game in the third with the Rangers leading 4-0.

Neither Myette nor Van Poppel had given up a hit through the first two innings. Benoit extended the no-hitter to the ninth inning, when he gave up a triple to Jerry Hairston Jr., who scored on a hit by Chris Richard. In seven innings, Benoit struck out four while walking no one. Van Poppel was credited with the win and Benoit with the first save of his career. At seven innings, it was the major leagues' longest credited save.15

Benoit had a rough spring training in 2003, starting the year at Oklahoma City. On May 2 he made a spot start with the Rangers in a game the Cleveland Indians won in the late innings.16 He soon found himself on the disabled list, but other than rehab innings following injury, Benoit was at the major-league level to stay. While his path to the majors had often come through injuries to others, the new pattern for Benoit was to try to maintain his spot on the major-league roster in spite of his own injuries.

Benoit spent June 1-22, 2003 (elbow inflammation), on the 15-day disabled list, including five days with Oklahoma City. Over the next few years, he would go the list again with right shoulder tendinitis in

2004 and 2005, right elbow tendinitis in 2005, right shoulder inflammation in 2008, and finally the most serious injury to that point, a torn right rotator cuff in April 2009 that cost him the rest of the season.17

As injuries seemed to become more regular, Benoit shifted toward becoming a set-up reliever. In 2004 only 15 of Benoit's 28 appearances were starts, and in 2005, only 9 of his 32 appearances. In the middle of the 2005 season, he settled into a set-up role. Benoit cemented that position in September, recording a hold in five consecutive appearances between September 15 and 25. In 2006 Benoit pitched in 56 games for the Rangers, 35 of them in the sixth, seventh, or eighth inning. He had no credited saves, and only seven credited holds. He ended 2006 with a 4.86 ERA and 85 strikeouts in 79⅔ innings.

By 2007 Benoit had another healthy year and was able to cement his place in the majors, appearing in 70 games with 82 innings pitched. His highlights that year included 87 strikeouts, only 28 walks, 17 holds, 7 blown saves, and 6 saves while going 7-4 and putting up a 2.85 ERA. Benoit went the entire month of August without giving up a run. However, 2008 was a more difficult year for Benoit, including time on the disabled list. He appeared in only 44 games for the Rangers, throwing 45 innings while putting up a 5.00 ERA. Although he had returned to the big-league club at the end of July, and made a run of appearances in August, he had only two appearances in September before returning the disabled list.18 After 2007, the Rangers had high hopes for Benoit, but his right shoulder had been acting up in spring training, limiting him to only four innings in Cactus League play. He attempted to play through that pain, but was shut down by September.

Diagnosed with a torn rotator cuff, Benoit had surgery in January 2009. The procedure was performed by the Cincinnati Reds' medical director, Dr. Timothy Kremcheck. According to Rangers GM Jon Daniels, "[M]ultiple doctors recommended rehab over surgery late last season. Unfortunately, [he] didn't respond to the rehab process as we'd hoped. That's a risk any time you rehab a shoulder."19 Although projected to possibly return for the second half of the season, Benoit ended up sitting out all of 2009. It also turned out to be the end of his career with the Texas Rangers; the team cut him on November 5, 2009. For his future, the often-injured pitcher would have to try his luck in the free-agent market to find a roster spot for the 2010 season.

Having only one truly successful season under his belt and a history of injury, Benoit was only able to secure a one-year minor-league deal for the 2010 season with the Tampa Bay Rays.[20] This proved to be a wise move by the Rays, as Benoit not only recovered from his surgery, but came back with his strongest season to that point. Appearing in 63 games as a set-up specialist in front of Rays closer Rafael Soriano, Benoit posted a 1.34 ERA over 60⅓ innings, allowing only 30 hits and giving up only 11 walks. In addition to his ERA being the best among all relievers in the American League, he led the league's relief corps with a .147 batting average against, as well as 4.48 hits and 6.12 baserunners per nine innings. He attained all of this despite starting the year with the Rays' Triple-A International League affiliate Durham Bulls. It wasn't until April 29 that the Rays' brought Benoit up.

The Rays finished 96-66 and made the playoffs. Benoit found himself in the American League Division Series against his former team, the Rangers. Although the Rangers took the series (on their way to the AL pennant before losing the 2010 World Series to the San Francisco Giants), Benoit himself had a good playoff series. Benoit didn't see any action until the seventh inning of Game Three, but was able to pick up a win in the game. In three games, he pitched 3⅔ innings with three strikeouts, and no hits, runs, or walks allowed.

After the 2010 season, the Boston Red Sox announced that Benoit had been voted the winner of the 21st annual Tony Conigliaro Award. Citing Benoit's performance after missing an entire season to injury, the Red Sox noted that the "honor is presented to a Major League player who has overcome adversity through the attributes of spirit, determination and courage that were trademarks of Tony C." The award was presented on January 20, 2011, at the annual dinner of the Boston chapter of the Baseball Writers Association of America.[21]

Benoit had the highest velocity of his career following his surgery, and he sustained this for several seasons.[22] Looking back on his 2010 season, he said, "The first full month I was in the big leagues, I was really inconsistent. I was getting outs because people were swinging. After the first month, my arm responded great."[23] Benoit was able to convert that season into a three-year, $16 million deal with the Detroit Tigers.

For the next three seasons, Benoit was a key member of the Tigers bullpen. He had 66 appearances in 2011, 73 in 2012, and 66 in 2013. He stepped into the closer role at times in 2013, saving 24 games as part of a career-high 43 games finished. The Tigers went to the playoffs each year. In 2011 Benoit was on the losing side against the Rangers again as they went on to win the AL pennant for the second year in a row. Both years, the Rangers lost the World Series.

The Tigers made the Series themselves in 2012, losing to the San Francisco Giants. In 2013 the Tigers lost the American League Championship Series to the Boston Red Sox, four games to two. Benoit finished both Tigers wins, but also gave up an eighth-inning grand slam to David Ortiz, allowing the Red Sox to tie a Game Two they later won in the ninth.

After the 2013 season Benoit was a free agent once more. He signed with the San Diego Padres on December 28 for two years, totaling $15.5 million, with a third-year option on the 2016 season for $8 million, if he pitched in at least 55 games in 2015. Benoit performed well in 2014, appearing in 53 games with a 1.49 ERA in 54⅓ innings, and followed that in 2015 with a 2.34 ERA in 65⅓ innings. He was traded on November 12, 2015, by the Padres to Seattle. His shoulder problems resurfaced in spring training with Seattle.[24] After a return to the 15-day disabled list for the first time since the end of the 2008 season, Benoit appeared in only 26 games with a 5.18 ERA with Seattle in 2015.

On July 26, 2016, Benoit was traded (on his 39th birthday) to the Toronto Blue Jays for Drew Storen and cash. Pitching on a team contending to win the

AL East, he appeared in 25 games during the final two months of the season, giving up only one earned run in 23⅔ innings. His 0.38 ERA in a set-up role proved him to be a timely late-season acquisition for the Blue Jays. Just before the end of the season, on September 26, he tore a calf muscle in a brawl during a 7-5 loss to the New York Yankees.[25]

At every stage of his career, Benoit had encountered adversity and opportunity through injury, and each year had come back stronger. Then, remarkably, when injury loomed greatest, Benoit was able to respond with his best season ever. Although time will eventually catch up with all players of the game, certainly the way Benoit responded to adversity extended his career and brought him and his teams to a remarkable run of success.

SOURCES

In addition to the sources cited in the Notes, the author also consulted Retrosheet.org, Baseball-Reference.com, Benoit's biographical information on MLB.com, and a number of other sources including:

Lagesse, David. "Baseball Is a Field of Dreams and Dashed Hopes For Dominicans," National Public Radio, npr.org/sections/goatsandsoda/2016/04/03/472699693/baseball-is-a-field-of-dreams-and-dashed-hopes-for-dominicans.

Historia del Equipo, Águilas Cibaeñas, aguilas.lidom.com/home/historia-del-equipo/.

NOTES

1   Major League Baseball, Joaquin Antonio Benoit biographical information, mlb.com, m.mlb.com/player/276542/joaquin-benoit, Accessed September 9, 2016.

2   Ibid.

3   Barry Lewis, "Drillers Starting With Rare Roster," *Tulsa World*, April 5, 2001 (tulsaworld.com/archives/drillers-starting-with-rare-roster/article_e4022f0c-9876-5745-8c18-db17aec46e85.html), accessed September 9, 2016.

4   Player bio, mlb.com.

5   Bob Hersom, "Competition Refines Opening Day Roster," *The Oklahoman* (Oklahoma City), April 3, 2001 (newsok.com/article/2736172), accessed September 9, 2016.

6   Bob Hersom, "Zephyrs Take a Stroll in RedHawks' Park," *The Oklahoman*, May 24, 2001 (newsok.com/article/2742502), accessed September 8, 2016.

7   Associated Press, "AL roundup — August 9, 2001," *Lubbock Avalanche-Journal*, August 9, 2001 (lubbockonline.com/sto-ries/080901/pro_0809010075.shtml#.V5b6VI-cE2w), accessed September 4, 2016.

8   Cibao Eagles, "Pitcher of the Year," Águilas Cibaeñas BBC (aguilas.lidom.com/home/premios-obtenidos-por-jugadores-de-aguilas-cibaenas-en-premiacion-de-producciones-apolo/), accessed September 8, 2016.

9   Josh Goldfine, "Rangers 2002 Prospect Report," *USA Today*, April 1, 2002 (usatoday30.usatoday.com/sports/baseball/rangers/prospect.htm), accessed September 17, 2016.

10   Gerry Fraley, "Texas Rangers Top 10 Prospects," *Baseball America* 2002 (baseballamerica.com/online/leagues/mlb/rangers/02top10.html), accessed September 17, 2016.

11   Stephen Hawkins, "Rangers' Benoit Stymies Sox," *Northwest Indiana Times* (Munster, Indiana), May 10, 2002 (nwitimes.com/uncategorized/rangers-benoit-stymies-sox/article_7ad15f4f-a2af-5305-85c2-370dfda28f83.html), accessed September 30, 2016.

12   Associated Press, "Rangers' Benoit Silences Sox," *Northwest Indiana Times*, May 10, 2002 (nwitimes.com/uncategorized/rangers-benoit-silences-sox/article_da0667b5-a454-575b-8591-d46c4d6d3de1.html), accessed September 9, 2016.

13   ESPN, "MLB Transactions," ESPN.com, June 7, 2002 (espn.go.com/mlb/transactions/_/date/20020607), accessed September 17, 2016.

14   Joe Christensen, "Nearly No-Hit, O's Drop 10th in a Row, 7-1," *Baltimore Sun*, September 4, 2002 (articles.baltimoresun.com/2002-09-04/sports/0209040378_1_texas-rangers-orioles-inning), accessed September 8, 2016.

15   Ibid.

16   Game Log, Texas Rangers at Cleveland Indians, May 2, 2003, CBS Sports (cbssports.com/mlb/gametracker/recap/MLB_20030502_TEX@CLE), accessed September 17, 2016.

17   *2016 Seattle Mariners Media Information Guide* (marinersblog.mlblogs.com/2016/02/18/2016-mariners-media-guide/), accessed September 4, 2016.

18   Ken Daley, "Benoit Trying to Turn Around Tough Start," MLB.com (texas.rangers.mlb.com/news/print.jsp?ymd=20080430&content_id=2619181&vkey=news_tex&fext=.jsp&c_id=tex), accessed September 17, 2016.

19   Joe Zedalis, "Texas Reliever Benoit Has Rotator Cuff Surgery," Yahoo Sports (sports.yahoo.com/mlb/rumors/post/Texas-reliever-Benoit-has-rotator-cuff-surgery?urn=mlb,137825), accessed September 17, 2016.

20   Adam J. Morris, "Rays Sign Joaquin Benoit to Minor League Deal," Lonestarball.com, February 15, 2010 (lonestarball.com/2010/2/15/1311453/rays-sign-joaquin-benoit-to-minor), accessed September 18, 2016.

21   Boston Red Sox, "Joaquin Benoit Wins 2010 Tony Conigliaro Award," Redsox.com, December 7, 2010 (boston.redsox.mlb.com/content/printer_friendly/bos/y2010/m12/d07/c16272496.jsp), accessed September 18, 2016.

22   Jeff Sullivan, "Mariners Get Joaquin Benoit, Who Won't Go Away," Fangraphs.com, November 12, 2015 (fangraphs.com/blogs/mariners-get-joaquin-benoit-who-wont-go-away/), accessed September 18, 2016.

23   Matt Chaprales, "Benoit Receives Boston's Tony C. Award," MLB News (m.mlb.com/news/article/16474306//), accessed September 18, 2016.

24   Bob Dutton, "Mariners Notebook: Benoit Placed on Disabled List Because of Sore Shoulder," *Tacoma News-Tribune*, April 25, 2016 (thenewstribune.com/sports/mlb/seattle-mariners/mariners-insider-blog/article73826107.html), accessed September 18, 2016.

25   Associated Press, "Blue Jays Lose 2 to Injury in Brawl-Marred Loss to Yankees," *USA Today*, September 27, 2016 (usatoday.com/story/sports/mlb/2016/09/27/blue-jays-lose-2-to-injury-in-brawl-marred-loss-to-yankees/91152846/), accessed October 1, 2016.

TONY CAMPANA

BY MARK S. STERNMAN

THE 2011 TONY CONIGLIARO Award winner, Anthony Edward "Tony" Campana, overcame cancer and a lack of size to make the major leagues as a backup outfielder known mostly for speed.[1]

Only 5-feet-8 and 165 pounds, the left-handed Campana exuded self-confidence. After spending a month in the majors, he boasted, "I'd like to challenge anyone in the league to a race."[2] Campana "said he could oppose Nyjer Morgan, Michael Bourn, Dee Gordon, and 'Got to add another white guy, so put Brett Gardner in there.'"[3]

Campana had a great deal of faith in his ability to steal bases in large quantities. "[I]f I played every day and did what I hope I could do at the plate, I could give myself a chance to get close to 100," he said.[4]

Campana was born into an athletic family in Kettering, Ohio, on May 30, 1986. His mother, Faye, was a gymnast at Indiana State University and has coached and judged gymnastics.[5] His father, Mike (a steel salesman), and his uncle Tom played football at Eastern Illinois University and Ohio State University respectively. Faye and Mike's two daughters Alex and Nikki, also went in for sports.

Bald as a boy due to chemo treatments he endured to fend off Hodgkin's lymphoma, a diagnosis he received as a 7-year-old[6] at Vanderbilt University Medical Center,7 Campana said in 2015, "I was just a sick kid and knew I needed to get better. It was probably scarier for my parents than for me. As a result, I have fun doing everything I do and no regrets about anything."[8]

At the time, of course, Campana had some scary moments. He "once rolled over while sleeping in his hospital bed, dislodging a needle and waking in a pool of blood. But six months of treatment worked, and after years of regular checkups, Campana was declared cancer-free during high school."[9]

Campana used his illness as a self-motivational tool. "That's how I grew up—being a fighter," he said. "People tell me I can't do something because I'm sick, because I'm too small, I'm not going to listen to them. I'm going to show them I can."[10]

Attending Springboro High near Dayton, Ohio, Campana had a .418 batting average his senior year and made all-area in football. In college, he batted over .300 each of his four years. "After calling everyone I could out of high school," Campana walked-on at the University of North Carolina-Asheville[11] and played there for two years before transferring to the University of Cincinnati for two more. In his freshman year, he hit .321 before falling off slightly as a sophomore to .315. As a junior, he batted .329 and set a school record that still stands with an NCAA-leading 60 stolen bases while making second team all-Big East. In his senior year, his one scholarship season, he upped his hitting to .338[12] and made first team all-Big East along with future Pittsburgh star and minor-league teammate Josh Harrison. At the end of the 2015 season, Campana held three other University of Cincinnati records, for career stolen bases (104), at-bats in a season (263), and steals in a game (6).[13]

The Chicago Cubs drafted Campana in the 13th round of the June 2008 free-agent draft, with his signing credited to scout Lukas McKnight. The Cubs sent Campana to the short-season Boise Hawks, where he broke his hand stealing second in the first inning. "I finished the game, went back to my host family, and iced my hand all night, but it blew up like a balloon. The rest of the year I stopped sliding headfirst into second and didn't resume doing so until two years later at Double A."

This unfortunate beginning notwithstanding, at each level Campana stole lots of bases, swiping 22 in 25 games in 2008, 66 in 2009, and 48 in 2010. Off to a strong start with Triple-A Iowa in 2011, Campana joined the plodding Cubs in May 2011.[14] "I got called up with [pitcher] Scott Maine," Campana said. "He had been up to the majors before and thought we would cab from the airport to the park, but my parents picked us up. My mom was crying. I left 50 tickets for the game, but didn't know I had to pay for them. Kerry Wood ended up taking care of it."

The Cubs' manager at the time, Mike Quade, said, "He can fly. So if we have a lead and I can inject him somewhere to make a difference defensively or come up and steal a base, we're going to do that."[15]

Campana saw his call-up as a blow for the little guy: "When I was in high school, all the coaches I talked to said, 'You're a little too small to play college ball,'" he told the *Chicago Tribune*. "Then once I transferred to Cincinnati, they were like, 'Well, he's probably a little too small to play pro ball.' Then finally I got drafted and they were like, 'Well, he's fast. Let's see if anything else happens.'"[16]

Campana immediately contributed with his bat, legs, and glove. On May 17 he debuted against Cincinnati, the big-league team closest to his hometown. Pinch-running for Alfonso Soriano, Campana scored on a bases-loaded walk to put the Cubs up 4-3 in the seventh inning. Facing Jordan Smith with two on and one out in the eighth, he "got a first-pitch fastball that was probably a ball and pulled a double past Joey Votto" to put Chicago up 5-3. (In the eighth the Reds got four unearned runs off Kerry Wood.)

The next day Campana pinch-ran, stole a base, and scored on a groundout. On May 26, he got his first start, had three hits, and made two sliding catches. "He got an ovation … for nearly beating out a grounder to first," the *Tribune* reported.[17] On May 30 Campana turned 25, and celebrated by becoming the first Cub in nearly five seasons to steal four bases in a game.[18]

Campana homered on August 5 against Cincinnati. According to the *Tribune*, he was "the first Cub to have his first career home run be an inside-the-park-homer at Wrigley Field,"[19] on a hit that "barely cleared the infield,"[20] then "bounced off the left-field wall and past a fielder."[21] "When I got back in the locker room, I had, like, 64 text messages, something outrageous like that," he said. "I had to turn my phone on silent because I was still getting text messages at 2 o'clock in the morning."[22]

The hit was Campana's lone homer in 477 plate appearances through 2015. His bat quickly cooled, and Quade used the youngster irregularly. A trade-deadline analysis of the Chicago roster said of Campana: "Cubs like his speed, though not enough to play him. Not much market for a designated pinch-runner."[23]

Campana had so little power that he rarely even homered in batting practice. When he did so in September 2011, the Cubs commemorated the occasion by smashing pie in his face,[24] a sure sign of a bad team with little to celebrate. Chicago finished 25 games out of first place at 71-91.

A fan favorite, Campana mostly appreciated the attention: "It's kind of an honor. I hope it's because of the way I play and not because I'm a small guy. I like that people enjoy watching me play. It's cool."[25]

Campana swiped 24 bases in 26 attempts in his rookie year, finishing second in the NL in stolen-base percentage. He sought to get stronger before the 2012 season and reported in January that he had "gained 10 pounds of muscle working out since November in Mesa, Ariz."[26]

The added bulk did not help Campana make the 2012 Cubs to start the season; Chicago kept nonroster invitee Joe Mather instead.[27] Campana was sent to Iowa. The Cubs recalled recalled him in April after selling fellow outfielder Marlon Byrd to Boston. Under new skipper Dale Sveum, who planned to give him 80 percent of the starts in center field,[28] Campana helped Chicago beat rival St. Louis on April 24 with a 10th-inning single, a controversial stolen base,[29] and a walk-off run scored.

On April 27 Campana had two infield hits, two more runs, and a stolen base in a 5-1 win over the Philadelphia Phillies. On April 29, in another 5-1 victory against Philadelphia, he again had two hits, two runs, and a steal. He won praise from his manager for tallying on an infield weed-killer: "It's going to be very, very difficult to ever throw him out when you let him go on contact on a ground ball, You've got to be perfect with the throw because he's so fast," Sveum said.[30]

L to R: Anthony Conigliaro, Tony Campana, and Anthony's father Richie Conigliaro.

In a May 22 loss to the Houston Astros, in what a beat reporter later called "the Cubs' play of the year"[31] and Campana called "the coolest play I've ever been a part of," he sped from first to third after an errant pickoff throw to first. As he rounded second, "third baseman Matt Downs took a throw from Carlos Lee, but Campana leaped over Downs, [clearing] Downs' glove with enough room to spare that umpire Bill Welke could see it. His momentum carried him past third base, but he reversed course and scrambled back before Downs could tag him."[32]

By June 24 Campana was leading the majors with 24 steals, but was losing playing time to other outfielders.[33] In August, to get him more playing time and to shake up a losing roster, the Cubs returned Campana to Iowa, then recalled him in September after the rosters expanded. Despite the time in the minors, Campana set career highs in plate appearances, at-bats, runs, hits, doubles, steals, walks, and sacrifices. His 30 stolen bases ranked ninth in the National League.

Caught just three times, he again finished second in stolen-base percentage.

The Cubs had dipped to 61-101 in 2012. After the season, Campana returned to Venezuela, where he had also played in 2010. Back in the United States, he would not long remain with Chicago. After picking up outfielder Scott Hairston, Chicago designated Campana for assignment in February 2013. The Cubs hoped to keep him in the organization but wound up trading him to the Arizona Diamondbacks for a pair of minor-league pitchers. Campana played in just 29 games for the Diamondbacks in 2013. In one memorable game, he walked five times and scored the winning run in an 18-inning marathon against Philadelphia on August 24.

On December 7, 2013, Campana married Whitney Lawson, whom he met through a teammate, in Knoxville, Tennessee.

On April 10, 2014, Campana put together the only four-hit game of his career, at San Francisco. One of the hits was a two-out, two-strike single in the 10th off

Yusmeiro Petit that gave Arizona a 6-5 victory." But overall, Campana struggled for Arizona. Batting only .143 coming into a June 18 game against Milwaukee, he did deliver a walk-off hit to beat the Milwaukee Brewers. "My first career walk-off," he said. "Probably (at any level). I don't think I've ever done it in the minor leagues either."[34]

Nevertheless, the Diamondbacks the next morning sent Campana back to the minors. "I told him going out the door, 'You can be better than that,' manager Kirk Gibson said. "I emphasized to him hitting the ball on the ground more. Not to say he can't hit line drives, but if he hits the ball in the air, it's going to be an out."[35]

"Gibson treated me really well," Campana said. "He was really intense. I liked his football mentality, having grown up around it."

Campana did not stay with the Arizona organization long, going to the Angels as part of a four-player trade soon after being sent down. While he inspired a sportswriter to describe him in spring training in 2014 as "a spitfire sparkplug with a pretty good glove who can get on base and steal bags about as easy as a purse snatcher in a room full of blind grannies,"[36] he stole just nine bases in 18 attempts for Salt Lake, the Triple-A affiliate of the Angels.

Recalled again after rosters expanded and used mostly as a pinch-runner, Campana did have a second 2014 batting highlight, on September 15. Hitting in the slot of Albert Pujols, who had been injured, Campana knocked in two runs that helped cement an 8-1 win over Seattle that made the Angels the first team to clinch a spot in the 2014 playoffs.[37]

After the season Campana became a free agent after turning down a minor-league assignment.[38] He came back to Chicago via an invitation to spring training with the White Sox, but tore his ACL while box jumping in February before spring training had even begun.[39] "I knew right away that something was wrong," he said.

On March 3, 2015, Chicago released Campana. Several months after the injury, he seemed most scarred by his having lost his health-care coverage. "I never knew how much health insurance was until I had to pay for it," he said.

Relieving the financial burden and professional uncertainty, on August 11, 2015, Washington signed Campana to a two-year minor-league contract. In a close division race, the Nationals would have activated Campana and used him as a late-season pinch-runner, but after the Mets surged, he ended up sitting out the entire 2015 season.[40]

Going into the 2016 season, Campana seemed a longshot to make a major-league roster. "I'm going to try to compete for a spot in Washington," he said. "If I don't make it, I will work my butt off in Syracuse to get to Washington."

In spite of his small size and lack of power, Campana strikes out much more than he walks—in 76 plate appearances in 2014, he failed to draw a single base on balls while fanning 16 times. His speed also appeared to be fading from exceptional to above average. (His stolen-base percentage dropped from 92.3 percent in 2011 to 90.9 percent in 2012, 80.0 percent in 2013, and 66.7 percent in 2014.) Regardless of whether he ever donned a big-league uniform again, Campana admirably overcome adversity with a winning personality and a career characterized by a handful of memorable moments, most of which his blazing speed made possible.

NOTES

1 "Send Tony Campana back to his gnome world to make sure wizards cast spells on opposing pitchers," suggested a group of wits. Brian Moore, Phil Thompson, Scott Bolohan, Clark Jones, and John Dooley, "GET A W," *Chicago Tribune*, May 15, 2012. When Chicago pitcher Matt Garza borrowed an idea from his Tampa days and proposed the Cubs dress up as superheroes, Campana appropriately went as the Flash. Paul Sullivan, "Nothing heroic about weekend," *Chicago Tribune*, July 23, 2012.

2 Paul Sullivan, "A Blue Blazer," *Chicago Tribune*, June 15, 2011.

3 John Shea, "Jim Thome Has Clean Reputation Amid Steroid Era," *San Francisco Chronicle*, August 14, 2011.

4 Paul Sullivan, "Campana Thinking Triple Digits," *Chicago Tribune*, May 3, 2012.

5 See gtcohio.com/gtco-info/coaches-page/10-faye (accessed December 17, 2015).

6   Patrick S., "Determination, Hustle and Tony Campana," January 18, 2011 at chicagocubsonline.com/archives/2011/01/cubstonyc-ampana.php (accessed December 17, 2015).

7   Nick Gates, "Campana Determined to Succeed," *Knoxville News Sentinel*, May 4, 2010.

8   Unless otherwise indicated, all quotations attributed to Campana come from a telephone interview conducted December 19, 2015. The author thanks Campana for taking the time to talk and to Brett Bick of Pro Star Management for arranging the interview.

9   Tyler Kepner, "The Cubs' Cincinnati Kid," *New York Times*, June 4, 2011.

10   Tom Haudricourt, "After Their Plunge, Pirates Hope to Stay Afloat," *Milwaukee Journal Sentinel*, August 13, 2011.

11   In the 10th game of his freshman year, Campana singled off future big leaguer Darren O'Day and scored the winning run as UNC-Asheville beat Florida 8-5. "Asheville Holds Back Florida Late," *Gainesville Sun*, March 10, 2005.

12   All batting averages in this paragraph come from gobearcats.com/sports/m-basebl/mtt/campana_tony00.html (accessed December 17, 2015).

13   See issuu.com/ucbearcats/docs/2015_media_giude_-_final (accessed December 17, 2015).

14   Chicago had just 69 stolen bases as a team in 2011. Playing part-time for just part of the season, Campana had 24 with the Cubs.

15   "Campana Fills Cubs' Big Need for Speed," *Chicago Tribune*, May 19, 2011.

16   "Major Setback in Cashner's Rehab," *Chicago Tribune*, May 18, 2011.

17   Paul Sullivan, "Another Veteran Arm Joins the Mix," *Chicago Tribune*, May 27, 2011.

18   Paul Sullivan, "Add Sori to the Story," *Chicago Tribune*, May 31, 2011.

19   Toni Ginnetti, "Cubs' Tony Campana Hears Buzz About Historic Homer," *Chicago Sun-Times*, August 7, 2011.

20   Dave van Dyck, "'Z' Hits His Tee-Off Time," *Chicago Tribune*, August 7, 2011.

21   Dave van Dyck, "This Homer an Inside Job," *Chicago Tribune*, August 6, 2011.

22   Dave van Dyck, "Big Day, Then Back to Bench," *Chicago Tribune*, August 7, 2011.

23   Paul Sullivan, "Blowing Through the Trade Winds," *Chicago Tribune*, July 29, 2011.

24   Paul Sullivan, "2011's Best? (Crickets)," *Chicago Tribune*, September 23, 2011.

25   Paul Sullivan, "Following No Small Thing," *Chicago Tribune*, February 22, 2012.

26   Paul Sullivan, "Epstein: Wood a 'No-Brainer,'" *Chicago Tribune*, January 12, 2012.

27   Paul Sullivan, "Sveum Confident Rotation Is Better," *Chicago Tribune*, March 31, 2012.

28   Paul Sullivan, "Cubs Have Leg Up on Halladay," *Chicago Tribune*, April 28, 2012.

29   "Umpire Bill Welke ruled that Campana got past [Tyler] Greene's tag after a dart from catcher Yadier Molina beat the speedy Campana to the base. Before teammate Rafael Furcal pushed him away and [manager Mike] Matheny arrived, Greene argued that Campana still hadn't touched the bag. 'He was out 100 percent,' Greene insisted after the game. 'For one, I tagged him. Two, he never touched the bag. He missed it, plain and simple. He had my foot the whole time. So he was out.'" Derrick Goold, "Umpires Confound Cardinals," *St. Louis Post-Dispatch*, April 25, 2012.

30   Paul Sullivan, "Now That's 'Cool,'" *Chicago Tribune*, April 30, 2012.

31   Phil Rogers, "All-City Pretty Gritty," *Chicago Tribune*, June 17, 2012.

32   Phil Rogers, "Campana Flying High on the Run," *Chicago Tribune*, May 24, 2012.

33   Paul Sullivan, "Running Game Hits Skids in Last Month," *Chicago Tribune*, June 24, 2012.

34   Nathan Brown, "Tony Campana's RBI Single Lifts Arizona Diamondbacks Over Milwaukee Brewers," *Arizona Republic*, June 19, 2014.

35   Scott Bordow, "Arizona Diamondbacks Send Tony Campana Back to Minors," *Arizona Republic*, June 19, 2014.

36   Bob McManaman, "Arizona Diamondbacks' Tony Campana Hopes to Parlay Speed Into Job," *Arizona Republic*, March 12, 2014.

37   Mike DiGiovanna, "Angels Clinch Playoff Berth in 8-1 Win Over Mariners," *Los Angeles Times*, September 15, 2014.

38   Mike DiGiovanna, "Angels Pick Up Closer Huston Street's 2015 Option for $7 Million," *Los Angeles Times*, October 30, 2014.

39   Colleen Kane, "The Lineup," *Chicago Tribune*, February 11, 2015.

40   Chelsea Janes, "Nationals Sign Outfielder Tony Campana to a Minor League Deal," *Washington Post*, August 11, 2015.

R.A. DICKEY

By Skip Nipper

"**F**OR ME, IT'S NOT ABOUT AN All-America award or other accolades, it's about my experiences," R.A. Dickey told a baseball luncheon audience at Lipscomb University in Nashville, Tennessee, in 2007. "Sometimes you are not as bad as you feel nor are you as good as you might think you are. It is more important to have a purpose, be it in faith or in baseball, but in all things to have joy in it.

"I try to glean wisdom from a game and apply it to my life."[1]

His purpose is being a husband, father, competitor, and philanthropist. But it all began when he became a star athlete in high school as a quarterback, shooting guard, and pitcher/shortstop.[2]

Robert Allen Dickey was born in Nashville on October 29, 1974, to Harry Dickey, a construction worker, and his wife, Leslie, a receptionist.

His athletic talent shined brightly. On June 30, 1993, R.A. tossed a seven-inning perfect game for Nashville's Montgomery Bell Academy, striking out 14, to improve his record to 8-1. It was his third no-hit game of the season.[3] A football and basketball star, in his 1993 senior season he struck out 112 in 60 innings[4] and had a 15-3 record for the AAA state championship Big Red.

The accolades continued to pour in: *Tennessean* All-Metro (twice), All-State, Tennessee Baseball Player of the Year, Most Valuable Player in the AAA tournament.[5] Dickey's success caught the attention of the baseball scouts, and he was drafted by Detroit in the 10th round of the 1993 June Amateur Draft. He passed up the Tigers opportunity to fulfill another dream: to pitch for the University of Tennessee.

College meant taking on a weight-training regimen, something he had never participated in. "I go from 175 pounds to 210 pounds, and my fastball jumps from the 87- to the 89- to the 93- to the 94-miles-per-hour range. I'm still not a prototypical, strike-out-the-side power pitcher, but I can bring enough heat that it makes my breaking pitches and changeup more effective."[6]

Travis Copley, a Vols teammate, called Dickey one of the fiercest competitors he ever knew. "He had to win at everything: team basketball, conditioning tests, everything. He did more for me in understanding how to compete, and really had a fierce, built-in bulldog mentality about winning."[7]

Dickey's college career record was 38-10 with a 3.40 ERA; the Volunteers won three SEC baseball titles and made an appearance in the College World Series. He was named *Baseball America's* 1994 Freshman of the Year, was All-SEC twice, was a three-time All American, an Academic All-SEC, and Academic All-American.[8] He was named to the U.S. national baseball team for the 1996 Olympics, which won a Bronze Medal.

The Texas Rangers made Dickey the 18th player selected in the 1996 amateur draft, and were ready to reward his signing with an $810,000 contract. The 6-foot-3, 215-pound right-hander would throw out the first ball at a Rangers home game, and the signing was scheduled to happen before the event.

But when the Rangers' trainer, Danny Wheat, noticed a peculiar position of Dickey's elbow in a *Baseball America* cover photo,[9] he notified Dr. John Conway, the team orthopedist.[10]

It was discovered that the pitcher had no ulnar collateral ligament in his right elbow, and doctors were baffled that he could throw at all.[11] The Rangers backed off their offer. Surgery was imminent, and Dickey decided to go back to college and play baseball his senior year.

The day before Dickey was to head back to college, the Rangers replaced their offer with one for $75,000 and medical help.[12] Dickey accepted it. His journey to the majors would be a long one.

Assigned to Port Charlotte to begin his professional career, in 1997 and 1998, Dickey won only one game in each season, but struck out nearly one batter an inning. Oklahoma City and Tulsa were his destinations for the next two seasons, and in 2001 he was called up to the Rangers.

On April 22, 2001, Dickey made his major-league debut in the top of the ninth inning at Arlington Stadium facing the Oakland third baseman, Mark Bellhorn. A flyout and two popups later, he had played in his first game to aid an 11-2 win over the A's.

With three relief appearances under his belt, on May 7 Dickey entered a game against the Chicago White Sox with no outs in the top of the first inning. Starting pitcher Darren Oliver had been hit on the thumb by a line drive by leadoff batter Tony Graffanino, and manager Jerry Narron called on Dickey. He allowed six runs in 4⅔ innings and collected his first career loss as Chicago won 7-4 over Texas.

Returned to Oklahoma City, Dickey was 11-7 with a 3.75 ERA for the season, striking out 120 in 163 innings. He began 2003 with Oklahoma but was called up after three appearances, and won a position on the Rangers pitching staff as a long reliever. By July he was in the starting rotation.[13]

Dickey had begun to throw an unusual forkball he named "the thing." In truth, it was a hard knuckleball. Former knuckleballer Charlie Hough began to work with him to change his grip.[14]

In an interview in 2012, Dickey explained Hough's knuckleball experience: "Charlie Hough told me the first day that I met with him: "It took me one day to learn how to throw a knuckleball and a lifetime to learn how to throw it for strikes.""[15]

On August 20 at Detroit's Comerica Park, Dickey pitched his first career shutout, holding the Tigers to six hits and a walk, and moving his record to 8-5. Two days earlier, he had earned his first career save, also against Detroit, retiring Bobby Higginson, Dmitri Young, and Carlos Peña on 11 pitches in the 16th inning.[16] The Rangers had scored two runs in the top of the inning, and won the game, 4-2.

By the end of the 2003 season Dickey was 9-8 but his ERA had ballooned to 5.09. In spring training in

2004 he earned a roster spot and made his first start of the new season on April 9 at home against Anaheim. Holding the Angels to six hits in seven innings, he won and allowed no earned runs although the opposition scored three runs in the second inning on two errors by Michael Young and a home run by Adam Kennedy.

On May 2 at Arlington Stadium against the Boston Red Sox, Dickey pitched well for 8⅔ innings before giving way to Francisco Cordero with the bases loaded. The Rangers won 4-1, and Dickey's record improved to 4-1. In August he was sent to Frisco (Double-A Texas League) and pitched in four games before being recalled to complete the season with the Rangers at 6-7, 5.61.

In May 2005, after spending time on the 15-day disabled list, Dickey was optioned to Oklahoma once again, and was 10-6 before being being recalled again. In four September appearances, he gave up 17 earned runs, winning one and losing one. His velocity was beginning to slow down.

"When Orel [Hershiser] was a pitching coach in 2003 and, you know, there was some real hope for me to become maybe a fourth or fifth starter, a really good swingman, I was low 90s—you know, high 80s, low 90s, and could really change speeds well. But in 2004, 2005, I just started—the velocity started dropping from low 90s to max 88, to max 86. I'd run out of gas as a conventional pitcher [with the Rangers] and was kind of just hanging on, just trying to survive as long as I could before I felt like the inevitable call would come."[17]

In the fourth game of the 2006 season, Dickey started against Detroit at Ameriquest Field in Arlington, and lasted 3⅓ innings. After giving up home runs to Brandon Inge and Magglio Ordonez in the first, Chris Shelton in the second, and Shelton (again), Craig Monroe, and Marcus Thames in the third, he was yanked. It was Dickey's last appearance in a Texas Rangers uniform.

Again he spent the balance of the year at Oklahoma. He was let go on October 11 after going 9-8 with only 61 strikeouts in 131⅔ innings.

On January 10, 2007, Dickey signed with the Milwaukee Brewers and was assigned to Triple-A Nashville. By then he had perfected his knuckleball grip, and his reputation as a solid pitcher returned. With a 13-6 record, he lowered his ERA to 3.72 with 6.3 strikeouts per nine innings. Dickey was named the Pacific Coast League pitcher of the year.

"The Brewers say that they don't have a roster spot for me but tell me to stay ready in case they need me for the pennant race in September," he recalled in an autobiography published in 2012. "They are fighting for a divisional title and I am their top minor-league pitcher and they don't want me. You try not to take it personally, but how can you not?"[18]

He did not receive a call from the Brewers, and was let go on October 29. A curious chain of events soon occurred.

With hints of an offer to play for the Samsung Lions in the Korean Baseball League, Dickey signed with the Minnesota Twins for $525,000 in November 2007, and on December 6 was drafted by the Seattle Mariners from Minnesota in the Rule 5 draft. On March 29, 2008, he was returned to the Twins by the Mariners, then traded back to the Mariners for Jair Fernandez.

Dickey wondered about plot twists in his baseball life.

"I report to Mariners spring training in Peoria, Arizona, and have one of the best springs of my life. I pitch as both a starter and a reliever. They put me out there in every situation they can. My knuckleball holds up well, and I know it's dancing because Kenji Johjima, the Mariners catcher, catches about three of every ten knuckleballs I throw," he said in the 2012 autobiography.[19]

But disappointment followed, as Dickey failed to make the club and was sent to Triple-A Tacoma. Then he was recalled by the Mariners in mid-April. With Boston due to appear in Seattle at the end of May, he knew Red Sox knuckleballer Tim Wakefield was on the club.

"He's the best knuckleballer in the game—and the only full-time one besides me. I get to the park early on Memorial Day afternoon and write a note to Tim, asking if we might get together and talk for a bit…

"Meet me behind the plate in ten minutes, Tim says."

They talked for 45 minutes, discussing grip, spin, even how he keeps his fingernails.

"Knuckleballers don't keep secrets."[20]

Dickey finished the 2008 season 5-8. He was non-tendered on December 9 and a few weeks later, at the age of 34, was signed by the Twins and invited to spring training. He pitched in 35 games (one as starter) for Minnesota before being sent to Rochester, ending the season with five starts for the Red Wings but without a September call-up. Instead, he became a free agent once again before the New York Mets came calling.

On December 21 Dickey signed a minor-league deal with the Mets. When the season began he was with the Triple-A Buffalo Bisons. On April 29, in a home game against the Durham Bulls, Dickey threw a knuckler to leadoff batter Fernando Perez on an 0-and-2 count. He recalled:

"He gets under it and pops it weakly over second base. It plops in for a single.

"I retire the next twenty-seven hitters in order. A perfect game, with one mulligan."[21]

Five weeks into the season, Dickey had a 4-2 record with a much-improved 2.23 ERA, striking out 37 batters in 60⅔ innings and walking only eight. The Mets called him up, and on May 19 in Washington, he started against the Nationals. He pitched six innings, allowing five hits, and gave up two earned runs before giving way to Raul Valdes in relief. Dickey got a no-decision but he was in the major leagues to stay.

On August 13 he held the Phillies to one hit, by pitcher Cole Hamels, in a 5-1 home win. By season's end he had started 26 games, appearing in relief only once. He finished 11-9 with an ERA of 2.84, seventh-best in the National League.

In 2011 Dickey's record fell to 8-13 and his ERA climbed to 3.28, but he had 134 strikeouts. In his last start of the season, against Philadelphia at Citi Field on September 24, Dickey tossed 6⅓ innings of no-hit ball until Shane Victorino drove a double to left field.

Once the season was over, Dickey prepared for a journey of another kind: Mount Kilimanjaro — to benefit Red Light District Outreach Mumbai, which combats human trafficking in India. He included two friends, Kevin Slowey from the Minnesota Twins and Dave Racaniello, bullpen catcher for the New York Mets organization.

"I always thought it would be a fantastic pilgrimage to hike to the summit," Dickey said.[22]

Though the Mets advised Dickey to reconsider the climb, even telling him there would be risk of voiding his $4.25 million contract for 2012 if he were injured.[23]

Undaunted, he and his friends reached the summit on January 14.

On March 29, 2012, Dickey's first book, *Wherever I Wind Up: My Quest for Truth, Authenticity and the Perfect Knuckleball* (Penguin Press), was published. It includes a descriptive incident when, as an 8-year-old boy, he was sexually assaulted by his babysitter. In another occurrence, the offender was a teenage male.

In terms of Dickey's baseball success, the 2012 season was memorable. He led the National League with 223⅔ innings pitched, 230 strikeouts, 33 starts, five complete games, and three shutouts. He was 20-6, had a 2.73 ERA, and was named to the National League All-Star team. Selected NL Pitcher of the Year by

The Sporting News, he also won the Branch Rickey Award in recognition of his community service. He captured the Cy Young Award as best pitcher in the National League, taking 27 of the 32 first-place votes and finishing with 209 points, well in front of 2011 winner Clayton Kershaw of the Dodgers (96 points).

On December 6, 2012, Dickey was named to receive the Tony Conigliaro Award. The award goes to a player "who has overcome adversity through the attributes of spirit, determination and courage that were trademarks of Tony C."[24] Dickey obtained the recognition for confronting child sexual abuse, and prevailing over the lack of the ulnar collateral ligament in his right arm.[25]

As successful as 2012 may have been, the Mets finished in fourth place in the N.L. East division again, and on December 17, 2012, Dickey was traded to the Toronto Blue Jays.

His second book, *Throwing Strikes: My Quest for Truth and the Perfect Knuckleball* (Penguin Press), was published on March 26, 2013.

Dickey won 14 games while losing 13 for Toronto in 2013, and won the AL Gold Glove Award after leading the league in assists by a pitcher with 40. He duplicated his won-lost record in 2014 as his salary increased from $5 million to $12 million. In 2015 he was 11-11, but his record fell to 10-15 in 2016 as the Blue Jays won the AL East.

The team beat the Texas Rangers three games to two in the Division Series. Dickey started Game Four, allowing five hits and one run in 4⅔ innings as the Blue Jays beat the Rangers, 8-4. In the American League Championship Series he started Game Four and was the losing pitcher in the 14-2 loss to the Royals. He lasted only 1⅔ innings. Beating the Blue Jays in six games, the Royals went on to win the 2015 World Series.

In 2016 Toronto earned a wild-card slot against Baltimore, winning 5-2. The Blue Jays swept the ALDS from Texas, but lost the Championship Series to the Cleveland Indians in five games.

Dickey was not on the active roster for the post-season. Tom Dakers, Toronto blogger for SB Nation, explained why:

"After a crappy April, he was pretty good in the first half. His second half was terrible, and on a team with an embarrassment of riches in the starting pitching department, he was left off the playoff roster."[26]

As he pondered retirement, on November 3, 2016, Dickey was granted free agency for the fifth time. Atlanta wasted little time scooping him up: On November 10 he signed a two-year contract with the Braves worth $15,500,000.

Dickey's life and his faith walk have been committed to the "bulldog" mentality his former Tennessee teammate Travis Copley spoke of.

"You may hit me. You may knock me around and knock balls out of the park.

"But I am always going to get back up and keep coming at you."[27]

R.A. and his wife, Anne, have four children and as of 2016 resided in the Nashville area. He was selected to the Tennessee Sports Hall of Fame in 2013.

NOTES

1   Skip Nipper, "The Pride of Nashville: R.A. Dickey," 262downright.com, January 5, 2014. [Blog post]. Retrieved October 6, 2016, from 262downright.com/2014/01/05/the-pride-of-nashville-r-a-dickey/.

2   R.A. Dickey, *Wherever I Wind Up: My Quest for Truth, Authenticity and the Perfect Knuckleball* (New York: Penguin Group, 2012), 65.

3   *The Tennessean* (Nashville), May 1, 1993: 66.

4   *The Tennessean*, May 6, 1993: 26.

5   *The Tennessean*, June 1, 1993: 13.

6   Dickey, *Wherever I Wind Up*, 80.

7   Telephone interview with R.A. Dickey, December 1, 2016.

8   2015-16 University of Tennessee Baseball Media Guide

9   Ross Newhan, "Case of Missing Ligament Gets Draftee Out of Joint," *Los Angeles Times*, August 25, 1996. Retrieved October 9, 2016, from articles.latimes.com/1996-08-25/sports/sp-37663_1_collateral-ligament/.

10 R.A. Dickey, *Throwing Strikes: My Quest for Truth and the Perfect Knuckleball* (New York: Penguin Group, 2013), 84.

11 Alan Schwarz, "New Twist Keeps Dickey's Career Afloat," *New York Times*, February 27, 2008. Retrieved October 9, 2016, from nytimes.com/2008/02/27/sports/baseball/27dickey.html/.

12 Newhan.

13 *The Sporting News*, August 25, 2003: 46.

14 Schwarz.

15 Tim Kurkjian, "The Knuckleball Experiment," ESPN.com, December 1, 2012. espn.com/mlb/story/_/id/8677078/mets-pitcher-ra-dickey-orel-hershiser-making-knuckleballer-espn-magazine-interview-issue/. Accessed November 2, 2016.

16 *The Tennessean* (box score), August 19, 2003: 18.

17 Kurkjian.

18 *Wherever I Wind Up*, 230.

19 *Wherever I Wind Up*, 246.

20 *Wherever I Wind Up*. 252.

21 *Wherever I Wind Up*, 283.

22 Jonathan Zeller, "R.A. Dickey on Embracing the Knuckleball and Preparing to Climb Mount Kilimanjaro," *New York Magazine*, November 1, 2011. ,nymag.com/daily/sports/2011/11/ra-dickey-on-preparing-to-climb-kilimanjaro.html. Accessed November 1, 2016.

23 Wayne Coffey, "NY Mets Starting Pitcher R.A. Dickey Completes Grueling Journey and Gets to the Top of Mt. Kilimanjaro," *New York Daily News*, January 15, 2012. nydailynews.com/sports/baseball/mets/ny-mets-starting-pitcher-dickey-completes-grueling-journey-top-mt-kilimanjaro-article-1.1006343. Accessed October 30, 2016.

24 Matt Pepin, "R.A. Dickey wins Tony Conigliaro Award," Boston.com. December 6, 2012. boston.com/sports/extra-bases/2012/12/06/ra_dickey_wins. Accessed November 27, 2016.

25 http://www.baseball-reference.com/bullpen/Tony_Conigliaro_Award, accessed November 5, 2016.

26 Tom Dakers, "On R.A. Dickey," Bluebird Banter.com. October 25, 2016. bluebirdbanter.com/2016/10/25/13406972/on-r-a-dickey. Accessed December 5, 2016.

27 *Wherever I Wind Up*, 3.

JOHN LACKEY

BY SUSAN LANTZ

THE WINNER OF 176 MAJOR-league games through 2016 despite years of arm problems, John Lackey as of 2016 was only the second rookie to start and win a World Series-clinching game. He has won World Series rings with three different teams.

John Derran Lackey was born in Abilene, Texas, to Derran and Sharon Lackey on October 23, 1978. (In 2016, Derran Lackey was listed as a teacher/coach at Mesquite Independent School District in the Dallas/Fort Worth area.) John attended Abilene High School and lettered in football, basketball, and baseball. In baseball, he was a two-time first-team All-District honoree, and as a senior, he was an All-State selection.

At the University of Texas at Arlington, Lackey played one season of baseball, usually at first base, but sometimes as a reliever. The first summer after attending UTA, he pitched in the Kansas Jayhawk Summer League. In 1999, while attending Grayson County College in Denison, Texas, Lackey played on the school's Junior College World Series championship team, which went 50-13. In 100 innings pitched, he posted a 10-3 record and a 4.23 ERA. He also excelled at the plate, batting .428 with 15 home runs and 81 runs batted in. In the Junior College World Series, he had eight hits, two of them homers, and seven RBIs.

Lackey was drafted by the Anaheim Angels in the second round (68th overall) of the June 1999 free-agent draft. His professional career began with the Boise Hawks (short-season Class-A Northwest League), where he had a 6-2 record and a 4.98 ERA. He was known for his competitiveness. Tom Kotchman, the veteran manager, recalled "one particular game when he tried to replace Lackey only to have the tall Texan tell him otherwise. Sure enough, Kotchman trotted back to the dugout, and Lackey kept dominating."[1]

Lackey quickly ascended through the minor leagues. After a 6-2 season with Boise (Northwest League) in 1999, he posted a combined 15-9 record with a 3.15 ERA in 2000 with Cedar Rapids (Class-A Midwest League), Lake Elsinore (Class-A California League), and Erie (Double-A Eastern League), and was chosen as the Angels' Minor League Pitcher of the Year. He began 2001 with Arkansas of the Double-A Texas League, and in July was promoted to Triple-A Salt Lake (Pacific Coast League), where he struggled somewhat, posting a 3-4 record and a 6.71 ERA. In 2002 season, however, Lackey went 8-2 with a 2.57 ERA, and was called up by the Angels on June 24. He lost to the Texas Rangers. 3-2, in his first major-league start and was optioned back to Salt Lake, then recalled on June 28. Two days later he replaced Scott Schoeneweis in the Angels' rotation and defeated the Los Angeles Dodgers, 5-1, for his first major-league win. His 9-4 record over the remainder of the season helped make the Angels a wild-card team.

The Angels faced the New York Yankees in the American League Division Series. Lackey pitched three scoreless innings of relief in a 9-6 Angels win. He got his first postseason victory in Game Four of the American League Championship Series against the Minnesota Twins, pitching seven scoreless innings and allowing only three hits. The Angels won their first American League pennant, beating the Twins in five games.

The Angels' opponent in the World Series was the San Francisco Giants. Lackey entered Game Two when starter Kevin Appier was pulled in the third inning. He pitched 2⅓ innings, giving up two runs on two hits in the Angels' 11-10 victory. He started Game Four and pitched gave up three runs in five innings as the Angels lost, 4-3.

Lackey was the winning pitcher in Game Seven, allowing one run on four hits in five innings. He was only the second rookie in World Series history to start and win a Game Seven. (Babe Adams of the 1909 Pittsburgh Pirates was the other.)[2]

Lackey struggled his second year, posting a 10-16 record with a 4.63 ERA while leading the team in hits and earned runs allowed, strikeouts, and wild pitches. In 2004, he had a record of 14-13 and a 4.67 ERA, and he helped the Angels win their first division title since 1986. Lackey continued to mature during the 2005 season; he worked into the sixth inning in 30 of his 36 starts, had a 14-5 record with a 3.44 ERA, ranked second in the AL in strikeouts per nine innings (8.6) and third in strikeouts (199), but also third in wild pitches.

In 2006 Lackey was 13-11, 3.56. On July 7 he retired 27 consecutive batters after Mark Kotsay of the Oakland Athletics led off the first inning with double. Those nine innings were part of 31⅓ consecutive scoreless innings he pitched from June 26 through July 19. (The streak ended when he gave up a home run to Ben Broussard of the Cleveland Indians.)

On June 13, 2007, Lackey became the first pitcher to win 10 games in the 2007 season.[3] He was named to the American League team in the All-Star Game, but did not pitch in the game. Finishing the season with a 19-9 record and a league-best 3.01 ERA, he took third place in the AL Cy Young Award voting.

In 2008 Lackey didn't pitch for the Angels until May 14 after spending time on the disabled list after straining a triceps muscle in spring training. On July 10 he allowed six runs on 15 hits in 5⅔ innings, tying an Angels franchise record for the most hits allowed by a starter in a game.[4]

On July 29, pitching against the Red Sox at Fenway Park, Lackey had a no-hitter with one out in the ninth inning. But Dustin Pedroia singled and Kevin Youkilis, hit a two-run homer. Lackey finished the game, and the Angels won, 6-2.

In Game One of the 2008 ALDS, Lackey gave up a two-run homer to Jason Bay of the Red Sox as he lost, 4-1, to future teammate Jon Lester.

Lackey began the 2009 season on the disabled list with tightness in his pitching forearm.[5] On May 16, in his first start of the season, against the Texas Rangers, Lackey was ejected after throwing only two pitches. His first pitch was behind Ian Kinsler's head, and he hit Kinsler in the side with his second pitch and was ejected by home-plate umpire Bob Davidson. (Kinsler had hit two home runs against the Angels the night before.)

Lackey got a no-decision in that game and ended the season 11-8 with a 3.83 ERA. The Angels made the postseason again and in Game One of the American League Division Series against the Red Sox, Lackey defeated Lester, 3-0, as the Angels swept the series in three games. Lackey lost one game and got a no-decision in another as the New York Yankees defeated the Angels in six games in the Championship Series,

A free agent after the 2009 season, Lackey was widely regarded as the best starting pitcher on the market. *Baseball Prospectus* declared: "Lackey stands alone as the best of the best, a relatively young righty who carries significantly less risk than the other high-upside hurlers." The writer noted that Lackey faced a tough division and tougher league and that his statistics would likely have been better if he were a National League pitcher.[6] It was predicted that he would receive a deal of about $70 million to $80 million. He drew interest from many teams. The Angels pursued Lackey aggressively but hesitated to offer a five-year deal because of the elbow injuries that had sidelined him for the first six weeks of the 2008 and 2009 seasons.[7]

Lackey is known for his fierce competitiveness. In a radio interview in November 2009, Boston Red Sox manager Terry Francona said of him, "John Lackey is one of the best. Every year, there are a couple of guys that seems like they can sway the fortunes of an organization. I think he's that type of pitcher."[8]

On December 14 Lackey signed a five-year contract worth $82.5 million with the Red Sox. The contract included a clause that if he missed a full season due to injury, the Red Sox would have a team option at the end of the contract worth the league minimum.[9] On April 7, 2010, he made his debut for Boston at Fenway Park against the Yankees, pitching six innings of three-hit, shutout ball. After a 10-5 record and a 4.26 ERA during the first half of the season, Lackey finished with a 14-11 record, a 4.40 ERA, and 215 innings pitched.

In his first seven starts in 2011, Lackey went 2-5 with an 8.01 ERA. In May he was placed on the disabled list with tightness in his right elbow.[10] After returning to the rotation, Lackey finished the season 12-12 with a 6.41 ERA and 1.62 WHIP (walks and hits per inning pitched), both career worsts. His 114 earned runs allowed were the worst in the American League, and his ERA set a new high mark for the Red Sox for a starter with at least 150 innings pitched. Near the end of the season, Lackey and starting pitchers Josh Beckett and Jon Lester were at the center of a controversy after the disclosure that the three (and sometimes others) drank beer and ate fried chicken in the clubhouse during games in which they were not pitching.[11] The Red Sox' precipitous slide toward the end of the season cost manager Francona his job.

General manager Ben Cherington was reluctant to cast too much blame on the pitcher for the team's disastrous 2011 season. "John Lackey pitched through circumstances this year that I don't think any of us can fully understand, and he got beat up for it a little bit," Cherington said. "This guy was dealing with stuff both on the field and off the field that were very difficult, and he showed tremendous toughness pitching through that." (In addition to his problems on the field and in the clubhouse, Lackey and his wife, who was battling breast cancer, filed for divorce.)[12]

On November 1 Lackey underwent Tommy John surgery. (He was the third Red Sox pitcher to have the surgery in 2011, following lefty reliever Rich Hill and starter Daisuke Matsuzaka.) He did not pitch for the entire 2012 season. He was later seen drinking beer in the clubhouse during his rehabilitation, causing further controversy.[13]

The Tommy John surgery, technically known as ulnar collateral ligament replacement surgery, was first performed by Dr. Frank Jobe on Tommy John in 1974. Jobe took part of a ligament from elsewhere in the body and used it to reattach the torn one in the pitcher's elbow. The surgery was followed by months of rehabilitation.

If the rehab — building up strength in every area around the elbow — is successful, when the elbow heals itself enough to start throwing again, the rest of the arm should be strong. Lackey and others who have undergone the procedure feel that their shoulder got stronger than ever.[14]

On April 6, 2013, Lackey injured his arm in his first start since September 2011. In the fifth inning, he tossed an errant pitch, then immediately grabbed his arm, jumping around the mound in pain.[15] The Red Sox announced it was a right biceps strain.[16]

As the 2013 season progressed, Lackey's biceps muscle healed, and his elbow started to feel the way it used to. "The arm strength was coming," Lackey said. "It was coming out of my hand like I remembered it. And I could definitely feel the difference."[17]

Major-league hitters noticed the difference, too. Lackey, at 35, was still one of the hardest-throwing pitchers in the majors. He threw a fastball as often as 90 percent of the time in some games, putting it in the strike zone about 70 percent of the time. Lackey's four-seamer was averaging 92 mph, 3 mph faster than he had thrown in 2004, when he was 23. One could question how long it could last, considering that Lackey had thrown more than 2,000 career innings.

"I'm going to chuck it as hard and fast as I can until it breaks again," he said. "And then we'll call it a day."[18]

Despite a lackluster 10-13 season, Lackey contributed to the Red Sox, particularly at midseason when Clay Buchholz went on the disabled list and Jon Lester was going through a rough stretch.[19] Lackey had a 3.52 ERA and was plagued by a lack of run support throughout the season, He pitched two complete games — the first time he had multiple complete games in a season since 2008.

Lackey was much better in the postseason. He beat Detroit's David Price in the Division Series and Justin Verlander in the ALCS. He pitched a pivotal eighth inning of relief in Game Four of the World Series against the St. Louis Cardinals, one he all but begged his manager to let him throw. Fans who loathed Lackey the year before were chanting, "Lackey, Lackey, Lackey" as he pitched in the seventh inning of Game Six on October 30.[20]

When manager John Farrell came to the mound with two outs in the seventh inning, Lackey refused to leave the game, telling Farrell, "This is my guy" (referring to the next batter, Matt Holliday). Farrell allowed Lackey to stay in the game, and he walked Holliday to load the bases. Lackey exited to a standing ovation from the fans at Fenway Park. The Red Sox won the game and the Series, 6-1. Lackey became the first major-league starting pitcher to win World Series-clinching games with two different teams.[21] In his four 2013 postseason starts, he was 3-1 and in his five appearances, he recorded a 2.77 ERA.

After Game Six, Farrell said of Lackey, "His turn-around mirrored the organization, no question. ... It was fitting that he was on the mound tonight."[22]

After the season, Lackey received the Tony Conigliaro Award, award given annually to the major-league player "who has overcome adversity through the attributes of spirit, determination, and courage that were trademarks of Tony C."

In an interview in June 2014, teammate Clay Buchholz praised Lackey for his decision to have Tommy John surgery and undergo the rehab process. "He knew he was pitching with a broken arm," Buchholz said. "He fought and got through about 2½, 3 years of doing that. I think he knew the right thing to do was to have the surgery and put in the time and the work to get back to where he's familiar with being. And as big of a competitor is he is, that's really the only way he was going to do it."[23]

Lackey began the 2014 season as the Red Sox' number-two starter behind Lester. He made six starts in April, four of them quality starts and two in which he gave up six runs in less than six innings. By the end

of July, he'd started 21 games, pitched 137⅓ innings with 116 strikeouts, and had an 11-7 record and a 3.60 ERA.

On July 31 the Red Sox traded Lackey and minor-league pitcher Corey Littrell to the St. Louis Cardinals for outfielder Allen Craig and pitcher Joe Kelly.[24] In his Cardinals debut on August 3 against the Brewers, Lackey pitched seven innings, but St. Louis trailed 2-0 when he left the game. His teammates rallied for three runs in the bottom of the inning and won the game 3-2, crediting him with the win, the 150th of his career. Lackey, who wore uniform number 41 during his tenure with Anaheim and Boston, acquired the number from new teammate Pat Neshek in exchange for an autographed Babe Ruth baseball.[25]

Lackey made 10 regular-season starts for the Cardinals in 2014 and allowed two or fewer runs in seven of them. He finished the season with three wins and three loses, 60⅔ innings pitched, and a 4.30 ERA. His totals for the 2014 season with both of his teams were a 14-10 record, a 3.82 ERA, and 164 strikeouts in 198 innings. He made the postseason for the seventh time in his career, starting once each against the Los Angeles Dodgers in the NLDS, a 3-1 victory, and the San Francisco Giants in the NLCS, a 5-4 loss. The Giants defeated the Cardinals in five games, ending their season.

Many people expected Lackey to retire to avoid being paid the league minimum, in accordance with his December 2009 contract, although he had told the Cardinals before he was dealt to them that he would honor the contract. On October 30 the Cardinals announced they had picked up the option.[26] With a guaranteed base salary of $507,000, the club added performance bonuses.[27]

In 7⅔ innings against the Chicago Cubs on May 7, 2015, Lackey struck out 10 in a 5-1 win. He also drove in his third career run with a double, his third career extra-base hit. On July 12, despite the Cardinals losing to the Pittsburgh Pirates, 6-5 in 14 innings, Lackey had his sixth consecutive quality start (three earned runs or fewer in at least seven innings), and his 12th in his most recent 15 appearances. He lost to the Cincinnati Reds on July 29, but gave up just one run with eight strikeouts while allowing one walk and two hits. It was the fewest hits he had allowed that season. He had given up three runs or less in all but one of his 17 prior starts.

When he pitched seven scoreless innings against the Milwaukee Brewers on September 17, Lackey reached 200 innings pitched for the sixth time in his career and for the first time since 2010. He had a career-best 2.77 ERA and 218 innings pitched, his highest total since 2010. His average fastball speed for the 2014 season was 91.6 miles per hour, his highest since 2009.[28] Also, 2015 was the 12th consecutive year in which he'd played (not including 2012), in which he won at least 10 games.

The Cardinals won 100 games and the National League Central Division crown in 2015, and made Lackey the Game One starter of the NLDS against the Cubs. He opposed Jon Lester, with whom he had faced the Cardinals in the 2013 World Series when they were teammates with the Red Sox. Lackey held the Cubs hitless through the first five innings and pitched 7⅓ innings in a 4-0 win. For Game Four, the elimination game, the Cardinals started Lackey on three days' rest. He gave up a three-run homer to Javier Báez, It was the first home run Lackey had tossed in the playoffs since 2008, a span of 77⅔ innings. The Cubs won the game and the series, ending the Cardinals' season. At the end of the season, Lackey became a free agent. On December 8 he signed a two-year, $32 million contract with the Cubs.

In a game against the Cardinals on April 18, 2016, Lackey earned his third win of the season by striking out 11 in seven innings. It was his first regular-season win against St. Louis, and with it he became the 16th player to defeat all 30 major-league teams.[29]

On September 21, 2016, with a 9-2 win over the Cincinnati Reds, Lackey reached a double-digit win total for his 13th consecutive season. In his 29 starts in 2016, he finished 11-8 with a 3.35 ERA. The Cubs finished the season 103-58 and won the NL Central Division.

Lackey started Game Four of the NLDS at San Francisco, tossing four innings in the Cubs' 6-5 come-from-behind win that gave them the series. He pitched four innings of Game Four of the NLCS against the Los Angeles Dodgers, which the Cubs won, 10-2. In Game Four of the World Series against the Cleveland Indians, he pitched five innings and gave up three runs (two earned), taking the loss in the Indians' 7-2 win.

When the Cubs beat the Indians in Game Seven, ending the North Siders' 108-year championship drought, Lackey received his third World Series ring, with a third team. Unlike the previous occasions, he did not pitch the clinching game.

NOTES

1   Brittany Ghiroli, "Path of the Pros: John Lackey: Always Unflappable, the Angels' Ace Never Wavered in His Winning Ways," MiLB.com, October 5, 2009. (milb.com/news/article.jsp?ymd=20090924&content_id=7138436&vkey=news_milb&fext=.jsp)..

2   Baseball's Best: 2002 World Series, Game 7, MLB.com. (m.mlb.com/video/v5061435/2002-ws-gm7-rookie-lackey-earns-win-in-clincher/?query=2002+world+series+game+7).

3   Associated Press, "Lackey Pitches Streaking Angels Past Reds," ESPN.com, June 13, 2006.

4   "Angels Hang on for Wild Win Over Rangers," SportingNews.com, July 10, 2008.

5   The Week That Was in Baseball: March 23-29, 2009. (thisgreatgame.com/comebacker033009.html).

6   Eric Seidman, "So You Need: Starting Pitching," baseballprospectus.com, November 24, 2009. (baseballprospectus.com/article.php?articleid=9799).

7   Mike DiGiovanna, "Angels About to Lose Out on John Lackey and Roy Halladay," Los Angeles Times, December 15, 2009. (articles.latimes.com/2009/dec/15/sports/la-sp-lackey-halladay15-2009dec15).

8   Ian Browne, "Red Sox Welcoming Cameron, Lackey," mlb.com, December 16, 2009. (m.redsox.mlb.com/news/article/7814688).

9   Rob Bradford, "John Lackey on Salary Structure for 2015: 'It's Going to Be Different,'" WEEI.com, February 28, 2014. (fullcount.weei.com/sports/boston/baseball/red-sox/2014/02/28/john-lackey-on-salary-structure-for-2015-its-going-going-to-be-different/).

10   Steven Krasner, "John Lackey Shelved With Elbow Strain," ESPN.com, May 17, 2011. (sports.espn.go.com/boston/mlb/news/story?id=6557306). See also Joe McDonald, "John Lackey to Have Elbow Surgery," ESPN.com, October 26, 2011. (espn.com/boston/mlb/story/_/id/7148697/boston-red-sox-john-lackey-tommy-john-surgery).

11   Ian Browne, "Lester: We Did Drink In Clubhouse During Games," MLB.com, October 17, 2011. (m.redsox.mlb.com/news/article/25692288//).

12 McDonald.

13 "Jon Heyman On Gresh & Zo: John Lackey 'Just a Big Disappointment.'" August 14, 2012, Boston.CBSlocal.com. (boston.cbslocal.com/2012/08/14/jon-heyman-on-gresh-zo-john-lackey-just-a-big-disappointment/).

14 Ibid.

15 Associated Press, "Red Sox pitcher Lackey Leaves Game Against Blue Jays With Apparent Arm Injury," CTVnews.ca, April 6, 2013. (ctvnews.ca/sports/red-sox-pitcher-lackey-leaves-game-against-blue-jays-with-apparent-arm-injury-1.1227067/comments-7.385121).

16 Nick Cafardo, "John Lackey Suffers Biceps Strain, Leaves Game," *Boston Globe,* April 6, 2013. (boston.com/sports/extra-bases/2013/04/06/lackey_injured).

17 Ibid.

18 Ibid.

19 Mike Shalin, "Lackey Sharp as Red Sox Beat Rockies," *Bangor* (Maine) *Daily News,* June 27, 2013. (bangordailynews.com/2013/06/27/sports/professional-sports/pitcher-john-lackey-sharp-as-boston-red-sox-beat-colorado-rockies/).

20 Joel Sherman, "John Lackey Goes From Chump to Champ," *New York Post,* October 30, 2013. (nypost.com/2013/10/30/john-lackey-goes-from-chump-to-champ/).

21 Joe McDonald, "Lackey Caps Comeback Season in Style," ESPN.com, October 31, 2013. . (espn.com/blog/boston/red-sox/post/_/id/33218/lackey-caps-comeback-season-in-style). See also Joel Sherman.

22 Sherman.

23 Jason Mastrodonato, "John Lackey's Difficult, but Successful Recovery From Tommy John Surgery and Why He'll Never Do It Again," MassLive.com, June 4, 2014. (masslive.com/redsox/index.ssf/2014/06/john_lackeys_difficult_but_suc.html).

24 Ian Browne, "Lackey to Cards as Sox get Kelly, Craig," MLB.com, July 31, 2014. (m.mlb.com/news/article/87232200/red-sox-trade-john-lackey-for-joe-kelly-allen-craig/).

25 Ted Berg, "John Lackey traded a Babe Ruth Autograph for a Uniform Number," *USA Today,* August 20, 2014. (ftw.usatoday.com/2014/08/john-lackey-pat-neshek-uniform-number-babe-ruth-st-louis-cardinals).

26 Molly Geary, "Cardinals Exercise 2015 Option on Veteran Pitcher John Lackey," *Sports Illustrated,* October 30, 2014. (si.com/mlb/2014/10/30/cardinals-pick-2015-option-john-lackey).

27 Derrick Goold, "Offense Backs Lackey as Cards Sweep," *St. Louis Post-Dispatch,* September 17, 2015. (stltoday.com/sports/baseball/professional/offense-backs-lackey-as-cards-sweep/article_263a16f4-1ff5-50d5-9245-3ee371c41f0b.html).

28 Zach Rymer, "John Lackey Showcases Late-Career Renaissance With Dazzling NLDS gem," Bleacher Report, October 9, 2015. (bleacherreport.com/articles/2577700-john-lackey-showcases-late-career-renaissance-with-dazzling-nlds-gem).

29 Carrie Muskat, "John Lackey Beats Cardinals in First Matchup." MLB.com, April 19, 2016. (m.mlb.com/news/article/173145090/john-lackey-beats-cardinals-in-first-matchup/). Besides Lackey, the other pitchers who have defeated all 30 major-league teams are Al Leiter, Randy Johnson, Kevin Brown, Barry Zito, Terry Mulholland, Curt Schilling, Woody Williams, Jamie Moyer, Javier Vazquez, Vicente Padilla, Derek Lowe, Dan Haren, A.J. Burnett, Kyle Lohse, and Tim Hudson,

WILSON RAMOS

BY JOEL RIPPEL

WILSON RAMOS HAS persevered through a plethora of injuries during his decade-plus career in professional baseball.

In his second professional season (2007), he missed games because of a thumb injury. In 2009, injuries limited him to 59 games. After reaching the majors in 2010, he suffered a torn ACL in 2012, a hamstring injury in 2013, and a broken hand in 2014.

That succession of injuries made the Washington Nationals catcher, wonder if his career would end prematurely.

"It was very difficult going through all the injuries I've been through the last few seasons," said Ramos in August of 2016. "At one point in my career I felt like it could be over because of those same injuries, but I kept a strong faith over everything. My family was very key in supporting me and God blessed me to this point and I was able to get through all of this. Just keeping my head held high through this whole adversity that has led me to this season I'm having. I just thank God and everyone involved helping me get through this."[1]

After being healthy for much of the 2015 and 2016 seasons, Wilson suffered another injury—a torn right ACL in his right knee—in the final week of the 2016 regular season. The injury, the same as the injury in 2012, was expected to sideline him until at least mid-2017.

But none of the injuries compare to what Ramos experienced in November of 2011.

While in Venezuela to play for the Tigres de Aragua of the Venezuelan Winter League, Ramos was abducted on November 9 by four armed men in front of his mother's house in Valencia, Venezuela. It would be nearly 24 hours before it was known if he was unharmed. Ramos was rescued on the 11th after being held captive for 51 hours.

After being rescued by Venezuelan government forces in the remote mountains of Montalban in Carabobo State, Ramos said, "What they did was laugh, joke about my pain. I'm very thankful and I feel like I've been born again."[2]

Because of what he has endured, Ramos said being named the 25th winner of the annual Tony Conigliaro Award in January of 2015 was special.

"Receiving the award meant a lot to me. I tried to keep my head up during all the injuries and everything that I went through," said Ramos. "It meant a lot to be recognized for my achievement, especially with everything I've been through. I kept my faith forward and stayed strong through this whole thing. Receiving this award meant a lot, achieving what I had achieved and being recognized for it."[3]

Prior to his season-ending injury in 2016, the resilient Ramos was enjoying the best season of his major-league career. He had established career highs in at least nine categories and was the best offensive catcher in the majors. Ramos batted .307 with 22 home runs and 80 RBIs in 131 games, all career highs.

One highlight for Ramos was being named an All-Star for the first time. In the Nationals' NL East Division-clinching victory over the Pittsburgh Pirates on September 24, 2016, Ramos had three hits in his next-to-last appearance of the season as the Nationals earned their third division title in five seasons.

"There have been several points in this season that I've seen as highlights, starting off with the All-Star Game," said Ramos, who underwent Lasik eye surgery after the 2015 season. "It was a dream come true for me. It was something I've strived for and finally got to participate in. It was a great honor. Some of the numbers I have put up this season, they are all career highlights. It's obviously something I've been working hard to achieve and it's been made possible this season. I just thank God for the season I'm having and hopefully it continues."[4]

showed promise defensively by throwing out 17 of 45 of would-be base stealers (38 percent).

In 2006 Ramos played for the Gulf Coast League Twins. In 46 games, he hit .286 with 3 home runs and 26 RBIs.

Ramos was promoted to Class A in 2007. After joining Beloit on June 2, he hit .291 with 8 home runs and 42 RBIs in 73 games. Ramos missed the final week of the Midwest League season with a sprained right thumb. After the season he played for Aragua in the Venezuelan Winter League.

Ramos got off to a slow start with Fort Myers of the Class-A Florida State League in 2008. Playing in the league's pitcher-friendly parks, he hit .203 with one home run in April. But he warmed up in May, hitting .257 with seven home runs. He finished the season with a .288 batting average in 126 games. He had 23 doubles (fourth best in the league), 13 home runs, and 78 RBIs. After the season Ramos played in the Venezuelan Winter League and was named to the Caribbean Series all-star team.

Also after the 2008 season, *Baseball America* rated Ramos as the "best defensive catcher" and the number-8 prospect in the Florida State League. In November of 2008, the Twins added Ramos to their 40-man roster. (Players signed at age 18 or younger are eligible for the Rule 5 draft after four years. Players signed at 19 or older are eligible after three years.)

For 2009 Ramos was promoted to the Twins' New Britain farm team in the Double-A Eastern League. He was limited to 54 games because of injuries. He hit .317 and had a slugging percentage of .454 (both best among Twins full-season minor leaguers). In a five-game injury rehab assignment with the Gulf Coast League Twins, he was 6-for-19 with 3 home runs and six RBIs. After the season he was named the number-8 prospect in the Eastern League by *Baseball America*.

In 2010 Ramos went to his first big-league training camp. Coming off a great winter in the Venezuelan Winter League (hitting .332 and earning Winter Player of the Year honors by *Baseball America*), he batted .400 (12-for-30) in exhibition games with four doubles, two home runs, and six RBIs—a performance that left the Twins with a question about his future. They had

The latest injury also put a damper on the pending free agency for Ramos, who was in the final year of a three-year contract. Four days before the injury, he was reportedly offered a three-year contract worth $30 million by the Nationals. He turned down the offer.[5]

Ramos signed his first professional contract (with the Minnesota Twins) in July of 2004, one month before his 17th birthday.

Ramos, one of eight children of Abraham Ramos and Maria Campos de Ramos, grew up in Valencia, Venezuela. Valencia, the capital city of Carabobo State and the third largest city in Venezuela, is a city of 900,000 near the country's Atlantic coast.

Ramos and his brothers grew up playing baseball in the street. Ramos learned the game from his maternal grandfather, Jesus Campos. Campos, who owned a fruit store, hadn't played baseball professionally but knew and understood the game.

Ramos made his professional debut in the Dominican Summer League in 2005. He batted .252 with one home run and 15 RBIs in 39 games. He

to decide whether keeping the 22-year old Ramos, whom manager Ron Gardenhire described as the "the package," on their Opening Day roster as a backup to Joe Mauer would slow his development.[6]

Ramos, who had played just 54 games above Class A, told reporters he could "learn just by watching."[7]

Mauer said, "I don't know if he needs my help, he's doing really well. He's pretty good, pretty polished already."[8]

But in what Gardenhire called an "extremely tough decision," the Twins kept Drew Butera as Mauer's backup and optioned Ramos to Rochester of the Triple-A International League.[9]

After his solid spring training, Ramos started the regular season slowly. He hit just .179 in the first month of the season for the Red Wings. But when a bruised left heel sidelined Mauer, Ramos was recalled by the Twins on May 1.

Ramos initially didn't know he was being summoned by the Twins. Before telling him the news, Rochester manager Tom Nieto (a former big-league catcher) met with Ramos and told him it didn't look like he was "cut out for Class AAA."[10]

"Then he said, 'No, congratulations, you're going to the big leagues,'" said Ramos.[11]

Ramos said his 12-for-67 start at Rochester was a result of "thinking too much."[12]

"He was struggling in Triple-A, probably because he did so well in spring training and used up all his hits," Gardenhire said. "Normally you'd keep a guy [in the majors] after a spring like that."[13]

Ramos made his major-league debut in Cleveland on May 2, 2010. Even though he played in pain after fouling a ball off his left foot in the fourth inning, Ramos went 4-for-5 in the Twins' 8-3 victory over the Indians. Ramos was the first Twins rookie to get four hits in his major-league debut since Kirby Puckett in 1984.

"He said, 'No way I'm coming out,'" Gardenhire said. "And I agreed with him."[14]

The next night, at Target Field in Minneapolis, Ramos went 3-for-4 with two doubles in the Twins' 10-3 victory over the Detroit Tigers. Ramos became the first big leaguer to get seven hits in his first two

major-league games since Nanny Fernandez of the Boston Braves did it in April of 1942.

After going 7-for-9 in his first two games, Ramos went 1-for-18 over his next five games. On May 12, with Mauer healthy enough to return to the lineup, Ramos was sent back to Rochester.

"He's a big-league baseball player with a chance to be one for a long time," Gardenhire said. "He needs to play, not watch Joe Mauer play."[15]After returning to Rochester, he went 55-for-211 to raise his average to .241 in 71 games with the Red Wings.

On July 29, 2010, two weeks shy of his 23rd birthday, the Twins traded Ramos and minor-league pitcher Joe Testa to the Washington Nationals for closer Matt Capps and $500,000 in cash.

The Nationals assigned Ramos to Syracuse of the International League. He was recalled by the Nationals for a three-game stint in August. (He went 0-for-4 against the Braves in his Nationals debut on August 19.) He was returned to Syracuse but then was recalled in September. On September 8 he hit his first major-league home run, a two-run shot off the New York Mets' R.A. Dickey, in a 3-2 home loss to the Mets. In 15 games with the Nationals, he hit .269.

After the season Ramos played in the Venezuelan Winter League, hitting .322 in 47 games with 17 doubles, 9 home runs, and 36 RBIs.

Ramos was healthy in 2011, playing in 113 games for the Nationals. He batted .267 with 15 home runs (a franchise record for home runs by a rookie catcher) and 52 RBIs. Defensively, he threw out 23 of 71 (32 percent) would-be base stealers. Ramos finished fourth in the NL Rookie of the Year voting.

Ramos got off to a solid start in 2012, batting .265 with 3 home runs and 10 RBIs in 25 games before an injury ended his season on May 12. In a game in Cincinnati, Ramos, who had homered in the game, injured his knee while chasing a passed ball in the seventh inning. He had two surgeries—on June 1 to repair a medial meniscus and on July 18 on the ACL in his right knee.

An injury to Ramos's left hamstring caused him to go on the disabled list twice in 2013. Despite missing 59 games, he set a Nationals season record for catchers with 16 home runs (in 287 at-bats). He finished with 59 RBIs in 78 games.

After missing 44 games, Ramos returned to the lineup on July 4 and hit a three-run home run to break a 5-5 tie and lift the Nationals to an 8-5 victory over the Brewers. He had a career-high five RBIs in the game. Between August 22 and September 17, Ramos started 24 consecutive games at catcher—the major-league high in 2013.

The 2014 season brought two more stints on the disabled list. On Opening Day, Ramos suffered a fractured hamate bone in his left wrist. The injury kept him out of the lineup for about six weeks. He returned on May 7 and batted .270 with 11 RBIs in 23 games before suffering a strained right hamstring on June 10. That injury kept him out of the lineup for 15 days.

Ramos was sidelined again for three days in early August under more positive terms. He was on maternity leave from August 5 to 7. His wife, Yely, gave birth to daughter Antonella on August 5. For the season, Ramos batted .267 with 11 home runs and 47 RBIs in 88 games. He threw out 38 percent of would-be basestealers and caught Jordan Zimmerman's 1-0 no-hit victory over the Miami Marlins on September 28 at Nationals Park. In his first appearance in the postseason, Ramos went 7-for-19 in four games in the Nationals' 3-1 loss to San Francisco in the National League Division Series.

After the 2014 season, Ramos hit just .224 in 18 games with the Tigres de Aragua. A highlight of his stint with the Tigres was getting to play in a game with his younger brothers, David and Natanael. David Ramos, a pitcher, signed with the Nationals in June of 2012. Natanael, a catcher, signed in November of 2010 with the New York Mets.

Healthy in 2015, Wilson Ramos had career highs in RBIs (68) and hits (109) in 128 games, with a 19-game hitting streak from April 24 to May 19. He was second among NL catchers with a career-best catcher caught-stealing percentage of 44.4 percent (24 of 54). Ramos caught Max Scherzer's two no-hitters that season (over the Pirates and Mets).

Several days after Ramos's season-ending injury in September 2016, he addressed his uncertain future with reporters. "I've received the opportunity that I always wanted in my career here," he said. "I feel happy, very proud of the opportunities they've given me. My career grew in this organization and I would like to stay here for a lot of years. Unfortunately, this happened with my knee and it's very difficult at my position to be in the National League, but I'd really like to be here for a lot of years. I hope to get out of the operation fine and get back very strong to stay here with this team."[16]

Still, Ramos remained upbeat. "I'm very happy with the season that I had," he said. "To be able to do what I did makes me feel super happy after a year that wasn't very good. This year, I worked very hard for that and I achieved it and I feel super happy with that. It's a difficult moment now that I was on the verge of playing in another playoffs and this happened. But you have to look at the positives over the negatives."[17]

In December 2016, the Tampa Bay Rays agreed to a two-year, $12.5 million contract with Ramos, giving him the opportunity to earn an additional $5.75 million in incentives.

SOURCES

In addition to the sources cited in the Notes, the author consulted Baseball-Reference.com, Retrosheet.org, mlb.com, milb.com, and the Washington Nationals 2016 media guide.

NOTES

1   Author interview with Wilson Ramos, August 10, 2016.

2   Associated Press via Fox News Latino, "Eight Arrested in Wilson Ramos Kidnapping," November 17, 2011.

3   Wilson Ramos interview.

4   Wilson Ramos interview.

5   Jorge Castillo, "Wilson Ramos Declines Nationals' Contract Offer," *Washington Post*, September 22, 2016.

6   Joe Christensen, "There's Someone Blocking His Path," *Minneapolis Star Tribune*, March 27, 2010.

7   Ibid.

8   Ibid.

9   Joe Christensen, "Butera Beats Out Ramos as Backup," *Minneapolis Star Tribune*, April 1, 2010.

10 Joe Christensen, "Who Needs Mauer?" *Minneapolis Star Tribune*, May 3, 2010.

11   Ibid.

12   Ibid.

13   Ibid.

14   Ibid.

15   La Velle E. Neal III, "Hudson Bunt Was Big Surprise,"
     Minneapolis Star Tribune, May 13, 2010.

16   Jorge Castillo, "Wilson Ramos Knows His Future Might
     Not Be With the Nationals—Or in the National League,"
     Washington Post, September 29, 2016.

17   Ibid.

MITCH HARRIS

BY MIKE HUBER

MANY MAJOR LEAGUERS follow a twisting path to the major leagues, but none can say they traveled the same road as Mitch Harris. The right-handed pitcher's major league debut was interrupted by graduation from the US Naval Academy and five years of active duty. A 2008 graduate of the Naval Academy, Harris finally realized his dream of reaching the major leagues in 2015.

Mitchell Andrew Harris was born on November 7, 1985, in Ocala, Florida, to Cy and Cindy Harris. With two younger sisters, he was the oldest of three children. Cy Harris was a minister, and the family moved around while Mitchell was young, from Florida to South Carolina, to Atlanta, to Charlotte, North Carolina, before settling in Cleveland, Tennessee.

Harris attended South Point High School in Mount Holly, North Carolina, near Charlotte. He earned all-conference and all-state honors in the 2003 and 2004 seasons (his junior and senior years). He played for the North Carolina State Games team in 2003. Harris described himself as a "utility guy,"[1] able to play different positions and pitch as well. Buddy Green, a US Navy Academy football coach and recruiter on a visit to South Point High School, strolled past the baseball field, saw Harris throwing a bullpen session and later connected him with Academy admissions officials. After a visit to Annapolis, Harris became part of the Brigade of Midshipmen.

There is a military gene running in the family. Harris's two grandfathers served in World War II. Louin Harris, his paternal grandfather, was in the Navy and fought in the Battle of Midway. James Chamberlain, his maternal grandfather, was a soldier in the Battle of the Bulge. Once Harris decided to attend the Naval Academy, his grandfathers would tell him stories of their experiences in the military, and Harris recalled that his father and uncle said it was the first time they had heard those tales.

In his first season at Navy, 2005, Harris played in 40 games, 37 of them as the starting pitcher. He batted .283 and tied for the team lead with 12 multihit games. As a pitcher, he held Patriot League hitters to a .214 batting average against him. Despite these fancy figures, his pitching record was 0-and-3 with a 6.46 earned-run average and two saves.

As a sophomore at Annapolis, Harris set a Navy record with 113 strikeouts in 82⅔ innings. His 12.30 strikeouts per nine innings were still a Patriot League record as of 2016. He earned Patriot League Pitcher of the Year honors in 2006, posting a 10-3 record with a 1.74 ERA and claiming the league's pitching Triple Crown.

The next year, 2007, Harris struck out 119 batters, as of 2016 still the record for Patriot League pitchers. In addition, he led the Patriot League with four triples and eight home runs. He was named a third-team All-American by Baseball America, and was drafted by the Atlanta Braves in the 24th round of the major-league amateur draft. He had to remain at the Naval Academy; sophomores are required to commit themselves to graduate and serve five years on active duty.[2] One more honor was added when Harris received the Thompson Trophy Cup recipient, presented to a midshipman, male or female declared to have "done the most during the year for the promotion of athletics at the Naval Academy."[3]

By 2008, his senior year, 15 to 20 major-league scouts were attending Navy baseball games.[4] The St. Louis Cardinals' assistant general manager, John Abbamondi, a former Navy pilot who flew 40 combat missions over Iraq,[5] was instrumental in drafting Harris with the Cardinals' 13th-round pick in the 2008 free-agent draft. Abbamondi and GM John Mozeliak tried to get the Navy to waive Harris's five-year service commitment. However, with the nation at war, all requests were denied. Harris never lost hope of pitching in the major leagues, and Mozeliak "wanted to make sure he had an opportunity."[6] So, after graduation from the Naval Academy, Ensign Harris began his service to the country. On March 2, 2009, Harris did sign an agreement with the Cardinals.

As a naval surface warfare officer, Harris traveled to the Middle East twice aboard the amphibious transport USS Ponce, which performed exercises with Marines. He then spent time aboard the frigate USS Carr, going to Russia for a diplomatic mission and then to South America on drug operations. But he never lost sight of his goal of pitching in the major leagues. "It would be a dream come true," he said in 2014, while playing in the minor leagues.[7] "Growing up, you have a dream of playing pro baseball. And when you get the opportunity to go to the Naval Academy, you can't pass that up. Once I got there, I realized what it meant to have that brotherhood and to be able to serve your country. That moved to the forefront, but in the back of my mind, I still had the dream of playing pro ball."

While Harris was aboard the Ponce, Victor Nunez, a cook on the ship who had played baseball, became his batterymate, catching him.[8] "He was about the only person I trusted to throw with, because I was scared I'd hurt anybody else," Harris said.[9] He pitched to Nunez on the ship's flight deck, with the Persian Gulf as his "ballpark." He lost more than a few balls into the ocean, but his father kept him supplied with bags of balls.

After his naval service ended, the Cardinals honored their promise to give Harris a shot at making the major leagues. In 2013, at the age of 27, the right-hander made his pro-ball debut with the State College Spikes of the short-season New York-Penn League. His fastball had initially lost its zip, but he worked hard to regain his form. He finished the season with a minuscule 0.81 ERA and a 4-1 record. He struck out 29 batters in 33⅓ innings.

In 2014 Harris raced through three levels of the minor leagues. He pitched in eight games for the Palm Beach Cardinals in the Class-A Florida State League, 33 games for the Springfield Cardinals in the Double-A Texas League, and one game for the

Richie Conigliaro and Mitch Harris

Memphis Cardinals in the Triple-A Pacific Coast League.

Harris's work at Springfield impressed pitching coach Randy Niemann, who said, "There's no doubt the younger guys look up to him. I made a point of making sure our younger players know where Mitch has been and what he's done."[10] In 57 innings in the minors in 2014, used mostly as a late-inning relief pitcher, Harris posted an ERA of 3.95. He struck out 45 and walked 19. His WHIP (walks and hits per inning pitched) was 1.158. According to Niemann, "Not only was he hitting 94 mph almost every outing, but he perfected the cutter and I got him throwing a splitter as a third pitch. I don't think age is a factor for Mitch."[11]

Harris returned to Memphis at the beginning of the 2015 campaign. After earning two saves in the first two weeks of the season, he got the call of his life: "Report to Washington, DC. You're joining the Cardinals. You made the big leagues."[12] On April 21 a roster opening developed when outfielder Peter Bourjos was given paternity leave. The Cardinals put Harris on their 40-man roster, making room for him by designating outfielder Gary Brown for assignment. His pitching coach in Memphis, Bryan Eversgerd, said, "Mitch dedicated his life to our country for five years. It's nice to have this great game of baseball to give back to him a little bit."[13]

Harris made his major-league debut on April 25 at Milwaukee, relieving Adam Wainwright to start the bottom of the fifth inning with the Cardinals leading, 2-0. His first pitch, to Brewers first baseman Adam Lind, was a 95-mph fastball for a called strike. Three pitches later, Lind struck out. Harris then gave up a walk and a hit, but retired two more Brewers to end the inning. He faced three batters in the sixth inning, giving up a walk and a hit before yielding to Matt Belisle. Harris had pitched 1⅓ innings and yielded no runs. The Cardinals went on to beat the Brewers, 5-3.

Harris notched his first major-league victory on May 5. Before 41,613 fans at Busch Stadium, he relieved Seth Maness in the top of the sixth inning against the Chicago Cubs with the score tied, 4-4. He faced four batters, allowing a two-out double to Addison Russell, and then got the third out. Harris was lifted for a pinch-hitter in the bottom of the inning as the Cardinals scored two runs and held on to defeat the Cubs, 7-4.

Over the rest of the season, Harris went back and forth between the Cardinals and Memphis. With the Redbirds he was 0-4 with a 3.38 ERA, striking out 20 in 26⅔ innings. With the Cardinals, Harris was 2-1. His earned-run average was 3.67 in 27 innings pitched (26 appearances).

Harris pitched in one spring training game in 2016. In March he underwent a nerve test to clarify a diagnosis of compression syndrome,[14] and began the season on the disabled list.

Harris's coach at Navy, Paul Kostacopoulos, said he knew exactly how hard the pitcher had to work. "He did the full five years of service and he truly is an officer and a baseball player. He's fulfilled every promise he's made. He promised his parents he'd graduate from the Naval Academy. He did that. He promised his country he would serve his time, and he did that. And he made a promise to himself that he was going to hang in there as long as he could to be a baseball player."[15]

Harris became the second Naval Academy graduate to play in the major leagues. Nemo Gaines played four games in 1921 before heading back to the Navy. Gaines pitched 4⅔ innings in four games, with a 0.00 ERA, facing 19 batters and yielding five hits and two walks but no runs.

Harris said he appreciated the Cardinals' organization for their support. He said, "The Cardinals said, 'Hey look, we believe in you, we think this is going to happen and however much time it takes we'll be here whenever you are ready.' I can't say enough about this organization."[16] For his part, Cardinals manager Mike Matheny said, "For a guy who's made that kind of sacrifice, and then (to) be able to make that kind of jump into our world, it's just so rare."[17]

In 2015 Harris was voted the recipient of the 26th annual Tony Conigliaro Award. The honor is bestowed on a major leaguer who "has overcome adversity through the attributes of spirit, determination, and courage that were the trademarks of Tony C."[18] Members of the Conigliaro family presented the award to Harris at the Boston Baseball Writers' dinner on January 21, 2016. The event was co-hosted by the BBWAA and the Sports Museum, based at the TD Garden in Boston.

As of 2016 Harris was still a lieutenant in the US Naval Reserve, assigned to the Navy Operational Support Center in Hialeah, Florida. He was fulfilling his military obligation during the offseason. He had spent four years, eight months, and eight days on active duty, and this required three years of reserve time to complete his obligation. As a serviceman, Harris stood at attention when the national anthem was played before games, and when "the color guard is still on the field, no one returns to the dugout until they get their cue from Harris."[19]

Mitch and his wife, Mandi, were wed on November 21, 2015, in Athens, Georgia.

Harris said he was proud of his service to his country. "I want everyone who served to be recognized, too," he said. "When I see those guys, whether in an airport or somewhere else, I'll go out of my way to say hello, just to say, 'Hey, I've been there with you. Thank you for what you are doing.'"[20] But he said believed he belonged in the major leagues, commenting, "I'm not here because I have a good story. I'm here because I'm a good pitcher."[21] In a 2015 interview with the *Navy Times*, Harris said, "The Naval Academy and the Navy made me who I am, developed me into the person and the leader that I hope I am, and I wouldn't take that back for anything."[22]

NOTES

1   Author interview with Harris, March 3, 2016.

2   Author interview with Harris, April 13, 2016. Midshipmen may leave the Naval Academy after their sophomore year, but they must reimburse the Navy for its costs in educating them.

3   navysports.com/trads/thompson-trophy.html. Accessed March 4, 2016.

4   Bob Nightengale, "After Naval Stint 'Much Bigger Than Me,' Mitch Harris Takes on Major Leagues," *usatoday.com/story/ sports/mlb/2015/05/21/mitch-harris-st-louis-cardinals-naval-acade- my-graduate/27660855/*, May 21, 2015. Accessed January 21, 2016.

5   Nightengale.

6   Nightengale.

7   Spencer Fordin, "Navy Grad Harris Finally Pursuing MLB Dream," *m.mlb.com/news/article/99298562/naval_academy-grad- mitch-harris-finally-pursuing-mlb-dream*, October 23, 2014. Accessed January 21, 2016.

8   Author interview with Harris, March 3, 2016.

9   Tom Schad, "With Service Commitment Fulfilled, Navy Grad Realizes His Big League Dreams," *washingtontimes.com/ news/2015/apr/22/mitch-harris-cardinals-pitcher-and-navy-grad- reali/?page=all*. Accessed January 21, 2016.

10   Jeff Bradley, "After Five Years in the Navy, Mitch Harris Chases His Big League Dream, *si.com/mlb/2014/10/28/mitch-harris- arizona-fall-league-st-louis-cardinals-navy-midshipmen*, October 28, 2014. Accessed January 21, 2016.

11   Bradley.

12   Nightengale.

13   Anna McDonald, "From the Navy to the Majors, Cardinals Pitcher Mitch Harris Carries on, *espn.go.com/blog/sweetspot/ post/_/id/57570/mitch-harris-from-u-s-naval-academy-to-the major-leagues*, November 11, 2015. Accessed January 21, 2016.

14   Jennifer Langosch, "Reliever Harris Likely to Begin Season on DL," *mlb.com*, March 23, 2016. The article says Harris had a stem test, but he told the author on April 13, 2016, that it was a nerve test.

15   Fordin.

16   McDonald.

17   "Former Navy Lieutenant Mitch Harris Called Up by Cardinals," *espn.go.com/mlb/story/_/id/12734785/st-louis-cardinals- call-former-navy-lieutenant-mitch-harris*, April 23, 2015. Accessed January 21, 2016.

18   "Cardinals Pitcher Mitch Harris Wins 2015 Tony Conigliaro Award," *foxsports.com/Midwest/story/st-louis-cardinals-pitcher- mitch-harris-wins-2015-tony-conigliaro-award-121515*, December 15, 2015. Accessed January 21, 2016.

19   Nightengale.

20   Nightengale.

21   McDonald.

22   Meghann Myers, "Academy Grad Makes History in MLB Debut," *navytimes.com/story/sports/2015/05/02/navy-naval-acad- emy-st-louis-cardinals-baseball-mitch-harris/26636619/*. Accessed January 21, 2016.

YANGERVIS SOLARTE

BY GORDON EDES

YANGERVIS ALFREDO Solarte was 26 years old and had played eight seasons in the minor leagues. Three times, he could have been added to a 40-man major-league roster. Three times, he was passed over, becoming a minor-league free agent each time.

Sometimes, more often than we care to acknowledge, hard work and perseverance go unrewarded. The will was there, no doubt. The opportunity, however, remained elusive. There was little reason to believe that was going to change in the spring of 2014, when Solarte came to the New York Yankees' camp as a nonroster invitee, after six seasons in the Minnesota Twins' organization and two with the Texas Rangers, who had hinted at making him a late-season call-up the previous summer but didn't follow through.

But when the Yankees broke camp that April, there was a new infielder on their roster, a switch-hitting Venezuelan with a unique first name, a combination of his parents' names (mother Yanmili, father Gervis).[1] In Houston, where Solarte would draw his first big-league start in the Yankees' third game of the season, he circulated through the visitors' clubhouse with the lineup card, asking his teammates to sign.

"There were times I dreamed big for my debut," he said after collecting three hits and a walk, scoring twice and driving in a run. "When you see players like [Derek] Jeter, you expect big things for yourself."[2]

Four days later, on April 7, 2014, Solarte was in Yankee Stadium, playing third base alongside Jeter, who admonished the rookie to pay attention and wave when the Bleacher Creatures in right field chanted his name during their first-inning "roll call."

"I'm going to remember all of it," Solarte said, "from the moment they gave me the news I had made the team, to my first major-league game, to my first defensive play when I had Derek Jeter and Brian Roberts next to me.

"I've had so many experiences already, and one starts to think: 'How was I able to accomplish this?' I know one of the reasons was because I worked so hard. I never let up. I just kept going and working. All the things that happened to me previously, and yet here I am."[3]

A player who had dared hope he might catch on as a utilityman was, for the first two months of the 2014 season, one of the best stories in baseball. Yangervis Solarte was the Yankees' everyday third baseman, hitting over .300, starting a triple play (April 17 against the Tampa Bay Rays in Tropicana Field), winning over skeptics with his performance.

"It's become a running joke in our dugout — 'best player I've ever seen'—at this point," Roberts said after a game against the Mets in mid-May in which Solarte hit a home run and led the team in RBIs (23) after the season's first six weeks. "It's a great story, fun to watch. To do what he is doing is tough to do. It's tough to hit .350 in this league for two months."[4]

In the end, Solarte could not maintain that torrid pace, and following a prolonged slump and brief demotion to the minors, he was traded with minor-league pitcher Rafael De Paula on July 22, 2014, to the San Diego Padres for a veteran third baseman, Chase Headley, who was two years removed from a 31-homer season, and cash.

The trade, however, did not signal a return to obscurity for Solarte. Instead, he found a home in San Diego, which became the place where in 2016 he would experience his most prolonged success and encounter heartbreaking tragedy, when his wife, Yuliett, the mother of his three daughters, succumbed to cancer in September at the age of 31.

Yuliett Pimentel Solarte, like her husband, was from Venezuela, where his odyssey took shape and was inspired by the example of his cousin, Roger Cedeño, who played 11 seasons in the big leagues with five teams, his longest stint the four seasons he spent

with the Los Angeles Dodgers, the team that signed him as an amateur free agent in 1991.

Cedeno recalled how a 4-year-old Solarte watched, inconsolable, from the window of an airport terminal as his then-16-year-old uncle walked toward the plane that would be taking him far from home in pursuit of his big-league dream. Cedeño said his sister, Vilma, later told him Solarte cried for hours.

"She never saw a baby cry that long," he said.[5]

Solarte, his parents, and more than a dozen other relatives would one day live in a house Cedeño provided for them in Valencia, where he attended Tomas Alba Edison High School. Before Cedeño embarked on his pro career, he had doted on Solarte.

"I was one of the favorites because I was the oldest nephew," Solarte said. "I was always a class apart from everyone in how he treated me. Since I've been a kid, he's been an inspiration."[6]

Solarte said that when he was 13, he was denied a visa to visit Cedeño in the United States. But he saw plenty of him on television and, even better, got to spend time with his uncle in winter ball, where

he played for Caracas and introduced his nephew to some of Venezuela's most celebrated major leaguers.

"He'd tell me to come with him into the dugout," said Solarte, ticking off the names of such players as Omar Vizquel, Bobby Abreu, Andres Galarraga, and Alex Gonzalez as players he was able to meet through Cedeño.[7]

Even as Cedeño used the wealth he accumulated in the big leagues to take care of his extended family, Solarte began to attract the attention of scouts with his own play, although he wasn't signed until just three weeks before his 18th birthday, a relatively advanced age for a Latin American prospect. Solarte was signed on June 16, 2005, by Minnesota Twins scout Jose Leon.

A variety of injuries allowed Solarte to have as many as 400 at-bats only once in his first six pro seasons. He began his professional career with the Twins' entry in the Dominican Summer League, amassing a slash line of .278/.373/.376 in 53 games. He spent the next season in Fort Myers (Florida) in the Gulf Coast League, batting .303/.342/.377 with 53 hits in 52 games while playing all three outfield positions as well as second, short, and third. He continued in a utility role in 2008, which he split between Fort Myers in the Florida State League and Beloit in the Midwest League, and was back in Fort Myers in 2009, where he underwent surgery on his right shoulder in May after appearing in just four games, went on rehab assignment in August, and played three games for Double-A New Britain in September. In 2010, he tore the meniscus cartilage in his right knee, missing six weeks, though he eventually was promoted back to New Britain, batting .276 in 32 games.

Solarte had a breakout season for New Britain in 2011, when he posted a .329/.367/.466 slash line with 36 doubles and 7 home runs and was the second baseman on the Eastern League All-Star team. But at the end of the season, the Twins left him off their 40-man roster, and he became a minor-league free agent for the first time.[8]

"That year could have been explained as a blip in a rather unspectacular stint with the Twins," *Baseball America* wrote in 2014. "[But] he was notable enough that [*BA*] highlighted him as a minor-league free agent with upside after the 2011 season."[9]

Solarte also returned home after each season to play in the Venezuelan Winter League for the Aragua Tigers, where he was teammates with former big leaguer Edgardo Alfonzo, who offered the benefit of his experience to his younger teammate.

"He was impatient," Alfonzo said. "He would get mad and frustrated at little things and get out of control. He would go 0 for 4 and get so mad at himself, he'd carry it over to the next game. I would tell him, 'It's OK, you're going to have bad days.'

"We played together for two years, and I just told him, once he controlled his emotions, he could be a really good player."[10]

Solarte signed as a minor-league free agent with Texas and in 2012 primarily played second base for the Rangers' affiliate in Round Rock, the first time he had played at the Triple-A level. He had a .288/.340/.405 slash line with 11 home runs in 130 games, putting together a 22-game hitting streak while ranking as the second hardest player in the Pacific Coast League to strike out, averaging one K per 12.91 plate appearances.[11]

Even so, the Rangers did not promote him to their 40-man roster, re-signing him as a minor-league free agent for another go-round in 2013 at Round Rock, where he batted .276 and set career highs in home runs (12) and RBIs (75), while also hitting 31 doubles, tied for the team high.[12]

Those numbers did not stand out in the hitter-friendly PCL. Fifteen players logged at least 150 plate appearances for the Express in 2013, and Solarte ranked just 13th in wOBA (weighted on-base average).[13]

But when Solarte became a minor-league free agent for the third time, he was championed by Yankees assistant GM Billy Eppler, with support from the team's statistical analyst, Michael Fishman. They were rewarded when Solarte hit .429 in spring training, beating out Eduard Nunez for the team's utility spot.[14]

"I think the overall feeling [at first] was I was really happy for a kid that had persevered to get to this point," Yankees manager Joe Girardi would say six weeks later, in the midst of Solarte's hot start. "But now, you expect him to have good at-bats, and you don't think much about it. He smokes a double, he hits a home run, it's just, 'That's Solo.'"[15]

Solarte's career with the Yankees lasted 75 games. At the time of his trade, after he batted just .164 (10-for-61) in June,[16] his average had faded to .254, with 6

Jersey honoring Yuliett Solarte, in the Padres dugout, September 19, 2016.

home runs and 31 RBIs. San Diego's expectations for Solarte were modest.

"The Solarte acquisition helps the Padres fill in for the loss of Headley and second baseman Jedd Gyorko (disabled list) while potentially buying time for [second-base prospect Taylor] Lindsey to get more reps at Triple-A before he's called upon," *Baseball America* wrote at the time of the deal.[17]

But Solarte made a strong first impression on the Padres, leading the team in plate appearances (246) for the duration of the season while playing four different positions. He batted .267 over the 56 games he played for San Diego.

"It's about his bat," Padres third-base coach Glenn Hoffman said. "When you hit, you find a place to play."[18]

When Solarte came to camp in 2015, he brought eight different gloves. Will Middlebrooks, acquired from the Boston Red Sox, was projected as the team's starting third baseman. But with Middlebrooks slumping, Solarte became the everyday third baseman by midseason, starting 64 of the Padres' last 72 games at third base and appearing in a career-high 152 games overall. The added playing time resulted in his best numbers to date: career highs in hits (142), runs (63), doubles (33), home runs (14), RBIs (63), and batting average (.270). His average led the club.

"When I was in the minors, this was my dream," he said. "I saw my uncle in the majors all the time. I never forgot my dream. The big difference for me and my family is there's just so much happiness because my family saw me fight a lot of fights for my dreams."[19]

By 2016, Solarte had established himself as one of the most popular players in the Padres' clubhouse, which made it all the more frustrating when he missed 38 games early in the season with a strained right hamstring. His return in May was hailed by Padres manager Andy Green.

"He's obviously a left-handed bat with a ton of life and a ton of energy," Green said. "He's just a guy that everybody loves being around; he's got an infectious personality."[20]

Solarte did not disappoint, building off his 2015 season to put up even better numbers, with a

.286/.341/.467/.808 slash line, along with 15 home runs and 71 RBIs. But in late July Solarte left the club for nearly a week for what was described at the time as a "family medical matter."[21]

Less than two months later, the magnitude of that medical matter was revealed. On Saturday, September 17, Solarte's wife, Yuliett, died after a nearly yearlong battle with cancer.

"What he's going through right now as a dad of three girls and losing his wife, it's tragic," Green said. "I got calls and texts from coaches in other organizations. Everybody's heart breaks for him right now. There's nothing that replaces a wife and a mother. All we can do is love him and support him."[22]

That night, in the Padres' game in Denver against the Rockies, Padres utilityman Adam Rosales hit a home run. When he approached home plate, he opened his arms wide before clapping his hands, emulating Solarte's signature home-run celebration.

"We talked about it before the game," Rosales said. "If somebody hit a home run, we'd do the 'alligator arm' for Solarte. We miss Solarte right now, and our hearts definitely go out to him and his family."[23]

On Thursday, September 22, several Padres club officials attended the memorial service for Yuliett Solarte in Miami. The next day, Solarte returned to San Diego with his daughters and his mother. On September 24, a week after his wife died, Solarte was back with the ballclub. In that night's game in Petco Park, he pinch-hit in the seventh inning, his appearance greeted with a standing ovation. He singled, pointing to the sky as he reached first base.

"From the beginning of the season, my wife has always pushed me and hadn't wanted her illness to get in the way of things," Solarte said. "She always wanted me to play and to remember I have three daughters. She was always reminding me of that. To think of them, to think of her."[24]

Solarte said he considered the Padres a "second family."

"[Yuliett] is in a better place now," he said, "so I just need to focus on what I need to focus on, and that's being back with my team.

"It feels a little bit different, and she's gone now, but at the end of the day those things are out of our control. Those things are up to God, and that was his decision."[25]

Megan Otto, the Padres' manager of player and family relations, nominated Solarte for the Tony Conigliaro Award. "For Yangervis, 2016 has been one of the most personally challenging years that he will have in his lifetime," she wrote. "Dealing with personal loss and missing time to due to injury, and yet he still managed to produce the best year of his career."[26] In December 2016 the 20-person committee selected Solarte as the award recipient; the honor was to be presented in January 2017, in the 50th-anniversary year of the tragic accident that befell Conigliaro.

NOTES

1   Brendan Kuty, "The Strange Explanation as to How Yangervis Solarte Got His First Name," NJ Advance Media for NJ.com, April 9, 2014.

2   Dan Martin, "Taking Third Prize Solarte Solid in First Start," New York Post, April 4, 2014: 52.

3   Jorge Arangure Jr., "Rookie Answers Yankees' Needs, If Not Fans' Chants," New York Times, April 8, 2014.

4   George A. King III, "Solarte Thrills in A-Big Way," New York Post, May 15, 2014: 49.

5   David Waldstein, "For the Newest Yankee, Reaching the Majors Was a Family Affair," New York Times, April 16, 2014.

6   Ibid.

7   Ibid.

8   Yangervis Solarte, BR Bullpen, Baseball-Reference.com.

9   J.J. Cooper, "Ask BA: Can Yangervis Solarte Keep This Up?" BaseballAmerica.com, May 21, 2014.

10   Waldstein.

11   San Diego Padres Media Guide, 146.

12   Ibid.

13   Chris Mitchell, "It's Time to Start Believing in Yangervis Solarte," Pinstripealley.com, May 15, 2014.

14   Waldstein.

15   Ken Davidoff, "Solo Continues to Make Impact," New York Post, May 24, 2014: 47.

16   George A. King III, "Demotion for Solarte," New York Post, July 4, 2014: 51.

17   Matt Eddy, "Trade Central: Padres Trade Headley to Yankees," BaseballAmerica.com, July 22, 2014.

18   Jeff Sanders, "Solarte Making New Home With Padres," San Diego Union-Tribune, August 8, 2014.

19   Jeff Sanders, "He's Entrenched as Third Baseman," San Diego Union-Tribune, August 30, 2015.

20   Dennis Lin, "Solarte Back From Hamstring Strain," San Diego Union-Tribune, May 22, 2016.

21   Dennis Lin, "Solarte on Leave as Part of Shuffle," San Diego Union-Tribune, July 28, 2016.

22   Dennis Lin, "Loss of Solarte's Wife Hurts," San Diego Union-Tribune, September 19, 2016.

23   Ibid.

24   Dennis Lin, "Padres Lose in 10th as Solarte Returns," San Diego Union-Tribune, September 25, 2016.

25   Ibid.

26   Press release, Boston Red Sox, December 15, 2016.

MAJOR LEAGUE BASEBALL AND TOPPS HONOR PLAYERS WHO OVERCAME DISABILITIES

BY BILL NOWLIN

IN OCTOBER 2015, ABOUT FIVE months after this book was conceived, Major League Baseball, working with Topps, released a set of baseball cards titled "Pride & Perseverance." Wendy Lewis, MLB Senior Vice President of Diversity, Inclusion & Strategic Alliance, said, "As a game for all, baseball is proud to be the sport of Jim Abbott, Curtis Pride and many world-class athletes who have overcome obstacles en route to success in the Major Leagues. This special set from Topps is a terrific way not only to honor all individuals who have faced challenges and reached the highest level of their chosen sport, but also to inspire anyone who dreams of one day being a part of the 'National Pastime'."

The 12-card set was released on October 21, timed to the 70th anniversary of National Disability Employment Awareness month, and honoring 25 years of Americans with disabilities legislation.

In MLB's press release, Chicago Cubs medical director Mark O'Neal was quoted saying, "People with disabilities are often looked at for what they can't do instead of being appreciated for what they can do. We hope these cards will help people take a closer look at the potential of people with disabilities. Imagine if a child or the parent of a child with a disability, by simply opening a pack of baseball cards, discovers that one of their heroes was legally blind or deaf or has battled cancer? They would truly feel empowered and encouraged."

David Hochman, Specialist, Business Communications for MLB, credited Topps for spearheading the idea.

The 12-card set featured current and former major-league ballplayers, weighted more toward recent players. The checklist:

1—Buddy Carlyle, New York Mets reliever diagnosed with diabetes in 2009.

2—Curtis Pride, born deaf but a 13-year major-league veteran.

3—George Springer, Houston Astros outfielder George Springer, who has overcome stuttering.

4—Jake Peavy, San Francisco Giants pitcher, legally blind without corrective lenses. Peavy pitched for the 2013 World Champion Boston Red Sox.

5—Jason Johnson, an 11-year veteran former pitcher and a Type 1 diabetic who was the first to receive permission to wear an insulin pump on the field.

6—Jim Abbott, who won 87 major-league games in 10 seasons, and who threw a no-hitter for the New York Yankees in 1993, despite being born without his right hand.

7—Jim Eisenreich, born with Tourette's syndrome but who went on to play 15 years in the majors, including a World Championship with the 1997 Florida Marlins. He hit .500 in the Series.

8—Jon Lester, diagnosed and treated for anaplastic large cell lymphoma, who came back in 2007 and won the clinching Game Four of the World Series for the Red Sox. He won two games in the 2013 Series (and, after the Topps set was released) won Game Five in the 2016 Series for the Chicago Cubs, winning a third ring.

9 — Pete (Wyshner) Gray, former outfielder who played for the St. Louis Browns in 1945 and spent six seasons in the minor leagues, despite having lost an arm in a childhood accident.

10 — Sam Fuld, an eight-year veteran outfielder for four different teams, who had been battling Type 1 diabetes since he was 10 years old.

11 - William "Dummy" Hoy, one of the first deaf players to play the game, a centerfielder with a 14-year career from 1888-1902.

12 — Anthony Rizzo, Chicago Cubs first baseman treated for Hodgkins' lymphoma in 2008. Like Jon Lester, the year after the set was released he was a key player for the 2016 World Champion Chicago Cubs.

CURTIS PRIDE
DETROIT TIGERS
OF

JASON JOHNSON
BALTIMORE ORIOLES
P

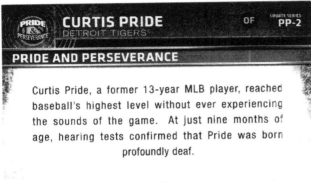

CURTIS PRIDE
DETROIT TIGERS
OF — UPDATE SERIES PP-2

PRIDE AND PERSEVERANCE

Curtis Pride, a former 13-year MLB player, reached baseball's highest level without ever experiencing the sounds of the game. At just nine months of age, hearing tests confirmed that Pride was born profoundly deaf.

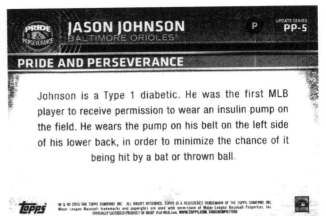

JASON JOHNSON
BALTIMORE ORIOLES
P — UPDATE SERIES PP-5

PRIDE AND PERSEVERANCE

Johnson is a Type 1 diabetic. He was the first MLB player to receive permission to wear an insulin pump on the field. He wears the pump on his belt on the left side of his lower back, in order to minimize the chance of it being hit by a bat or thrown ball.

"The importance of this set cannot be overstated," said David Leiner, VP & General Manager of North American Sports and Entertainment for Topps. "These men had to overcome great odds to not only make it to the Majors, but at times with what could have been a disadvantage. Instead, they are an inspiration and we are honored to showcase them in our product."

Five of the 12 players in the set are Tony Conigliaro Award recipients: Abbott, Eisenreich, Johnson, Lester, and Rizzo.

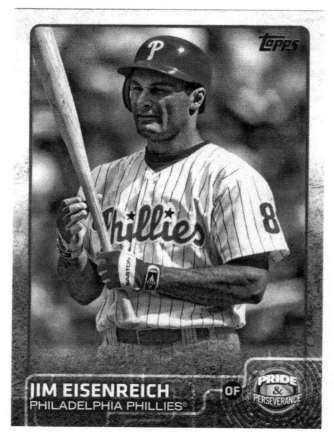

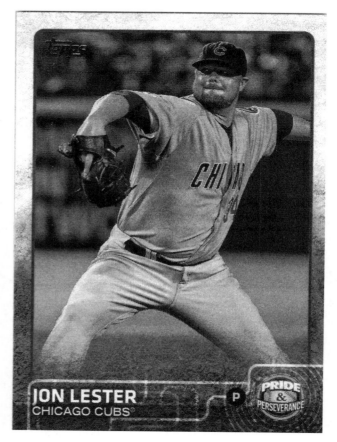

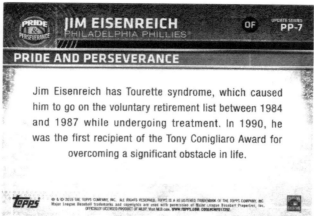

JIM EISENREICH · OF · UPDATE SERIES PP-7
PHILADELPHIA PHILLIES

PRIDE AND PERSEVERANCE

Jim Eisenreich has Tourette syndrome, which caused him to go on the voluntary retirement list between 1984 and 1987 while undergoing treatment. In 1990, he was the first recipient of the Tony Conigliaro Award for overcoming a significant obstacle in life.

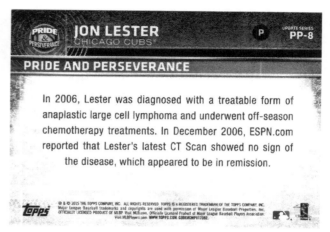

JON LESTER · P · UPDATE SERIES PP-8
CHICAGO CUBS

PRIDE AND PERSEVERANCE

In 2006, Lester was diagnosed with a treatable form of anaplastic large cell lymphoma and underwent off-season chemotherapy treatments. In December 2006, ESPN.com reported that Lester's latest CT Scan showed no sign of the disease, which appeared to be in remission.

THE HUTCH AWARD

By Clayton Trutor

LIKE THE **TONY CONIGLIARO** Award, the Hutch Award honors major-league baseball players who persevere through personal hardship. Conigliaro himself was the 1970 recipient of the award, an accolade he received after his great comeback season.

Established in 1965, the Hutch Award was created to pay tribute to the life of Fred Hutchinson, the former Detroit Tigers pitcher (1939-1940, 1946-1953) and manager of the Tigers (1952-1954), St. Louis Cardinals (1956-1958), and Cincinnati Reds (1959-1964). Late in 1963, doctors told the Reds manager that he had advanced-stage lung cancer. Hutchinson told few people about his illness and continued to manage the Reds well into the 1964 season. Eventually, Hutchinson was overcome by the illness and forced to stop managing in August 1964. He died on November 12, 1964, in Bradenton, Florida.

The Cincinnati Reds honored Hutchinson, who had led the Reds to the 1961 NL pennant, by retiring his jersey number, 1. Fred Hutchinson's brother, Dr. William B. Hutchinson, was a well-known surgeon who had founded the Pacific Northwest Research Foundation in their hometown of Seattle in 1956. The PNRF was quickly emerging as one of the nation's leading medical research institutions. In 1965, Dr.

Hutchinson established a cancer research wing in the foundation named in his brother's honor, the Fred Hutchinson Cancer Research Center.

After Hutch's death, three of his friends worked together to create the award that bears his name as well as a scholarship fund that supports medical students engaged in cancer research. The triumvirate of Pirates broadcaster Bob Prince, sportswriter and Hall of Fame basketball official Jim Enright, and *Dayton Journal Herald* sports editor Ritter Collett did the legwork that brought the award and scholarship program into being the following year. The Hutch Award, they decided, would honor a major-league baseball player "who best exemplifies the fighting spirit and competitive desire of Fred Hutchinson."

The inaugural Hutch Award banquet was held in 1965 in Pittsburgh under the auspices of Dapper Dan Charities, founded in 1936 by Al Abrams, the sports editor of the *Pittsburgh Post-Gazette*. Dapper Dan Charities had supported a number of youth-focused charities in the Pittsburgh area since its founding. Mickey Mantle, who famously overcame a series of serious knee injuries during his career, received the inaugural Hutch Award.

In 1987 the Fred Hutchinson Cancer Research Center took over the sponsorship of the award. It is now presented every January at a luncheon at Safeco Field. Since 2000 the Hutch Award Luncheon has raised more than $5 million for its scholarship program and for cancer research at the "Fred Hutch," as the center is known locally. For more information on the award, visit the Fred Hutchinson Cancer Research Center at fredhutch.org.

HUTCH AWARD RECIPIENTS

1965 Mickey Mantle, Yankees
1966 Sandy Koufax, Dodgers
1967 Carl Yastrzemski, Red Sox
1968 Pete Rose, Reds

1969 Al Kaline, Tigers
1970 Tony Conigliaro, Red Sox
1971 Joe Torre, Cardinals
1972 Bobby Tolan, Reds
1973 John Hiller, Tigers
1974 Danny Thompson, Twins
1975 Gary Nolan, Reds
1976 Tommy John, Dodgers
1977 Willie McCovey, Giants
1978 Willie Stargell, Pirates
1979 Lou Brock, Cardinals
1980 George Brett, Royals
1981 Johnny Bench, Reds
1982 Andre Thornton, Indians
1983 Ray Knight, Astros
1984 Don Robinson, Pirates
1985 Rick Reuschel, Cubs
1986 Dennis Leonard, Royals
1987 Paul Molitor, Brewers
1988 Ron Oester, Reds
1989 Dave Dravecky, Giants
1990 Sid Bream, Pirates
1991 Bill Wegman, Brewers
1992 Carney Lansford, Athletics
1993 John Olerud, Blue Jays
1994 Andre Dawson, Red Sox
1995 Jim Abbott, Angels

1996 Omar Vizquel, Indians
1997 Eric Davis, Orioles
1998 David Cone, Yankees
1999 Sean Casey, Reds
2000 Jason Giambi, Athletics
2001 Curt Schilling, Diamondbacks
2002 Tim Salmon, Angels
2003 Jamie Moyer, Mariners
2004 Trevor Hoffman, Padres
2005 Craig Biggio, Astros
2006 Mark Loretta, Astros
2007 Mike Sweeney, Royals
2008 Jon Lester, Red Sox
2009 Mark Teahen, White Sox
2010 Tim Hudson, Braves
2011 Billy Butler, Royals
2012 Barry Zito, Giants
2013 Raúl Ibañez, Mariners
2014 Alex Gordon, Royals
2015 Adam Wainwright, Cardinals

SOURCES

Hutch Award Luncheon Website: .fredhutch.org

Clay Eals, "SABR Biography: Fred Hutchinson": sabr.org/bioproj/
person/8584a2d4

THE LOU GORMAN AWARD

BEGINNING IN **2011**, THE **R**ED Sox also initiated the Lou Gorman Award.

In making the announcement on September 17, 2011, the Red Sox issued this press release:

Red Sox announce winner of first annual Lou Gorman Award

BOSTON, MA-The Boston Red Sox today announced left-handed pitcher **Tommy Hottovy** as the winner of the first annual Lou Gorman Award. The award is given to a Red Sox minor-league player who has demonstrated dedication and perseverance in overcoming obstacles while working his way to the Major League team. The award was presented today during an on-field ceremony recognizing the organization's 2011 Minor League Awards held prior to the Red Sox game against the Tampa Bay Rays.

Gorman was the Red Sox vice president/general manager from 1984-1993 and later served as vice president of baseball operations and executive consultant until his death in April 2011. He was a staunch advocate of player development throughout his professional baseball career, particularly during his time with the Red Sox.

"Lou Gorman was a force within baseball and impacted the game in so many ways," said Larry Lucchino, President/CEO. "His dedication to player development had a significant and lasting effect on both the Red Sox and Major League Baseball. This award will give us an opportunity to annually honor Lou's legacy and to recognize a minor-league player who embodies the characteristics that he so admired."

Hottovy made his Major League debut at 29-years-old on June 3 in his eighth professional season and appeared in eight games in relief for the Red Sox. He combined for a 2.47 ERA (15 ER/54.2 IP) with two saves, 47 strikeouts and 13 walks in 32 relief appearances between Double-A Portland and Triple-A Pawtucket this season. Boston's third pick (fourth round, 125th overall) in the 2004 First-Year Player Draft, Hottovy posted a 1.93 ERA (4 ER/18.2 IP) with the Sea Dogs prior to joining the PawSox on May 14.

2012: Outfielder **Daniel Nava** was the organization's winner of the Lou Gorman Award.

2013: Right-handed pitcher **Steven Wright** was named the winner of the Lou Gorman Award.

2014: Catcher **Dan Butler** was honored as the 2014 recipient of the Award.

2015: Right-handed pitcher **Jonathan Aro was** named as the 2015 recipient.

2016: Left-handed pitcher **Robby Scott** was recognized as the 2016 recipient.

CONTRIBUTORS

RICHARD BOGOVICH is the author of *Kid Nichols: A Biography of the Hall of Fame Pitcher* and *The Who: A Who's Who*, both published by McFarland & Co. For SABR he most recently wrote a chapter in *Tigers by the Tale: Great Games at Michigan and Trumbull* and provided biographies of Dave Sax for *The 1986 Boston Red Sox: There Was More Than Game Six* and Jorge Comellas of the Cubs for *Who's on First: Replacement Players in World War II*. Earlier he contributed chapters to *Inventing Baseball: The 100 Greatest Games of the Nineteenth Century*. He lives in Rochester, Minnesota.

RYAN BRECKER has been a SABR member since 2004. Founder and chair of the Luke Easter SABR Chapter, he is an Emergency Physician by night and lives in Rochester with his wife Stephanie and daughters Cadence and Quinn.

MARK BRUNKE was not a week past his 10th birthday when the Seattle Mariners made their debut. He became a lifelong fan when they finally scored two days later. A human resources executive from Seattle, Washington, he is chapter secretary for Pacific Northwest SABR, belongs to SABR's Origins of Baseball Committee, is a contributor to Protoball. org, and specializes in pre-1890 baseball in the Puget Sound region. He is also a painter, poet, composer/ performer, and filmmaker. Recent works include his poem "Artificial Light" in *The Edinburgh Companion to Twentieth-Century British and American War Literature* from the Edinburgh University Press and his poem "Mothers Go To War" being adapted by Timothy J. Brown for Aquarius Kamerkoor in Ghent, Belgium as part of a commission of new choral work, *Siempre lloran las madres en las guerras*. He presented on his current research project, *John C. Keenan, Jack Levy, and the Plausible Migration of Baseball to the Pacific Northwest*, at the 2015 Frederick Ivor-Campbell 19th Century Base Ball Conference at the Baseball Hall of Fame in Cooperstown. Mark also wrote about Jack Levy for the book *Distant Replay! Washington's Jewish Sports Heroes*. He is a father of two sons, and once hit six consecutive batters in coach pitch Little League.

ALAN COHEN has been a SABR member since 2011, and serves as Vice-President/Treasurer of the Connecticut Smoky Joe Wood Chapter of SABR. He has written over 30 biographies for SABR's bioproject, and has contributed to 16 SABR books. He is expanding his research into the Hearst Sandlot Classic (1946-1965), an annual youth All-Star game which launched the careers of 88 major-league players. His research on the subject first appeared in the Fall 2013 edition of the *Baseball Research Journal*, and was followed with a poster presentation at the SABR Convention in Chicago. He is currently expanding his research and is looking forward to having a book published. He lives in Connecticut with his wife Frances, a cat, and two dogs.

RORY COSTELLO grew up in New England and became a baseball fan in 1969, so his awareness of Tony Conigliaro and his comeback was high. Rory has contributed many stories to SABR BioProject efforts, and diversity is his watchword. He lives in Brooklyn, New York with his wife Noriko and son Kai.

SABR member **GORDON EDES** is a native of Lunenburg, Massachusetts, who spent 35 years as a sports reporter, 18 covering the Boston Red Sox, before becoming the team's historian and communications advisor for Fenway Sports Group.

GREG ERION is retired from the railroad industry and currently teaches history part-time at Skyline Community College in San Bruno, California. He has written several biographies for SABR's BioProject and is currently working on a book about the 1959 season. Greg is one of the leaders of SABRs Baseball Games Project. He and his wife Barbara live in South San Francisco, California.

CHARLES F. FABER was a native of Iowa who lived in Lexington, Kentucky, until his passing in August 2016. He held degrees from Coe College, Columbia University, and the University of Chicago. A retired public school and university teacher and administrator, he contributed to numerous SABR projects, including editing *The 1934 St. Louis Cardinals*. Among his publications are dozens of professional journal articles, encyclopedia entries, and research reports in fields such as school administration, education law, and country music. In addition to textbooks, he wrote 10 books (mostly on baseball) published by McFarland. His last book, co-authored with his grandson Zachariah Webb, was *The Hunt for a Reds October*, published by McFarland in 2015.

ERIC FROST is a neonatal intensive care nurse at a children's hospital in Houston. A graduate of Texas A&M University and Excelsior College, one of his best childhood memories was watching the 1986 Astros clinch a division pennant. Largely because of Eric's background in nursing and emergency medical services, he is intrigued by the ways that medicine intersects with baseball. His research interests include players who suffered from career-limiting injuries and illnesses.

JOY HACKENMUELLER is a healer/writer. She holds a Master of Science degree in Acupuncture and a Bachelor of Arts degree in Photography and African Studies. Joy credits her father Gary for her ability to strategize for the win, especially when the game runs long; because of him the thread of continuity between sport and spirituality was always a clearly presented package for human betterment. Joy encourages us all to tell it like it is, and never ever allow an edit in favor of a Hollywood ending. Her first book, *When At War The Soldier Never Sleeps*, published by Endless Press Publications in 1994, included her favorite interview of all time with former Black House of David African-American Semi-League "barnstorming" team member, Wilbert Lamar, who always told her like it was. Joy's first novel is due out in 2017.

DONNA L. HALPER is an Associate Professor of Communication and Media Studies at Lesley University, Cambridge, Massachusetts. A media historian who specializes in the history of broadcasting, Dr. Halper is the author of six books and many articles. She is also a former broadcaster and print journalist.

MIKE HUBER is Professor of Mathematics at Muhlenberg College in Allentown, Pennsylvania. He has been a SABR member for 20 years and was fortunate to watch Mitch Harris pitch in college for Navy and in the Major Leagues for St. Louis. He enjoys researching and modeling rare baseball events, such as hitting for the cycle and pitching no-hitters.

SCOT JOHNSON wrote the biography of Jim Eisenreich for the book *Minnesotans in Baseball*, edited by Stew Thornley, a publication of the Society for American Baseball Research issued by Nodin Press in 2009. His contributor biography in that book read: Scot Johnson lives in Oakdale, Minnesota, with his wife and son. He is currently working on his master of arts degree in education though he spends a lot of time writing about baseball and Minnesota Twins history at coffeywhirlwind.wordpress.com. That site seems to no longer be functional, and we have been unable to locate him.

NORM KING lives in Ottawa, Ontario, and has been a SABR member since 2010. He has contributed to a number of SABR books, including, *"Thar's Joy in Braveland" — The 1957 Milwaukee Braves* (2014), *Winning on the North Side. The 1929 Chicago Cubs* (2015), and *A Pennant for the Twins Cities: The 1965 Minnesota Twins* (2015). He was also the senior editor and main writer for: *Au jeu/Play Ball: The 50 Greatest Games in the History of the Montreal Expos* (2016). He thought he was crazy to miss his beloved Expos after all these years until he met people from Brooklyn.

SUSAN A. LANTZ, PH.D., a forensic mechanical, biomechanical, and biomedical engineer, and former college professor, attended her first baseball game at the ripe old age of 26 and was immediately and forever hooked on baseball, Wrigley Field, and the Cubs. She began her professorial career in Detroit, in the days when cable TV was limited to a few channels, and since Cubs games were few and far between, she began following the Detroit Tigers, watching their games every evening while writing lecture notes for Thermodynamics. Much to her husband's dismay, she will watch any baseball game, but she prefers to see her beloved Cubs or Tigers play.

DAVID LAURILA grew up in Michigan's Upper Peninsula and now writes about baseball from his home in Cambridge, Massachusetts. A co-chapter leader at SABR-Boston and a member of the BBWAA, he has written for FanGraphs since 2011. He has also been a regular contributor to *Baseball Digest, New England Baseball Journal, Red Sox Magazine,* and other publications.

BOB LEMOINE grew up in South Portland, Maine and became a Red Sox fan well after the time of Tony C. Nevertheless, he soon became a student of Red Sox and baseball history. Digging deep into Boston's baseball history, he co-edited *Boston's First Nine: the 1871-75 Boston Red Stockings* with Bill Nowlin in 2016, and has contributed to several SABR publications. When he isn't scanning an old Boston newspaper on his laptop or digging into an old baseball book found in an antique store, he is working as a high school librarian. He became a SABR member in 2013, after decades of looking for a community that could understand him.

LEN LEVIN has been the copyeditor for most of SABR's recent books. He retired as an editor at the *Providence Journal,* currently has a part-time job editing the decisions of the Rhode Island Supreme Court, and follows the Red Sox through thick and thin.

SKIP NIPPER is author of *Baseball in Nashville* (2007, Arcadia Publishing), and shares is thoughts on his blog, www.262downright.com, and historical website, www.sulphurdell.com. Born and raised in Nashville, his interest in local baseball is deeply-rooted in his life-long love for the National Game, interlaced with fond memories of Nashville's famous ballpark, Sulphur Dell. A graduate of Memphis State University, Skip serves as secretary of the Nashville Old Timers Baseball Association and chapter leader of

the Grantland Rice-Fred Russell (Nashville) chapter of SABR (Society for American Baseball Research). He and his wife Sheila reside in Mt. Juliet, Tennessee.

BILL NOWLIN somewhat vaguely remembers seeing Tony C play in 1967 (these were the Sixties, after all). He even remembers *hearing* Tony's singles (that's a music term, too.) Bill spent closing in on 50 years in the music business, but as his responsibilities wore down, he dove in to writing about baseball. This is one of many books he has been pleased to help edit for SABR.

JOEL RIPPEL, a Minnesota native and graduate of the University of Minnesota, is the author or co-author of eight books on Minnesota sports history.

From an early age **DAVID E. SKELTON** developed a lifelong love of baseball when the lights from Philadelphia's Connie Mack Stadium shone through his bedroom window. Long removed from Philly, he resides with his family in central Texas where he is employed in the oil & gas industry. An avid collector, he joined SABR in 2012.

MARK S. STERNMAN works in Boston for MassDevelopment, a quasi-governmental agency that, among other tasks, issues tax-exempt bonds to hospitals for capital projects. He joined SABR in 1990, less than a decade after the death of his aunt from cancer and a little more than a decade before the death of his mom from cancer. He dedicates his Campana profile to their memories.

RICK SWAINE is the author of *Beating the Breaks: Major League Ballplayers Who Overcame Disabilities* (McFarland, 2004). He is a semi-retired CPA who lives near Tallahassee, Florida. A past contributor to various SABR publications, he enjoys writing about baseball's unsung heroes. He teaches a class in baseball history for FSU's Oscher Lifelong Learning Institute and still plays competitive baseball in various leagues and senior tournaments. His recently released *Baseball's Comeback Players* (McFarland 2014) is his fourth historical baseball book.

CLAYTON TRUTOR is a history instructor at Northeastern University's College of Professional Studies. He is also a PhD candidate in US History at Boston College. He has participated in SABR's Biography Project since 2012. He is a staff writer for *Down the Drive*, SB Nation's University of Cincinnati athletics website. You can follow him on twitter @ ClaytonTrutor

SAUL WISNIA joined SABR around the time he saw future Tony C. Award winner Jim Abbott throw a 1989 shutout at Fenway Park, and has contributed to numerous biography book projects since — most notably on Boston's "almost perfect" baseball summer of 1948 and the '67 Impossible Dream Red Sox. He is also the author of several non-SABR books including *Fenway Park: The Centennial* and *Miracle at Fenway* (on the Curse-busting Sox of 2004). He lives 5.7 miles from his favorite ballpark and works a deep fly ball from Yawkey Way chronicling the stories of off-the-field heroes as senior publications editor at Dana-Farber Cancer Institute. His wife Mic̄ kids Jason and Rachel have grown used to the never leaves ballgames early.

A lifelong Pirates fan, **GREGORY H. WOLF** born in Pittsburgh, but now resides in the Chicagoland area with his wife, Margaret, and daughter, Gabriela. He remembers vividly listening to a 45 of Sister Sledge's "We Are Family" before attending a few games at Three Rivers in 1979, decked out in black and gold and topped off with a Pirates pill box cap. A professor of German studies and holder of the Dennis and Jean Bauman Endowed Chair in the Humanities at North Central College in Naperville, Illinois, he has edited several SABR books, most recently *From the Braves to the Brewers: Great Games and Exciting History at Milwaukee's County Stadium* and *When Pops Led the Family: The 1979 Pittsburgh Pirates* (2016). He is currently working on projects about the Houston Astrodome and Sportsman's Park in St. Louis.

SABR BioProject Team Books

...ican Baseball Research launched an effort to write and publish biographies of every player,
...s made a contribution to baseball. Over the past decade, the BioProject Committee has
... articles. Many have been part of efforts to create theme- or team-oriented books, spear-
...ommittees of SABR.

...ME SIX
...es on the rivals that met in
...s, the Boston Red Sox and the
..., including biographies of every
...broadcaster, and other important fig-
...op organizations in baseball that year. .
...by Leslie Heaphy and Bill Nowlin
...5 paperback (ISBN 978-1-943816-19-4)
...99 ebook (ISBN 978-1-943816-18-7)
8.5"X11", 420 pages, over 200 photos

THE MIRACLE BRAVES OF 1914
BOSTON'S ORIGINAL WORST-TO-FIRST CHAMPIONS
The other book in the "rivalry" set from the 1986
World Series. This book re-tells the story of that
year's classic World Series and this is the story of
each of the players, coaches, managers, and broadcasters, their lives in baseball and the way the
1986 season fit into their lives.
Edited by Leslie Heaphy and Bill Nowlin
$19.95 paperback (ISBN 978-1-943816-13-2)
$9.99 ebook (ISBN 978-1-943816-12-5)
8.5"X11", 392 pages, over 100 photos

SCANDAL ON THE SOUTH SIDE:
THE 1919 CHICAGO WHITE SOX
The Black Sox Scandal isn't the only story worth
telling about the 1919 Chicago White Sox. The team
roster included three future Hall of Famers, a 20-
year-old spitballer who would win 300 games in the
minors, and even a batboy who later became a
celebrity with the "Murderers' Row" New York
Yankees. All of their stories are included in Scandal
on the South Side with a timeline of the 1919 season.
Edited by Jacob Pomrenke
$19.95 paperback (ISBN 978-1-933599-95-3)
$9.99 ebook (ISBN 978-1-933599-94-6)
8.5"x11", 324 pages, 55 historic photos

WINNING ON THE NORTH SIDE
THE 1929 CHICAGO CUBS
Celebrate the 1929 Chicago Cubs, one of the most
exciting teams in baseball history. Future Hall of
Famers Hack Wilson, '29 NL MVP Rogers
Hornsby, and Kiki Cuyler, along with Riggs
Stephenson formed one of the most potent quartets
in baseball history. The magical season came to an
ignominious end in the World Series and helped
craft the future "lovable loser" image of the team.
Edited by Gregory H. Wolf
$19.95 paperback (ISBN 978-1-933599-89-2)
$9.99 ebook (ISBN 978-1-933599-88-5)
8.5"x11", 314 pages, 59 photos

DETROIT THE UNCONQUERABLE:
THE 1935 WORLD CHAMPION TIGERS
Biographies of every player, coach, and broadcaster
involved with the 1935 World Champion Detroit
Tigers baseball team, written by members of the Society for American Baseball Research. Also includes a season in review and other articles about
the 1935 team. Hank Greenberg, Mickey Cochrane,
Charlie Gehringer, Schoolboy Rowe, and more.
Edited by Scott Ferkovich
$19.95 paperback (ISBN 9978-1-933599-78-6)
$9.99 ebook (ISBN 978-1-933599-79-3)
8.5"X11", 230 pages, 52 photos

THE TEAM THAT TIME WON'T FORGET:
THE 1951 NEW YORK GIANTS
Because of Bobby Thomson's dramatic "Shot Heard
'Round the World" in the bottom of the ninth of the
decisive playoff game against the Brooklyn
Dodgers, the team will forever be in baseball pub-
lic's consciousness. Includes a foreword by Giants
outfielder Monte Irvin.
Edited by Bill Nowlin and C. Paul Rogers III
$19.95 paperback (ISBN 978-1-933599-99-1)
$9.99 ebook (ISBN 978-1-933599-98-4)
8.5"X11", 282 pages, 47 photos

A PENNANT FOR THE TWIN CITIES:
THE 1965 MINNESOTA TWINS
This volume celebrates the 1965 Minnesota Twins,
who captured the American League pennant in just
their fifth season in the Twin Cities. Led by an All-
Star cast, from Harmon Killebrew, Tony Oliva, Zoilo
Versalles, and Mudcat Grant to Bob Allison, Jim
Kaat, Earl Battey, and Jim Perry, the Twins won 102
games, but bowed to the Los Angeles Dodgers and
Sandy Koufax in Game Seven
Edited by Gregory H. Wolf
$19.95 paperback (ISBN 978-1-943816-09-5)
$9.99 ebook (ISBN 978-1-943816-08-8)
8.5"X11", 405 pages, over 80 photos

MUSTACHES AND MAYHEM: CHARLIE O'S
THREE TIME CHAMPIONS:
THE OAKLAND ATHLETICS: 1972-74
The Oakland Athletics captured major league baseball's crown each year from 1972 through 1974. Led
by future Hall of Famers Reggie Jackson, Catfish
Hunter and Rollie Fingers, the Athletics were a
largely homegrown group who came of age together. Biographies of every player, coach, manager,
and broadcaster (and mascot) from 1972 through
1974 are included, along with season recaps.
Edited by Chip Greene
$29.95 paperback (ISBN 978-1-943816-07-1)
$9.99 ebook (ISBN 978-1-943816-06-4)
8.5"X11", 600 pages, almost 100 photos

*SABR Members can purchase each book at a significant discount (often 50% off) and receive the ebook
edtions free as a member benefit. Each book is available in a trade paperback edition as well as ebooks
suitable for reading on a home computer or Nook, Kindle, or iPad/tablet.*
To learn more about becoming a member of SABR, visit the website: sabr.org/join

THE SABR DIGITAL LIBRARY

The Society for American Baseball Research, the top baseball research organization in the world, disseminates some of the best in baseball history, analysis, and biography through our publishing programs. The SABR Digital Library contains a mix of books old and new, and focuses on a tandem program of paperback and ebook publication, making these materials widely available for both on digital devices and as traditional printed books.

GREATEST GAMES BOOKS

TIGERS BY THE TALE:
GREAT GAMES AT MICHIGAN AND TRUMBULL
For over 100 years, Michigan and Trumbull was the scene of some of the most exciting baseball ever. This book portrays 50 classic games at the corner, spanning the earliest days of Bennett Park until Tiger Stadium's final closing act. From Ty Cobb to Mickey Cochrane, Hank Greenberg to Al Kaline, and Willie Horton to Alan Trammell.
Edited by Scott Ferkovich
$12.95 paperback (ISBN 978-1-943816-21-7)
$6.99 ebook (ISBN 978-1-943816-20-0)
8.5"x11", 160 pages, 22 photos

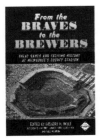

FROM THE BRAVES TO THE BREWERS: GREAT GAMES
AND HISTORY AT MILWAUKEE'S COUNTY STADIUM
The National Pastime provides in-depth articles focused on the geographic region where the national SABR convention is taking place annually. The SABR 45 convention took place in Chicago, and here are 45 articles on baseball in and around the bat-and-ball crazed Windy City: 25 that appeared in the souvenir book of the convention plus another 20 articles available in ebook only.
Edited by Gregory H. Wolf
$19.95 paperback (ISBN 978-1-943816-23-1)
$9.99 ebook (ISBN 978-1-943816-22-4)
8.5"X11", 290 pages, 58 photos

BRAVES FIELD:
MEMORABLE MOMENTS AT BOSTON'S LOST DIAMOND
From its opening on August 18, 1915, to the sudden departure of the Boston Braves to Milwaukee before the 1953 baseball season, Braves Field was home to Boston's National League baseball club and also hosted many other events: from NFL football to championship boxing. The most memorable moments to occur in Braves Field history are portrayed here.
Edited by Bill Nowlin and Bob Brady
$19.95 paperback (ISBN 978-1-933599-93-9)
$9.99 ebook (ISBN 978-1-933599-92-2)
8.5"X11", 282 pages, 182 photos

AU JEU/PLAY BALL: THE 50 GREATEST GAMES IN THE
HISTORY OF THE MONTREAL EXPOS
The 50 greatest games in Montreal Expos history. The games described here recount the exploits of the many great players who wore Expos uniforms over the years—Bill Stoneman, Gary Carter, Andre Dawson, Steve Rogers, Pedro Martinez, from the earliest days of the franchise, to the glory years of 1979-1981, the what-might-have-been years of the early 1990s, and the sad, final days.and others.
Edited by Norm King
$12.95 paperback (ISBN 978-1-943816-15-6)
$5.99 ebook (ISBN978-1-943816-14-9)
8.5"x11", 162 pages, 50 photos

ORIGINAL SABR RESEARCH

CALLING THE GAME:
BASEBALL BROADCASTING FROM 1920 TO THE PRESENT
An exhaustive, meticulously researched history of bringing the national pastime out of the ballparks and into living rooms via the airwaves. Every play-by-play announcer, color commentator, and ex-ballplayer, every broadcast deal, radio station, and TV network. Plus a foreword by "Voice of the Chicago Cubs" Pat Hughes, and an afterword by Jacques Doucet, the "Voice of the Montreal Expos" 1972-2004.
by Stuart Shea
$24.95 paperback (ISBN 978-1-933599-40-3)
$9.99 ebook (ISBN 978-1-933599-41-0)
7"X10", 712 pages, 40 photos

BIOPROJECT BOOKS

WHO'S ON FIRST:
REPLACEMENT PLAYERS IN WORLD WAR II
During World War II, 533 players made the major league debuts. More than 60% of the players in the 1941 Opening Day lineups departed for the service and were replaced by first-times and oldsters. Hod Lisenbee was 46. POW Bert Shepard had an artificial leg, and Pete Gray had only one arm. The 1944 St. Louis Browns had 13 players classified 4-F. These are their stories.
Edited by Marc Z Aaron and Bill Nowlin
$19.95 paperback (ISBN 978-1-933599-91-5)
$9.99 ebook (ISBN 978-1-933599-90-8)
8.5"X11", 422 pages, 67 photos

VAN LINGLE MUNGO:
THE MAN, THE SONG, THE PLAYERS
Although the Red Sox spent most of the 1950s far out of contention, the team was filled with fascinating players who captured the heart of their fans. In *Red Sox Baseball*, members of SABR present 46 biographies on players such as Ted Williams and Pumpsie Green as well as season-by-season recaps.
Edited by Bill Nowlin
$19.95 paperback (ISBN 978-1-933599-76-2)
$9.99 ebook (ISBN 978-1-933599-77-9)
8.5"X11", 278 pages, 46 photos

NUCLEAR POWERED BASEBALL
Nuclear Powered Baseball tells the stories of each player—past and present—featured in the classic Simpsons episode "Homer at the Bat." Wade Boggs, Ken Griffey Jr., Ozzie Smith, Nap Lajoie, Don Mattingly, and many more. We've also included a few very entertaining takes on the now-famous episode from prominent baseball writers Jonah Keri, Joe Posnanski, Erik Malinowski, and Bradley Woodrum.
Edited by Emily Hawks and Bill Nowlin
$19.95 paperback (ISBN 978-1-943816-11-8)
$9.99 ebook (ISBN 978-1-943816-10-1)
8.5"X11", 250 pages

SABR Members can purchase each book at a significant discount (often 50% off) and receive the ebook edtions free as a member benefit. Each book is available in a trade paperback edition as well as ebooks suitable for reading on a home computer or Nook, Kindle, or iPad/tablet.
To learn more about becoming a member of SABR, visit the website: sabr.org/join

Society for American Baseball Research

Cronkite School at ASU
555 N. Central Ave. #416, Phoenix, AZ 85004
602.496.1460 (phone)
SABR.org

Become a SABR member today!

If you're interested in baseball — writing about it, reading about it, talking about it — there's a place for you in the Society for American Baseball Research. Our members include everyone from academics to professional sportswriters to amateur historians and statisticians to students and casual fans who enjoy reading about baseball and occasionally gathering with other members to talk baseball. What unites all SABR members is an interest in the game and joy in learning more about it.

SABR membership is open to any baseball fan; we offer 1-year and 3-year memberships. Here's a list of some of the key benefits you'll receive as a SABR member:

- Receive two editions (spring and fall) of the *Baseball Research Journal*, our flagship publication
- Receive expanded e-book edition of *The National Pastime*, our annual convention journal
- 8-10 new e-books published by the SABR Digital Library, all FREE to members
- "This Week in SABR" e-newsletter, sent to members every Friday
- Join dozens of research committees, from Statistical Analysis to Women in Baseball.
- Join one of 70 regional chapters in the U.S., Canada, Latin America, and abroad
- Participate in online discussion groups
- Ask and answer baseball research questions on the SABR-L e-mail listserv
- Complete archives of *The Sporting News* dating back to 1886 and other research resources
- Promote your research in "This Week in SABR"
- Diamond Dollars Case Competition
- Yoseloff Scholarships

- Discounts on SABR national conferences, including the SABR National Convention, the SABR Analytics Conference, Jerry Malloy Negro League Conference, Frederick Ivor-Campbell 19th Century Conference
- Publish your research in peer-reviewed SABR journals
- Collaborate with SABR researchers and experts
- Contribute to Baseball Biography Project or the SABR Games Project
- List your new book in the SABR Bookshelf
- Lead a SABR research committee or chapter
- Networking opportunities at SABR Analytics Conference
- Meet baseball authors and historians at SABR events and chapter meetings
- 50% discounts on paperback versions of SABR e-books
- 20% discount on MLB.TV and MiLB.TV subscriptions
- Discounts with other partners in the baseball community
- SABR research awards

We hope you'll join the most passionate international community of baseball fans at SABR! Check us out online at SABR.org/join.

SABR MEMBERSHIP FORM

	Annual	3-year	Senior	3-yr Sr.	Under 30
U.S.:	❑ $65	❑ $175	❑ $45	❑ $129	❑ $45
Canada/Mexico:	❑ $75	❑ $205	❑ $55	❑ $159	❑ $55
Overseas:	❑ $84	❑ $232	❑ $64	❑ $186	❑ $55

Add a Family Member: $15 each family member at same address (list names on back)
Senior: 65 or older before 12/31 of the current year

All dues amounts in U.S. dollars or equivalent

Participate in Our Donor Program!

Support the preservation of baseball research. Designate your gift toward:
❑General Fund   ❑Endowment Fund   ❑Research Resources   ❑_____
❑ I want to maximize the impact of my gift; do not send any donor premiums
❑ I would like this gift to remain anonymous.

Note: Any donation not designated will be placed in the General Fund.
SABR is a 501 (c) (3) not-for-profit organization & donations are tax-deductible to the extent allowed by law.

Name _____

E-mail* _____

Address _____

City _____ ST_____ ZIP_____

Phone _____ Birthday _____

* Your e-mail address on file ensures you will receive the most recent SABR news.

Dues $_____

Donation $_____

Amount Enclosed $_____

Do you work for a matching grant corporation? Call (602) 496-1460 for details.

If you wish to pay by credit card, please contact the SABR office at (602) 496-1460 or visit the SABR Store online at SABR.org/join. We accept Visa, Mastercard & Discover.

Do you wish to receive the *Baseball Research Journal* electronically?: ❑ Yes   ❑ No
Our e-books are available in PDF, Kindle, or EPUB (iBooks, iPad, Nook) formats.

Mail to: SABR, Cronkite School at ASU, 555 N. Central Ave. #416, Phoenix, AZ 85004

Made in the USA
Middletown, DE
08 July 2017